AI-Assisted Programming Web and Machine Learning

Improve your development workflow with ChatGPT and GitHub Copilot

Christoffer Noring
Anjali Jain
Marina Fernandez
Ayşe Mutlu
Ajit Jaokar

AI-Assisted Programming for Web and Machine Learning

Copyright © 2024 Packt Publishing

All rights reserved. No part of this book may be reproduced, stored in a retrieval system, or transmitted in any form or by any means, without the prior written permission of the publisher, except in the case of brief quotations embedded in critical articles or reviews.

Every effort has been made in the preparation of this book to ensure the accuracy of the information presented. However, the information contained in this book is sold without warranty, either express or implied. Neither the authors, nor Packt Publishing or its dealers and distributors, will be held liable for any damages caused or alleged to have been caused directly or indirectly by this book.

Packt Publishing has endeavored to provide trademark information about all of the companies and products mentioned in this book by the appropriate use of capitals. However, Packt Publishing cannot guarantee the accuracy of this information.

Senior Publishing Product Manager: Bhavesh Amin

Acquisition Editor – Peer Reviews: Gaurav Gavas

Project Editor: Meenakshi Vijay

Content Development Editor: Deepayan Bhattacharjee

Copy Editor: Safis Editing

Technical Editor: Tejas Mhasvekar

Proofreader: Safis Editing

Indexer: Tejal Soni

Presentation Designer: Rajesh Shirsath

Developer Relations Marketing Executive: Sohini Ghosh

First published: August 2024

Production reference: 1270824

Published by Packt Publishing Ltd.
Grosvenor House

11 St Paul's Square
Birmingham
B3 1RB, UK.

ISBN 978-1-83508-605-6

www.packt.com

Contributors

About the authors

Christoffer Noring works as a Senior Advocate at Microsoft and focuses on application development and AI. He's a Google Developer Expert and a public speaker on 100+ presentations across the world. Additionally, he's a tutor at the University of Oxford on cloud patterns and AI. Chris is also a published author on Angular, NGRX, and programming with Go.

Anjali Jain is a London-based AI and ML professional with a career spanning over two decades. Currently working as a data architect for Metrobank, she brings her expertise in AI, data, architecture, data governance, and software development to the financial sector. Anjali holds a bachelor's degree in electrical engineering and boasts certifications, including TOGAF 9.1 and ITIL 2011 Foundation. In her role as Senior AI and ML tutor at Oxford, she shares cutting-edge knowledge on various technologies.

Marina Fernandez is a data science and Databricks consultant with expertise in financial risk management. She contributes to the academic team at the University of Oxford, where she holds the positions of senior AI and ML tutor and guest lecturer. Throughout her 20-year career, Marina has worked on the development of large-scale enterprise systems for various business domains. Her experience encompasses e-commerce, e-learning, software security, commodity trading, commodity trading and risk management systems, and regulatory reporting. Marina obtained her MSc in Software Engineering from the University of Oxford. Additionally, she has earned professional certifications, including Microsoft Certified Professional and Certified Scrum Master.

Ayşe Mutlu is a data scientist working on Azure AI and DevOps technologies. Based in London, Ayşe's work involves building and deploying Machine Learning and Deep Learning models using the Microsoft Azure framework (Azure DevOps and Azure Pipelines). She enjoys coding in Python and contributing to open-source initiatives in Python.

Ajit Jaokar is a data scientist for Feynlabs, building AI prototypes for complex applications. He is also a course director for AI at the University of Oxford. Besides this, Ajit is a visiting fellow in Engineering Sciences at the University of Oxford and conducts AI courses at the London School of Economics, Universidad Politécnica de Madrid, and the Harvard Kennedy School of Government as part of The Future Society. His work at Oxford and his company is based on interdisciplinary aspects of AI, including AI with digital twins, quantum computing, metaverse, Agtech, and life sciences. His teaching is based on a methodology for AI and cyber-physical systems, which he is developing as part of his research.

About the reviewers

Maxim Salnikov is a tech and cloud community enthusiast based in Oslo. With over two decades of experience as a web developer, he shares his extensive knowledge of the web platform, cloud computing, and AI by speaking at and providing training for developer events worldwide. By day, Maxim plays a crucial role in supporting the development of cloud and AI solutions within European companies, serving as the leader of developer productivity business at Microsoft. During evenings, he can be found running events for Norway's largest web and cloud development communities. Maxim is passionate about exploring and experimenting with Generative AI possibilities, including AI-assisted development. To share his insights and connect with like-minded professionals globally, he founded and organized the inaugural Prompt Engineering Conference, the first of its kind on a global scale.

Şaban Kara is an AI and ML software engineer who graduated from Gebze Technical University Electronics Engineering. Throughout his career, Şaban has developed several NLP projects and worked on various probabilistic statistics-based ML algorithms. Şaban is especially known for his interest in LLM and LangChain models. His work on these models focuses on improving spontaneous learning abilities. He started his career working at TUBITAK. Currently, he is developing ML algorithms on LLM models in a private company and making a self-learning AI.

I would like to thank my family, friends, and colleagues for their contributions to the preparation of this book. Their support played an important role in the success of this project.

Join our community on Discord

Join our community's Discord space for discussions with the author and other readers:

https://packt.link/aicode

Table of Contents

Chapter 7: Support Multiple Viewports Using Responsive Web Layouts   85

Chapter 8: Build a Backend with Web APIs   101

Chapter 9: Augment Web Apps with AI Services   129

Chapter 10: Maintaining Existing Codebases   143

Chapter 11: Data Exploration with ChatGPT   175

Chapter 14: Building an MLP Model for Fashion-MNIST with ChatGPT 301

Chapter 15: Building a CNN Model for CIFAR-10 with ChatGPT 335

Preface

Who this book is for

The target audience for this book is professionals in the web development, machine learning, and data science fields. You should be a professional with at least 1-3 years of experience. This book means to empower you by showcasing how AI assistants can be leveraged in different problem domains. It describes overall features but also gives recommendations on effective prompting for best results.

What this book covers

Chapter 1, *It's a New World, One with AI Assistants, and You're Invited*, looks at how we started using large language models and how it constitutes a paradigm shift for many, not just IT workers.

Chapter 2, *Prompt Strategy*, explains the strategy used throughout the book in terms of breaking down a problem and some guiding principles on how to effectively prompt your chosen AI tool.

Chapter 3, *Tools of the Trade: Introducing Our AI Assistants*, is where we explain how to work with our two chosen AI assistants, GitHub Copilot and ChatGPT, covering everything from installation to how to get started using them.

Chapter 4, *Build the Appearance of Our App with HTML and Copilot*, focuses on building the frontend for our e-commerce app (a narrative you will see featured throughout the book).

Chapter 5, *Style the App with CSS and Copilot*, is where we keep working on our e-commerce app but now focus specifically on CSS and ensuring the appearance is appealing.

Chapter 6, *Add Behaviour with JavaScript*, is where we add behavior to our e-commerce app using JavaScript.

Chapter 7, *Support Multiple Viewports Using Responsive Web Layouts*, is where we address the fact that an app needs to work for different device types, whether it's a smaller mobile screen, a tablet, or a desktop screen. Therefore, this chapter focuses on responsive design.

Chapter 8, *Build a Backend with Web APIs*, looks at how, for the app to actually work, it needs to have a backend, consisting of code that's able to read and write data and persist it. This chapter therefore focuses on building a Web API for our e-commerce app.

Chapter 9, Augment Web apps with AI Services, covers training a machine learning model and how to expose it via a Web API for consumption by anyone with a browser or other type of client capable of using the HTTP protocol.

Chapter 10, Maintaining Existing Codebases, covers how most developers work on existing code and maintain existing codebases rather than creating new projects. Therefore, this chapter focuses on various aspects of maintaining code, like dealing with bugs, performance, working with tests, and more.

Chapter 11, Data Exploration with ChatGPT, is where we work with a review dataset and learn to identify insights into distribution, trends, correlation, and more.

Chapter 12, Building a Classification Model with ChatGPT, looks at the same review dataset as in *Chapter 11,* this time performing classification and sentiment analysis.

Chapter 13, Building a Regression Model for Customer Spend with ChatGPT, attempts to predict the yearly amount spent by customers and uses regression to create a model capable of making this prediction.

Chapter 14, Building an MLP Model for Fashion-MNIST with ChatGPT, looks at building an MLP model based on a fashion dataset, still sticking to our general theme of e-commerce.

Chapter 15, Building a CNN Model for CIFAR-10 with ChatGPT, focuses on building a CNN model.

Chapter 16, Unsupervised Learning: Clustering and PCA, focuses on clustering and PCA.

Chapter 17, Machine Learning with Copilot, covers conducting machine learning using GitHub Copilot to contrast it with ChatGPT.

Chapter 18, Regression with Copilot Chat, is where we develop a regression model. Also, this chapter uses GitHub Copilot.

Chapter 19, Regression with Copilot Suggestions, like the preceding chapter, focuses on regression using GitHub Copilot. The difference between this and the preceding chapter is that here we use the suggestions from writing prompts as comments in a text file, rather than writing our prompt in a chat-like interface.

Chapter 20, Increasing Efficiency with GitHub Copilot, focuses on getting the most out of GitHub Copilot. This chapter is a must read if you want to master GitHub Copilot.

Chapter 21, Agents in Software Development, takes a look at what's coming next within AI, namely, agents. Agents are able to assist you to a much higher degree by acting autonomously based on a high-level goal. This is definitely worth a read if you're curious about future trends.

Chapter 22, Conclusion, wraps up the book by drawing some conclusions as to the greater lessons learned about working with AI assistants.

To get the most out of this book

You'll get more out of this book if you've built a few projects in each domain as opposed to being a complete beginner. Therefore, the book focuses on empowering you in your existing development workflows. We recommend other titles by Packt if you are completely new to web development or machine learning. See the below list for recommendations:

- https://www.packtpub.com/en-us/product/html5-web-application-development-by-example-beginners-guide-9781849695947
- *Machine Learning with Python: Unlocking AI Potential with Python and Machine Learning* by Oliver Theobald (https://www.packtpub.com/en-US/product/machine-learning-with-python-9781835461969)

The book is built in such a way that you're shown the prompts you're recommended to write followed by the results from the chosen AI tool.

- To follow along with the chapters on web development, we recommend installing Visual Studio Code. There are dedicated chapters in the book pointing out how to install GitHub Copilot and leverage it. See the installation instructions for Visual Studio Code here: https://code.visualstudio.com/download
- For the machine learning chapters, the majority of those chapters use ChatGPT, which can be accessed through a web browser. We do recommend solving those problems using notebooks, which can be viewed through a variety of different tools. For more detailed instructions on Notebook setup, refer to this page: https://code.visualstudio.com/docs/datascience/jupyter-notebooks
- To use GitHub Copilot, you need a GitHub account to log in to. Refer to this page on the setup process for GitHub Copilot: https://docs.github.com/en/copilot/quickstart

Download the example code files

The code bundle for the book is hosted on GitHub at https://github.com/PacktPublishing/AI-Assisted-Software-Development-with-GitHub-Copilot-and-ChatGPT. We also have other code bundles from our rich catalog of books and videos available at https://github.com/PacktPublishing/. Check them out!

Download the color images

We also provide a PDF file that has color images of the screenshots/diagrams used in this book. You can download it here: https://packt.link/gbp/9781835086056.

Conventions used

There are a number of text conventions used throughout this book.

CodeInText: Indicates code words in text, database table names, folder names, filenames, file extensions, pathnames, dummy URLs, user input, and X(formerly known as Twitter) handles. For example: "Now that the product.css is created with the above content, we can include said CSS file in an HTML file."

Bold: Indicates a new term, an important word, or words that you see on the screen. For instance, words in menus or dialog boxes appear in the text like this. For example: "**Create new user:** It should be possible to create a new user."

 Warnings or important notes appear like this.

 Tips and tricks appear like this.

Get in touch

Feedback from our readers is always welcome.

General feedback: Email feedback@packtpub.com and mention the book's title in the subject of your message. If you have questions about any aspect of this book, please email us at questions@packtpub.com.

Errata: Although we have taken every care to ensure the accuracy of our content, mistakes do happen. If you have found a mistake in this book, we would be grateful if you reported this to us. Please visit http://www.packtpub.com/submit-errata, click **Submit Errata**, and fill in the form.

Piracy: If you come across any illegal copies of our works in any form on the internet, we would be grateful if you would provide us with the location address or website name. Please contact us at copyright@packtpub.com with a link to the material.

If you are interested in becoming an author: If there is a topic that you have expertise in and you are interested in either writing or contributing to a book, please visit http://authors.packtpub.com.

Share your thoughts

Once you've read *AI-Assisted Programming for Web and Machine Learning*, we'd love to hear your thoughts! Scan the QR code below to go straight to the Amazon review page for this book and share your feedback.

https://packt.link/r/1835086055

Your review is important to us and the tech community and will help us make sure we're delivering excellent quality content.

Download a free PDF copy of this book

Thanks for purchasing this book!

Do you like to read on the go but are unable to carry your print books everywhere?

Is your eBook purchase not compatible with the device of your choice?

Don't worry, now with every Packt book you get a DRM-free PDF version of that book at no cost.

Read anywhere, any place, on any device. Search, copy, and paste code from your favorite technical books directly into your application.

The perks don't stop there, you can get exclusive access to discounts, newsletters, and great free content in your inbox daily.

Follow these simple steps to get the benefits:

1. Scan the QR code or visit the link below:

https://packt.link/free-ebook/9781835086056

2. Submit your proof of purchase.
3. That's it! We'll send your free PDF and other benefits to your email directly.

1

It's a New World, One with AI Assistants, and You're Invited

Introduction

In November 2022, ChatGPT arrived from seemingly nowhere. Over time, ChatGPT gained momentum, gradually evolving into a widely embraced tool. Eventually, millions actively incorporated ChatGPT into their workflows, leveraging its capabilities for generating insights, summarizing text, crafting code, and more.

Its arrival changed many people's workflow and improved it a lot in tasks like quickly understanding large bodies of text, writing emails, and more. Here you are, having bought this book, and hoping that you can learn how to use an AI tool like **ChatGPT** or **GitHub Copilot** to make you more efficient. That's exactly the mission of this book: to teach you not only how to use these two AI tools but also to be able to apply them across various problem domains.

Before we start solving problems using an AI assistant, let's back up a bit; how did we get here? ChatGPT just didn't arrive out of nowhere, right?

How ChatGPT came to be, from NLP to LLMs

To tell the story of how we got here, to AI tools like ChatGPT, powered by **large language models (LLMs)**, let's first cover **natural language processing (NLP)**.

NLP is a field of computer science, artificial intelligence, and computational linguistics. It's concerned with the interactions between computers and human language, and how to program computers to process and analyze large amounts of natural language data. NLP is a hugely interesting area that has a range of useful applications in the real world. Here are some:

- **Speech recognition:** If you have a modern smartphone, you've likely interacted with voice assistants like Siri or Alexa, for example.

- **Machine translation:** Google Translate is perhaps what comes to mind when thinking of machine translation, the ability to translate from one language to another automatically.

- **Sentiment analysis:** A very useful area is understanding the sentiment in areas like social media, for example. Companies want to know how brands are perceived; e-commerce wants to quickly understand product reviews to boost their business.

- **Chatbots and virtual assistants:** You've likely seen chatbots being integrated on web pages even before the advent of ChatGPT. These chatbots can answer simpler questions, and companies have them to ensure you quickly get an answer to simpler questions and provide a more natural experience than an FAQ page, among other usage areas.

- **Text summaries:** Search engines come to mind again when thinking about text summaries. You might have seen how, when you use search engines like Bing or Google, it's able to summarize a page and show the summary together with the link to the page in a search result page. As a user, you get a better understanding of what link to click.

- **Content recommendation:** This is another important area used by a variety of different domains. E-commerce uses this to present products you're likely to be interested in, Xbox uses this to recommend what games to play and buy, and video streaming services display content you might want to watch next.

As you can see already, with NLP, both companies and end users benefit greatly from adopting it.

The rise of LLMs

How did we evolve from NLP to LLMs, then? Initially, NLP used rule-based systems and statistical methods underneath. This approach, although working well for some tasks, struggled with human language.

This changed for the better when deep learning, a subset of machine learning, was introduced to NLP, and we got models like RNN, recurrent neural networks, and transformer-based models, capable of learning patterns in data. The result was a considerable improvement in performance. With transformer-based models, we're starting to lay the foundations of large language models.

LLMs are a type of transformer model. They can generate human-like text and, unlike NLP models, they're good at a variety of tasks without needing specific training data. How is this possible, you ask? The answer is a combination of improved architecture, a vast increase in computational power, and gigantic datasets.

LLMs rest on the idea that a large enough neural network can learn to do anything, given enough data and compute. This is a paradigm shift in how we program computers. Instead of writing code, we write prompts and let the model do the rest.

GPT models

There are many different types of LLMs out there, but let's focus on GPT for a second, a type of LLM on which the book's chosen tools are based (even if GitHub Copilot uses a specific subset known as Codex).

There have been several different versions developed in the last few years. Here are some models developed by the company OpenAI:

- GPT-1: The first one, with 117 million parameters using transformer architecture.
- GPT-2: This model has 1.5 billion parameters and is able to generate coherent and relevant text.
- GPT-3: This model has 175 billion parameters and is considerably better than its predecessor with features like answering questions, fiction generation, and even writing code.
- GPT-4: This model has been quoted to have 1.76 trillion parameters.
- The number of parameters allows the model to understand more nuanced and coherent text. It should also be said that the larger the model, the larger the computational resources that are needed to train it.
- ChatGPT recently switched to GPT-4 and the difference compared to GPT-3 is significant.

How LLMs are better

Now that we have a better understanding of how LLMs came to be and where they came from, what makes LLMs great? What are some good examples of why we really should adopt AI assistants based on LLMs?

Because LLMs are bigger and more advanced, there are some areas in which they clearly outperform traditional NLP models:

- **Context**: LLMs can understand not just the recent input but can produce responses based on a longer conversation.
- **Few-shot learning**: To perform a task, LLMs usually just need a few examples to produce a correct response. This should be contrasted with NLP models, which usually use a large amount of task-specific training data to perform properly.
- **Performance**: LLMs are better than traditional NLP models in areas like translations, questions, and summarization.

It's worth mentioning that LLMs aren't perfect; they do generate incorrect responses and can sometimes make up responses, also known as hallucinations. It's our hope though that by reading this book, you will see the advantages of using LLM-based AI assistants and you will feel the pros clearly outweigh the cons.

The new paradigm, programming with natural language

Probably the biggest game changer with using LLM-based AI assistants is that you're able to interact with them using nothing but natural language. There's no need to learn a programming language to get the response you need. This change constitutes a new paradigm in interacting with AI. We're moving away from writing in specific languages for producing apps, data retrieval, or even how we produce images, presentations, and more to express at a high level what we want through a prompt.

Here is an example of things that are now possible to do using prompts, where it before needed considerably more effort:

- **Programming**: With a prompt, you express what app you want to build or what changes you want to make with the code.

- **Image generation:** Where you before needed a designer or artist, you can now generate via prompts.
- **Videos:** There are tools out there that, once given a prompt, will generate videos where an avatar reads out your written text.
- **Text tasks:** LLM-based AI assistants can generate emails, summarize large bodies of text, author interview ads, and much more; anything you can imagine with text really.

All these application areas mentioned above make it clear that LLM-based AI tools are useful not only to programmers and data scientists but numerous different professions.

Challenges and limitations

Is everything working perfectly at this point? AI assistants aren't able to replace "you" just yet, and should be considered more of a "thinking partner." Microsoft has even, through conscious naming, called their AI assistants "Copilots" where you're clearly the pilot that sets out the direction. These tools can generate text and other modalities in seconds, but you need to verify the correctness. Often, the first response you get from a tool is something you need to iterate over. The good news is that it just takes seconds to redo the instruction.

An important thing to realize about AI assistants is that the more skilled you are at a certain topic, the more intelligent questions you can ask of it, and you'll be able to better assess the correctness of the response.

About this book

The goals of this book are to:

- Introduce you to the new paradigm of programming with natural language.
- Provide you with the tools to get started using AI assistants.
- Empower you to use AI assistants effectively and responsibly by teaching you prompt engineering and specifically a set of prompting strategies (covered in *Chapter 2*) and some sound practices (covered in *Chapter 8*).

We believe that with these tools, prompting strategies, and practices, you will be able to use AI assistants effectively and responsibly to augment your work and increase your productivity.

Who this book is for

This book is for professional developers within both the web and machine learning space. It is for those who want to learn how to use AI assistants like GitHub Copilot and ChatGPT to augment their work and increase their productivity.

Evolution of programming languages

Programming has gone through a series of changes and paradigm shifts throughout history:

- Ada Lovelace wrote the first algorithm for a machine, the Analytical Engine, in the 1840s. Lovelace is considered the first computer programmer and the first to recognize that the machine had applications beyond pure calculation.

- In the 1940s, the first programmable computers were created. These computers were programmed using punch cards. One such computer was the Harvard Mark I, which was used to calculate the trajectory of artillery shells. Also, Bombe is worth mentioning, which was used to crack the Enigma code during World War II and was instrumental in the Allies winning the war.

- In the 1950s, the first high-level programming languages were created. This time period saw the birth of FORTRAN, LISP, COBOL, and ALGOL. Some of these languages are still in use today, especially in banking systems, scientific computing, and defense.

- In the 1970s, the first object-oriented programming languages were created. The 1970s meant we got Smalltalk, C++, and Objective-C. Except for Smalltalk, these languages are heavily in use today.

- In the 1990s, the first functional programming languages were created. The 1990s gave us Haskell, OCaml, and Scala. The benefit of these languages is that they encourage immutability and pure functions, which makes them easier to reason about and test.

- In the 2000s, the first declarative programming languages were created. Declarative programming languages are used to describe what you want to do, rather than how you want to do it. The 2000s gave us SQL, HTML, and CSS.

- In the 2010s, the first low-code and no-code platforms were created. These platforms opened programming to a wider audience, and allowed anyone, regardless of technical background, to build applications.

- In the 2020s, the first AI assistants were created that leveraged natural language. If you can write a sentence, you can write code.

In summary, programming has gone through a series of changes and paradigm shifts. Prompt-first programming is the latest paradigm shift and mastering it will be key to staying relevant in the immediate future.

Looking ahead

If changes and paradigm shifts took years or decades in the past, they now take months or even weeks. We're moving toward a new world at breakneck speed.

There's reason to be excited, as we're moving faster than before, but as always, we should exercise caution. We should be aware of the risks and the dangers of using these tools irresponsibly, but most of all we should be aware of the opportunities.

As Alan Kay once said, "The best way to predict the future is to invent it."

How to use this book

We believe the best way to use this book is to follow the chapters in order.

Chapter 2, with the prompting strategies, is the most important chapter in the book. These patterns and strategies are referred to throughout the book and are the foundation for how to use AI assistants effectively and responsibly.

The book is written in the following format:

- **Introduction:** The first chapter aims to provide you with an overview of what this book is about, its goals, and who it is for.
- **Prompt strategy:** The idea is to lay the foundation on how to break down problems within the domains of data science and web development. From this chapter, you will learn strategies you can adopt for your own problems.
- **Tools of the trade:** The third chapter introduces you to our tools, GitHub Copilot and ChatGPT, what they are, how they work, and how to install them. However, the book is written in such a way that you can take any of the prompts we suggest and feed those into any AI assistant, and get a similar experience.
- The remaining chapters of the book show how we use the prompt strategies from *Chapter 2* and apply them to various domains from web development to data science and machine learning.

Happy reading!

Join our community on Discord

Join our community's Discord space for discussions with the author and other readers:

`https://packt.link/aicode`

2

Prompt Strategy

Introduction

In the previous chapter, we gave some historical context to how AI has developed over the years, how we've gone from **natural language processing (NLP)** to **large language models (LLMs)**, and how the latter serves as the underlying machine learning model in AI assistants. To use these AI assistants, you use natural language prompts as input. However, to ensure you "prompt" in an efficient way, so that you get what you want, it's important to have a strategy, and that's what this chapter aims to give you.

How to "prompt" efficiently is commonly known in the industry as a "prompt strategy" or "prompt engineering." It's not an engineering practice in the common sense of the word but rather an art form where practitioners of AI assistants have discovered patterns and practices that seem to work well. We, the authors of this book, are building upon those discovered practices and aim to describe our findings for two domains: full-stack web development and data science. This book turns to you as either a web developer or data scientist and aims to empower you by describing how you can best approach problem solving in your domain using an AI assistant.

This chapter constitutes a central piece of the book. It's central in the sense that the approach being taught will be exemplified by other chapters in the book. As such, see this chapter as a guide you can refer to, providing the theory and thinking that is used in future chapters that solve specific problems within data science and full-stack web development.

In this chapter, we will:

- Provide a strategy for solving problems with prompts and validating the solution.
- Illustrate the strategy with examples from data science and full-stack web development.
- Identify some basic principles for writing prompts.

Where you are

As a reader and a practitioner of data science and/or full-stack web development, you know your craft. Knowing your craft means you know the tools and techniques to solve problems. At this point, you're looking at an AI assistant and realize it's controlled by natural language, so-called prompts. What you may not realize is that there's more to it than just writing a prompt and getting an answer. An AI assistant is trained on a large corpus of text, so it's quite flexible on what it can generate text on and how to respond to prompts. Because of this flexibility, it's important to understand how to write prompts that are effective and efficient.

Guidelines for how to prompt efficiently

Prompts are input to AI tools. Depending on what you're trying to achieve, you need to adjust your prompts for the scenario you're solving for. Therefore, how you "prompt" matters. For example, if your prompt is too vague, you won't get what you need. Or, let's say you're trying to use a prompt to generate company slogans; you don't want to use the same prompt for generating code for an app. Conversely, in a discipline like data science, it's important you perform tasks in a certain order and your prompt should reflect what you want done and, if needed, the steps to do so.

What you need to succeed is an approach, a strategy, that you can use in general to be efficient with AI assistants. Additionally, such a strategy should be specific enough to present "best practices" for chosen problem domains. As mentioned earlier in this chapter, we've developed a prompt strategy specifically for the domain's full-stack web development and data science.

At a high level, we suggest the guidelines for general problem-solving using AI assistants; it's our belief it holds true regardless of what problem domain you're applying prompts to:

1. **Break down the problem** so that it's fully understood. Within this guideline, there might be several steps like the following:

   - **Understand the problem:** For any problem, it's important to understand what the problem is and what it's not. For example, are we building a machine learning model to predict sales or a web page to track inventory? These are two different problems and require different approaches.

   - **Identify the parts:** A problem is usually complex and consists of many parts that need to be solved. For example, if we're building a machine learning model to predict sales, we need to identify the data, the model, the training, and the evaluation. Each of these parts can be broken down into smaller parts and so on. Once you find the right detail level for your problem, you can start solving it by writing prompts.

   - **Break down the problem into smaller pieces:** If needed, break down your problem into smaller more manageable pieces.

   - **Identify and understand the data:** Especially with machine learning, it's crucial to identify a dataset to work with, what it contains, and how it's structured. Within web development, data also plays a central role, but the goal is usually to ensure you can read, write, and present data in a way that's useful for the user.

2. **Generate prompts** at a suitable level. Once you've understood the problem fully, you should have a list of tasks, and for each task, you should be able to author and run a prompt that solves said task.

3. **Validate the solution.** Just like without AI assistants, validation plays a crucial part in building systems or apps. Traditionally, that means writing tests, testing various components together, and letting users try out various parts. Using prompts is no different. A side effect of LLMs is that they can generate text that's not relevant to the problem or solve the problem in a less-than-optimal way. Because you're relying on prompts that end up generating code for you, it becomes extra important to validate the solution to ensure it is correct and relevant.

In the upcoming sections, we will describe a detailed strategy for each chosen problem domain's full-stack web development and data science.

Prompt techniques

There are some techniques that are extra useful when instructing the AI assistant to ensure you get the most out of it. The general advice is to provide enough context to the AI assistant but what that means exactly can be made more concrete via the below suggested patterns:

- Task-Action-Guideline Prompt Pattern
- Persona-Instruction-Content Prompt Pattern
- Exploratory prompt

Task-Action-Guideline prompt pattern (TAG)

To explain how this pattern works, let's break down the parts and the show an example prompt with an example response:

Intent: To instruct an AI assistant on what task to solve, what actions to take, and what guidelines to adhere to.

- **Task:** Clearly define the task you want the AI to accomplish
- **Action:** Specify the steps or actions the AI should take to complete the task
- **Guideline:** Provide any rules, constraints, or guidelines the AI should follow while performing the task

Example:

[Prompt]

Task: Generate a summary of the latest news article about climate change.

Action:

1. Search for the most recent news articles on climate change.
2. Select the article with the highest relevance and credibility.
3. Summarize the key points of the article in 3-4 sentences.

Guideline:

1. Ensure the summary is concise and accurate.
2. Avoid using technical jargon; keep the language simple and accessible.
3. Cite the source of the article at the end of the summary.

[End of prompt]

[Prompt response]

Summary: A recent article from BBC News highlights the alarming increase in global temperatures over the past decade. Scientists warn that if current trends continue, we could see unprecedented climate events. The article emphasizes the urgent need for international cooperation to combat climate change. [Source: BBC News]

This pattern helps ensure that the AI assistant understands the task, knows the steps to take, and adheres to any specific guidelines, leading to more accurate and useful outputs.

[End of response]

Here's what a prompt example could look like for web development:

[Prompt]

Task: Develop a RESTful API for a simple blog application using Node.js and Express.

Action:

1. Set up a new Node.js project.
2. Create an Express server.
3. Define routes for CRUD operations on blog posts.
4. Implement middleware for JSON parsing and error handling.
5. Connect to a MongoDB database using Mongoose.
6. Write tests for the API endpoints.

Guideline:

1. Ensure the project setup is clear and straightforward.
2. Provide concise and accurate code examples.
3. Avoid using overly complex terminology; keep the language simple and accessible.
4. Include comments in the code to explain each step.

[End prompt]

Persona-Instruction-Context prompt pattern (PIC)

Let's describe this pattern in the same way as the preceding one, let's define it, followed by an example prompt and an example response:

Intent: To instruct an AI assistant on the persona it should assume, what instructions to carry out, and provide enough context to generate a correct response.

- **Persona:** Define the persona or character traits the AI should embody while responding
- **Instruction:** Specify the tasks or actions the AI should perform
- **Context:** Provide relevant background information or context to help the AI understand the situation and generate an appropriate response

Example:

[Prompt]

Persona: Assume the persona of a friendly and knowledgeable travel guide.

Instruction:

1. Recommend three must-visit attractions in Paris.
2. Provide a brief description of each attraction.
3. Suggest the best time to visit each attraction.

Context: The user is planning a trip to Paris for the first time and is interested in both historical sites and local culture.

[End of prompt]

[Prompt response]

As your friendly and knowledgeable travel guide, I'd love to recommend three must-visit attractions in Paris:

1. **Eiffel Tower**: This iconic landmark offers breathtaking views of the city. It's best to visit in the early morning or late evening to avoid the crowds and enjoy the stunning sunrise or sunset.

2. **Louvre Museum**: Home to thousands of works of art, including the Mona Lisa, the Louvre is a treasure trove of history and culture. Plan your visit on a weekday morning to experience the museum with fewer visitors.

3. **Montmartre**: This charming neighborhood is known for its artistic history and vibrant street life. Visit in the late afternoon to explore the quaint streets and enjoy a leisurely dinner at a local café.

Enjoy your trip to Paris!

[End of response]

This pattern ensures that the AI assistant adopts the right persona, follows specific instructions, and uses the provided context to deliver a relevant and helpful response.

Here's what such a prompt could like for web development:

[Prompt]

Persona: Assume the persona of a friendly and knowledgeable software development mentor.

Instruction:

1. Set up a new Node.js project.
2. Create an Express server.
3. Define routes for CRUD operations on blog posts.
4. Implement middleware for JSON parsing and error handling.
5. Connect to a MongoDB database using Mongoose.
6. Write tests for the API endpoints.

Context: The user is a beginner in web development and is looking to build their first RESTful API for a blog application. They need clear, step-by-step guidance and code examples.

[End of prompt]

Exploratory prompt pattern

You might find yourself in situations where you're not building a project from start to finish, or you only want to build a smaller part of and then evaluate the response. In those cases, your prompts will be more exploratory in nature and can for example look like the below:

[Prompt]

Clean the data.

[End of prompt]

An assumption here is that we have a Notebook open with existing code that has already fetched the data.

Or, something more for web development:

[Prompt]

Add CSS for this product list.

[End of prompt]

Prompts for this pattern are usually a lot shorter in length, has context (derived from existing code or in some other way) and the developer line of sight is seldom beyond the next step.

Learn-Improvise-Feedback-Evaluate prompt pattern (LIFE)

This pattern, like TAG and PIC helps frame the problem and provides a good start to a solution that you can further refine.

*   **Learn:** Highlight the need to understand data through various analytical techniques, from basic statistics to complex correlations and temporal analysis.
*   **Improvise:** Adapt the analysis based on initial findings. For instance, if certain categories of products show unusual trends, deepen the analysis in these areas

- **Feedback:**
  - Share code and model outputs for feedback to ensure effective learning and understanding.
  - Incorporate suggestions and critiques to refine the model and the approach.
  - Provide errors to troubleshoot and resolve the issues
- **Evaluate:** Execute the code provided by ChatGPT to ensure accuracy and validity.

An example prompt from this pattern might look like so:

[Prompt]

Project Title: Building a Web-Based Search Results Page. You must suggest steps and code

Objective: Create a dynamic and interactive search results page that efficiently displays and filters search results based on user queries. Steps:

- **Learn:** Understand the importance of displaying search results effectively. Analyze user interaction data to identify key metrics such as click-through rates, average time spent on results pages, and user satisfaction scores. Use various analytical techniques, from basic statistics to complex correlations and temporal analysis, to gain insights into user behavior and preferences.
- **Improvise:** Based on initial findings, adapt the search results page to highlight the most relevant results. For instance, if users frequently click on certain types of results, prioritize these in the display. Implement features such as filters, sorting options, and pagination to enhance user experience.
- **Feedback:** Share your code and the search results page with peers or mentors for feedback. This will help ensure effective learning and understanding. Incorporate their suggestions and critiques to refine the search results page and improve its functionality. Provide errors: Document any errors encountered during the development process, such as issues with data retrieval or display. Troubleshoot and resolve these issues, learning from the process to enhance your skills.
- **Evaluate:** Execute the code provided by ChatGPT to ensure its accuracy and validity. Validate the search results page by comparing its performance with real-world data and user feedback. Make necessary adjustments to improve accuracy and user satisfaction.

[End of prompt]

You might end up with a prompt response similar to:

[Prompt response]

Great! Let's break down the steps and provide some code snippets to help you build a dynamic and interactive search results page.

- **Project Title:** Building a Web-Based Search Results Page
- **Objective:** Create a dynamic and interactive search results page that efficiently displays and filters search results based on user queries.

Steps:

Learn:

- **Understand the importance of displaying search results effectively:**

    - Analyze user interaction data to identify key metrics such as click-through rates, average time spent on results pages, and user satisfaction scores.
    - Use various analytical techniques, from basic statistics to complex correlations and temporal analysis, to gain insights into user behavior and preferences.

Improvise:

- **Adapt the search results page based on initial findings:**

    - Highlight the most relevant results based on user interaction data.
    - Implement features such as filters, sorting options, and pagination to enhance user experience.

Feedback:

- **Share your code and the search results page with peers or mentors for feedback:**

    - Incorporate their suggestions and critiques to refine the search results page and improve its functionality.

Provide errors:

- **Document any errors encountered during the development process:**

    - Troubleshoot and resolve these issues, learning from the process to enhance your skills.

Evaluate:

- **Execute the code provided by ChatGPT to ensure its accuracy and validity:**

    - Validate the search results page by comparing its performance with real-world data and user feedback. Make necessary adjustments to improve accuracy and user satisfaction.

Code Snippets:

HTML Structure:

```html
<!DOCTYPE html>
<html lang="en">
<head>
    <meta charset="UTF-8">
    <meta name="viewport" content="width=device-width, initial-scale=1.0">
    <title>Search Results Page</title>
    <link rel="stylesheet" href="styles.css">
</head>
<body>
```

```html
    <div class="search-container">
        <input type="text" id="search-input" placeholder="Search...">
        <button onclick="performSearch()">Search</button>
    </div>
    <div class="results-container" id="results-container"></div>
    <script src="script.js"></script>
</body>
</html>
```

CSS Styling:

```css
/* styles.css */
body {
    font-family: Arial, sans-serif;
}

.search-container {
    margin: 20px;
}

.results-container {
    margin: 20px;
}

.result-item {
    border: 1px solid #ccc;
    padding: 10px;
    margin-bottom: 10px;
}
```

JavaScript Functionality:

```javascript
// script.js
function performSearch() {
    const query = document.getElementById('search-input').value;
    const resultsContainer = document.getElementById('results-container');
    resultsContainer.innerHTML = ''; // Clear previous results

    // Simulate search results
    const results = [
        { title: 'Result 1', description: 'Description for result 1' },
        { title: 'Result 2', description: 'Description for result 2' },
        { title: 'Result 3', description: 'Description for result 3' },
```

```
    ];

    results.forEach(result => {
        const resultItem = document.createElement('div');
        resultItem.className = 'result-item';
        resultItem.innerHTML = `<h3>${result.title}</h3><p>${result.
description}</p>`;
        resultsContainer.appendChild(resultItem);
    });
}
```

Additional Features:

- **Filters and Sorting:** Add dropdowns or checkboxes to filter and sort results.
- **Pagination:** Implement pagination to handle large sets of results.
- **Error Handling:** Add error handling to manage issues with data retrieval or display.

This should give you a solid foundation to start building your web-based search results page. Let me know if you need further assistance or more detailed code examples!

[End of response]

Which pattern to choose?

The general answer it depends on the situation which pattern to choose. The reason for choosing between the TAG and PIC is that you have a clearly defined problem that you want to solve from start to finish and you're looking for the AI assistant to do the "heavy lifting". The reason to go for the exploratory pattern is when you're working on an existing codebase, or you want to try out various approaches and steps. Our general recommendation is to try out all three patterns to see what suits your approach and problem the best.

Prompt strategy for web development

Let's apply the different guidelines presented in the former section, and through using these guidelines, we will step by step work ourselves toward a prompt strategy.

Break down the problem: "web system for inventory management"

Let's use a real example, "inventory management" within web development, to see if we can understand the general problem. To "manage" an inventory, you need to read and write data to it. Most likely, you will have different roles in this system/app, everything from administrators to normal users. You might also need to consider how this system fits in with other systems, should you, for example, integrate it with other systems, what parts it consists of in that case and how.

The domain seems pretty straightforward so let's move on to understand what parts it consists of.

At a high level, we understand what the system should do. But to solve the problem, we need to divide it into smaller parts, which in web development usually entails the following components:

- **Frontend:** The frontend is the part of the system that the user interacts with. The frontend is responsible for presenting data to the user and receiving input from the user.
- **Backend:** This part of the system communicates with the frontend. The backend is responsible for reading and writing data to a database. There could additionally be different frontends and different apps altogether that communicate with the backend in a more complex system.
- **Database:** The database is the part of the system that stores data. It's a data store, for example, a relational database such as MySQL or PostgreSQL. The database is responsible for storing data in a way that's efficient and easy to read and write.
- **Reporting:** There's often a reporting part that presents insights. It takes its data from the data store and may need to transform the data to make it presentable from a reporting perspective.

Further breakdown of the frontend into features

Having an overview like this is useful but usually not enough of a breakdown for us to start writing prompts. We need to break it down further, usually by features. At this point, a further breakdown of the frontend into features may look like the following list:

- **Login:** The user needs to be able to log in to the system.
- **Logout:** The user needs to be able to log out of the system.
- **View inventory:** The user needs to be able to view the inventory.
- **Add inventory:** The user needs to be able to add the inventory.
- **Remove inventory:** The user needs to be able to remove the inventory.
- **Update inventory:** The user needs to be able to update the inventory.

Generate prompts for each feature

At this point, it's granular enough for us to start writing prompts. Let's take the first feature, login, and see how we can start thinking about how to craft a prompt.

You may start with a prompt, using a tool like ChatGPT or GitHub Copilot (more on that in an upcoming next chapter) like the following:

[Prompt]

Create a login page for the user to log in to the system.

[End of prompt]

While this may work, you're leaving out a lot of context, such as what exactly is needed here and what's not, what technologies are you using, what the user experience is, and so on.

Let's try to improve the prompt by adding more context:

[Prompt]

Create a login page with fields for the username and password. It should have a link for creating a user and a login button, be vertically and horizontally centered, and work well on a mobile phone and tablet. It should be written in React and use the Material UI library.

[End of prompt]

Identify some basic principles for web development, a "prompt strategy"

As you have seen so far, we broke down the problem into smaller, more "manageable" pieces and we suggested some prompts for how to solve a specific feature. So what exactly are we suggesting in terms of "prompt strategy" now that we understand more about our example "inventory management"? For one, we realize that our strategy will be context-dependent. Because we're in web development, we need to use keywords within that domain, together with libraries and architecture suitable for a specific area. Here are some guides we suggest you use:

- **Provide context – fields:** A login screen can be as simple as username and password fields. Most screens however have more fields, such as a password confirmation field, a link to reset a password, a field to create a new user, and so on. Depending on your needs, you may need to be very detailed.

- **Specify how – design, and tech choices:** A login screen can be designed in many ways. It's quite common today to optimize for different devices like tablets, mobile, large screens, and so on. For tech choices, web development has a lot of choices, from frameworks like React, Vue, and Angular to plain HTML and CSS. Specify according to the needs of the project.

- **Iterate:** Different tools react differently to the same prompt. Throughout this book, we will show you how to use different tools like GitHub Copilot and ChatGPT. Each tool has its own strengths and weaknesses and may offer different results. Try to iterate on the prompt by adding separators like commas and colons, and try rephrasing the prompt.

- **Be context-aware:** When you use tools like ChatGPT and GitHub Copilot, you do so with pre-existing context. For ChatGPT, that means you're having an ongoing conversation of prompts and responses, and for GitHub Copilot, it means it sees not only what you've written in your open file but also your entire workspace if you let it. The response to your prompts looks at this context and decides what to generate. It's important to be aware of this context and if you're not getting the response you want, try to change the context, in ChatGPT, start a new conversation, and in GitHub Copilot, close the open files, start writing in a blank file, and so on.

Prompt strategy for data science

Let's do a similar thought experiment for data science as we did for web development. We'll use the presented guidelines "problem breakdown" and "generate prompts," and just like in the web development section, we'll draw some general conclusions on the domain and present those as a prompt strategy for data science.

## Chapter 2

Problem breakdown: predict sales

Let's say we're building a machine-learning model to predict sales. At a high level, we understand what the system should do. To solve the problem though, we need to divide it into smaller parts, which in data science usually entails the following components:

- **Data:** The data is the part of the system that stores information. The data can come from many places like databases, web endpoints, static files, and more.
- **Model:** The model is responsible for learning from the data and producing a prediction that's as accurate as possible. To predict, you need an input that produces one or more outputs as a prediction.
- **Training:** The training is the part of the system that trains the model. Here, you typically have part of your data as training and a part being sample data.
- **Evaluation:** To ensure your model works as intended, you need to evaluate it. Evaluation means taking the data and model and producing a score that indicates how well the model performs.
- **Visualization:** Visualization is the part where you can gain insights valuable for the business via graphs. This part is very important, as it's the part that's most visible to the business.

Further breakdown into features/steps for data science

At this point, you're at too high a level to start writing prompts. We can break it down further by looking at each step:

- **Data:** The data part has many steps, including collecting the data, cleaning it, and transforming it. Here's how you can break it down:
    1. **Collect data:** The data needs to be collected from somewhere. It could be a database, a web endpoint, a static file, and so on.
    2. **Clean data:** The data needs to be cleaned. Cleaning means removing data that's not relevant, removing duplicates, and so on.
    3. **Transform data:** The data needs to be transformed. Transformation means changing the data to a format that's useful for the model.
- **Training:** Just like the data part, the training part has many steps to it. Here's how you can break it down:
    1. **Split data:** The data needs to be split into training and sample data. The training data is used to train the model and the sample data is used to evaluate the model.
    2. **Train model:** The model needs to be trained. Training means taking the training data and learning from it.
- **Evaluation:** The evaluation part is usually a single step but can be broken down further.

Generate prompts for each step

Note how our breakdown for data science looks a bit different from web development. Instead of identifying features like **Add inventory**, we instead have a feature like Collect data.

However, we're on the correct level to author a prompt, so let's use the **Collect data** feature as our example:

[Prompt]

Collect data from `data.xls` and read it into a DataFrame using Pandas library.

[End of prompt]

The preceding prompt is both general and specific at the same time. It's general in the sense that it tells you to "collect data" but specific in that it specifies a specific library to use and even what data structure (DataFrame). It's entirely possible that a simpler prompt would have worked for the preceding step like so:

[Prompt]

Collect data from data.xls.

[End of prompt]

This is where it may vary depending on whether you use a tool like ChatGPT or GitHub Copilot.

Identify some basic principles for data science, "a prompt strategy for data science"

Here, we've identified some similar principles as in the web development example:

- **Provide context – filename:** A CSV file can have any name. It's important to specify the name of the file.

- **Specify how – libraries:** There are many ways to load a CSV file, and even though Pandas library is a common choice, it's important to specify it. There are other libraries to work with and you might need a solution for Java, C#, and Rust, for example, where libraries are named differently.

- **Iterate:** It's worth iterating on the prompt, rephrasing it, and adding separators like a comma, a colon, and so on.

- **Be context-aware:** Also here, context matters a lot; if you're working in Notebook, previous cells will be available to GitHub Copilot, previous conversations will be available to ChatGPT, and so on.

As you can see from the preceding guidance, the strategy is very similar for web development. Here we're also listing "Provide," "Specify how," "Iterate," and "Be context-aware." The big difference lies in the details. However, there's an alternate strategy that works in data science and that's lengthy prompts. Even though we've broken down the data science problem into features, we don't need to write a prompt per feature. Another way of solving it could be to express everything you want to be carried out in one large prompt. Such a prompt could therefore look like so:

[Prompt]

You want to predict sales on the file `data.xsl`. Use Python and Pandas library. Here are the steps that you should carry out:

- Collect data
- Clean data
- Transform data
- Split data
- Train model
- Evaluation

[End of prompt]

You will see examples in future chapters on data science and machine learning where both smaller prompts as well as lengthier prompts are being used. You decide which approach you want to use.

Validate the solution

The most important part of this strategy is verifying correctness and that the text and code created by the AI assistant are correct. There are two general approaches we can take to verify our outcome:

- **Verification via prompts:** The first approach is to use prompts to verify the outcome. This means writing prompts that question the outcome of specific results. This can be a good strategy to employ at the beginning of your verification process. What you're looking for are situations where the AI assistant isn't consistent in its responses.
- **Classical verifications:** The second approach is to use classical verification techniques. What those techniques are varies depending on the problem domain. At a high level, though, it boils down to testing code, comparing output, and relying on your own knowledge, and the knowledge of your peers, to verify the outcome.

The AI tool doesn't really know what it's doing. The responses provided are responses that likely depend on its training corpus. At all times, you should be aware of this and rely on your expertise to verify the outcome.

In the next subsections, let's explore various approaches for manual and classical verification.

Verification via prompts

You can use prompts to both produce results that take you closer to resolving the problem but also to verify the results. Let's take an example where we're building the previously mentioned login screen. We've written a prompt that looks like the following:

[Prompt]

Create a login page with fields for username and password; it should have a link for creating a user and a login button. It should be vertically and horizontally centered and work well on a mobile phone and tablet. It should be written in React and use the Material UI library.

[End of prompt]

To verify this outcome, we can write a prompt like the following:

[Prompt]

Given the below code, what does it do?

```
.login {
  <!-- should include CSS to center horizontally and vertically and be
responsive -->
  @media (min-width: 768px) {
    <!-- should include CSS to center horizontally and vertically and be
responsive -->
  }
}

<div class="login">
  <TextField id="username" label="Username" />
  <TextField id="password" label="Password" />
  <Button variant="contained" color="primary">
    Login
  </Button>
</div>
```

[End of prompt]

An app could look at the code provided and realize you don't need a prompt to deduce what it does, and that it's in fact missing CSS code to make it responsive. The point here though is that by writing prompts, you can have the AI assistant tell you what it thinks the code does via questions.

Using prompts this way, to pose queries on the output, is a good first step to verifying the outcome. However, it's not enough and you need to rely on classical verification techniques, so let's cover that next.

Classical verification

How you verify the outcome depends on the problem domain. In web development, you can use a variety of different tools and techniques, for example:

- **Testing:** With end-to-end testing or frontend testing, you can verify that the code works as intended. Usually, this type of test involves using a programmatic approach to simulate user interaction with the web page, using something like Selenium, for example.

- **Manual testing:** You can manually test the web page by opening it in a browser and interacting with it. This is a good approach to use at the beginning of your verification process. Apart from interaction, you can also visually inspect the web page to see if it looks correct according to your requirements.

- **Code review:** You can review the code and see if it looks correct. This is a good approach to use at the beginning of your verification process. It allows not only you but also your peers to verify the outcome.

- **Tools:** Tools can test a variety of different scenarios like accessibility, performance, and so on. These tools are most likely a part of your development process already.

Conducting data science, you may rely on all of the preceding approaches, but you may also use other approaches. Some common approaches are:

- **Unit testing:** You can use unit testing to verify that the code works as intended.
- **Integration testing:** You can use integration testing to verify that the code works as intended.
- **Validation of results:** This type of validation means you compare the results of your analysis or model to known results or benchmarks.
- **Cross validation:** This type of validation means you split your data into training and sample data, train your model on the training data, and evaluate it on the sample data. This is a good approach to use at the beginning of your verification process.

Summary

Throughout this chapter, we've provided a strategy for solving problems with prompts and validating the solution.

You've seen how both web development and data science can be broken down into smaller parts that can be solved with prompts. We also identified some basic principles for writing prompts.

Finally, we looked at how to validate the solution using prompts and classical verification techniques.

It's our hope that you will revisit this chapter when you're looking at solving a problem within web development or data science and you're looking for an approach.

There's more to prompting than writing a prompt and getting a response. You will see throughout this book how we use these principles in various domains to solve problems. Try typing these prompts as you read, adapt to your own needs, and see what happens.

In the next chapter, we are going to learn more about the two AI assistants of our choice, GitHub Copilot and ChatGPT.

Join our community on Discord

Join our community's Discord space for discussions with the author and other readers:

`https://packt.link/aicode`

3

Tools of the Trade: Introducing Our AI Assistants

Introduction

Writing code or text takes time, at least if you want it to be well organized and readable. But what if you could have a tool that would help you write code faster and with less effort? That's what GitHub Copilot and ChatGPT are really all about.

Before you start using an AI assistant, it's a good idea to get a mile-high view of its capabilities and limitations. You want to see what you can and can't use it for, or at least understand where the tool performs less well.

In this chapter, we will cover the following:

- Understanding what GitHub Copilot and ChatGPT are and how they work
- Learning about Copilot's capabilities and limits
- Installing GitHub Copilot
- Generating code completions via GitHub Copilot

Understanding Copilot

Pair programming is the idea of (usually two) developers working together, often in front of the same screen, also sometimes called "pairing." GitHub Copilot can be seen as an "AI pair programmer" that helps you write code, enabling you to get more done, faster. It's based on OpenAI's Codex model, a new AI system trained on publicly available source code and natural language. But in reality, it has gone beyond this. Let's denote GitHub Copilot as Copilot for the remainder of the book. Copilot suggests whole lines or entire functions right inside your editor.

How Copilot knows what to generate

The idea behind Copilot is that it learns from the code you and others have written and uses that knowledge to suggest new lines of code as you type.

How does Copilot work? It uses machine learning to build a model of the code you and others have written and suggests the best text for you to use next. There are two parts of importance, the trained model and the so-called in-memory context. The model is trained on public repositories on GitHub and the context is something it assembles at runtime from looking at your files. Using the context and the underlying model, it provides you with text suggestions. Copilot uses some of the following to build its context (i.e., its in-memory capability that it uses together with the trained model to provide suggestions):

- **Your active file:** The code you're working on.
- **Comments:** Copilot uses comments to understand the context of your code.
- **Open files and your workspace:** It not only looks at the code in your active file but also at the code in other files in your workspace.
- **Import statements:** Even import statements are factored into Copilot's suggestions.
- **The underlying model and its training data:** The code in public GitHub repositories constitutes the base of what it's trained on.

Copilot capabilities and limits

So, what can Copilot do? It can do a lot, but here's a non-exhaustive list of capabilities:

- **Code completion:** Copilot can complete lines of code for you.
- **Code generation:** Copilot can generate whole functions for you.
- **Tests, comments, and documentation:** Copilot can generate tests, comments, and documentation for you.
- **Suggest improvements:** Copilot can suggest improvements to your code. Improvements can come in many forms, from suggesting a better variable name or a better way to write a function to how to organize code better.
- **Translate code:** Copilot can translate code from one language to another. For example, it can translate Python code to JavaScript code.
- **Answer questions:** Copilot can answer questions about your code. For example, it can tell you what a function does or what a variable is used for, and answer questions about a domain such as "What is machine learning?", for example.

Setup and installation

How can you get started? You can use Copilot from a variety of places and editors including Visual Studio, Visual Studio Code, GitHub Codespaces, and GitHub's web-based editor. In this chapter, we'll use Visual Studio Code.

Installing Copilot

To install Copilot, you need to install the GitHub Copilot extension for Visual Studio Code and also need to allow access.

Let's review the steps in more detail (as outlined on the official Copilot docs page).

You can install the GitHub Copilot extension for Visual Studio Code from the Visual Studio Code Marketplace or from within Visual Studio Code. We will show the latter here:

1. In the **Extension: GitHub Copilot** tab in Visual Studio Code, select **Install**.
2. If you have not previously authorized Visual Studio Code in your GitHub account, you will be prompted to sign in to GitHub in Visual Studio Code.
3. If you have previously authorized Visual Studio Code for your account on GitHub, GitHub Copilot will be automatically authorized.
4. If you don't get the prompt to authorize, select the bell icon in the bottom panel of the Visual Studio Code window.
5. In your browser, GitHub will request the necessary permissions for GitHub Copilot. To approve these permissions, select **Authorize Visual Studio Code**.
6. To confirm the authentication, in Visual Studio Code, select **Open** in the **Visual Studio Code** dialog box.

Refer to this page if you have any problems getting Copilot to work: `https://docs.github.com/en/copilot/getting-started-with-github-copilot`.

Getting started with Copilot

How do we get started? Well, provided you have installed Copilot and there's a Copilot icon in the bottom-right corner of your Visual Studio Code window, you're good to go.

Here's a suggestion to get started:

1. Create a new file in Visual Studio Code named `app.js`.
2. Start typing the text prompt "Express web api with routes products and customers" as a comment at the top of the file like so, and press *Enter*:

    ```
    //Express web api with routes products and customers
    ```

3. Give it a few seconds and you should see a suggestion from Copilot as follows:

    ```
    const express = require('express');
    ```

 If nothing appears, try pressing *Ctrl* + *Spacebar* to trigger a suggestion or start typing the start of the code, i.e., *const*, and wait for a suggestion to appear.

4. You will have to press the *Tab* key to accept the suggestion. At this point, Copilot can keep generating code for you. To ensure it does, press *Enter* and watch as Copilot generates more code for you. Repeatedly press *Enter* and press *Tab* to accept the suggestions until you have code similar to the following:

```
const app = express();

app.get('/products', (req, res) => {
  res.send('products');
});

app.get('/customers', (req, res) => {
  res.send('customers');
});

app.listen(3000, () => {
  console.log('Server listening on port 3000');
});
```

5. Congratulations, you've just written your first lines of code with Copilot. Feel free to experiment with Copilot and try adding comments, so-called prompts, in the middle of your code and see what happens. Also, try varying the prompts and see what happens.

Assignment: improve the code

As an assignment, you're asked to improve the code generated by Copilot. Here are a few suggestions:

*   Add a route for the root of the web API.
*   Add a route for a specific product.
*   Add documentation for one of the routes.

Solution

Here's a possible solution:

```
const express = require('express');

app = express();

// add default route
app.get('/', (req, res) => {
  res.send('Hello world');
});

app.get('/products', (req, res) => {
```

```
    res.send('products');
});

// document route
/**
 * Get a product by id
 * @param {number} id - The id of the product
 */
app.get('/products/:id', (req, res) => {
  res.send(`product with id ${req.params.id}`);
});

app.get('/customers', (req, res) => {
  res.send('customers');
});

app.listen(3000, () -> {
  console.log('Server listening on port 3000');
});
```

Challenge

See if you can add a test for one of the routes.

In the next chapter, we will look at how to use Copilot in more detail. To use any AI assistant well, you need to understand how it works and how to use it. There's a skill associated with using these tools well and it's called prompt engineering. Prompt engineering is the art of writing prompts, not only to make it understand your intentions but also to produce an output you're happy with. It's more than just writing a comment; you can instruct your AI assistant to solve something, apply a form of reasoning to it, and much more. The next chapter presents the central theme of this book, prompt engineering.

References

- Copilot landing page: https://github.com/features/copilot
- Copilot docs: https://docs.github.com/en/copilot/getting-started-with-github-copilot

Understanding ChatGPT

ChatGPT, an OpenAI development, is a specialized version of the GPT model designed to simulate human-like conversations. It excels in creating human-like text in dialogues, handling a variety of topics. It's available for free at chat.openai.com, with a premium ChatGPT Plus option (also known as GPT-4), and can draft essays, generate art prompts, and program code. The premium version offers enhanced features such as visual and audio input and output handling, file uploads, code execution, data visualization with select Python libraries, and customizable GPT capabilities.

You can access ChatGPT simply by visiting `chat.openai.com` and creating an OpenAI account. It is also available as an app for both Android and iOS. More details can be found on the official website (`https://openai.com/`).

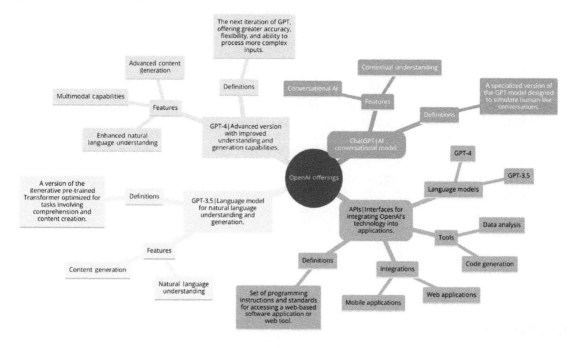

Figure 3.1: Offerings of OpenAI

How does ChatGPT work?

ChatGPT, paralleling Copilot's code-oriented approach but in natural language processing, is adept at content generation, challenging traditional search engines. It excels in tasks such as essay writing and summarizing texts. The quality of ChatGPT's responses heavily depends on the prompts it receives.

ChatGPT leverages extensive training data including books, websites, and a variety of textual sources for comprehensive language understanding.

It employs sophisticated machine learning algorithms, such as deep learning neural networks based on the Transformer architecture, to predict accurate and contextually relevant text responses.

ChatGPT's contextual understanding is honed through advanced techniques, enabling it to interpret and respond to varying conversation threads intelligently. This approach mirrors the principles used in Copilot for code, adapted here for nuanced, human-like text interaction.

ChatGPT capabilities and limits

Capabilities of ChatGPT:

- **Content creation:** Generates creative content including marketing material, blog posts, stories, and poems
- **Educational explanations:** Offers detailed explanations on complex topics for educational purposes
- **Coding assistance:** Assists developers with code optimization, error debugging, and algorithm design
- **Learning aid:** Acts as a companion in online learning, offering real-time assistance and clarification of concepts
- **Conversational AI:** Enhances user experience in virtual assistants and chatbots through natural language interactions

Limitations and concerns of ChatGPT:

- **Accuracy issues:** ChatGPT may generate responses with factual inaccuracies or biases from training data, also known as hallucinations. These outputs often emerge from the AI model's inherent biases, lack of real-world understanding, or training data limitations. In other words, the AI system "hallucinates" information that it has not been explicitly trained on, leading to unreliable or misleading responses. Hence, users should always verify and validate the responses and should not use them blindly.
- **Ethical implications:** Raises concerns about the misuse of AI-generated content for fraudulent activities or harmful information gathering.
- **Employment impact:** Fear of AI replacing human jobs in certain sectors.
- **Security risks:** Potential use in phishing, creating malware, and cybercriminal activities.
- **Data privacy:** Concerns about the use of vast internet data in training, impacting user privacy.
- **Message cap:** At the time of writing the book, GPT-4 was capped to offer a maximum of 40 responses over 3 hours.
- **Limited Python libraries for code execution:** The Code Interpreter and Advanced Data Analysis features of ChatGPT use limited sets of libraries, heavily featuring machine learning libraries but not such great support for other libraries, such as Keras or TensorFlow, required for deep learning.

Setup and installation

Setting up and installing ChatGPT involves a few steps:

1. **Create an OpenAI account:** Visit the OpenAI website and sign up for an account.
2. **API access:** Developers need to obtain API access by applying on the OpenAI platform.

For non-developers, using ChatGPT is as simple as visiting the ChatGPT website or installing the Android or iOS app and logging in with your OpenAI account. No installation is required for general use. For more detailed steps and information, please refer to OpenAI's official documentation and website.

Getting started with ChatGPT

Once you've logged in to your OpenAI account on the ChatGPT side of the website, it's time to get to know the AI tool's window. Here's a breakdown of what you will see:

- **New chat and hide sidebar buttons:** On the left side of your screen, the New chat button can be used to start fresh conversations at any time. It creates a new discussion without context. There's also an option to hide the sidebar.
- **Chat history:** The left sidebar keeps your previous conversations accessible. You can edit chat titles, share your chat history, or delete it. Optionally, you can turn off chat history.
- **Account:** Click your name at the bottom left to access your account information. This includes settings, log out, help, and FAQs. If you don't have ChatGPT Plus, you'll see an **Upgrade** button here.
- **Your prompts:** Your questions or prompts appear in the middle of the chat window, accompanied by your account photo or initials.
- **ChatGPT's responses:** ChatGPT's responses display the logo on the left. On the right, you'll see options such as Copy, Thumbs Up, and Thumbs Down. Copy text to your clipboard for use elsewhere and provide feedback on response accuracy.
- **Regenerate response:** Click Regenerate response if you encounter issues or unsatisfactory answers. It prompts ChatGPT to generate a new reply based on your latest prompt.
- **Text area:** This is where you enter your prompts and questions.
- **ChatGPT version:** Below the text input area, you'll find fine print, including a disclaimer: "ChatGPT can make mistakes. Consider checking important information." Note that the display of the ChatGPT model version has been discontinued.

The following screenshot illustrates how this looks.

In the top-left corner, you can see the GPTs you have access to if you have the premium version.

At the bottom are your previous conversations.

If you have the premium version, you can choose **GPT-4** from the dropdown along with plugins.

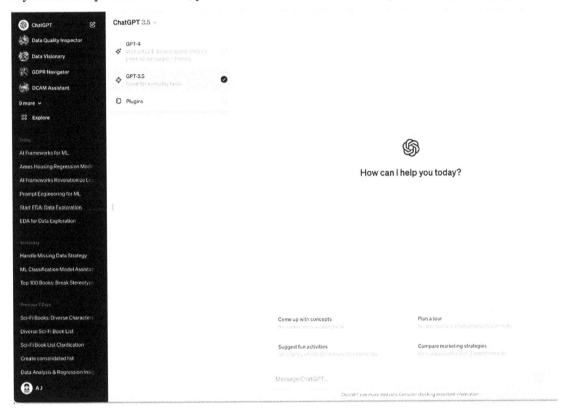

Figure 3.2: Selecting different versions of ChatGPT

You can even set custom instructions at the profile level if you wish to apply your configuration to all new conversations.

Figure 3.3: ChatGPT custom instructions

Prompting

Let's draft our first prompt with ChatGPT.

You just have to ask questions in your natural language and converse with it like you would with a human and it will start sharing its knowledge with you.

[Prompt]

Can you please explain the process of machine learning in bullet points to me?

[End of prompt]

You should see a response similar to the following screenshot. Note that the responses are never identical, and you will not get the exact same text each time.

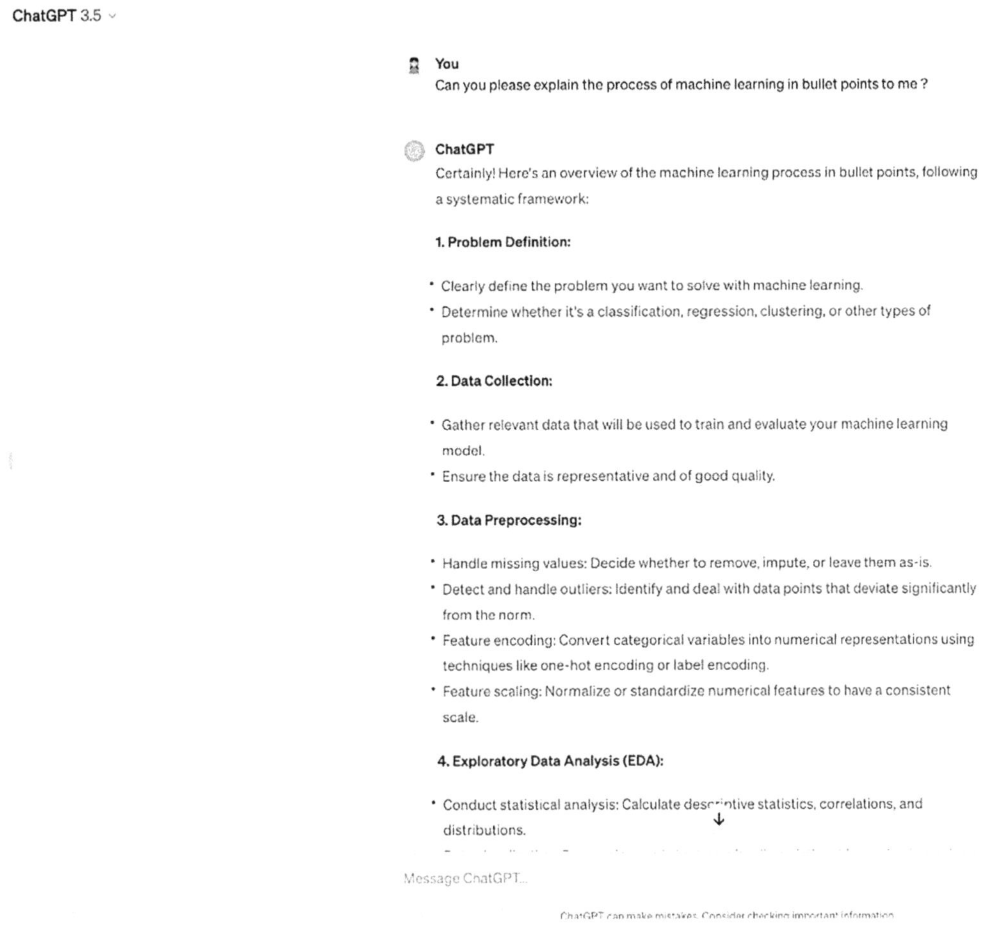

ChatGPT 3.5 ⌄

> **You**
> Can you please explain the process of machine learning in bullet points to me ?

> **ChatGPT**
> Certainly! Here's an overview of the machine learning process in bullet points, following a systematic framework:
>
> **1. Problem Definition:**
>
> * Clearly define the problem you want to solve with machine learning.
> * Determine whether it's a classification, regression, clustering, or other types of problem.
>
> **2. Data Collection:**
>
> * Gather relevant data that will be used to train and evaluate your machine learning model.
> * Ensure the data is representative and of good quality.
>
> **3. Data Preprocessing:**
>
> * Handle missing values: Decide whether to remove, impute, or leave them as-is.
> * Detect and handle outliers: Identify and deal with data points that deviate significantly from the norm.
> * Feature encoding: Convert categorical variables into numerical representations using techniques like one-hot encoding or label encoding.
> * Feature scaling: Normalize or standardize numerical features to have a consistent scale.
>
> **4. Exploratory Data Analysis (EDA):**
>
> * Conduct statistical analysis: Calculate descriptive statistics, correlations, and distributions.

Message ChatGPT...

ChatGPT can make mistakes. Consider checking important information

Figure 3.4: ChatGPT prompt screen

Summary

In this chapter, we've looked at GitHub Copilot and ChatGPT, including what they are, how they work, and how to get started with them.

We've also looked at some of their capabilities and limitations.

Finally, we've looked at how to install them and work with them. You were also given some idea of how to use them via prompts. 3

Join our community on Discord

Join our community's Discord space for discussions with the author and other readers:

`https://packt.link/aicode`

4

Build the Appearance of Our App with HTML and Copilot

Introduction

Building a web app involves the usage of HTML for markup, CSS for styling, and JavaScript for making it interactive.

We've come a long way from building a web app from static pages in the 1990s to now using frameworks to build large apps. Regardless of whether you use a framework or a library, it still rests on the same foundation, HTML, CSS, and JavaScript.

To tackle these three markup and programming languages, we can use an AI assistant. There's more to using an AI assistant than generating text, given text input. You also need working knowledge of the area you're trying to tackle. For markup languages like HTML and CSS, "working knowledge" means you should know how to structure a web page or configure the styling with CSS. In short, you know how to do the task at hand, and the AI assistant is there to make you faster and more efficient.

 The output from the prompts mentioned in this chapter may vary based on training data, what files you have open, and what you typed previously.

You will see throughout the different chapters of this book how we will follow a specific method of first discussing a business problem we're looking to solve, with web development or data science merely being approaches that help us solve the problem. We will then focus on the problem, which varies depending on whether we're a web developer or data scientist, followed by dividing up our problem into smaller more manageable parts. Finally, we will recommend a "prompt" strategy that works well for this particular type of problem.

In this chapter, we will:

- **Generate basic HTML**: GitHub Copilot is capable of generating different kinds of code, including HTML.
- **Apply prompting techniques**: There are different techniques we can use to get the desired content.

Business problem: e-commerce

E-commerce is quite an interesting domain. There are many problems to be solved within this domain. For example, you need to provide a technical platform that allows users to purchase items. That in itself means you need to build various solutions for taking payments as well as products to buy and also some logistics that allow for shipping and more.

If you look at this business from the data side of things, you see that you need to analyze customer behavior to ensure you have the right number of items in stock, the correct prices on the items, and so on. In short, e-commerce is an intriguing domain that you will see mentioned throughout the book.

Problem domain

This chapter focuses on the role of the web developer, so let's discuss what type of problems await a web developer in e-commerce. There are usually two to three major roles you need to solve for as a web developer:

- The customer and all the actions that a customer can take like browsing and purchasing items to managing their account.
- Back office: This is the company behind the e-commerce application. Here, you need to ensure there exist technical solutions so that company employees can manage inventory, product information, payment solutions, and more.
- From a data standpoint, you, as a web developer, need to ensure that data can be stored and updated on areas like products, purchase orders, and customer information.

Problem breakdown: identify the features

To start breaking down this problem domain into something we can write prompt input for, let's again turn to the roles we mentioned, customer and back office. Here's an attempt at breaking the problem down into features we can build.

Let's start with the customer role and the major area, "Authentication." Let's attempt to break it down into things the customer should be able to do. Here are the actions we should support:

- **Login:** The user should be able to log in.
- **Logout:** The user should be able to log out.
- **Create a new user:** It should be possible to create a new user.
- **Update password:** An existing user should be able to update their password.

- **Password:** If a user forgets their password, it should be possible to reset it in a safe way.

Now, we have a set of features for a specific domain, "Authentication," and we have a better grasp of the different actions we should support. We'll leave it to you to further break down your problem domain like this, but see the preceding list as the detail level you should preferably be on before you start using your AI assistant.

Given the preceding breakdown into features, you could now, for example, type a prompt like so to attempt solving the first feature we identified above:

[Prompt]

Generate a login page, with fields for username, password, and repeat password and login button.

[End of prompt]

As a web developer, you've usually already done this breakdown of the problem domain into features before you start developing and even called these "user stories" if you use a development methodology like Scrum, for example.

With web development, though, you know it's a matter of looking at this problem from three different layers, the frontend, backend, and the data layer, usually a database where you store the data. The rest of this chapter will focus on the frontend when using the AI assistant. In later chapters, we will focus on other layers of the e-commerce example.

Prompt strategy

So, how do we select a prompt strategy and what do we mean by prompt strategy? Our strategy is about how we will prompt; will we write one prompt per feature or many short ones? It's also about how we use our chosen AI assistant, GitHub Copilot, and how we choose to input the prompts into the tool.

In GitHub Copilot, there are two major choices for how you write your prompts, either using the chat functionality or via typing comments or code directly in a text file. In this chapter, we will use the latter approach of typing directly in the text file. The general recommendation is that both approaches are valid and, it's our experience that you vary between these two approaches as you solve a problem.

Now that we've chosen our GitHub Copilot approach, what about the prompts themselves? We will choose a prompt strategy here where we type shorter prompts – we refer to this pattern as "Exploratory prompt pattern" in *Chapter 2* of the book. We will let GitHub Copilot build up its runtime context and learn from our code as we type it.

In the upcoming section, we will showcase how you can start generating markup code while being inside an open text file. At the end of this chapter, you will see how we revisit our e-commerce use case.

Page structure

A web page is defined in HTML, and all such pages are made up of a tree called a **document object model (DOM)**. The DOM has the following parts:

```
<html>
```

```
        <head>
        </head>
        <body>
        </body>
    </html>
```

You can see how the markup of the page consists of elements. The top elements need to be laid out hierarchically with HTML being the root element having the inner nodes HEAD and BODY. In the HEAD node, we define things like styling, instructions for search engines, page title, and more. In the BODY element, we place content we want to be visible.

Add AI assistance to our page structure

How can we leverage GitHub Copilot for this? Normally, web apps should have an `index.html` as an entry point for the app. To leverage GitHub Copilot, create a comment, `<!-- my comment -->`, on the page. You need to replace `my comment` with your prompt. So, what do you type instead of `my comment`? The answer is to provide GitHub Copilot with enough context for it to know what to generate in response.

 GitHub Copilot builds a runtime context not only based on its training model but also based on file endings like `.js` or `.html`, and what text is in both open or closed files in the directory you're in. This context is what decides what text should be generated based on what prompt you type.

Your first prompt, simple prompting, and aiding your AI assistant

Let's try writing our first prompts in an open text file.

 If you want to try the following prompts yourself while reading this, create an `index.html` page. Prompts are comments that you write. The comment should use the assigned comment format for the chosen type of file, meaning `<!-- -->` is how you comment in an HTML page, and `//` is how you write a comment in a JavaScript file.

Here's a prompt you can try adding as an HTML comment at the top of the page:

[Prompt]

Create a page with a title and list.

[End of prompt]

`<!-- create a page with a title and list -->`.

In this case, this prompt generates another prompt, namely, `<!-- the list should contain 3 items -->`.

At first glance, this might look confusing. Why would GitHub Copilot give me another comment as output? The explanation is that your AI assistant is trained on code and comments. In this case, GitHub Copilot provides you with the most likely response given its training data.

So, how do you get HTML markup as a response instead? The answer is that you start typing HTML, which narrows it down for GitHub Copilot, so the code in your text file should look like the following:

```
<!-- create a page with a title and list -->
<HTML
```

GitHub Copilot now generates code that should look similar to the following output:

[Prompt response]

```
<html lang="en">
```

[End of response]

If you keep hitting the *Return* key, and accepting the suggestions with *Tab*, more and more code will be generated so you end up with an output like so:

[Prompt response]

```
<!-- create a page with a title and list -->
<html lang="en">
<head>
    <title>My First Page</title>
</head>
<body>
    <h1>My First Page</h1>
    <ul>
        <li>First item
        <li>Second item
        <li>Third item
    </li>
</body>
</html>
```

[End of response]

Your second prompt: adding more context

Let's erase what we've done so far and start with a new prompt. The objective is to understand how writing a better-written prompt, with more context, yields a better output.

Let's try a second prompt, with more context and have it look like the following text:

[Prompt]

Create a page with a title and list, each item should have fields title, description and completed.

[End of prompt]

Note how we're now saying that the list consists of items and that each item has separate fields. So, what's the output of this prompt? Like before, use the *Return* key to generate a prompt response and *Tab* to accept the completion provided by GitHub Copilot.

[Prompt response]

```
<!-- create a page with a title and list, each item should have fields title,
description and completed -->
<html>
<head>
    <title>Todo List</title>
</head>
<body>
    <h1>Todo List</h1>
    <ul>
        <li>
            <h2>Item 1</h2>
            <p>Item 1 description</p>
            <p>Completed: <input type="checkbox" checked></p>
        </li>
        <li>
            <h2>Item 2</h2>
            <p>Item 2 description</p>
            <p>Completed: <input type="checkbox"></p>
        </li>
    </ul>
```

[End of response]

Our AI assistant is able to guess that we're trying to build a so-called "Todo app," a common type of app where we have tasks we're looking to complete. It was also able to generate a header element h2 for the title, a p for the description, and a checkbox for the Completed field. By adding more context, our AI assistant was able to provide a better output.

Your third prompt: accept prompt suggestions

So far, you've seen the difference between the two prompts, but what happens if we add even more context like so?

[Prompt]

create a page with a header, main part, and a footer. Use dark theme.

[End of prompt]

At this point, the output consists of more comments (suggestions), and if you accept several of them by entering the *Return* key (to get a new suggestion) and the *Tab* key (to accept the completion), your text file should now have content similar to the following output:

 It's also possible to reject the suggestion by, for example, continuing to type.

[Prompt response]

```
<!-- create a page with header, main part and footer use dark theme -->
<!-- header should have a navigation with 3 links -->
<!-- main part should have 3 sections with some text and images -->
<!-- footer should have 3 columns with some text and images -->
<!-- use flexbox for layout -->
<!-- use css variables for colors -->
<!-- use css variables for font sizes -->
<!-- use css variables for paddings and margins -->
<!-- use css variables for font family -->
<!-- use css variables for border radius -->
<!-- use css variables for border width -->
<!-- use css variables for border color -->
<!-- use css variables for background color -->
```

[End of response]

GitHub Copilot can suggest prompts that you might not even consider like navigation, images, and the use of CSS variables. If you type <html at this point, you see an output similar to:

[Prompt response]

```
<!-- create a page with header, main part and footer use dark theme -->
<!-- header should have a navigation with 3 links -->
<!-- main part should have 3 sections with some text and images -->
<!-- footer should have 3 columns with some text and images -->
<!-- use flexbox for layout -->
<!-- use css variables for colors -->
<!-- use css variables for font sizes -->
<!-- use css variables for paddings and margins -->
<!-- use css variables for font family -->
<!-- use css variables for border radius -->
<!-- use css variables for border width -->
<!-- use css variables for border color -->
```

```html
<!-- use css variables for background color -->
<html>
<head>
    <title>06.6 solution</title>
    <link rel="stylesheet" href="style.css">
</head>
<header>
        <nav>
            <a href="#">Home</a>
            <a href="#">About</a>
            <a href="#">Contact</a>
        </nav>
    </header>
<body>
    <main>
        <section>
            <h1>Section 1</h1>
            <p>Lorem ipsum dolor sit amet consectetur adipisicing elit.
Quisquam, voluptatum.</p>
            <img src="https://picsum.photos/200/300" alt="random image">
        </section>
        <section>
            <h1>Section 2</h1>
            <p>Lorem ipsum dolor sit amet consectetur adipisicing elit.
Quisquam, voluptatum.</p>
            <img src="https://picsum.photos/200/300" alt="random image">
        </section>
        <section>
            <h1>Section 3</h1>
            <p>Lorem ipsum dolor sit amet consectetur adipisicing elit.
Quisquam, voluptatum.</p>
            <img src="https://picsum.photos/200/300" alt="random image">
        </section>
    </main>
    <footer>
        <div>
            <h1>Column 1</h1>
            <p>Lorem ipsum dolor sit amet consectetur adipisicing elit.
Quisquam, voluptatum.</p>
            <img src="https://picsum.photos/200/300" alt="random image">
        </div>
        <div>
```

```
        <h1>Column 2</h1>
        <p>Lorem ipsum dolor sit amet consectetur adipisicing elit.
Quisquam, voluptatum.</p>
        <img src="https://picsum.photos/200/300" alt="random image">
    </div>
    <div>
        <h1>Column 3</h1>
        <p>Lorem ipsum dolor sit amet consectetur adipisicing elit.
Quisquam, voluptatum.</p>
        <img src="https://picsum.photos/200/300" alt="random image">
    </div>
</footer>
```

[End of response]

View this output in a browser and it should display the preceding sections that contain the title, description, and image for a number of items (exactly what you will see varies as these images are random).

As a web developer, you take this for what it is: a nice first scaffold that you need to add styling to at a later stage to make it look better.

Section 1
Lorem ipsum dolor sit amet consectetur adipisicing elit. Quisquam, voluptatum.

Section 2
Lorem ipsum dolor sit amet consectetur adipisicing elit. Quisquam, voluptatum.

Figure 4.1: Page with images (without the header and footer)

Challenge: vary the prompt

You can vary the output by adding or removing context. As a suggestion, see if you can change the prompt to add tables, forms, a multi-column layout, and more.

Use case: build a front for an e-commerce

Now that we've learned how to use GitHub Copilot for creating HTML markup, let's use it for a more challenging project: an e-commerce website. The requirements are that it should be a site with the following parts:

- A login page
- A user creation page
- A products page for products to put in a basket
- A basket page to show items you mean to purchase
- A checkout page showing your basket content and form for payment information and address info for shipping
- An admin page that allows you to edit your products

Let's start with these pages as they are commonly found on e-commerce websites.

Login page

The requirements for a login page are that you as a user can enter a username and password and that there's a button verifying your credentials. Optionally, you can add links for creating a user and a link if you forgot your password.

Try the following prompt as a comment at the top of a page called `login.html`:

[Prompt]

```
<!-- a page with input fields user name and password and a login button and
links to create a user and link for if you forgot your password, should look
good for mobile and desktop -->
```

[End of prompt]

 You may need to start typing `<html>` for the completion to be generated. Also, ensure you close all files except for the current one to make sure that your AI assistant is not distracted by other files that might be open.

You should see an output similar to:

[Prompt response]

```
<html>
<head>
```

```
    <title>Login</title>
    <link rel="stylesheet" href="css/login.css">
</head>
<body>
    <div class="container">
        <div class="login">
            <h1>Login</h1>
            <form action="login.php" method="post">
                <input type="text" name="username" placeholder="Username"
required="required" />
                <input type="password" name="password" placeholder="Password"
required="required" />
                <button type="submit" class="btn btn-primary btn-block btn-
large">Login</button>
            </form>
            <a href="register.php">Create User</a>
            <a href="forgot.php">Forgot Password</a>
        </div>
    </div>
```

[End of response]

This renders like so:

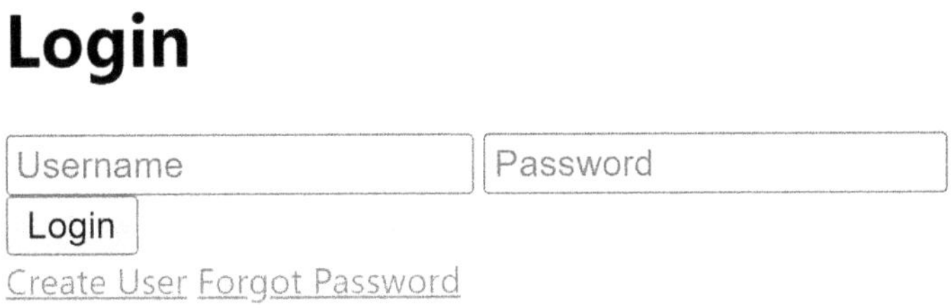

Login

| Username | Password |

Login

Create User Forgot Password

Figure 4.2: Login page

Product list page

On this page, we want to see a list of products we can buy, some details on each product, and an "**Add to Cart**" button. For this, we will create a `products.html` page and give it the following prompt:

```
<!-- list of products as div elements where each item has fields text, link to
detail page, random image, description and "add to cart button" -->
```

You should see an output similar to:

[Prompt response]

```
<!-- list of products as div elements where each item has fields text, link to
detail page, random image, description and "add to cart button" -->
```

```html
<html>
<head>
    <title>Products</title>
    <link rel="stylesheet" href="css/products.css">
</head>
<body>
    <div class="container">
        <div class="products">
            <h1>Products</h1>
            <div class="product">
                <div class="product-image">
                    <img src="https://picsum.photos/200/300" alt="product
image">
                </div>
                <div class="product-text">
                    <h2>Product 1</h2>
                    <p>Lorem ipsum dolor sit amet consectetur adipisicing elit.
Quisquam, voluptatum.</p>
                    <a href="product.php">View Product</a>
                    <button type="submit" class="btn btn-primary btn-block btn-
large">Add to Cart</button>
                </div>
            </div>
            <div class="product">
                <div class="product-image">
                    <img src="https://picsum.photos/200/300" alt="product
image">
                </div>
                <div class="product-text">
                    <h2>Product 2</h2>
                    <p>Lorem ipsum dolor sit amet consectetur adipisicing elit.
Quisquam, voluptatum.</p>
                    <a href="product.php">View Product</a>
                    <button type="submit" class="btn btn-primary btn-block btn-
large">Add to Cart</button>
                </div>
```

```
                </div>
                <div class="product">
                    <div class="product-image">
                        <img src="https://picsum.photos/200/300" alt="product
image">
                    </div>
                    <div class="product-text">
                        <h2>Product 3</h2>
                        <p>Lorem ipsum dolor sit amet consectetur adipisicing elit.
Quisquam, voluptatum.</p>
                        <a href="product.php">View Product</a>
                        <button type="submit" class="btn btn-primary btn-block btn-
large">Add to Cart</button>
                    </div>
                </div>
                <div class="product">
                    <div class="product-image">
                        <img src="https://picsum.photos/200/300" alt="product
image">
                    </div>
                    <div class="product-text">
                        <h2>Product 4</h2>
                        <p>Lorem ipsum dolor sit amet consectetur adipisicing elit.
Quisquam, voluptatum.</p>
                        <a href="product.php">View Product</a>
                        <button type="submit" class="btn btn-primary btn-block btn-
large">Add to Cart</button>
                    </div>
                </div>
            </div>
        </div>
</body>
</html>
```

[End of response]

This should render something like so:

Products

Product 1

Lorem ipsum dolor sit amet consectetur adipisicing elit. Quisquam, voluptatum.

View Product Add to Cart

Figure 4.3: Product list page

Remaining pages

We will leave it as an exercise for you to produce the remaining pages. Remember to create a dedicated HTML page and put a prompt comment at the top of the page.

Here's some suggested prompts for the remaining pages:

- A user creation page.

    Here is a suggested prompt:

    ```
    <!-- a page with fields username, password, repeat password and
    create button -->
    ```

- A basket page to show items you mean to purchase.

    Here is a suggested prompt:

    ```
    <!-- a page showing a list of items in a basket, each item should
    have title, price, quantity, sum and buttons to increase or
    decrease quantity and the page should have a link to "checkout" at
    the bottom  -->
    ```

- A checkout page showing your basket content and form for payment information and address info for shipping.

    Here is a suggested prompt:

    ```
    <!-- a checkout page containing a section for payment info with a
    credit card and a section below for shipping address  -->
    ```

- An admin page that allows you to edit your products.

    Here is a suggested prompt:

    ```
    <!--
    a section that's a list of products, each item has fields title
    and price, quantity, should also have an action for adding a new
    product, remove a product -->
    ```

Assignment

In this assignment, you will create a resume website. What context you provide GitHub Copilot with is up to you but start by creating an index.html and an HTML comment, <!-- my prompt -->.

Remember the techniques you were taught.

Write a prompt

Write a prompt and start typing the code/markup on the next line to help your assistant. Use the *Return* key to generate a response and the *Tab* key to accept the suggested text. Rewrite the prompt and add or change what it says to get the desired result.

You can find the solution to this assignment in the GitHub repository: https://github.com/PacktPublishing/AI-Assisted-Software-Development-with-GitHub-Copilot-and-ChatGPT/tree/main/04

Challenge

Given your built resume, you can improve it further by adding colors. How would you prompt to do so?

Quiz

Here's a set of questions to ensure you've grasped the key concepts:

1. The text you send to your AI assistant is called:

    a. text

    b. instruction

    c. prompt

2. Your AI assistant builds a context from:

    a. what you type

    b. what you type, the file ending, and the open and closed files in your working directory

    c. what you type and the file ending

You can find the solution to this quiz in the GitHub repository: `https://github.com/PacktPublishing/` `AI-Assisted-Software-Development-with-GitHub-Copilot-and-ChatGPT/tree/main/04`

Summary

In this chapter, we covered how to generate HTML markup using GitHub Copilot. We also covered how to use prompting techniques and how to add context to your prompts. As part of learning these prompting techniques, we discovered that the more context you give your AI assistant, the better the output. You also build up context over time as you add more content to your page.

Additionally, we started on a use case where we started building an e-commerce website. This use case is something we will continue to build on in the coming chapters.

For the next chapter, we will continue to cover web development but shift our focus to CSS and styling. You will see how the same or similar prompting techniques can be used for CSS as well.

Join our community on Discord

Join our community's Discord space for discussions with the author and other readers:

`https://packt.link/aicode`

5

Style the App with CSS and Copilot

Introduction

Styling an app well can make a huge difference in how a user perceives it. Well-thought-out styling includes catering to multiple devices, the smart use of graphics, and colors with great contrast.

CSS styling is a big topic, and we will not cover it in detail. However, we will show how you can start using it. Just like in the previous chapter, we will use our AI assistant to help us generate code. You will see how we will keep using comment-based prompting to generate code but also a new technique where nothing but the file's context is used for code generation.

You will also see how we will keep building on our e-commerce project and style it.

In this chapter, we will see how we can generate the CSS we need and how to keep applying the prompting patterns and strategies we've used in previous chapters. We will continue to build on the e-commerce project and give it an appealing appearance.

In this chapter, we will:

- **Generate CSS**: GitHub Copilot can generate styling, and we will show how AI assistance can generate CSS both by looking at surrounding code in a text file and based on a CSS comment.
- **Apply prompting techniques**: There are different techniques we can use to get the desired content.
- **Add CSS to our e-commerce project**: We will select a couple of pages in our e-commerce project to show how it benefits from styling.

Business problem: e-commerce

Just like the previous chapter, we will keep working in the e-commerce domain and through its many interesting problems. As this chapter focuses on visualization with CSS, what's the connection to the business, you might wonder? A bad UX, or user experience, or an ill-designed site that doesn't work on devices other than desktop or doesn't cater to accessibility can cost you money as, because of this, customers might choose to do business with your competitors.

Problem and data domain

This chapter continues with the e-commerce business domain and dives specifically into a basket page that lists products a customer aims to purchase. The data is therefore product data; not only that, but from a data aspect, we need to consider how to showcase detailed data relating to products, such as quantity and total cost, so the customer can decide what and how many items to buy. These considerations should be reflected in the chosen design.

Breaking the problem down into features

In the previous chapter, we chose to identify a larger area, "Authentication," and break that down into specific features. Let's recall what that feature breakdown looked like. After that, we'll see if we need to change it to instead be more design oriented. But first, let's show the list of features:

- **Area:** Authentication
- **Log in:** User should be able to log in.
- **Log out:** User should be able to log out.
- **Create new user:** It should be possible to create a new user.
- **Update password:** An existing user should be able to update their password.
- **Reset password:** If a user forgets their password, it should be possible to reset it in a safe way.

The above list of features constitutes a good high-level list of what we need to support. However, from a design viewpoint, we need to consider things like catering to different devices or support accessibility, for example. Therefore, a prompt for, let's say, the first feature might need to be tweaked to look like so:

[Prompt]

Generate a login page. It should have fields for username, password, and repeat password, as well as a login button. It should also support accessibility via tooltips and ARIA keys so that it can be used with just the keyboard and mouse.

[End of prompt]

As you can see from the above prompt, our concern is not only with what UI elements we need, like inputs and buttons, but also how it should work.

As before, we recommend that you break down the web app you're about to build into areas and each area into features so as to make prompting easier.

Prompting strategy

We mentioned in the previous chapter that you can both use the Chat mode of GitHub Copilot as well as typing inside of a file, and that you're recommended to use both approaches. As for how to prompt, you're recommended to write shorter prompts that you add context to as needed. By doing so, you rely on how GitHub Copilot works and how it builds a runtime context based on its underlying model, what's in your open directory, and your open file, among other things. You will also see another facet of prompting that doesn't rely on whether the prompt is long or short but rather on how your specific AI tool works. In this chapter, we use the "Exploratory prompt pattern" as described in *Chapter 2*.

CSS, or Cascading Style Sheets

CSS, or Cascading Style Sheets, is used to style HTML pages. It contains various constructs that allow you to change things such as fonts, sizes, colors, and layouts.

> To follow along with the below-mentioned prompts, you're recommended to create a `product.css` file, or you can just wait until the *Assignment* section later in this chapter; it is up to you.

First CSS

To leverage our AI assistant, we can place a CSS-type comment in a CSS file just like we do with code, for example:

```css
.product {
    /* apply padding and margin */
    padding: 10px;
    margin: 10px;
}
```

> As was mentioned in the previous chapter, comment styles are different depending on the type of file. HTML comments look like so: `<!-- -->`. CSS comments use `/**/` and JavaScript understands both CSS-type comments and `//`. In this chapter, you will be using `/**/` as you're dealing with CSS.

In GitHub Copilot, you can keep pressing the *Return* key, followed by the *Tab* key, to generate and accept new suggestions without needing to type a new prompt. Your AI assistant can provide suggestions based on the first typed prompt and what code exists in your file.

How this affects our CSS file above is that once we type our first CSS comment, we can keep pressing *Return* and *Tab* and the AI assistant will generate CSS properties that usually go together with padding and margin. The following output is the result of using this technique of pressing the *Return* and *Tab* keys and relying on the open file's context.

This is how it looks for `product.css`:

```css
.product {
    /* apply padding and margin */
    padding: 10px;
    margin: 10px;
    /* apply border */
    border: 1px solid #ccc;
    /* apply border radius */
    border-radius: 5px;
    /* apply background color */
    background-color: #fff;
    /* apply box shadow */
    box-shadow: 0 0 5px #ccc;
    /* apply display */
    display: inline-block;
    /* apply width */
    width: 200px;
    /* apply text align */
    text-align: center;
    /* apply text decoration */
    text-decoration: none;
    /* apply color */
    color: #333;
}
```

Now that `product.css` is created with the above content, we can include said CSS file in an HTML file. Switch to said HTML file (if you're typing along, create an `index.html` file), then add the following prompt at the end of the new file:

[Prompt]

Page that includes `product.css`.

[End of prompt]

[Prompt response]

```html
<!-- page that includes product.css -->
<!DOCTYPE html>
<html lang="en">
<head>
    <meta charset="UTF-8">
    <title>Product</title>
    <link rel="stylesheet" href="product.css">
</head>

<body>
    <div class-"product">
        some text
        <div class="product__image">
            <img src="https://via.placeholder.com/200x200" alt="Product Image">
        </div>
        <div class="product__info">
            <h2 class="product__name">Product Name</h2>
            <p class="product__description">Lorem ipsum dolor sit amet
consectetur adipisicing elit. Quisquam, voluptatum.</p>
            <p class="product__price">$9.99</p>
            <button class="product__buy">Buy</button>
        </div>
    </div>
</html>
```

[End of response]

Observe how it not only correctly adds a link tag to include `product.css` but it also generates HTML that might fit a product.

The following is the output:

Figure 5.1: Product CSS showing a product image, title, and description

CSS by name

So far, we've added a comment to generate suggestions. But there's another way we can generate suggestions for our CSS file rather than placing a comment for Copilot to react to. The "other" way consists of creating an empty CSS class, `.product`, and placing the cursor inside of it. Then use the *Return* key and the *Tab* key and see what Copilot generates until you're happy.

Here's how you start off your CSS file:

```
.product {

}
```

Now place the cursor inside of the curly brackets, {}, and use the *Return* and *Tab* keys for each new line you want suggestions for.

Here's what the end result could look like:

[Prompt response]

```
.product {
  display: flex;
  flex-direction: column;
  align-items: center;
  justify-content: center;
```

```
    width: 100%;
    margin: 0 auto;
    padding: 0 0 50px 0;
    background-color: #f5f5f5;
}
```

[End of response]

Assignment

In this assignment, you will create an image gallery app. The gallery should show 10 images with 5 images per row. Use what you learned in the previous chapter to generate both an HTML file and a separate CSS file.

Use "placeholder" as a keyword to get images.

Your HTML file should add a reference to the generated CSS file to correctly apply the CSS.

Solution

You can find the solution to this assignment in the GitHub repository: `https://github.com/PacktPublishing/AI-Assisted-Software-Development-with-GitHub-Copilot-and-ChatGPT`

Use case: style the e-commerce app

Now that you've carried out an assignment where you created both a CSS file and an HTML file, you should have a better understanding of how to write prompts and generate and accept suggestions from GitHub Copilot. Let's now recall the beginning of this chapter, where we talked about the business problem and the e-commerce domain. We will now continue to solve problems in this domain but focus on visualization using CSS.

We will continue with the use case we started with in the previous chapter: our e-commerce store. We will focus on the basket page and leave the remaining pages for you to implement.

Basket page

To style our basket HTML page, we create a `basket.css` file and then we observe what CSS classes we introduced in the `basket.html` file. Let's take a look at a representative snippet:

```
<div class="container">
        <div class="basket">
```

```
<h1>Basket</h1>
<div class="basket-item">
    <div>
        <h2>Product 2</h2>
        <p>Price: 200</p>
        <p>Quantity: 2</p>
        <p>Sum: 400</p>
    </div>
</div>
```

In the preceding code, we see the classes basket and basket-item. Let's create CSS classes for those in basket.css:

Start with a blank basket.css and start typing .basket. You should see output similar to the following when using the *Return* and *Tab* keys repeatedly. When you're happy with the output, type } to finish the CSS class.

[Prompt response]

```css
.basket {
    width: 100%;
    height: 100%;
    display: flex;
    flex-direction: column;
    align-items: center;
    padding: 20px;
}
```

[End of response]

To create the basket-item class, type .basket-item and use *Return* and *Tab* repeatedly. Like before, type } when you're happy with the number of generated CSS properties for this CSS class. You should now have generated a CSS output similar to the below text:

```css
.basket-item {
    width: 100%;
    height: 100%;
    display: flex;
    flex-direction: row;
    align-items: center;
    padding: 20px;
    border-bottom: 1px solid #ccc;
}
```

If we continue looking at our HTML file, we will see yet another snippet of interest:

```
<div class="basket-item-buttons">
    <button type="submit" class="btn btn-primary btn-block btn-large">+</
button>
    <button type="submit" class="btn btn-primary btn-block btn-large">-</
button>
</div>
```

Use the same prompting technique as before by typing the name of the CSS class (.basket-item > .basket-item-button) and repeatedly using RETURN and TAB to generate the below text:

```
.basket-item > .basket-item-buttons {
    display: flex;
    flex-direction: column;
    align-items: center;
    justify-content: center;
    margin-left: auto;
}

.basket-item-buttons button {
    margin: 5px;
    /* set width, large font size, business color background */
    width: 50px;
    font-size: 20px;
    background-color: #f5f5f5;
    border: 1px solid #ccc;
    border-radius: 4px;

}
```

 You may need to type the .basket-item-buttons button class separately and, like before, use *Return* and *Tab* repeatedly.

Viewing the impact of the applied CSS in a browser, you should see something similar to the below appearance:

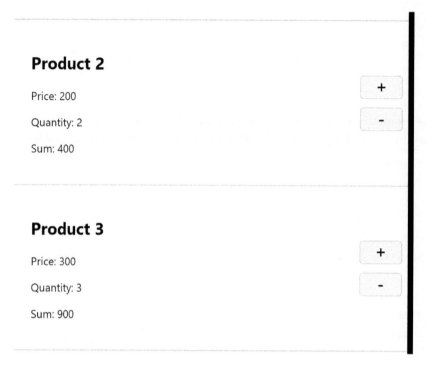

Figure 5.2: List of items in a shopping basket

Challenge

How would you change the prompts to create a dark-themed version of your basket page?

Quiz

How you can generate CSS using your AI assistant?

    a.   Create a comment in a CSS file.

    b.   Create a class and place the cursor in the class.

    c.   Both A and B.

You can find the solution to this quiz in the GitHub repository: `https://github.com/PacktPublishing/`
`AI-Assisted-Software-Development-with-GitHub-Copilot-and-ChatGPT`

Summary

In this chapter, we covered how you can generate CSS using your AI assistant. You saw how prompting techniques introduced in the previous chapters can be applied to CSS as well.

Furthermore, we showed how we could generate text in two different ways, by placing a comment at the top of the file or near the area we wanted help with or placing the cursor inside a CSS class and letting it generate CSS based on the name of the CSS class.

In the next chapter, we will show how you can add behavior to your app using JavaScript. You will see how JavaScript, from a prompting aspect, is similar to HTML and CSS. However, you still need to understand the subject matter, which is the underlying problem you're trying to solve.

Join our community on Discord

Join our community's Discord space for discussions with the author and other readers:

https://packt.link/aicode

6

Add Behavior with JavaScript

Introduction

It's perfectly fine to have a web page consisting of nothing but HTML markup and CSS, but if you want interactivity, you need JavaScript.

With JavaScript, you can apply a little, for example, posting a form to a backend, to a lot, like building a **Single-Page Application (SPA)** with a framework like Vue.js or React.js. Regardless, there's a common denominator, namely that you need to write code and reference that code or code file from your HTML markup.

You will see that Copilot can help with both common tasks like adding a script tag to your HTML markup to more advanced tasks like adding a JavaScript framework like Vue.js to your web app.

In this chapter, we will:

- Generate JavaScript using prompts to add behavior to our app.
- Add interactivity to our e-commerce application.
- Introduce a JavaScript framework like Vue to ensure we set ourselves up with a solid foundation.

Business problem: e-commerce

We'll keep working on our e-commerce domain in this chapter as well. In the previous chapters, you saw how we worked with HTML to try to lay out what information should be on each page and identify what pages we need in the process. In this chapter, we're adding the missing component, JavaScript, which is what makes it all work. JavaScript will play the roles of both adding interactivity and reading and writing data.

Problem and data domain

There are a few problems you need to address, as follows:

- **Data flow:** How do we add code to our application so that we can read and write data?

- **Handling user interaction:** The user will want to interact with your application. You will need to configure the part of the site that the user will want to use and ensure this will work. Not all user interactions lead to data being read or written, but many do, so therefore you need to figure out when that's the case and "connect" a user interaction with your data flow, as mentioned above.
- **Data:** The data will vary depending on what parts of the app you're addressing. If you implement a basket page, for example, you will need to deal with both product data as well as orders as the user is looking to "check out" their basket so they can purchase the products and get them delivered to a chosen address.

Breaking the problem down into features

We understand the business domain and roughly what type of problems we're likely to encounter, so how can we break this down into features? From the previous chapters, we have an idea of how to do this, but the main difference is that instead of just creating a basket page, for example, that looks like it works, this should work. We can therefore break down a basket page, for example, into the following features:

- Read the basket information from the data source.
- Render the basket information.
- Add the item to the basket.
- Adjust the selected number of items for a specific item in the basket.
- Remove an item from the basket.
- Support checking out a basket, taking the user to an order page where they will be asked for purchase information and a delivery page.

An e-commerce site consists of many different pages. It's therefore recommended to do a similar feature breakdown for each page as you address a specific page.

Prompting strategy

The prompting strategy is a bit dependent on the chosen AI tool, how it works, and how we prompt. GitHub Copilot is our chosen AI tool for this chapter, and we will focus mostly on its in-editor experience where you type prompts in open files. The approaches we will show throughout this chapter are the following:

- **Inline comments:** This means we will write prompts directly in open files. You can add prompts this way at the top of the file and also add additional supporting prompts where you're trying to have your AI assistant build specific code blocks.
- **Chat:** We will not show this approach that much, but we do recommend using the chat just to compare and contrast or if you need to look up specific information or want advice on how to implement something.

The general recommendation throughout this book is that you use a blended approach of both using prompts directly in open files "in-editor" and typing prompts in the chat windows. These approaches come with their pros and cons. As for prompt pattern, we're going to be using the "Exploratory prompt pattern" as described in *Chapter 2*.

Adding JavaScript

To add JavaScript to a web page, there are two main approaches:

- Using a `script` tag in the `head` element: In this version, you would add a script tag to an existing HTML page, for example, named `index.html`.

```
<!-- Alt1 -->
<script>
  // JavaScript here
</script>
```

- Pointing to a stand-alone file: In this case, you would write your JavaScript in an existing file, `my-javascript-file.js`:

```
<!-- Alt2 -->
<script src="my-javascript-file.js"></script>
```

The role of JavaScript

When JavaScript was first added to the browser, it played the role of adding interactivity. Today, JavaScript often has an extended role as part of application frameworks like Vue.js, React, and Angular. In such frameworks, a developer can now declaratively define templates that, with the help of JavaScript, can be turned into static HTML, with event handling added, to respond to user interactions. Ultimately, all this is then sent to the browser to be rendered by it.

Adding JavaScript to a page

Let's show next how we can add JavaScript to a page by providing the following prompt:

[Prompt]

Create web page with a script tag.

[End of prompt]

We end up with a web page that also contains a `script` tag. Note how the prompt is added as a comment at the top of the page. That's how GitHub Copilot knows to suggest a text completion:

[Prompt response]

```
<!-- create web page with a script tag -->
<html>
<head>
```

```
    <title>My First Web Page</title>
</head>
<body>
    <script>
        alert("Hello World!");
    </script>
</body>
```

[End of response]

In this case, the code calls `alert("Hello World")`, which will show a dialog box with the text "Hello World."

A second example: adding a JavaScript library/framework

The first example might not be all that useful, but let's add something you're likely to do, like adding a framework like Vue.js. The reason for adding a framework like Vue.js is that you want to build a large application consisting of a lot of interactivity and many different pages. To keep things organized, and make it easy for other developers to contribute, you want a framework like Vue.js.

[Prompt]

Add Vue 3.

[End of prompt]

This time, we place ourselves in the header tag. See the HTML comment in the HEAD tag below to indicate the prompt we're using as input to GitHub Copilot:

```
<head>
<!-- add Vue 3 -->
</head>
```

This prompt results in the following suggestion:

[Prompt response]

```
<script src="https://unpkg.com/vue@next"></script>
```

[End of response]

You can easily build on this by adding a prompt that asks to set up an entry point (most SPA frameworks work on the idea of having an entry point, an element where the app will be rendered):

[Prompt]

Add Vue 3 entry point.

[End of prompt]

This results in the following code:

[Prompt response]

```html
<!-- add Vue 3 entry point -->
<div id="app">
    <h1>{{ message }}</h1>
</div>
```

[End of response]

Placing our cursor below the `script` tag that imported Vue.js will lead to our AI assistant generating instructions for what code we should add to further set up Vue.js. It's not enough to just add script to Vue.js; some additional code is needed.

Luckily, with our cursor placement like below, GitHub Copilot understands from existing HTML comments (prompts) what code is missing and will suggest that code at the location of our cursor (if a Copilot suggestion doesn't appear, try pressing the *Spacebar* key or the *Return* key):

[Prompt]

No prompt given

[End of prompt]

[Prompt response]

```html
<script src="https://unpkg.com/vue@next"></script>
<!-- below is rendered by just placing cursor here -->
<script>
    // create Vue 3 instance
    const app = Vue.createApp({
        data() {
            return {
                message: 'Hello World!'
            }
        }
    })
    // mount Vue 3 instance to DOM element
    app.mount('#app')
</script>
```

[End of response]

 It's worth calling out again that GitHub Copilot had enough context to generate more suggestions by us only using Tab and Return key without the need to provide an extra prompt..

Running this in a browser returns "Hello World," which is what's expected given the above code. The reason this code works, in case you're not familiar with Vue.js, is that it contains the bare minimum of what's needed for it to be referenced and configured:

- `script` tag, referencing Vue.js
- Creation of an app instance that also defines a data function with a `message` property
- A call to `mount()`, which ensures that the identified HTML tag (with `id = app`) is interpolated, and the HTML tag is replaced with the value of the property `message`

 When building a more advanced Vue.js project, please use the Vue CLI over the approach chosen above. For smaller proofs of concept, this approach could be OK.

Challenge

As a challenge, ask Copilot to add a button that increments a counter. You can use the following prompt:

[Prompt]

Add a button that increments a counter.

[End of prompt]

It is recommended that you place the cursor in the HTML markup where the DIV element with `id="app"` is located.

Use case: adding behavior

For this part of our e-commerce use case, let's work on rendering a cart page of items. In this case, we will mock calling a backend for the data and let the data be placed in a file called `cart.json` with the following structure:

```
{
   "cart": [

   ]
}
```

The above JSON content describes a JSON object (defined by {}), with the property `cart`, of the array type, as denoted by the square brackets, [].

In fact, let's use our AI assistant to generate the data we need. Let's create the `cart.json` file and the following structure and prompt:

```
{
   "cart": [
```

```
     // item with id name , quantity and price, total = quantity * price
   ]
}
```

Note the prompt `// item with id name, quantity and price, total = quantity * price`, which results in the following JSON:

```json
{
    "id": "1",
    "name": "item1",
    "quantity": "1",
    "price": "10",
    "total": "10"
},
{
    "id": "2",
    "name": "item2",
    "quantity": "1",
    "price": "20",
    "total": "20"
},
{
    "id": "3",
    "name": "item3",
    "quantity": "1",
    "price": "30",
    "total": "30"
}
```

 Adding a comment with `//` is OK when you try to generate more JSON code from Copilot, but it should be removed once you're happy with the output.

Next, we need a file, `app.js`, that calls this JSON file and ends up rendering. We can use the `basket.html` file from the previous chapter. It should look something like so:

```html
<!-- a page showing a list of items in a basket, each item should have title,
price, quantity, sum and buttons to increase or decrease quantity and the page
should have a link to "checkout" at the bottom  -->
<html>
<head>
    <title>Basket</title>
```

```html
        <link rel="stylesheet" href="css/basket.css">

</head>
<body>
    <div class="container">
        <div id="basket" class="basket">
        </div>
    </div>
    <!-- add app.js  -->
    <!-- add app.js, type javascript -->

    <script src="js/app.js"></script>
</body>
```

Let's add app.js by adding a prompt to the end of the body tag:

[Prompt]

Add app.js.

[End of prompt]

[Copilot Response]

```html
<!-- add app.js  -->
<script src="js/app.js"></script>
```

[End of response]

In app.js, add the following prompt:

[Prompt]

Read cart.json and render the content as div elements to the element with ID basket. Add the CSS class basket-item to each item.

[End of prompt]

It should give you a result similar to:

[Prompt response]

```javascript
fetch('cart.json')
    .then(response => response.json())
    .then(data => {
        let basket = document.getElementById('basket');
        data.forEach(item => {
```

```
            let div = document.createElement('div');
            div.classList.add('basket-item');
            div.innerHTML = item.name;
            basket.appendChild(div);
        });
    });
```

[End of response]

The above code locates the HTML element whose ID is basket and then proceeds to loop through the array data. For each element in data, a new HTML element of type DIV will be created, and the following will happen to said element:

- The CSS class basket-item will be added.
- Its innerHTML property will be assigned the value of the name property.
- The specific element will be added to the parent element basket.

You need to tweak the forEach portion of the code to data.cart.forEach to adjust it based on what the JSON file looks like (if your JSON says you have a description property instead of name, that should be reflected in the JavaScript code, etc.). The resulting output doesn't look like much, though, just three titles:

```
item1
item2
item3
```

Improving the output

To improve the output, there are a few things we want to do, like:

- Add a CSS class to each rendered property on an item:

    ```css
    .basket-item > div {
      margin: 5px;
      /* 25% width */
      width: 25%;
    }
    ```

 You don't always need to type a prompt to get the above response. Sometimes it's enough to type .basket-item and CSS will be suggested to you that you can accept using the *Tab* key. Be sure that you are in either a style tag or a .css file when writing this, though.

- Add prompts in the JavaScript code to make it render each item property as separate `div` elements:

[Prompt]

//Read `cart.json` and render the content as `div` elements to the element with `id` basket, add CSS class `basket-item` to each item

[End of prompt]

[Prompt response]

```
fetch('cart.json')
.then(response => response.json())
.then(data => {
    let basket = document.getElementById('basket');
```

[End of response]

- At this point, the above prompt has managed to call the `fetch` method to retrieve data from the `cart.json` file. It then proceeded to convert the retrieved data into JSON format and identified the HTML element we will want to render the JSON response on:

```
    // render name, quantity, total and price for each item in separate
div elements
    data.cart.forEach(item => {
        let div = document.createElement('div');
        div.classList.add('basket-item');

        // 1) render name as separate child div element
        let name = document.createElement('div');
        name.innerHTML = item.name;
        div.appendChild(name);

        // 2) render quantity, price and total as separate child div
elements, add header and value for each element on this format, header:
value
        let quantity = document.createElement('div');
        quantity.innerHTML = `Quantity: ${item.quantity}`;
        div.appendChild(quantity);
        let price = document.createElement('div');
        price.innerHTML = `Price: ${item.price}`;
        div.appendChild(price);

        let total = document.createElement('div');
        total.innerHTML = `Total: ${item.price * item.quantity}`;
```

```
        div.appendChild(total);

        basket.appendChild(div);
    });
```

- In this section of the code, we've added context on what fields (name, quantity, etc.) we want to read from the JSON content. From the code, you can see this prompt instruction is reflected in the generated code and each field gets its own DIV element and descriptive text:

```
// 3) calculate total price for all items and render it as separate
div element, display as Total price: value
        let totalPrice = document.createElement('div');
        totalPrice.innerHTML = `Total price: ${data.cart.reduce((total,
item) => total + item.price * item.quantity, 0)}`;
        basket.appendChild(totalPrice);

    });
```

- In this prompt, we're providing specific instructions to multiply certain fields (price x quantity) to produce a total price for the row. At the same time, we can see how a call to reduce calculates the basket's total price.

The end result looks like so. It's far from perfect but looks more like what we can expect:

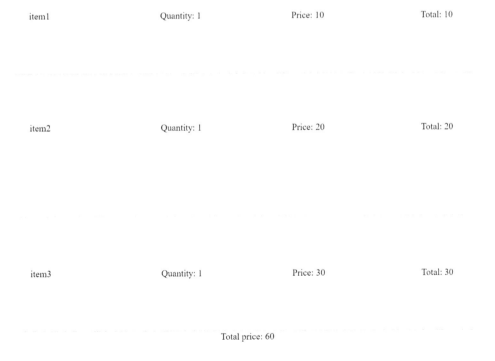

item1	Quantity: 1	Price: 10	Total: 10
item2	Quantity: 1	Price: 20	Total: 20
item3	Quantity: 1	Price: 30	Total: 30

Total price: 60

Figure 6.1: Rendered cart showing name, price, and total

Adding Bootstrap

In the previous section, we showed how we can add some basic CSS to our cart page. However, to really improve the looks of our basket page, we think adding a CSS framework like Bootstrap can be a good idea. Bootstrap is used by many teams across the world and has many different types of content, like "cards" and "menus," that will enable us to work faster in building our app.

To add Bootstrap, we place ourselves with a prompt comment in the head element like so:

[Prompt]

Add Bootstrap.

[End of prompt]

[Prompt response]

```
<!-- add bootstrap -->
    <link rel="stylesheet" href="https://stackpath.bootstrapcdn.com/
bootstrap/4.5.2/css/bootstrap.min.css">
</head>
```

[End of response]

At this point, we have added Bootstrap to our web app, but we need to use one of its classes. Previously, we mentioned the concept of "cards," when we discussed Bootstrap and its types of content, a layout that renders nicely.

To produce a card, we can give it a prompt like so on the web page:

[Prompt]

Create a card with the fields name, price, quantity, and total.

[End of prompt]

We get the following result:

[Prompt response]

```
<!-- Create a card with the fields name, price, quantity and total -->
<div class="card">
    <div class="card-body">
        <h2 class="card-title">Product 1</h2>
        <p class="card-text">Price: 100</p>
        <p class="card-text">Quantity: 1</p>
        <p class="card-text">Sum: 100</p>
        <button type="submit" class="btn btn-primary btn-block btn-large">+</button>
```

```
            <button type="submit" class="btn btn-primary btn-block btn-large">-</
button>
        </div>
    </div>
```

[End of response]

Above, we placed the prompt in our open text file as an HTML comment and accepted Copilot's suggestion via the *Tab* key.

OK, we had a good start. We have added Bootstrap to our web app. We also used Copilot to create an HTML card sample that we can use. The next step is to change our JavaScript code.

To change our JavaScript code, we will give Copilot a bit more context than usual, namely:

[Prompt]

See below:

```
// template:
// <div class="card">
//     <div class="card-body">
//         <h2 class="card-title">Product 1</h2>
//         <p class="card-text">Price: 100</p>
//         <p class="card-text">Quantity: 1</p>
//         <p class="card-text">Sum: 100</p>
//         <button type="submit" class="btn btn-primary btn-block btn-
large">+</button>
//         <button type="submit" class="btn btn-primary btn-block btn-
large">-</button>
//     </div>
// </div>

// for each item in cart.json, render name, quantity, total, use template above
```

[End of prompt]

This results in the following code:

[Prompt response]

```
    data.cart.forEach(item => {
    // target element with id basket
    let basket = document.getElementById('basket');


    let div = document.createElement('div');
    div.classList.add('card');
```

```
    basket.appendChild(div);

    let divBody = document.createElement('div');
    divBody.classList.add('card-body');
    div.appendChild(divBody);

    let name = document.createElement('h2');
    name.classList.add('card-title');
    name.innerHTML = item.name;
    divBody.appendChild(name);


    let price = document.createElement('p');
    price.classList.add('card-text');
    price.innerHTML = `Price: ${item.price}`;
    divBody.appendChild(price);

    let quantity = document.createElement('p');
    quantity.classList.add('card-text');
    quantity.innerHTML = `Quantity: ${item.quantity}`;
    divBody.appendChild(quantity);

    let total = document.createElement('p');
    total.classList.add('card-text');
    total.innerHTML = `Total: ${item.price * item.quantity}`;

    let buttonPlus = document.createElement('button');
    buttonPlus.classList.add('btn', 'btn-primary', 'btn-block', 'btn-large');
    buttonPlus.innerHTML = '+';
    divBody.appendChild(buttonPlus);

    let buttonMinus = document.createElement('button');
    buttonMinus.classList.add('btn', 'btn-primary', 'btn-block', 'btn-large');
    buttonMinus.innerHTML = '-';
    divBody.appendChild(buttonMinus);
});
```

[End of response]

All of this felt a tiny bit convoluted, going back and forth between JavaScript and HTML. This is the reason why many developers use a JavaScript framework in which they can augment the HTML, using templates, and just add instructions to it, like you do when you, for example, use a framework like Vue.js.

Adding Vue.js

At this point, we've realized that our approach wasn't so good. We let JavaScript handle the creation of HTML elements and populate them from a JSON response. What we're looking for is a cleaner approach. We will therefore start from the beginning. However, because we've been working with Copilot, it "remembers" that we're working with basket-type data, and the file we're working with, basket.html, helps provide additional context to Copilot. It might seem a bit like magic, what you're about to see, but it's really a result of Copilot having built up an in-memory context having worked with you.

 If you're starting fresh with just having opened Visual Studio Code, you would probably need to use a more detailed prompt.

It might sound like a big change to add a JavaScript framework at this point, but it really isn't. Let's show the needed changes step by step.

First, let's add support for Vue.js in our basket.html file. We add the below prompt at the end of the BODY tag:

[Prompt]

Add Vue 3.

[End of prompt]

[Prompt response]

```
<!-- add Vue 3 -->
<script src="https://unpkg.com/vue@next"></script>
```

[End of response]

The next thing we need is code that creates our Vue app.

[Prompt]

Add Bootstrap code for Vue 3.

[End of prompt]

The resulting code is as follows:

[Prompt response]

```
<!-- add bootstrap code for Vue 3 -->
<script>
let app = Vue.createApp({
    data() {
        return {
```

```
            basket: [
                {
                    id: 1,
                    name: 'Product 1',
                    price: 100,
                    quantity: 1
                },
                {
                    id: 2,
                    name: 'Product 2',
                    price: 200,
                    quantity: 2
                },
                {
                    id: 3,
                    name: 'Product 3',
                    price: 300,
                    quantity: 3
                },
                {
                    id: 4,
                    name: 'Product 4',
                    price: 400,
                    quantity: 4
                }
            ]
        }
    },
    methods: {
        increaseQuantity(index) {
            this.basket[index].quantity++;
        },
        decreaseQuantity(index) {
            if (this.basket[index].quantity > 0) {
                this.basket[index].quantity--;
            }
        }
    },
    computed: {
        total() {
            let total = 0;
```

```
            for (let i = 0; i < this.basket.length; i++) {
                total += this.basket[i].price * this.basket[i].quantity;
            }
            return total;
        }
    }
});


app.mount('#basket');
</script>
```

[End of response]

 Remember what we said about the in-memory context of Copilot. It remembers everything we've fed it so far on what fields the basket has, and it also looks at the name of the file basket.html; that's the result you see above.

Lastly, we need to state how we want to render the app:

[Prompt]

Render basket from Vue app.

[End of prompt]

[Prompt response]

```
<!-- render basket from Vue app -->
<div v-for="(item, index) in basket" class="basket-item">
    <div class="basket-item-text">
        <h2>{{ item.name }}</h2>
        <p>Price: {{ item.price }}</p>
        <p>Quantity: {{ item.quantity }}</p>
        <p>Sum: {{ item.price * item.quantity }}</p>
    </div>
    <div class="basket-item-buttons">
        <button type="submit" class="btn btn-primary btn-block btn-large" @
click="increaseQuantity(index)">+</button>
        <button type="submit" class="btn btn-primary btn-block btn-large" @
click="decreaseQuantity(index)">-</button>
    </div>
</div>
```

[End of response]

The cart will look like this:

Product 1

Price: 100

Quantity: 1

Sum: 100

Product 2

Price: 200

Quantity: 2   +

Sum: 400

Product 3

Price: 300

Quantity: 3

Sum: 900

Figure 6.2: Display of cart using Vue.js

 If you were to try out the page at this point and run it in a browser, you would notice how the + and - buttons increment and decrement products.

At this point, what's missing is ensuring our Vue app uses the Bootstrap CSS library. We can address that by modifying our prompt for generating the HTML markup from:

[Prompt]

Render basket from Vue app.

[End of prompt]

We can change it to a prompt with added context on Bootstrap, like so:

[Prompt]

Render basket from Vue app, using Bootstrap and the card class.

[End of prompt]

This results in the following HTML markup:

Figure 6.3: Cart in HTML markup

Assignment

Create a product list page. The page should show a list of products. Each product should have an **Add** button that will add the product to a cart. The cart should be represented as a cart icon in the top-right corner of the page and when clicked should display the number of items in the cart and the total value.

Use what you've been taught to craft a prompt to create the page, add JavaScript, and more. It's up to you if you want to add Vue.js to solve this or if you want to use plain JavaScript.

Solution

You can find the solution to this assignment in the GitHub repository: `https://github.com/PacktPublishing/AI-Assisted-Software-Development-with-GitHub-Copilot-and-ChatGPT`.

Summary

In this chapter, we've shown how to add JavaScript to a web page. Adding JavaScript to a web page is a common task and can be done in two ways, either by adding a `script` tag to the `head` element or by pointing to a standalone file.

We've also shown how we can build on our use case from previous chapters by adding behavior to our app. We first showed how to even let JavaScript generate the markup, which can become a bit unwieldy. Then, we made the case for using a JavaScript framework like Vue.js to make it easier to manage.

You've also seen how you can add a JavaScript framework like Vue.js. Exactly how you add a JavaScript framework varies by framework but it's generally recommended to add a prompt with wording including keywords like setup or initialize to ensure you not only add a `script` tag but also add code that triggers a setup process and makes the selected framework ready to use.

In the next chapter, we will show how we can add responsiveness to our app and cater to many different devices and viewports. We can no longer assume that everyone is using a desktop computer with a large screen. Many of our users will be using a mobile device with a smaller screen.

Join our community on Discord

Join our community's Discord space for discussions with the author and other readers:

`https://packt.link/aicode`

7

Support Multiple Viewports Using Responsive Web Layouts

Introduction

Building web pages is a challenge. Not only do you need to craft these pages with HTML, CSS, and JavaScript to perform the tasks you set out, but you also need to ensure they are accessible to most users. Additionally, you need to ensure the pages render nicely regardless of whether the device is a PC, tablet, or mobile device, which means you need to consider aspects like screen size; the orientation of the device; that is, landscape or portrait; and pixel density.

There are many different techniques to ensure your web pages look good on many devices, but it all starts with having a strategy, a vision for what the experience will be for the user depending on what device is used. Once you have that vision set, you can start to implement it.

Some choices you will need to make are how many columns should be listed, if your content is presented as columns. How should other things behave, like padding and margins? Should the content be centered or left-aligned? Should the content be stacked vertically or horizontally? Is there content that should be hidden on mobile devices? As you can see, there are many choices to make that affect what prompts you will need to use.

Using an AI assistant can be helpful when dealing with web layouts as there's a lot of information you need to remember, so not only can you have the AI assistant remember all those details for easy lookup, but you can also utilize it to suggest different designs.

In this chapter, we will:

- Explain technical terms like viewports and media queries.
- Apply different techniques to optimize rendering for different viewports.
- Leverage the Copilot chat feature to improve our code. This is the "other" modality you can use in GitHub Copilot; it's a chat window that lets you type the prompt and provides a response. This experience resembles an AI tool like ChatGPT.

Business problem: e-commerce

This chapter will continue to address the e-commerce use case that's been worked on in the last three chapters. Building the functionality is one thing, but you must assume your users will want to interact with your website from many different devices and that experience must be good or they will go to a competitor's website.

Problem and data domain

There are many different devices out there: tablets, mobile phones, and small desktop screens to large ones. Pixel density is different. It's not just a matter of shrinking or scaling up your site to fit this new device, but you might need to design a completely different experience that better suits the visual style of a specific device. There are also other concerns, like how much content we want to send to a smaller device if we assume the device has limitations, like how many concurrent downloads it can handle and what network speed it might have. It's not unusual that a desktop machine with a wide resolution often has a great connection to the internet. Conversely, a mobile device might be on a 3G network or worse and you therefore need to adjust to that by requiring a lot fewer graphical resources, smaller JavaScript bundles, and more.

Breaking the problem down into features

We've seen in several chapters before this one how a good approach is identifying the features we need to implement. These features are less about reading and writing data and more about ensuring the design and interaction work well on prioritized devices. You might therefore have a feature breakdown looking like the following list:

- Should render the basket page in a double-column design for landscape mode.
- Portrait mode:
    - Should render the basket page in a single column for portrait mode.
    - Should display menu actions at the bottom of the screen.
    - You should hide certain features, say, X, Y, Z (assuming X, Y, Z are available on a desktop with a wider screen). The point of this requirement is that you must "rethink" what a mobile experience is versus desktop, what features are central to the experience, and what features we only show if we have plenty of screen space to show it on.
    - Should support and render a visually appealing look for the following mobile devices: iPhone, X, Y, X, and Android.
- Should render the page in < 1 second on a 3G connection.

As you can see, the features are more connected to the user experience than any data domain.

Prompting strategy

Our prompting strategy is like before, a blended approach of using the in-editor experience and adding prompts in open text files to bring up the **Chat** window in Copilot; mix these approaches to your discretion.

As for prompts, there should be enough context in these prompts to make Copilot aware that it will need to suggest a design for specific devices. Thus, it should be able to infer from context what resolutions, pixel density, and other details should influence the suggestions it's about to generate. As for prompting pattern used, we will use the "Exploratory prompt pattern" described in *Chapter 2*.

Viewports

Gone are the days when you only had to develop a web page to look nice on a PC. Today, your web page can be rendered on multiple different devices and it needs to look good on all of them or your customers might go elsewhere.

The first step in understanding how to build web pages is being familiar with some key concepts. The first concept is a viewport. A viewport is a part of the page visible to the user. The difference between a viewport and a window is that a viewport is a part of the window.

Depending on what device is used, for example, a desktop screen or a mobile device, its size differs. When you write code to adjust to different sizes, to render nicely, it's known as making the page "responsive."

Media queries

OK, so I'm dealing with different sizes of the screen depending on what type of device I'm using, so how do I write code that ensures the visual interface adjusts to the size of the device I'm using?

The answer is to leverage a construct called media queries. A media query is a logical block in your CSS that identifies a specific condition and applies specific CSS if said condition is true.

Imagine if there were code like the following; that's basically how it works:

```
if(page.Width > 1024px) {
  // render this UI so it looks good for desktop
} else {
  // render this UI to look good for a mobile device
}
```

Below is an example of a media query:

```
body {
  background: blue;
}

@media (max-width: 600px) {
    body {
        background-color: lightblue;
    }
}
```

The preceding code identifies a condition that says, if the viewport is currently at most 600 pixels wide (which is true for most mobile devices), then set the background color to light blue.

This example might feel a bit contrived; why would I want a different background color when I'm on a mobile device over a normal desktop? You wouldn't, but the example above gives you an idea of how a media query identifies a viewport's size and can apply specific CSS under certain conditions on the viewport.

When to adjust to different viewports and make it responsive

A good reason for using responsive design is because you have a layout that looks great on desktop but might be too wide for mobile. For example, let's say you have a web page with a menu to the left and a main area to the right:

Figure 7.1: Page with a menu and a main area

Were we to try to view this page on a mobile device, it would not look nice. It would look something like this:

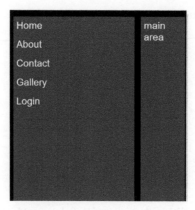

Figure 7.2: Non-responsive page on a mobile device

Above, we see how the device tries to view the page, but the main area is cut off. At this point, you as a designer need to consider how to solve this issue. One way is to align the content vertically using either flexbox or grid as techniques. The menu could go on top, for example, and the main area at the bottom.

Inspecting the styles used for this page, you see the following CSS:

```
<style>
    /* container, grid, left col is menu, right col is main area */
    .container {
        max-width: 1200px;
        margin: 0 auto;
        display: grid;
        /* 2 columns */
        grid-template-columns: 200px 1fr;
        background-color: #000;
        padding: 10px;
        /* space 5 px between columns */
        grid-gap: 10px;
        /* height 100% */
        height: 100%;
    }
```

In the preceding code, you can see how a grid, `display:grid`, is used to create the layout:

```
    /* menu items */
    .menu {
        /* background black shade */
        background-color: darkslategrey;

        padding: 0px;
        /* column 1 */
        grid-column: 1;


    }
```

You can also see how the menu is placed to the left, `grid-column: 1`:

```
    /* menu item */
    .menu-item {
        padding: 5px;
        background-color: darkslategrey;
        height: 20px;
    }
```

```
    .menu-item a {
        color: white;
        text-decoration: none;
        font-family: sans-serif;
    }


    /* main area, padding 5px, dark grey */
    .main {
        padding: 5px;
        background-color: darkslategrey;

        grid-column: 2;
        color: white;
        font-family: sans-serif;
    }
```

The main area is the second column, grid-column: 2:

```
    </style>
```

To improve this design so that it can be used on a device with a smaller screen, such as a mobile device, we can use the below prompt:

[Prompt]

If mobile, set menu to row 1 and main to row 2.

[End of prompt]

The resulting CSS is as follows:

[Prompt response]

```
@media (max-width: 768px) {
    .container {
        grid-template-columns: 1fr;
        grid-template-rows: 200px 1fr;
    }
    .menu {
        grid-row: 1;
        grid-column: 1;
    }
    .main {
        grid-row: 2;
        grid-column: 1;
    }
}
```

[End of response]

As you can see, Copilot can take this prompt instruction and adjust the CSS accordingly. The code shifts the layout to having one column and two rows. Also, it ensures the menu is placed at the top and the main area at the bottom:

The resulting page now renders in the following way on a mobile device:

Figure 7.3: Menu and main area rendered vertically in mobile viewport

Most browsers have built-in functionality for letting you resize the viewport, which helps you test your altered CSS. You can also change the window size.

Use case: make our product gallery responsive

In this use case, we will take an e-commerce application that renders OK on a desktop but not OK on a mobile device, and fix the issue.

First, here's the HTML code for it. If you want to follow along, you can save the following code in a products.html file:

```
<html>
<head>
    <title>menu</title>
    <link rel="stylesheet" href="css/style.css">
    <style>
        /* container, grid, left col is menu, right col is main area */
        .container {
            max-width: 1200px;
            margin: 0 auto;
            display: grid;
            /* 2 columns */
            grid-template-columns: 200px 1fr;
```

```css
    background-color: #000;
    padding: 10px;
    /* space 5 px between columns */
    grid-gap: 10px;
    /* height 100% */
    height: 100%;
}
/* menu items */
.menu {
    /* background black shade */
    background-color: rgb(25, 41, 41);


    /* background-color: #ddd; */
    padding: 0px;
    /* column 1 */
    grid-column: 1;

}
/* menu item */
.menu-item {
    padding: 5px;
    background-color: rgb(25, 41, 41);
    height: 20px;
}


.menu-item a {
    color: white;
    text-decoration: none;
    font-family: sans-serif;
}


/* main area, padding 5px, dark grey */
.main {
    padding: 5px;
    background-color: rgb(25, 41, 41);

    grid-column: 2;
    color: white;
    font-family: sans-serif;
}
/* if mobile, set menu to row 1 and main row 2 */
```

```
@media (max-width: 768px) {
    .container {
        grid-template-columns: 1fr;
        grid-template-rows: 200px 1fr;
    }
    .menu {
        grid-row: 1;
        grid-column: 1;
    }
    .main {
        grid-row: 2;
        grid-column: 1;
    }
}


/* gallery, 2 columns per row */
.gallery {
    display: grid;
    /* horizontal grid */
    grid-template-columns: auto auto auto;
    grid-gap: 20px;
}
/* gallery item */
.gallery-item {
    flex: 1 0 24%;
    margin-bottom: 10px;
    /* padding 10px */
    padding: 20px;

    /* margin 5px */
    margin: 5px;
    /* black shadow */
    box-shadow: 0 0 10px 0 black;

}
/* gallery image */
.gallery-image {
    width: 100%;
    height: auto;

    transition: transform 0.3s ease-in-out;
}
```

```
        /* gallery image hover */
        .gallery-image:hover {
            transform: scale(1.1);
        }


    </style>
</head>

<body>
    <div class="container">
        <!-- menu items -->
        <div class="menu">
            <div class="menu-item">
                <a href="index.php">Home</a>
            </div>
            <div class="menu-item">
                <a href="about.php">About</a>
            </div>
            <div class="menu-item">
                <a href="contact.php">Contact</a>
            </div>
            <div class="menu-item">
                <a href="gallery.php">Gallery</a>
            </div>
            <div class="menu-item">
                <a href="login.php">Login</a>
            </div>
        </div>
        <!-- main area -->
        <div class="main">
                <div class="gallery">
                <div class="gallery-item">
                    <img class="gallery-image" src="https://picsum.
photos/300/200/?random">
                    <h4>Product 1</h4>
                    <p>Description</p>
                    <p>Price</p>
                    <button>Add to cart</button>
                </div>
```

```
                    <div class="gallery-item">
                         <img class="gallery-image" src="https://picsum.
  photos/300/200/?random">
                         <h4>Product 2</h4>
                         <p>Description</p>
                         <p>Price</p>
                         <button>Add to cart</button>
                    </div>
                    <!-- code shortened -->
               </div>

     </div>
     </body>
     </html>
```

This should render something like the following (exact images may vary as these URLs produce random images) on desktop:

Figure 7.4: E-commerce product list page

However, trying to render the same page on a mobile device makes it look like the following:

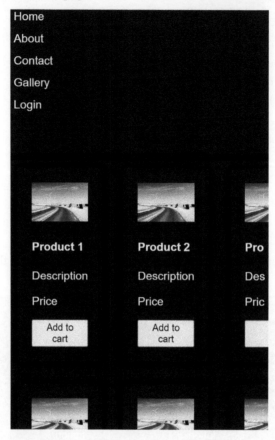

Figure 7.5: E-commerce product list, looks bad on mobile

To solve this problem, we need to place ourselves in the CSS code and ask our AI assistant what we should do.

Place a prompt at the bottom of the CSS like so:

[Prompt]

Switch from 3 columns to 1 on mobile device for gallery.

[End of prompt]

The result should be a media query like so:

[Prompt response]

```
@media (max-width: 768px) {
    .gallery {
```

```
        grid-template-columns: auto;
    }
}
```

[End of response]

Our new mobile rendering now looks like the image below, which is acceptable.

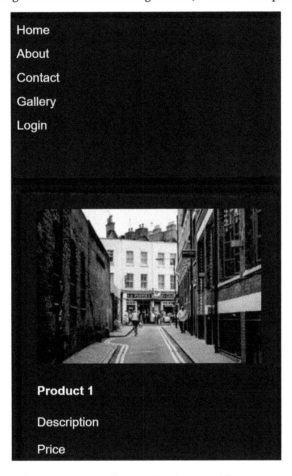

Figure 7.6: This shows an image gallery rendered on a mobile device in portrait mode

Assignment

As a newly hired frontend developer, you've been hired to maintain a memory game.

The game looks something like the below image:

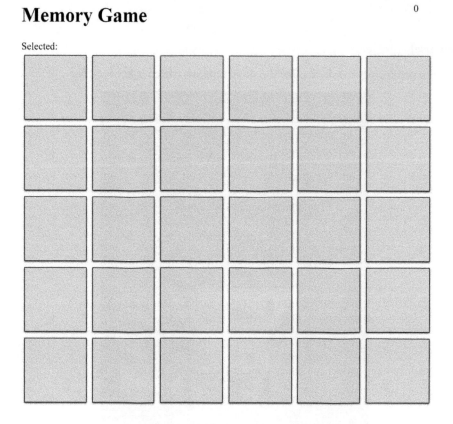

Figure 7.7: Grids in a memory game

Your company wants you to do the following:

- Ensure it renders as a 5x5 grid on desktop. For larger viewports, it doesn't work well, but you should address that problem.
- Support mobile devices, meaning that it should render as a 5x5 grid but with half as big tiles.
- While fixing it for mobile devices, ensure the score in the top-right corner is moved to the middle and is centered.

As a developer, it's now your job to adjust the code of this game using GitHub Copilot, using either inline editing of open text files or the Chat function in Copilot to ensure the code works well for different devices.

Solution

You can find the solution to this assignment in the GitHub repository: `https://github.com/PacktPublishing/AI-Assisted-Software-Development-with-GitHub-Copilot-and-ChatGPT`

Challenge

All the code for the assignment is in one file. See if you can split it up into different files. Additionally, see if you can experiment with matched cards; try removing them or adding a class that shows they're no longer part of the game.

Summary

In this chapter, we discussed viewports as the central concept for responsive web design. To help us tackle different viewports, we used media queries.

We also continued working on our use case, the e-commerce site, and tried to ensure a product list renders nicely on mobile devices. The first thing is to realize that you have a problem, and we managed to identify that. Second, we came up with a strategy to solve the problem, which was to use media queries. Third, we implemented the strategy. Finally, we tested it to ensure it worked.

In the next chapter, we will shift from the frontend to the backend. The backend is made up of a Web API. We will continue with our use case, the e-commerce site, and build a Web API that will serve the product list primarily. Hopefully, though, it will become apparent how to add other resources to the Web API as well.

Join our community on Discord

Join our community's Discord space for discussions with the author and other readers:

`https://packt.link/aicode`

8

Build a Backend with Web APIs

Introduction

When we say Web API, it's an application programming interface we develop that's meant for the client to consume. Said API uses HTTP to communicate. A browser can use a Web API to expose data and functionality to other browsers and applications.

When developing a Web API, you can use any programming language and framework you want. Regardless of the chosen tech, there are things you always need to consider, like data storage, security, authentication, authorization, documentation, testing, and more.

It's with this understanding of what things we need to consider that we can use an AI assistant to help us build a backend.

In this chapter, we will:

- Learn about Web APIs
- Create a Web API with Python and Flask
- Use our AI assistant to answer questions, suggest code, and create documentation and tests

Business domain: e-commerce

We will keep working on our e-commerce example in this chapter. This time, the focus is on the API. The API lets you read and write data that's important in the e-commerce domain. What's important to keep in mind as you develop this API is that there are a couple of important aspects to it:

- Logical domains: It's beneficial to divide up your app into different logical domains. Within the context of e-commerce, that usually translates to products, orders, invoices, and so on.
- What part of the business should handle each logical domain?
  - **Products:** Maybe there's a dedicated team. It's common for the same team to also manage all types of discounts and campaigns that might occur.

- **Invoices and payment:** There's usually a dedicated team that takes care of how the user can pay for things, for example, via credit cards, invoices, and other methods.
- **Inventory:** You need to have a certain amount of goods in stock. How do you know how much? You need to work with business analysts or data folk to make correct forecasts.

Problem and data domain

We've already mentioned a few different logical domains around products, orders, invoices, and so on. The problems you'll have in this domain are generally:

- Reading and writing: What data do you wish to read or write (or maybe both)?
- How will users access your data (all of it or maybe there will be filters applied to limit the output)?
- Access and roles: You can expect that different roles will need to have access to your system. An administrator role should probably have access to most of the data, whereas a logged-in user should only be able to see the part of the data that belongs to them. This is not something we will address in this chapter, but it's something you should consider when you build out this API.

Feature breakdown

Now that we understand that there are both business problems as well as data problems, we need to start to identify the features that we need. Once we get to this level of detail, it should be easier to come up with specific prompts.

A way to do this feature breakdown is as follows – for example, for products:

- Read all products.
- Read products given a filter: Usually, you won't want to read all products but maybe all products of a certain category, or maybe even limit it to a specific value such as 10 products or 20 products.
- Search for products: You should support the user looking for specific products, usually via a category, name, or perhaps part of a certain campaign.
- Retrieve detailed information on a specific product.

I'm sure there are more features for products, but now you have an idea of what granular detail you should have before you continue building the API.

Prompt strategy

In this chapter, you will see how we use both Copilot Chat and the in-editor mode. We will start with the Chat mode as it's quite useful for situations where you want to generate starter code. It's also quite efficient in that it lets you select certain lines of code and lets you update only those based on a prompt. Examples of the latter could be when you want to improve such code. You will see this use case later in the chapter when we improve a route to read from a database instead of reading static data from a list. There will also be cases in this chapter where we use the in-editor mode. This is the recommended approach when you're actively typing the code and want to make smaller tweaks. In this chapter, we will use the "Exploratory prompt pattern" as described in *Chapter 2*.

Web APIs

Using a Web API is a great way to ensure our front-end application has access to the data and functionality it needs to read and write data.

The expectations of a Web API are:

- It is accessible over the web.
- It leverages HTTP protocol and HTTP verbs such as GET, POST, PUT, DELETE, and others to communicate intentions.

What language and framework should you pick?

In this chapter, we already decided we will use Python and Flask. But why? What criteria do we use to pick a language and framework?

You can use any language and framework you want, but here are some criteria to consider:

- What languages and frameworks do you know?
- Are they easy to learn?
- Do they have a large community?
- Are they free and open source?
- How often are they updated?
- Do they have good documentation?
- Do they have good tooling?

These are just some of the criteria to consider.

The reason for picking Python and Flask is that they check many of the above boxes (so does the Express framework for Node.js, but the objective here is to just show how you can build a Web API using an AI assistant, so feel free to use whatever web framework you prefer). Also, the point of this book is to show how an AI assistant can help us build a backend; with what prompts and how and the framework and language is not the focus.

Planning the Web API

When you plan your Web API, you should consider the following:

- What data do you want to expose? For example, products and orders.
- What functionality do you want to expose? For example, reading order data.
- How will you structure your Web API?
- Security and authentication: You need to determine not only what areas of your app should require the user to log in but also what parts should be restricted to specific user types.
- Storage and database: Common choices are, for example, MySQL and Postgres.

Use the above points as a checklist when you plan your Web API.

Creating a Web API with Python and Flask

A key insight to working with an AI assistant is that we can use it to generate code, *but* we need to have a good understanding of the problem domain and the solution domain. This means that we should know how to create a Web API with Python and Flask before we ask our AI assistant to help us. Can we create it without an AI assistant? Yes, but we risk getting stuck and not knowing what to do next.

So, how much knowledge are we talking about? If you know Python in general and how to build a Web API in any language, you are good to go.

Let's begin.

Step 1: Create a new project

First, we need to create a new project. If you know Python, you know using a virtual environment is a good idea as it isolates the project from other Python projects on your computer. Using a virtual environment is not required but is recommended as different versions of Python and packages can cause issues.

Okay, so we know we need a virtual environment. How do we create one? Let's rely on our AI assistant to help us remember the syntax. For the prompt below, you can either open a text file or use the chat functionality in GitHub Copilot.

[Prompt]

How do I create a virtual environment for Python?

[End of prompt]

 The in-editor experience, typing a prompt in an open text file, prefers you to use q: at the start of a sentence. If you use the Chat functionality, there's no need to add q:.

[Prompt response]

The answer is on the same row as a:.

```
python -m venv venv
```

[End of response]

Here's how the output can look in an app.py file containing both the prompt and the response:

```
# q: How do I create a virtual environment for Python? a: python -m venv venv
```

To use the command the AI assistant responded with, we would need to open a terminal, paste the command, and run it.

At this point, you need enough conceptual knowledge to know that you need to activate the virtual environment to use it. But again, let's ask the AI assistant to help us.

[Prompt]

How do I activate a virtual environment for Python in Windows?

[End of prompt]

[Prompt response]

```
a: Venv\Scripts\activate
```

[End of response]

 If you are on a Mac or Linux, change the above prompt to reflect your operating system.

Step 2: Install Flask

The conceptual knowledge you need to have is that you can install packages – in this case, Flask – using pip. Let's ask the AI assistant to help us. Keep working with your app.py file and add your prompt as another comment.

[Prompt]

How do I install Flask with pip?

[End of prompt]

[Prompt response]

```
pip install Flask
```

[End of response]

Your app.py should now look like so:

```
# q: How do I create a virtual environment for Python? a: python -m venv venv
# q: How do I install Flask with pip? a: pip install Flask
```

 As you're using your AI tool to get quick answers on how to do something, it's up to you if you want to clear the text file from questions and responses.

Great, we now know how to install Flask.

Step 3: Create an entry point

We need to create an entry point for our Web API. This is the file that will be executed when we run our Web API. For Python, you usually name this file app.py.

Step 4: Create a Flask app

At this point, we have our project, we've installed Flask, and we have an entry point file, but the application is not a Flask application yet, so let's create one.

Let's ask the AI assistant to help us.

[Prompt]

How do I create a Flask app?

[End of prompt]

As usual, keep typing your questions as comments prepended with a q: in your open text file. Here's the response from your latest prompt:

[Prompt response]

```
from flask import Flask
```

[End of response]

We're not getting much back from the AI assistant. But we know we need to import Flask. Let's improve the prompt.

[Prompt]

How do I create a Flask app with a default route and a "hello" route?

[End of prompt]

Now you'll see an improved prompt response. The prompt contains more explicit instructions to create routes and logical areas in the app:

[Prompt response]

```
from flask import Flask

# create app
app = Flask(__name__)

# default route

@app.route('/')
def index():
    return 'Hello World!'

# hello route
@app.route('/hello')
def hello():
    return 'Hello World!'
```

```
# start app on port 5000
if __name__ == '__main__':
    app.run(debug=True, port=5000)
```

[End of response]

Now we have some starting code for our Flask app.

Next, let's focus on the use case for our Web API – e-commerce.

Use case: a Web API for an e-commerce site

So far, in this book, we've taken you through the process of building a front-end application for an e-commerce site. We used an AI assistant to help us with the front-end application. Now, we will build a Web API for the e-commerce site.

In the previous section, we used an AI assistant to help us create a Flask app. Now, we will use the AI assistant to help us create a Web API for an e-commerce site.

Step 1: Create a Web API for an e-commerce site

Let's plan this task first. Based on previous chapters, the e-commerce site has the following features:

- **Product catalog:** Containing the products we aim to sell.
- **Shopping cart:** With a shopping cart, we can add products to the cart, remove products from the cart, and update the quantity of products in the cart. Once we're happy with the products in the cart, we can check out and have the products paid for and shipped.
- **A checkout process:** In the checkout process, we need to collect payment information and shipping information.

With the above information in mind, let's craft a prompt for our AI assistant.

[Prompt]

Show me code to create a Flask Web API that includes routes for a product catalog, shopping cart, and checkout process.

[End of prompt]

[Prompt response]

```
from flask import Flask

# create app
app = Flask(__name__)

# default route
@app.route('/')
def index():
```

```
    return 'Hello World!'

# product catalog
@app.route('/products')
def products():
    return 'Products'

# shopping cart
@app.route('/cart')
def cart():
    return 'Cart'

# checkout
@app.route('/checkout')
def checkout():
    return 'Checkout'

# start app on port 5000
if __name__ == '__main__':
    app.run(debug=True, port=5000)
```

[End of response]

Okay, so we have some starting code for our Web API, but we need to improve it in the following ways:

- We need to return JSON instead of text.
- We want to add code to read and write to a database.
- We want to add tests.
- We want to document the Web API.

Step 2: Return JSON instead of text

JSON is a common format for data. It's a format that is easy to read and write for both humans and machines. To use JSON in Python, we need to import the `json` package. The method we will use is `jsonify()`, which is a method that will convert a Python dictionary to JSON.

Let's see how we can use `jsonify()` in our Web API. For this operation, we can keep using the AI assistant as prompt comments in the code, or we can use GitHub Copilot's Chat feature (this is a separate extension of GitHub Copilot).

Let's use the latter. To use GitHub Copilot's Chat feature (refer to this link for updated install instructions: `https://docs.github.com/en/copilot/github-copilot-chat/using-github-copilot-chat-in-your-ide`), we need to select the code we want to improve and click the chat icon on the left side of Visual Studio Code (if you are using the default orientation, where the icons are placed vertically – it depends what other extensions you have installed). Here's the icon to look for. Ensure the GitHub Copilot Chat extension has been correctly installed:

Figure 8.1: Chat icon for GitHub Copilot

Once we click the **Chat** icon, and the code selected, we can start chatting with GitHub Copilot. Let's ask GitHub Copilot to help us return JSON instead of text.

We add the following prompt to the chat window:

[Prompt]

Add code to respond with JSON for all routes.

[End of prompt]

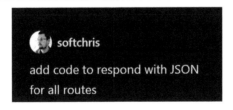

Figure 8.2: Prompt in Copilot chat window

The chat functionality generates an answer consisting of code including the `jsonify()` method.

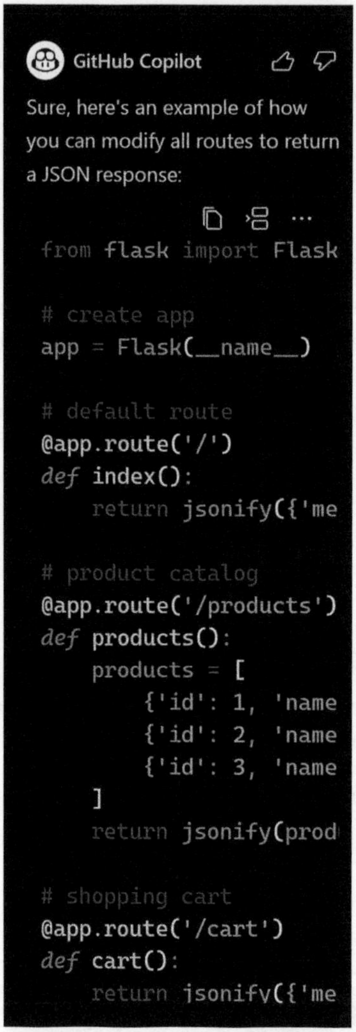

Figure 8.3: Copilot Chat response

Here's the code generated by GitHub Copilot:

```python
from flask import Flask, jsonify

# create app
app = Flask(__name__)

# default route
@app.route('/')
def index():
    return jsonify({'message': 'Hello World!'})
```

```
# product catalog
@app.route('/products')
def products():
    products = [
        {'id': 1, 'name': 'Product 1', 'price': 10.99},
        {'id': 2, 'name': 'Product 2', 'price': 5.99},
        {'id': 3, 'name': 'Product 3', 'price': 7.99}
    ]
    return jsonify(products)

# shopping cart
@app.route('/cart')
def cart():
    return jsonify({'message': 'Cart'})

# checkout
@app.route('/checkout')
def checkout():
    return jsonify({'message': 'Checkout'})

# start app on port 5000
if __name__ == '__main__':
    app.run(debug=True, port=5000)
```

Step 3: Add code to read and write to a database

Okay, so we have a Web API that returns JSON. Now, we need to add code to read and write to a database. Let's use the chat feature again to help us with this task.

[Prompt]

Add code to read and write to a database and apply it to all our routes.

[End of prompt]

Here's the code we end up with:

[Prompt response]

```
import sqlite3
from flask import Flask, jsonify

# create app
app = Flask(__name__)
```

```python
# connect to database
conn = sqlite3.connect('example.db')

# create table
conn.execute('''CREATE TABLE IF NOT EXISTS products
                (id INTEGER PRIMARY KEY AUTOINCREMENT,
                name TEXT NOT NULL,
                price REAL NOT NULL);''')

# insert data
conn.execute("INSERT INTO products (name, price) VALUES (?, ?)", ('Product 1',
10.99))
conn.execute("INSERT INTO products (name, price) VALUES (?, ?)", ('Product 2',
5.99))
conn.execute("INSERT INTO products (name, price) VALUES (?, ?)", ('Product 3',
7.99))
conn.commit()

# default route
@app.route('/')
def index():
    return jsonify({'message': 'Hello World!'})

# product catalog
@app.route('/products')
def products():
    cursor = conn.execute("SELECT id, name, price FROM products")
    products = []
    for row in cursor:
        product = {'id': row[0], 'name': row[1], 'price': row[2]}
        products.append(product)
    return jsonify(products)

# shopping cart
@app.route('/cart')
def cart():
    return jsonify({'message': 'Cart'})

# checkout
@app.route('/checkout')
def checkout():
```

```
        return jsonify({'message': 'Checkout'})
    # close connection
    conn.close()


    # start app on port 5000
    if __name__ == '__main__':
        app.run(debug=True, port=5000)
```

[End of response]

As you can see, we get quite a lot of code:

- Code to connect to a database – in this case, we get a connection to the common SQLite database.
- Code that creates a table and even reads from it in the /products route, but we don't get code to write to the database.
- We don't get code to read and write to the other routes either.

Based on the code above, we realize it's a good start, but there are things we'd like to improve, so we will change the prompt to address the shortcomings. We need the prompt to ensure all routes read their data from a database, not just one.

So, we can either adjust the code ourselves, knowing that most of the code is in place, or try to adjust the prompt. Let's try the latter.

[Prompt]

Add code to read and write to a database and apply it to all our routes.

[End of prompt]

[Prompt response]

```
    import sqlite3
    from flask import Flask, jsonify


    # create app
    app = Flask(__name__)


    # connect to database
    conn = sqlite3.connect('example.db')


    # create table
    conn.execute('''CREATE TABLE IF NOT EXISTS products
                (id INTEGER PRIMARY KEY AUTOINCREMENT,
                name TEXT NOT NULL,
                price REAL NOT NULL);''')
```

```python
# insert data
conn.execute("INSERT INTO products (name, price) VALUES (?, ?)", ('Product 1',
10.99))
conn.execute("INSERT INTO products (name, price) VALUES (?, ?)", ('Product 2',
5.99))
conn.execute("INSERT INTO products (name, price) VALUES (?, ?)", ('Product 3',
7.99))
conn.commit()

# default route
@app.route('/')
def index():
    return jsonify({'message': 'Hello World!'})

# product catalog
@app.route('/products')
def products():
    cursor = conn.execute("SELECT id, name, price FROM products")
    products = []
    for row in cursor:
        product = {'id': row[0], 'name': row[1], 'price': row[2]}
        products.append(product)
    return jsonify(products)

# shopping cart
@app.route('/cart')
def cart():
    cursor = conn.execute("SELECT id, name, price FROM products")
    products = []
    for row in cursor:
        product = {'id': row[0], 'name': row[1], 'price': row[2]}
        products.append(product)
    return jsonify(products)

# checkout
@app.route('/checkout')
def checkout():
    cursor = conn.execute("SELECT id, name, price FROM products")
    products = []
    for row in cursor:
        product = {'id': row[0], 'name': row[1], 'price': row[2]}
```

```
        products.append(product)
    return jsonify(products)

# close connection
conn.close()

# start app on port 5000
if __name__ == '__main__':
    app.run(debug=True, port=5000)
```

[End of response]

The improved prompt made the following changes:

- Added database code to the /checkout and /cart routes.
- All three routes read from the products table, which is incorrect. That's something we need to address in an upcoming prompt. The great news is that we can just tell Copilot Chat what the problem is with a prompt and expect the AI assistant to change the code accordingly.

The above code is better than our very first prompt but has issues still.

You could try to adjust the prompt in Copilot Chat, but let's fall back on our other approach – namely, prompts in the code. To add these prompts, put your cursor in the code and add the prompt as a comment. Here are some prompts we added:

- *# create tables*: We're repeating the comment we have already used, but because Copilot is now aware of all the routes, it does a better job this time, suggesting three database tables should be created rather than just the products one.
- *# add product to cart, productId and quantity in body, create cart if needed, else update*: This prompt is detailed as it asks what information should be added to each cart entry.
- *# product catalog* and *# shopping cart* are also repeated prompts (we remove the old prompt, and retype it to toggle a new suggestion). This time, we get Copilot to suggest the correct database tables to read from.

Note below how we reshape the code with various prompts in the code as comments:

```
import sqlite3
import json
import flask

# create app
app = flask.Flask(__name__)

# connect to database
db = sqlite3.connect('example.db')
```

```python
# create tables
db.execute('''CREATE TABLE IF NOT EXISTS products
             (id INTEGER PRIMARY KEY AUTOINCREMENT,
              name TEXT NOT NULL,
              price REAL NOT NULL);''')

db.execute('''CREATE TABLE IF NOT EXISTS cart
             (id INTEGER PRIMARY KEY AUTOINCREMENT,
              product_id INTEGER NOT NULL,
              quantity INTEGER NOT NULL);''')

db.execute('''CREATE TABLE IF NOT EXISTS checkout
             (id INTEGER PRIMARY KEY AUTOINCREMENT,
              cart_id INTEGER NOT NULL,
              total REAL NOT NULL);''')

db.commit()
db.close()

# default route
@app.route('/')
def index():
    return flask.jsonify({'message': 'Hello World!'})

# product catalog
@app.route('/products')
def products():
    db = sqlite3.connect('example.db')
    cursor = db.execute("SELECT id, name, price FROM products")
    products = []
    for row in cursor:
        product = {'id': row[0], 'name': row[1], 'price': row[2]}
        products.append(product)
    db.close()
    return flask.jsonify(products)

# shopping cart
@app.route('/cart')
def cart():
    db = sqlite3.connect('example.db')
    cursor = db.execute("SELECT id, product_id, quantity FROM cart")
```

```python
    cart = []
    for row in cursor:
        item = {'id': row[0], 'product_id': row[1], 'quantity': row[2]}
        cart.append(item)
    db.close()
    return flask.jsonify(cart)
# add product to cart, productId and quantity in body, create cart if needed,
else update
@app.route('/cart/', methods=['POST'])
def add_to_cart():
    db = sqlite3.connect('example.db')
    # get product id and quantity from body
    product_id = flask.request.json['productId']
    quantity = flask.request.json['quantity']

    # check if cart exists
    cursor = db.execute("SELECT id FROM cart")
    cart_id = None
    for row in cursor:
        cart_id = row[0]

    # if cart exists, update
    if cart_id:
        db.execute("UPDATE cart SET product_id = ?, quantity = ? WHERE id = ?",
(product_id, quantity, cart_id))
    # else create
    else:
        db.execute("INSERT INTO cart (product_id, quantity) VALUES (?, ?)",
(product_id, quantity))

    # close
    db.commit()
    db.close()

    return flask.jsonify({'message': 'Added to cart'})

# checkout POST, cartId in body
@app.route('/checkout', methods=['POST'])
def checkout():
    # insert cart into checkout
    conn = sqlite3.connect('example.db')
    # get cart id from body
```

```
    cart_id = flask.request.json['cartId']

    # write to checkout
    conn.execute("INSERT INTO checkout (cart_id, total) VALUES (?, ?)", (cart_
id, 0))
    # close
    conn.commit()
    conn.close()
```

Is this code good enough or do we need to adjust it further?

There's definitely room for improvement and here's what you should be looking for:

- The code is not DRY (Don't Repeat Yourself); we have a lot of duplicate code. We can solve this by creating a function that takes a query and returns the result.
- Authentication and authorization are missing. We should add this to the code.
- Documentation is missing.
- The code is not secure. We should add some security measures, especially when it comes to the database. As developers, having some knowledge of how to secure code, we can use prepared statements to prevent SQL injection attacks and also validate the data that we receive from the client.

Step 4: Improve the code

The best way to improve the code is to use the code that we have as a starting point and first just try to run it. We can then see what errors we get and what we need to fix.

After that, we work on architecture and design and separate the code into different files.

Lastly, we add authentication and authorization and security measures.

Run the code

Let's run the code. We need to set the Flask variable `FLASK_APP` to `app.py` and then run the app.

 If you are using Windows, you need to use **set** instead of **export** to set the variable.

```
# flask variable windows
set FLASK_APP=app.py
flask run
```

The app is working! We can now go to `http://localhost:5000` and see the message **Hello World!**.

Going to /products, /cart, and /checkout also works, but we don't have any data in the database yet. Let's add some data to the database. By inserting the above code at the top of the file and running the app again, we can do this:

```
db.execute("INSERT INTO products (name, price) VALUES (?, ?)", ('Apple', 1.99))

db.execute("INSERT INTO products (name, price) VALUES (?, ?)", ('Banana',
2.99))
```

Now, if you rerun the app and go to /products, you should see the products that we added as the following JSON output:

```
[
  {
    "id": 1,
    "name": "Apple",
    "price": 1.99
  },
  {
    "id": 2,
    "name": "Banana",
    "price": 2.99
  }
]
```

Refactor the code

Great – lots of progress so far! Now let's refactor the code and make it more DRY (Don't Repeat Yourself, a term for ensuring we don't duplicate code too much). We can use Copilot to help us with this.

Provide it with the following prompt:

[Prompt]

Improve the code by separating the database parts into a separate module db.py and expose the functions as follows: get_products, get_cart, add_to_cart, checkout.

[End of prompt]

We get two responses, one for the db.py file and one for the app.py file. Let's start with the db.py file.

[Prompt response]

```
import sqlite3

# connect to database
conn = sqlite3.connect('example.db')
```

```python
# create tables
conn.execute('''CREATE TABLE IF NOT EXISTS products
                (id INTEGER PRIMARY KEY AUTOINCREMENT,
                name TEXT NOT NULL,
                price REAL NOT NULL);''')

conn.execute('''CREATE TABLE IF NOT EXISTS cart
                (id INTEGER PRIMARY KEY AUTOINCREMENT,
                product_id INTEGER NOT NULL,
                quantity INTEGER NOT NULL);''')

conn.execute('''CREATE TABLE IF NOT EXISTS checkout
                (id INTEGER PRIMARY KEY AUTOINCREMENT,
                cart_id INTEGER NOT NULL,
                total REAL NOT NULL);''')

conn.execute("INSERT INTO products (name, price) VALUES (?, ?)", ('Apple',
1.99))

conn.execute("INSERT INTO products (name, price) VALUES (?, ?)", ('Banana',
2.99))

conn.commit()

def get_products():
    cursor = conn.execute("SELECT id, name, price FROM products")
    products = []
    for row in cursor:
        product = {'id': row[0], 'name': row[1], 'price': row[2]}
        products.append(product)
    return products

def get_cart():
    cursor = conn.execute("SELECT id, product_id, quantity FROM cart")
    cart = []
    for row in cursor:
        item = {'id': row[0], 'product_id': row[1], 'quantity': row[2]}
        cart.append(item)
    return cart

def add_to_cart(product_id, quantity):
```

```python
    # check if cart exists
    cursor = conn.execute("SELECT id FROM cart")
    cart_id = None
    for row in cursor:
        cart_id = row[0]

    # if cart exists, update
    if cart_id:
        conn.execute("UPDATE cart SET product_id = ?, quantity = ? WHERE id =
?", (product_id, quantity, cart_id))
    # else create
    else:
        conn.execute("INSERT INTO cart (product_id, quantity) VALUES (?, ?)",
(product_id, quantity))

    conn.commit()

def checkout(cart_id):
    # insert cart into checkout
    conn.execute("INSERT INTO checkout (cart_id, total) VALUES (?, ?)", (cart_
id, 0))
    conn.commit()
```

[End of response]

We need to improve the above code a bit, as it's using an open connection to the database. We should close the connection after we are done with it. Ensure you add code to close the connection after the commit. Also, ensure per route that you open and close the connection.

This looks good. Let's add it to our project. We can create a new file called db.py and copy the code into it.

Next, let's see what it suggested for the app.py file:

```python
import flask
import db

# create app
app = flask.Flask(__name__)

# default route
@app.route('/')
def index():
```

```python
    return flask.jsonify({'message': 'Hello World!'})

# product catalog
@app.route('/products')
def products():
    products = db.get_products()
    return flask.jsonify(products)

# shopping cart
@app.route('/cart')
def cart():
    cart = db.get_cart()
    return flask.jsonify(cart)

# add product to cart, productId and quantity in body, create cart if needed,
# else update
@app.route('/cart', methods=['POST'])
def add_to_cart():
    # get product id and quantity from body
    product_id = flask.request.json['productId']
    quantity = flask.request.json['quantity']

    db.add_to_cart(product_id, quantity)

    return flask.jsonify({'message': 'Added to cart'})

# checkout POST, cartId in body
@app.route('/checkout', methods=['POST'])
def checkout():
    # get cart id from body
    cart_id = flask.request.json['cartId']

    db.checkout(cart_id)

    return flask.jsonify({'message': 'Checkout successful'})

# start app on port 5000
if __name__ == '__main__':
    app.run(debug=True, port=5000)
```

As you can see, it has separated the database code into the db.py file and has also added the imports for the db.py file. Let's copy this code into our app.py file and replace its content.

Does it work? Let's run the app and see. It runs without any errors, and we get JSON output when we go to /products, /cart, and /checkout. If you want, you can also make a POST request to /cart to write cart content – great!

Step 5: Document the API

We can use Copilot Chat to help us document the API. Let's provide it with the following prompt:

[Prompt]

Document the API using Swagger. The API should have the following endpoints: GET /products, GET /cart, POST /cart/add, POST /checkout.

[End of prompt]

 Swagger or OpenAPI standard is a way to document your API routes. These route specifications can then be visualized, and you get a quick overview of what your API can do. Additionally, there's something called Swagger UI, a web page that not only lets you see what routes you have in your API but you can make requests and more, to ensure the API is working as it should.

Here's the output, which involves both code and documentation:

[Prompt response]

```
# app.py
import flask
import db
from flasgger import Swagger, swag_from

# create app
app = flask.Flask(__name__)
swagger = Swagger(app)

# default route
@app.route('/')
def index():
    return flask.jsonify({'message': 'Hello World!'})

# product catalog
@app.route('/products', methods=['GET'])
@swag_from('swagger/products.yml')
def products():
    products = db.get_products()
    return flask.jsonify(products)
```

```python
# shopping cart
@app.route('/cart', methods=['GET'])
@swag_from('swagger/cart.yml')
def cart():
    cart = db.get_cart()
    return flask.jsonify(cart)

# add product to cart, productId and quantity in body, create cart if needed,
else update
@app.route('/cart/add', methods=['POST'])
@swag_from('swagger/add_to_cart.yml')
def add_to_cart():
    # get product id and quantity from body
    product_id = flask.request.json['productId']
    quantity = flask.request.json['quantity']

    db.add_to_cart(product_id, quantity)

    return flask.jsonify({'message': 'Added to cart'})

# checkout POST, cartId in body
@app.route('/checkout', methods=['POST'])
@swag_from('swagger/checkout.yml')
def checkout():
    # get cart id from body
    cart_id = flask.request.json['cartId']

    db.checkout(cart_id)

    return flask.jsonify({'message': 'Checkout successful'})

# start app on port 5000
if __name__ == '__main__':
    app.run(debug=True, port=5000)
```

[End of response]

And it tells us to create the following files and folders:

```
folder: swagger
products.yml
file: cart.yml
file: add_to_cart.yml
```

```
file: checkout.yml
file: swagger.yml
```

Let's create these files manually and copy the content into them.

```yaml
products.yml
---
tags:
  - products
responses:
  200:
    description: A list of products
    schema:
      type: array
      items:
        type: object
        properties:
          id:
            type: integer
          name:
            type: string
          price:
            type: number
cart.yml
---
tags:
  - cart
responses:
  200:
    description: A list of items in the cart
    schema:
      type: array
      items:
        type: object
        properties:
          id:
            type: integer
          product_id:
            type: integer
          quantity:
            type: integer
add_to_cart.yml
---
```

```
tags:
  - cart
parameters:
  - in: body
    name: body
    required: true
    schema:
      type: object
      properties:
        productId:
          type: integer
        quantity:
          type: integer
responses:
  200:
    description: Added to cart
checkout.yml
---
tags:
  - checkout
parameters:
  - in: body
    name: body
    required: true
    schema:
      type: object
      properties:
        cartId:
          type: integer
responses:
  200:
    description: Checkout successful
```

What's missing is installing the `flassger` Swagger library:

```
pip install flasgger
```

Navigate to `http://localhost:5000/apidocs/` and you should see Swagger UI.

Figure 8.4: API doc generated by Swagger

You should verify that the API works as expected by interacting with generated docs and ensure the routes generate the expected output.

It's definitely possible to keep improving at this point but take a moment to realize how much we created with only prompts and a few lines of code. We have a working API with a database and documentation. We can now focus on improving the code and adding more features.

Assignment

Here's the suggested assignment for this chapter: A good assignment would be to add more features to the API, such as:

- Add a new endpoint to get a single product.
- Add a new endpoint to remove a product from the cart.
- Add a new endpoint to update the quantity of a product in the cart.

You can solve this by just adding the above to Copilot Chat as prompts and see what it generates. Expect both the code and documentation to change.

Solution

You can find the solution to this assignment in the GitHub repository: `https://github.com/PacktPublishing/AI-Assisted-Software-Development-with-GitHub-Copilot-and-ChatGPT/tree/main/08`

Challenge

Improve this API by adding more features. You can use Copilot Chat to help you with this.

Summary

In this chapter, we discussed how to plan out our API. Then we looked at how we can choose Python and Flask for the job but stressed the importance of having contextual knowledge on how to actually build a Web API. In general, you should always know how to do something before you ask an AI assistant to help you with it, at least at a high level.

Then we ended up crafting prompts for the AI assistant to help us with the Web API. We ended up working with our e-commerce site and created a Web API to serve it.

After that, we discussed how to improve the code and add more features to the API.

In the next chapter, we will discuss how to improve our app by adding artificial intelligence to it.

Join our community on Discord

Join our community's Discord space for discussions with the author and other readers:

`https://packt.link/aicode`

9

Augment Web Apps with AI Services

Introduction

There are several ways that a web app can be augmented with AI services: you could leverage an existing Web API exposing a model, or build it yourself and have it call a model.

The reason you would want to add AI to your app in the first place is to make it smarter. Not smarter for its own sake, but to make it more useful to the user. For example, if you have a web app that allows users to search for products, you could add a feature that suggests products based on the user's previous purchases. In fact, why limit yourself to previous purchases? Why not suggest products based on the user's previous searches? Or, what if the user could take a picture of a product and the app would suggest similar products?

As you can see, there are a lot of possibilities for augmenting your web app with AI that would improve the user experience.

In this chapter, we will:

- Discuss different model formats like Pickle and ONNX
- Learn how to use both Pickle and ONNX to persist your model as a file using Python
- Consume a model stored in ONNX format and expose it via a REST API using JavaScript

Business domain, e-commerce

We keep working on our e-commerce domain, but our business focus is on ratings. A good or bad rating can influence how many units are sold of a specific product. The logical domain consists of the following:

- **Products:** the products to be rated
- **Ratings:** the actual ratings and meta information like comments, dates and more

Problem and data domain

The problem to figure out is how we use this rating data and learn from it.

- **Insights:** We could, for example, get the insights that we should start/stop selling a certain product. There might be other insights as certain products sell well in certain parts of the world.
- **Technical problem:** The technical aspect of this is figuring out how to ingest the data, train a model from it, and then figure out how a web application can leverage said model.

Feature breakdown

Looking at this from a feature standpoint, we need to see this as consisting of three major parts.

- **Data ingestion and training:** this needs a separate interface, maybe it's done without a user interface and it's just static data being fed into code capable of training a model from it. With that understanding, we can outline the steps like so:

  - Load data
  - Clean data
  - Create features
  - Train model
  - Evaluate model
  - Run predictions

- **Consuming the model:** Once the model is trained, it needs to be exposed, preferably through a web endpoint. To get there, we think we need these set of steps:

  - Convert the model to suitable format if needed
  - Build a Web API
  - Expose model through Web API
  - Deploy model, there's a step here where we need to bring the API online

- **Prediction:** For the prediction part, this is a functionality that's meant for "back office" and not customer facing.

  - Build user interface to run predictions
  - Build underlying code that talks to the Web API to make predictions possible

Prompt strategy

You could go with either prompt approach here, either get suggestions from a prompt comment or use the chat interface.

For prompt pattern, we'll use the "Exploratory pattern" as described in *Chapter 2*.

Creating a model

Imagine we are dealing with the following data in the `sales_rating.csv` file that is the result of merging two datasets, one containing sales data and the other containing rating data. The data looks like this:

```
product_id,avg_rating,sold
1,2.5,100
2,3.7,200
3,4.2,300
4,1.3,50
5,4.9,800
6,3.2,150
7,2.1,80
8,4.8,500
9,3.9,400
10,2.4,200
11,4.1,300
12,3.2,100
13,2.9,150
14,4.5,500
15,3.8,400
16,2.7,200
17,4.3,300
18,3.4,100
19,2.3,150
20,4.7,500
```

The preceding data shows a dataset with `product_id`, `avg_rating`, and `sold` columns. Our theory is that the average rating of a product is correlated with the number of sales. It seems like a fair assumption that a product with a high rating will sell more than a product with a low rating. By creating a model, we can come closer to determining whether it's likely that our assumption is true or not.

Coming up with a plan

We can ask Copilot about the steps we need to take to create a model. We type these prompts as comments:

> If you want to ask Copilot to come up with text answers about something else other than code, you can type the text as a comment in a code file or inside of a Markdown file. It also helps to place yourself on the next row after the comment and start the row with "a:" for answer. You can also ask questions using Copilot Chat:

[Prompt]

Tell me the answer of life, the universe and everything.

[End of prompt]

[Prompt response]

```
a: 42
```

[End of response]

The above reference is from the book *Hitchhikers guide to the Galaxy* by Douglas Adams.

Next, let's ask Copilot to help us with the steps to create a model.

[Prompt]

What are the steps to create a model in Python given a CSV file?

[End of prompt]

Output:

- import pandas and scikit-learn
- read the CSV file
- create a test and training dataset
- create a model
- how good is the model?
- predict
- save the model to pkl

OK, we have a plan, so let's execute it and use Copilot to help us with the code.

Importing libraries

First, let's start by creating a new notebook in VS Code. Let's call it `sales.ipynb`.

 `.ipynb` is the file format for Jupyter Notebook that you as a data science practitioner are most likely familiar with. The idea is that you work on a file with cells, where some cells are text cells and others are code cells you can run.

To use certain libraries, we need to install them. We can use Copilot to help us with that. We can leverage the fact that we are data science practitioners and therefore have an understanding of what libraries we need. Therefore, we will suggest the pandas and scikit-learn libraries below to help us with our task.

[Prompt]

Install pandas and scikit-learn in a notebook.

[End of prompt]

[Prompt response]

```
! pip install pandas scikit-learn
```

[End of response]

Next, let's import the libraries we need.

[Prompt]

Import pandas and scikit-learn in a notebook.

[End of prompt]

[Prompt response]

```
# Import pandas and scikit-learn in a notebook.
import pandas as pd
import sklearn.linear_model
```

[End of response]

Reading the CSV file

Now that we have the libraries we need, let's read the CSV file.

[Prompt]

Read a CSV file in a notebook.

[End of prompt]

[Prompt response]

```
# Read a CSV file in a notebook.
df = pd.read_csv("sales_rating.csv")
```

[End of response]

The CSV file is now loaded into a pandas DataFrame, a structure holding columns and rows. Let's take a look at the first few rows.

```
df.head()
```

This will produce the following output:

```
   product_id  avg_rating  sold
0           1         2.5   100
1           2         3.7   200
2           3         4.2   300
```

| 3 | 4 | 1.3 | 50 |
| 4 | 5 | 4.9 | 800 |

Great, we have the data loaded into a DataFrame. Next, we need to split the data into test and training datasets.

Creating test and training datasets

In machine learning, we typically split the data into test and training datasets. The training dataset is used to train the model and the test dataset is used to test the model. We can use Copilot to help us with this.

[Prompt]

Create test and training dataset in a notebook, suggested test size of 0.2.

[End of prompt]

[Prompt response]

```
# Create a test and training dataset in a notebook, suggested test size of 0.2
test_size = 0.2
test = df.sample(frac=test_size)
training = df.drop(test.index)
```

[End of response]

0.2 is a good test size. It means that 20% of the data will be used for testing and 80% will be used for training.

 You may need to start typing "test_size" and "training" on the respective rows, then press *TAB* to accept the suggestion.

Now we have things set up, let's create a model next.

Creating a model

Creating a model involves selecting the algorithm we want to use and then training the model. Let's suggest a prompt:

[Prompt]

Create a model in a notebook using the `LinearRegression` algorithm.

[End of prompt]

[Prompt response]

```
# Create a model in a notebook using the LinearRegression algorithm.
```

```
model = sklearn.linear_model.LinearRegression()
model.fit(training[["avg_rating"]], training[["sold"]])
```

[End of response]

In the preceding code, we created a model using the `LinearRegression` algorithm and then trained the model using the training dataset with the `fit` method. Also, note how we are using the `avg_rating` column as the input and the `sold` column as the output. This is because we want to predict the number of sales based on the average rating.

How good is the model?

At this point, we want to find out how good the model is. To find this out, let's ask Copilot to help us.

 You can either use a comment style and get suggestions inline, or use Copilot Chat. In both cases, Copilot will understand from the context.

[Prompt]

How good is the model in a notebook? Show the code.

[End of prompt]

[Prompt response]

```
# How good is the model in a notebook? Show the code.
score = model.score(test[["avg_rating"]], test[["sold"]])
```

[End of response]

It seems that calling `score` on the model and passing in the `test` dataset is how we find out how good a model is. We can even ask Copilot about this:

[Prompt]

What does score do?

[End of prompt]

[Prompt response]

```
score returns the coefficient of determination R^2 of the prediction.
```

[End of response]

If you want, you keep querying and have things explained in more detail, like with the below prompt:

[Prompt]

What does that mean in simpler terms?

[End of prompt]

[Prompt response]

```
it returns a number between 0 and 1, where 1 is perfect prediction and 0 is no
prediction.
```

[End of response]

Predict

We won't know how good the model is until we try to predict something, even if we could refer to the score value. Let's craft a prompt for this task:

[Prompt]

Predict in a notebook. Show the code.

[End of prompt]

[Prompt response]

```
# Predict in a notebook. Show the code.
predictions = model.predict(test[["avg_rating"]])
```

[End of response]

OK, we got a variable called predictions that contains the predictions, but it is hard to understand if the predictions are reasonable. Let's try asking Copilot and see what it suggests.

[Prompt]

How do you suggest we show the predictions in a notebook?

[End of prompt]

[Prompt response]

```
print the predictions
```

[End of response]

[Prompt]

Any other ways you suggest we show the predictions in a notebook except for printing?

[End of prompt]

[Prompt response]

```
plot the predictions
```

[End of response]

Now that we've gotten more information on our various options, let's use that knowledge in a prompt:

[Prompt]

Show me how to print and plot predictions vs the actual data in a notebook.

[End of prompt]

[Prompt response]

```python
# Show me how to print and plot predictions vs actual data in a notebook.
import matplotlib.pyplot as plt
plt.scatter(test[["avg_rating"]], test[["sold"]],  color='black')
plt.plot(test[["avg_rating"]], predictions, color='blue', linewidth=3)
```

[End of response]

Running this code in a notebook will produce the following plot:

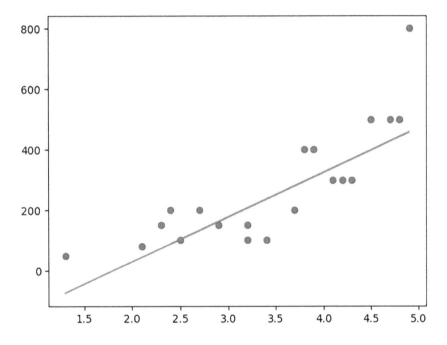

Figure 9.1: Plot showing predictions vs actual data

In the plot, it looks like the line is a good fit for the data. We can also print predictions to see the actual values:

```python
print(predictions)
```

Saving the model to a .pkl file

We have one step left: we need to save the model to a file. We have a few different choices for how to save the model. We can save it as a pickle file or an ONNX file, for example. Let's start with saving it as a pickle file.

As usual, let's craft a prompt for this task:

[Prompt]

Save the model to a pkl in the notebook.

[End of prompt]

[Prompt response]

```python
# Save the model to pkl in a notebook.
import pickle
pickle.dump(model, open("model.pkl", "wb"))
```

[End of response]

For the completion of the above, you may need to start typing "import" to get the suggestion. Additionally, it's a good bet it's going to use the pickle library, so on the next line you can start typing "pickle" and press *TAB* to accept the suggestion.

Creating a REST API in Python

At this point, we have a model.pkl file that contains our model. We can expose the model using this file via a REST API. Let's ask Copilot to help us with this.

[Prompt]

Create a REST API in Python that exposes the model in a pkl file.

[End of prompt]

[Prompt response]

```python
# Create a REST API in Python that exposes the model in a pkl file.
import pickle
import flask

# load the model
model = pickle.load(open("model.pkl", "rb"))

# app
app = flask.Flask(__name__)

# routes
@app.route('/', methods=['GET', 'POST'])
def predict():
    if flask.request.method == 'GET':
```

```
        return "Please POST a JSON object to this endpoint to get a
  prediction."
    else:
        data = flask.request.json
        prediction = model.predict([[data["avg_rating"]]])
        return flask.jsonify({"prediction": prediction[0][0]})
```

[End of response]

 Note how we use several prompts above. First, we set the context by adding the prompt "Create a REST API in Python that exposes the model in a pkl file" at the top of the file. Then we use various helper prompts like "load the model", "app", and "routes" to help us with the code. We end up with an API that exposes the model via a REST API.

Converting the model to ONNX

So far, you've seen how we can use Pickle to save a model and then load it in Python. However, Pickle has drawbacks, including being Python-specific. ONNX, on the other hand, is a format that is not Python-specific and can be used in other languages. Let's see how we can use the ONNX format to work with our model.

We need to solve our task in two steps:

- Convert the model to ONNX format.
- Load the model and create a REST API in JavaScript.

Creating a model in ONNX format

Because we're using a notebook, we need to install the dependencies, import the libraries we need, and then convert the model to ONNX format.

[Prompt]

What dependencies do I need for ONNX? Show me the Python code for installing those dependencies.

[End of prompt]

[Prompt response]

```
! pip install skl2onnx
```

[End of response]

[Prompt]

Show me how to import the libraries I need for ONNX and show me how to convert the model to ONNX format.

[End of prompt]

[Prompt response]

```
import skl2onnx
# convert the model to ONNX
skl2onnx.to_onnx(model, train[["avg_rating"]].astype("float32"), "model.onnx")
```

[End of response]

Now I should have a `model.onnx` file that contains the model in ONNX format. Let's see if we can load it in JavaScript next.

Loading the ONNX model in JavaScript

Next, we need to load the ONNX model in JavaScript and specifically Node.js, as we're doing this on the backend. We can use the `onnxruntime` library to do this. Let's ask Copilot to help us with this.

[Prompt]

Show me a step-by-step guide to load the ONNX model in JavaScript.

[End of prompt]

[Prompt response]

- install onnxruntime in JavaScript
- load the ONNX model in JavaScript
- predict using ONNX model in JavaScript

[End of response]

Now that we have a plan, let's execute it.

Installing onnxruntime in JavaScript

Because we're building a Node.js project, let's first, in a new folder, create an `app.js` file and run the `npm init -y` terminal command to create a new Node.js project.

The first step in our plan is to install `onnxruntime` in JavaScript. We can use npm to perform this task.

[Prompt]

Install onnxruntime in JavaScript.

[End of prompt]

[Prompt response]

```
npm install onnxruntime
```

[End of response]

Great, this installs the `onnxruntime` library in our project. Next, we need to load the ONNX model.

Loading the ONNX model in JavaScript

Now that we have onnxruntime installed, we can load the ONNX model.

[Prompt]

Load the ONNX model in JavaScript.

[End of prompt]

[Prompt response]

```
const rt = require("onnxruntime");

# load model from ONNX
model rt.InferenceSession("model.onnx");

# predict
model.run(null, {model.get_inputs()[0].name: [[4.5]]});
```

[End of response]

In the preceding code, we load the model from the ONNX file and then we make predictions using the model with the input 4.5 to represent the average rating to see what sales we can expect.

Assignment: Build a REST API in JavaScript that consumes the model

1. Take the model we created in the previous section and add the code to the notebook to turn it into an ONNX file.
2. Create a new folder in the repo called and create a new file called app.js in that folder.
3. Add the POST /predict route to the server.js file and ensure it returns a prediction given the input.

Here's some starter prompts you can try to help you with this assignment:

- **Prompt:** Create a REST API in JavaScript using Express
- **Prompt:** Create a POST /predict route in a REST API in JavaScript using Express
- **Prompt:** Load the model from ONNX in a REST API in JavaScript using Express
- **Prompt:** Predict using the ONNX model in a REST API in JavaScript using Express

Solution

See repo [https://github.com/PacktPublishing/AI-Assisted-Software-Development-with-GitHub-Copilot-and-ChatGPT/tree/main/09] and the *09* folder for the solution.

Quiz

What's the difference between Pickle and ONNX?

    a.   Pickle is Python-specific and ONNX is not.

    b.   Pickle can be used in JavaScript and ONNX can't.

    c.   ONNX is less efficient than Pickle.

Summary

In this chapter, we covered various model formats like Pickle and ONNX and how to persist your model as a file using Python. Storing a model as a file is useful because it allows you to integrate it with other applications.

Then we discussed the pros and cons of different formats for storing models like Pickle and ONNX. We came to the conclusion that ONNX is probably the better choice because it's not Python-specific and can be used in other languages.

Then we covered how to load a model stored in ONNX format using JavaScript and create a REST API to make the model available to other applications.

In the next chapter, we'll go into more detail of how we can use GitHub Copilot and get the most out of it. We'll cover both tips and tricks and features that help make you faster and more productive.

Join our community on Discord

Join our community's Discord space for discussions with the author and other readers:

`https://packt.link/aicode`

10

Maintaining Existing Codebases

Introduction

Brownfield is another word for working with existing code. In my career as a developer, most of the work carried out has been on existing code. The opposite of brownfield is **greenfield**, which is a new project with no existing code.

For that reason, it's important to cover how to work with existing codebases, and there's a lot to get excited about when working with an AI assistant like GitHub Copilot in a brownfield context.

In this chapter, we will:

- Learn about the different types of maintenance.
- Understand how we work with maintenance in a process to de-risk introduced changes.
- Use GitHub Copilot to help us with maintenance.

Prompt strategy

This chapter is a bit different from other chapters in the book. The focus is on describing various problems you may encounter in the space of existing codebases. You're recommended to use the prompt suggestion approach with which you're the most comfortable, be it prompt comments or the chat interface. As for patterns, you're encouraged to try out all three major patterns introduced, that is, PIC, TAG, or Exploratory patterns as described in *Chapter 2*. This chapter however focuses on using the "Exploratory pattern".

Different types of maintenance

There are different types of maintenance, and it's important to understand the differences between them. Here are some different types that you're likely to encounter:

- **Corrective maintenance:** This is when we're fixing bugs.
- **Adaptive maintenance:** In this case, we change code to adapt to new requirements.

- **Perfective maintenance:** When we improve code without changing the functionality. Examples of this could be refactoring or improving the performance of the code.
- **Preventive maintenance:** Changing the code to prevent future bugs or issues.

The maintenance process

Every time you change code, you introduce risk. For example, a bug fix could introduce a new bug. To mitigate this risk, we need to follow a process. A suggested process could be the following steps:

1. **Identify:** Identify the problem or the change that needs to be made.
2. **Inspect:** Inspect the test coverage and how well your code is covered by tests. The better it's covered, the more likely you are to detect any introduced bugs or other issues.
3. **Plan:** Plan the change. How are you going to make it? What tests are you going to write? What tests are you going to run?
4. **Implement:** Implement the change.
5. **Verify:** Verify that the change works as expected. Run the tests, run the application, check the logs, etc.
6. **Integrate:** This is about ensuring any change you make in a branch is merged into the main branch.
7. **Release/deploy the change:** You want to make sure the end customer can leverage the benefit of this change. For that to happen, you need to deploy it.

Do we need to cover all these steps for every change? No, it depends on the change; some changes might be so small that we might want to bundle many of them before we make a release that we want the end customer to have. The good news is that we have a great tool in GitHub Copilot that can help us with some of these minor steps, allowing us to focus on the more important steps.

Addressing a bug

Some bugs are more severe than others. In a best-case scenario, your bug is seldom encountered, or when it does occur it's not a big deal. In a worst-case scenario, your bug loses you money. Let's focus on a case where the bug loses you money in a scenario where you're running an e-commerce site.

Hopefully, this code has never been shipped in production, but it's a good example of a bug that could be catastrophic for an e-commerce site:

```python
def process_cart():
    # get cart from database
    cart = get_cart()

    card = cart.get_card()
    process_payment(card, cart)
    ship_order(cart)
```

The problem you might have is that `ship_order` is called even if `process_payment` fails, which means you ship orders without getting paid, losing you money.

Looking at this code, you might not have a problem if `process_payment` throws an error and you don't even get to `ship_order`.

What if it doesn't and, instead, returns a numerical code that depends on payment results, like so?

```python
def process_payment(card, cart):
    if card.is_valid():
        if card.has_funds(cart.total):
            charge_card(card, cart.total)
            return 0
        else:
            return 1
```

If you don't read the error code, you might not notice that the payment failed, and the order is shipped. So, what's our approach here?

1. Identify the problem

First, we need to identify the problem; in this case, there are two things you can do, namely:

- **Read the code:** What does our code look like? Are errors thrown, does it return a code, or something else entirely?
- **Check the tests:** Do we have a test that covers this scenario? If not, we need to write one. The test should show that we have a bug.

Let's use Copilot for this, with a prompt like so (here, we simulate `process_payment` to return error codes instead of throwing errors). Select the `ship_order` code in the main window, and then type a prompt as follows in the chat window:

[Prompt]

Write a test for the code; `ship_order` should not be called if `process_payment` returns 1.

[End of prompt]

 We're using the GitHub Copilot Chat function and selecting the `process_cart` code in our text editor.

You should see a response similar to the below code:

[Prompt response]

```python
import unittest
from unittest.mock import Mock, patch
from your_module import process_cart  # replace with the actual module name
```

```
class TestProcessCart(unittest.TestCase):
    @patch('your_module.get_cart')   # replace with the actual module name
    @patch('your_module.process_payment')
    @patch('your_module.ship_order')
    def test_order_not_shipped_if_payment_fails(self, mock_ship_order, mock_
process_payment, mock_get_cart):
        # Arrange
        mock_cart = Mock()
        mock_cart.get_card.return_value = 'test_card'
        mock_get_cart.return_value = mock_cart
        mock_process_payment.return_value = 1
        # Act
        process_cart()

        # Assert
        mock_ship_order.assert_not_called()

if __name__ == '__main__':
    unittest.main()
```

[End of response]

The above code contains a test that tests what happens if we get error code 1 from `process_payment`. What we want to have happen is for `ship_order` not to be called.

This test will fail, as we have a bug in our code, which is a good thing, as we've identified a bug and can prove it exists with a test.

2. Implement the change

Now that we have a test that shows we have a bug, we can implement the change. We can be confident to make the code change, as we have a test that shows that we have a bug, and we've hopefully also improved test coverage enough.

 Don't start refactoring unless you have good test coverage or the change is so small that you are confident that you won't introduce a bug.

How do we now improve the code? Simple – we can use GitHub Copilot to help us with the implementation. Let's use the following prompt to help us with the code change we need to do:

[Prompt]

Implement the change; `ship_order` should not be called if `process_payment` returns 1.

[End of prompt]

Your code for process_cart should now look like this:

[Prompt response]

```python
def process_cart():
    # get cart from database
    cart = get_cart()

    card = cart.get_card()
    payment_status = process_payment(card, cart)

    # Only ship the order if the payment was successful
    if payment_status != 1:
        ship_order(cart)
```

[End of response]

This code above is a step in the right direction, as it now contains an if statement that checks the payment status.

To further improve the code, we can use Copilot to help us make the code more robust and easier to read. Let's use the following prompt for additional improvements:

[Prompt]

Refactor the code, making it easier to maintain.

[End of prompt]

This might give you the following code:

[Prompt response]

```python
def get_payment_status(cart):
    card = cart.get_card()
    return process_payment(card, cart)

def process_cart():
    # get cart from database
    cart = get_cart()

    payment_status = get_payment_status(cart)

    # Only ship the order if the payment was successful
```

```python
    if payment_status != 1:
        ship_order(cart)
```

[End of response]

Here, Copilot has suggested that we extract the payment status into a separate function. This is a good suggestion, as it makes the code easier to read and maintain.

Adding a new feature

In this example, we'll look at an existing codebase and add a new feature. The codebase is like the one we used in the previous example, but it's a bit more complex. This is because it has a few more functions involving different types of payment methods. Here's the code:

```python
```python
import re

def validate_card(card):
    # Visa cards start with 4 and have 13 or 16 digits.
    # MasterCard cards start with 51 through 55 and have 16 digits.
    visa_pattern = r'^4[0-9]{12}(?:[0-9]{3})?$'
    mastercard_pattern = r'^5[1-5][0-9]{14}$'

    if re.match(visa_pattern, card):
        return 'Visa'
    elif re.match(mastercard_pattern, card):
        return 'MasterCard'
    else:
        return None

def process_payment(card, cart):
    card_type = validate_card(card)
    if card_type is None:
        return 1  # Invalid card
    else:
        # Process the payment here
        # Return 0 if the payment is successful, 1 otherwise
        pass

def process_cart():
    # Get cart from database
    cart = get_cart()

    card = cart.get_card()
```
```

```
    payment_status = process_payment(card, cart)

    # Only ship the order if the payment was successful
    if payment_status == 0:
        ship_order(cart)
```

In the above code, we have the following:

- `validate_card` validates the card number and returns the card type if valid; otherwise, it returns None.
- `process_payment` processes the payment and returns 0 if the payment was successful; otherwise, it returns 1.
- `process_cart` processes the cart, gets the card, processes the payment, and ships the order if the payment is successful.

1. Identify a problem and find the function/s to change

Our task is to make our code also support American Express cards. Implementing a new card means that we need to update the `validate_card` function to support American Express cards.

Now, we know what functions need to change, but does GitHub Copilot know?

Let's ask GitHub Copilot, with a prompt.

 In the identification step, we used our know-how to identify what and where to change. A good practice is to rely on a combination of your own skills and the Copilot tool to help analyze and identify problems.

2. Implement change, and add a new feature and tests

Let's use GitHub Copilot to help us with this. We can use the following prompt:

[Prompt]

Add support for American Express cards.

[End of prompt]

You will get code similar to this:

[Prompt response]

```
import re

def validate_card(card):
    # Visa cards start with 4 and have 13 or 16 digits.
```

```python
# MasterCard cards start with 51 through 55 and have 16 digits.
# American Express cards start with 34 or 37 and have 15 digits.
visa_pattern = r'^4[0-9]{12}(?:[0-9]{3})?$'
mastercard_pattern = r'^5[1-5][0-9]{14}$'
amex_pattern = r'^3[47][0-9]{13}$'

if re.match(visa_pattern, card):
    return 'Visa'
elif re.match(mastercard_pattern, card):
    return 'MasterCard'
elif re.match(amex_pattern, card):
    return 'American Express'
else:
    return None
```

[End of response]

In the above code, Copilot has made the following changes:

- Created a new regular expression in the `validate_card` function to support American Express cards.
- Added a new `elif` statement to return American Express if the card matches the new regular expression.

Of course, we're not done yet; we need to add a test to verify that the code works as expected. Let's use the following prompt:

[Prompt]

Write a test for the code; validate_card should return American Express for a valid card.

[End of prompt]

Your test should look like below:

[Prompt response]

```python
import unittest
from your_module import validate_card  # replace with the actual module name

class TestValidateCard(unittest.TestCase):
    def test_validate_card_returns_amex_for_valid_amex_card(self):
        # Arrange
        valid_amex_card = '378282246310005'

        # Act
```

```
        result = validate_card(valid_amex_card)

        # Assert
        self.assertEqual(result, 'American Express')

if __name__ == '__main__':
    unittest.main()
```

[End of response]

The new test, `test_validate_card_returns_amex_for_valid_amex_card`, was added by Copilot and tests that the `validate_card` function returns American Express for a valid American Express card.

At this point, it's a good idea to keep iterating; you not only want to test that the code works for a valid card but also for an invalid card, and so on.

 You can use Copilot as a challenge to write more tests.

Improving performance

Improving performance is a common task but can be tricky to achieve. Usually, you need specific tools to measure performance, and you need to know what to measure. A good way to find out how to improve your code in this way is to use a decorator to *profile* how long a method takes to execute. Then, you can measure specific methods and find out which methods to improve.

Here's an example of a decorator being used on a function that sleeps for 2 seconds:

```
import time

def profile(func):
    def wrapper(*args, **kwargs):
        start = time.time()
        result = func(*args, **kwargs)
        end = time.time()
        print(f'{func.__name__} took {end - start} seconds')
        return result
    return wrapper

@profile
def sleep_two_seconds():
    time.sleep(2)

sleep_two_seconds()
```

The `profile` function is a decorator that takes a function as input and returns a function that wraps the input function. The `wrapper` function measures the time it takes to execute the input function and prints the result.

Were you to run this code via the terminal, you would see output similar to the following:

```
sleep_two_seconds took 2.000000238418579 seconds
```

OK, so how do we use this to improve performance? Let's use GitHub Copilot and see how we can get advice on improving performance on a piece of code.

Here's the code we want to improve. This processes records and looks for duplicates:

```python
def process_records(records):
    for i in range(len(records)):
        for j in range(len(records)):
            if i != j and records[i] == records[j]:
                print(f'Duplicate record found: {records[i]}')
```

Most developers looking at this will refer back to their algorithms and data structures books and start thinking about things like *Big O notation*, a way to measure the performance of an algorithm. The main thing to focus on is reducing the number of costly operations to improve performance while retaining the same functionality.

So, the question we should ask GitHub Copilot is, how do we improve this code? Let's use the following prompt:

[Prompt]

Improve the performance of the code.

[End of prompt]

We get something like this back:

[Prompt response]

```python
def process_records(records):
    record_set = set()
    for record in records:
        if record in record_set:
            print(f'Duplicate record found: {record}')
        else:
            record_set.add(record)
```

[End of response]

So, why is this code better? Well, let's prove it:

1. First, by calculating the Big O notation for the original code and then for the new code.

2. Second, by using the decorator we created earlier.

Big O notation calculation

Try this prompt:

[Prompt]

What's the Big O complexity for this code? Show me how you calculated it as well.

[End of prompt]

You should get something like this:

[Prompt response]

The time complexity of the provided code is $O(n^2)$, where n is the number of records.

Here's how it's calculated:

- The outer loop runs n times, where n is the number of records. This is because it iterates over each record in the list.
- Inside the outer loop, there's an inner loop that also runs n times for the same reason.
- Since the inner loop runs n times for each iteration of the outer loop, the total number of iterations is $n * n$, or n^2.

Therefore, the time complexity is $O(n^2)$.

This means that if you double the number of records, the time it takes to process them will increase by about four times. This is a characteristic of quadratic time complexity.

[End of response]

OK, $O(n^2)$ is not great, but what about the new code?

Run the same prompt but on the new code:

[Prompt response]

The time complexity of the provided code is $O(n)$, where n is the number of records.

Here's how it's calculated:

- The loop runs n times, where n is the number of records. This is because it iterates over each record in the list.
- Inside the loop, the operations (checking if a record is in the set and potentially adding it to the set) are constant time, $O(1)$, because set operations in Python are typically constant time on average.

Therefore, the time complexity is $O(n) * O(1)$, which simplifies to $O(n)$.

This means that if you double the number of records, the time it takes to process them will also double, which is a characteristic of linear time complexity.

[End of response]

$O(n)$ is better than $O(n^2)$, but how much better? Let's measure this in the next section.

Measuring performance

OK, so algorithmically, we know that the new code is better, but how much better? Let's measure it by using the decorator and calling the code. Let's use the input of 1,000 records and 10,000 records and compare the time it takes to execute the code.

OK, let's see if the new code is faster than the old code. Let's try with 10,000 records:

```python
# old code
@profile
def process_records(records):
    for i in range(len(records)):
        for j in range(len(records)):
            if i != j and records[i] == records[j]:
                print(f'Duplicate record found: {records[i]}')


records_10000 = [i for i in range(10000)]
process_records(records_10000)
```

Running this code, you should see the following output:

```
process_records took 5.193912506103516 seconds
```

Now, let's run the new code:

```python
# new code
@profile
def process_records(records):
    record_set = set()
    for record in records:
        if record in record_set:
            print(f'Duplicate record found: {record}')
        else:
            record_set.add(record)


records_10000 = [i for i in range(10000)]
process_records(records_10000)
```

Running this code, you should see the following output:

```
process_records took 0.0011200904846191406 seconds
```

As you can see, by combining your knowledge with GitHub Copilot, you can improve your code.

Your code won't always look this obvious, and you might need to do more work to improve performance. You're recommended to use a profiler to measure performance, and then use GitHub Copilot to help you improve the code.

Improving maintainability

Another interesting use case is using GitHub Copilot to help you improve the maintainability of your code. So what are some things that you can do to improve the maintainability of your code? Here's a list:

- **Improve the naming** of variables, functions, classes, etc.
- **Separate concerns**: For example, separate business logic from presentation logic.
- **Remove duplication**: Especially in large codebases, you're likely to find duplication.
- **Improve readability**: You can improve readability by, for example, using comments, docstrings, event tests, and more.

Let's start with a codebase and see how we can improve it. Here's the code:

```python
def calculate_total(cart, discounts):
    # Define discount functions
    def three_for_two(items):
        total = 0
        for item in items:
            total += item.price * (item.quantity - item.quantity // 3)
        return total

    def christmas_discount(items):
        total = 0
        for item in items:
            total += item.price * item.quantity * 0.5
        return total

    def cheapest_free(items):
        items_sorted = sorted(items, key=lambda x: x.price)
        total = 0
        for item in items_sorted[1:]:
            total += item.price * item.quantity
        return total

    # Calculate totals for each discount
    totals = []
    for discount in discounts:
```

```
        if discount == '3 for 2':
            totals.append((discount, three_for_two(cart)))
        elif discount == 'Christmas Discount':
            totals.append((discount, christmas_discount(cart)))
        elif discount == 'Cheapest Free':
            totals.append((discount, cheapest_free(cart)))

    # Sort totals and return the lowest one
    totals_sorted = sorted(totals, key=lambda x: x[1])
    return totals_sorted[0][1] if totals_sorted else sum(item.price * item.
quantity for item in cart)

# Define discounts
discounts = ['3 for 2', 'Christmas Discount', 'Cheapest Free']

# Define cart
cart = [
    {'name': 'item1', 'price': 10, 'quantity': 3},
    {'name': 'item2', 'price': 20, 'quantity': 1},
    {'name': 'item3', 'price': 30, 'quantity': 1}
]

# Calculate total
total = calculate_total(cart, discounts)
print(f'Total: {total}')
```

The above codebase describes the following at a high level:

- A function, `calculate_total`, that calculates the total for a cart and a list of discounts
- A list of discounts
- A cart

What you can see from this codebase is that it's not very maintainable, as it's hard to understand what's going on.

1. Identify the problems. What problems do you see?

Let's first ask GitHub Copilot what it thinks about the code and decide what to do next. Let's use the following prompt:

[Prompt]

What do you think about the code? What would you do to improve it?

[End of prompt]

You get a lengthy response back with a bullet list and improved code. Let's look at the bullet list first:

[Prompt response]

- **Use Classes for Items and Discounts:** Right now, items and discounts are represented as dictionaries and strings, respectively. Using classes for these entities would make the code more readable and flexible.
- **Separate Discount Functions:** The discount functions are currently defined inside the `calculate_total` function. It would be better to define these functions separately to improve readability and make the code easier to test and maintain.
- **Use a More Extensible Approach for Applying Discounts:** The current approach for applying discounts involves a series of `if-elif` statements. This could be made more extensible by storing the discount functions in a dictionary or a list of `Discount` objects, and then iterating over that collection to apply the discounts.

[End of response]

The problems identified above all seem reasonable – using classes, separating functions, and using dictionary.

2. Add tests and de-risk change

Before we look at a suggested code change, we need to minimize the risk of introducing a bug. The first thing we should do is check our test coverage. In this case, we don't have any tests, so we need to write some. Let's use the following prompt:

[Prompt]

Write tests for this code, covering all possible execution paths.

[End of prompt]

[Prompt response]

```python
import unittest

class TestCalculateTotal(unittest.TestCase):
    def test_no_discounts(self):
        cart = [
            {'name': 'item1', 'price': 10, 'quantity': 3},
            {'name': 'item2', 'price': 20, 'quantity': 1},
            {'name': 'item3', 'price': 30, 'quantity': 1}
        ]
        discounts = []
        total = calculate_total(cart, discounts)
        self.assertEqual(total, 80)

    def test_three_for_two_discount(self):
```

```python
        cart = [
            {'name': 'item1', 'price': 10, 'quantity': 3},
            {'name': 'item2', 'price': 20, 'quantity': 1},
            {'name': 'item3', 'price': 30, 'quantity': 1}
        ]
        discounts = ['3 for 2']
        total = calculate_total(cart, discounts)
        self.assertEqual(total, 70)


    def test_christmas_discount(self):
        cart = [
            {'name': 'item1', 'price': 10, 'quantity': 3},
            {'name': 'item2', 'price': 20, 'quantity': 1},
            {'name': 'item3', 'price': 30, 'quantity': 1}
        ]
        discounts = ['Christmas Discount']
        total = calculate_total(cart, discounts)
        self.assertEqual(total, 40)


    def test_cheapest_free_discount(self):
        cart = [
            {'name': 'item1', 'price': 10, 'quantity': 3},
            {'name': 'item2', 'price': 20, 'quantity': 1},
            {'name': 'item3', 'price': 30, 'quantity': 1}
        ]
        discounts = ['Cheapest Free']
        total = calculate_total(cart, discounts)
        self.assertEqual(total, 70)


    def test_multiple_discounts(self):
        cart = [
            {'name': 'item1', 'price': 10, 'quantity': 3},
            {'name': 'item2', 'price': 20, 'quantity': 1},
            {'name': 'item3', 'price': 30, 'quantity': 1}
        ]
        discounts = ['3 for 2', 'Christmas Discount', 'Cheapest Free']
        total = calculate_total(cart, discounts)
        self.assertEqual(total, 40)


if __name__ == '__main__':
    unittest.main()
```

[End of response]

Now, you should never trust what an AI generates, so take your time to review the code, run a test coverage tool, and ensure that you're happy with the code before you proceed to the next step, which is to improve the code.

To improve the code from the first suggestion from Copilot, you want to ensure that it runs and uses classes like `Item` when you add items to a cart, for example. Below is the result of those alterations:

```python
import unittest
from discount_old import calculate_total, Item
from item import Item


class TestCalculateTotal(unittest.TestCase):
    def test_no_discounts(self):
        cart = [
            Item('item1', 10, 3),
            Item('item2', 20, 1),
            Item('item3', 30, 1)
        ]
        discounts = []
        total = calculate_total(cart, discounts)
        self.assertEqual(total, 80)

    def test_three_for_two_discount(self):
        cart = [
            Item('item1', 10, 3),
            Item('item2', 20, 1),
            Item('item3', 30, 1)
        ]
        discounts = ['3 for 2']
        total = calculate_total(cart, discounts)
        self.assertEqual(total, 70)

    def test_christmas_discount(self):
        cart = [
            Item('item1', 10, 3),
            Item('item2', 20, 1),
            Item('item3', 30, 1)
```

```python
        ]
        discounts = ['Christmas Discount']
        total = calculate_total(cart, discounts)
        self.assertEqual(total, 40)


    def test_cheapest_free_discount(self):
        cart = [
            Item('item1', 10, 3), #30
            Item('item2', 20, 1), # 20
            Item('item3', 30, 1) # 30
        ]
        discounts = ['Cheapest Free']
        total = calculate_total(cart, discounts)
        self.assertEqual(total, 60)


    def test_multiple_discounts(self):
        cart = [
            Item('item1', 10, 3),
            Item('item2', 20, 1),
            Item('item3', 30, 1)
        ]
        discounts = ['3 for 2', 'Christmas Discount', 'Cheapest Free']
        total = calculate_total(cart, discounts)
        self.assertEqual(total, 40)


if __name__ == '__main__':
    unittest.main()
```

And for the application code:

```python
from item import Item


def calculate_total(cart, discounts):
    # Define discount functions
    def three_for_two(items):
        total = 0
        for item in items:
            total += item.price * (item.quantity - item.quantity // 3)
        return total


    def christmas_discount(items):
        total = 0
```

```python
        for item in items:
            total += item.price * item.quantity * 0.5
        return total


    def cheapest_free(items):
        if not items:
            return 0


        items_sorted = sorted(items, key=lambda x: x.price * x.quantity)
        cheapest_item = items_sorted[0]
        total = 0
        for item in items:
            total += item.price * item.quantity
        total -= cheapest_item.price * cheapest_item.quantity if cheapest_item.
quantity > 0 else 0
        return total


    # Calculate totals for each discount
    totals = []
    for discount in discounts:
        if discount == '3 for 2':
            totals.append((discount, three_for_two(cart)))
        elif discount == 'Christmas Discount':
            totals.append((discount, christmas_discount(cart)))
        elif discount == 'Cheapest Free':
            totals.append((discount, cheapest_free(cart)))


    # Sort totals and return the lowest one
    totals_sorted = sorted(totals, key=lambda x: x[1])
    return totals_sorted[0][1] if totals_sorted else sum(item.price * item.
quantity for item in cart)


# if run as script,
if __name__ == '__main__':
    # Define discounts
    discounts = ['3 for 2', 'Christmas Discount', 'Cheapest Free']
    # Define cart
    cart = [
        Item('item1', 10, 3),
        Item('item2', 20, 1),
        Item('item3', 30, 1)
```

```
    ]

    # Calculate total
    total = calculate_total(cart, discounts)
    print(f'Total: {total}')
```

OK, so we now have a codebase that we're happy with and that's passing tests. Let's now look at the suggested code change from GitHub Copilot.

3. Implement change and improve maintainability

OK, we feel confident that we have good test coverage and we're ready to improve the code. Let's use the following prompt:

[Prompt]

Improve the maintainability of the code.

[End of prompt]

You should get something like this:

[Prompt response]

To improve the maintainability of the code, we can make the following changes:

- Move the discount functions out of `calculate_total` to make them standalone functions. This improves readability and makes it easier to test these functions individually.
- Use a dictionary to map discount names to their corresponding functions. This eliminates the need for multiple `if/elif` statements when applying discounts.

```
from item import Item

# Define discount functions
def three_for_two(items):
    total = 0
    for item in items:
        total += item.price * (item.quantity - item.quantity // 3)
    return total

def christmas_discount(items):
    total = 0
    for item in items:
        total += item.price * item.quantity * 0.5
    return total

def cheapest_free(items):
```

```python
    if not items:
        return 0

    items_sorted = sorted(items, key=lambda x: x.price * x.quantity)
    cheapest_item = items_sorted[0]
    total = 0
    for item in items:
        total += item.price * item.quantity
    total -= cheapest_item.price * cheapest_item.quantity if cheapest_item.
quantity > 0 else 0
    return total


def calculate_total(cart, discounts):
    # Map discount names to functions
    discount_functions = {
        '3 for 2': three_for_two,
        'Christmas Discount': christmas_discount,
        'Cheapest Free': cheapest_free
    }

    # Calculate totals for each discount
    totals = []
    for discount in discounts:
        if discount in discount_functions:
            totals.append((discount, discount_functions[discount](cart)))

    # Sort totals and return the lowest one
    totals_sorted = sorted(totals, key=lambda x: x[1])
    return totals_sorted[0][1] if totals_sorted else sum(item.price * item.
quantity for item in cart)

# if run as script,
if __name__ == '__main__':
    # Define discounts
    discounts = ['3 for 2', 'Christmas Discount', 'Cheapest Free']

    # Define cart
    cart = [
        Item('item1', 10, 3),
        Item('item2', 20, 1),
        Item('item3', 30, 1)
```

```
    ]

    # Calculate total
    total = calculate_total(cart, discounts)
    print(f'Total: {total}')
```

[End of response]

The code is now easier to maintain, as the following changes have been introduced:

*   `calculate_total` is a vastly smaller function, where each of the functions it used to contain has been moved out
*   The same method mentioned also now uses a dictionary to map names to functions

 The key to using Copilot effectively is to keep iterating, keep making small changes, and see what Copilot suggests. Change the prompt slightly, see what happens, and go with the output that best suits your needs.

Challenge

Try improving the code further using a prompt and GitHub Copilot. What should happen if there's a problem with the payment? Should you log it, maybe raise an error, etc.?

Updating an existing e-commerce site

Let's continue working on the e-commerce site that we presented in previous chapters. In this chapter, we'll focus on improving the codebase and adding new features.

For reference, let's show the `basket.html` file we've started to create:

```html
<!-- a page showing a list of items in a basket, each item should have title,
price, quantity, sum and buttons to increase or decrease quantity and the page
should have a link to "checkout" at the bottom  -->
<html>
<head>
    <title>Basket</title>
    <link rel="stylesheet" href="css/basket.css">


    <!-- add bootstrap -->
    <link rel="stylesheet" href="https://stackpath.bootstrapcdn.com/
bootstrap/4.5.2/css/bootstrap.min.css">
</head>
<body>
```

```
    <!-- add 3  basket items with each item having id, name, price, quantity,
use card css class -->


<!--
    <div class="container">
        <div id="basket" class="basket">
        </div>
    </div> -->
    <!-- add app.js  -->
    <!-- add app.js, type javascript -->



    <div id="basket" class="basket">
        <!-- render basket from Vue app, use Boostrap  -->
        <div v-for="(item, index) in basket" class="basket-item">
            <div class="basket-item-text">
                <h2>{{ item.name }}</h2>
                <p>Price: {{ item.price }}</p>
                <p>Quantity: {{ item.quantity }}</p>
                <p>Sum: {{ item.price * item.quantity }}</p>
            </div>
            <div class="basket-item-buttons">
                <button type="submit" class="btn btn-primary btn-block btn-
large" @click="increaseQuantity(index)">+</button>
                <button type="submit" class="btn btn-primary btn-block btn-
large" @click="decreaseQuantity(index)">-</button>
            </div>
        </div>
    </div>

    <!-- add Vue 3  -->
    <script src="https://unpkg.com/vue@next"></script>

    <!-- add boostrap code for Vue 3 -->
    <script>
        let app = Vue.createApp({
            data() {
                return {
                    basket: [
                        {
                            id: 1,
```

```
                              name: 'Product 1',
                              price: 100,
                              quantity: 1
                        },
                        {
                              id: 2,
                              name: 'Product 2',
                              price: 200,
                              quantity: 2
                        },
                        {
                              id: 3,
                              name: 'Product 3',
                              price: 300,
                              quantity: 3
                        },
                        {
                              id: 4,
                              name: 'Product 4',
                              price: 400,
                              quantity: 4
                        }
                  ]
            }
      },
      methods: {
            increaseQuantity(index) {
                  this.basket[index].quantity++;
            },
            decreaseQuantity(index) {
                  if (this.basket[index].quantity > 0) {
                        this.basket[index].quantity--;
                  }
            }
      },
      computed: {
            total() {
                  let total = 0;
                  for (let i = 0; i < this.basket.length; i++) {
                        total += this.basket[i].price * this.basket[i].
quantity;
```

```
                    }

    return total;
              }
          }
      });

      app.mount('#basket');
    </script>

    <!-- <script src="js/app.js"></script> -->
</body>
```

 This is an early version of a prototype; it's not meant to be production-ready code. However, we can use this code to improve it and make it production-ready.

Now that we know this code isn't great, let's improve it with Copilot and the following prompt:

[Prompt]

Improve the code, making it production-ready.

[End of prompt]

This prompt highlights some of the problems with the code, namely:

[Prompt response]

- **Separate JavaScript and CSS into external files:** This makes the code more maintainable and allows for caching of these resources.
- **Use a build tool or a module bundler:** Tools like Webpack or Parcel can help you manage dependencies, transpile modern JavaScript to older versions for better browser compatibility, and minify your code for production.
- **Error Handling:** Add error handling to your methods to ensure your application can gracefully handle unexpected situations.
- **Vue Component Structure:** Instead of creating the entire Vue app in one script, break it down into reusable components.
- **Accessibility:** Ensure that your HTML is accessible by using appropriate ARIA roles and properties.

[End of response]

That's a great list of things we can ask about next, but let's see what code changes it suggests. It suggests code separated into two different files, one for the HTML and one for the JavaScript:

```html
<!-- index.html -->
<html>
<head>
    <title>Basket</title>
    <link rel="stylesheet" href="css/basket.css">
    <link rel="stylesheet" href="https://stackpath.bootstrapcdn.com/
bootstrap/4.5.2/css/bootstrap.min.css">
</head>
<body>
    <div id="basket" class="basket"></div>

    <script src="https://unpkg.com/vue@next"></script>
    <script src="js/app.js"></script>
</body>
</html>
```

Now, let's look at how the JavaScript was improved:

```javascript
// app.js
let app = Vue.createApp({
    data() {
        return {
            basket: [
                { id: 1, name: 'Product 1', price: 100, quantity: 1 },
                { id: 2, name: 'Product 2', price: 200, quantity: 2 },
                { id: 3, name: 'Product 3', price: 300, quantity: 3 },
                { id: 4, name: 'Product 4', price: 400, quantity: 4 }
            ]
        }
    },
    methods: {
        increaseQuantity(index) {
            this.basket[index].quantity++;
        },
        decreaseQuantity(index) {
            if (this.basket[index].quantity > 0) {
                this.basket[index].quantity--;
            }
        }
    },
```

```
    computed: {
        total() {
            return this.basket.reduce((total, item) => total + item.price *
item.quantity, 0);
        }
    }
});
```

```
app.mount('#basket');
```

A great step forward. As a developer, you can see that the JavaScript code uses static data, so let's change that with the following prompt:

[Prompt]

Improve the code, use dynamic data by calling an API, and also generate a separate Python API with Flask that has the route /api/basket, containing the basket data.

[End of prompt]

Now, we get two files, the API and the JavaScript code. Let's look at the API first:

[Prompt response]

```python
# app.py
from flask import Flask, jsonify

app = Flask(__name__)

@app.route('/api/basket')
def get_basket():
    basket = [
        { 'id': 1, 'name': 'Product 1', 'price': 100, 'quantity': 1 },
        { 'id': 2, 'name': 'Product 2', 'price': 200, 'quantity': 2 },
        { 'id': 3, 'name': 'Product 3', 'price': 300, 'quantity': 3 },
        { 'id': 4, 'name': 'Product 4', 'price': 400, 'quantity': 4 }
    ]
    return jsonify(basket)

if __name__ == '__main__':
    app.run(debug=True)
```

Above you get a route /api/basket that returns the basket data. Let's look at the improved JavaScript code:

```javascript
let app = Vue.createApp({
    data() {
```

```
        return {
            basket: []
        }
    },
    methods: {
        increaseQuantity(index) {
            this.basket[index].quantity++;
        },
        decreaseQuantity(index) {
            if (this.basket[index].quantity > 0) {
                this.basket[index].quantity--;
            }
        }
    },
    computed: {
        total() {
            return this.basket.reduce((total, item) => total + item.price *
item.quantity, 0);
        }
    },
    mounted() {
        fetch('/api/basket')
            .then(response => response.json())
            .then(data => {
                this.basket = data;
            });
    }
});

app.mount('#basket');
```

[End of response]

Great! We're now getting data from the API. How can we improve the code? If you've built a Vue app before, you will know that it involves using the Vue CLI and has a build step. Let's ask GitHub Copilot about this with the following prompt:

[Prompt]

Improve the code, use the Vue CLI, and add a build step.

[End of prompt]

Now, we get both commands and file changes back as a response, as follows:

[Prompt response]

Install Vue CLI globally on your machine:

```
npm install -g @vue/cli
```

Create a new Vue project

```
vue create my-project
cd my-project
```

Now, let's create a new Vue component for the basket. Create a new file Basket.vue in the src/ components directory:

```vue
<!-- src/components/Basket.vue -->
<template>
  <div id="basket">
    <!-- Your basket template goes here -->
  </div>
</template>

<script>
export default {
  data() {
    return {
      basket: []
    };
  },
  methods: {
    increaseQuantity(index) {
      this.basket[index].quantity++;
    },
    decreaseQuantity(index) {
      if (this.basket[index].quantity > 0) {
        this.basket[index].quantity--;
      }
    }
  },
  computed: {
    total() {
      return this.basket.reduce((total, item) => total + item.price * item.
quantity, 0);
    }
  },
```

```
    mounted() {
      fetch('/api/basket')
        .then(response => response.json())
        .then(data => {
          this.basket = data;
        });
    }
};
</script>


<style scoped>
/* Your CSS goes here */
</style>
```

Then, import and use this component in your main `App.vue`:

```
<!-- src/App.vue -->
<template>
  <div id="app">
    <Basket />
  </div>
</template>


<script>
import Basket from './components/Basket.vue';

export default {
  name: 'App',
  components: {
    Basket
  }
};
</script>


<style>
/* Your CSS goes here */
</style>
```

Now, you can use the Vue CLI's build command to create a production-ready version of your app:

```
npm run build
```

This will create a dist directory with a production-ready version of your app.

[End of response]

This looks like a step in the right direction. However, you should always test the code to make sure it works as expected.

As a challenge, see if the above code works and if you can improve it further.

 Code is likely to change between versions of a framework. In this case, we're using Vue.js, so make sure to consult the documentation for the version that you use.

Assignment

Find a piece of code you want to improve. Follow the process outlined in this chapter to:

1. Identify the problems. What problems do you see?
2. Add tests and de-risk changes.
3. Implement the changes and improve maintainability.

If you don't have a piece of code you want to improve, try using the code from this chapter or the code from the Kata (Gilded Rose) GitHub page: `https://github.com/emilybache/GildedRose-Refactoring-Kata`.

Knowledge check

1. What's the difference between greenfield and brownfield development?

   A: Greenfield development is when you start coding from scratch; brownfield development is when you update existing code.

2. What's the best way to update existing code?

   A: The best way is to make small changes and have plenty of tests in place.

Summary

In this chapter, we established that a very important aspect of writing code is to update existing code, which is known as brownfield development. We also looked at how GitHub Copilot can help you with this task.

The most important message to take away from this chapter is to ensure that you have an approach to updating code that de-risks the changes you're about to make. It's better to make a small change several times than a big one once. It's also strongly recommended to have plenty of tests in place before you start changing code.

Join our community on Discord

Join our community's Discord space for discussions with the author and other readers:

`https://packt.link/aicode`

11

Data Exploration with ChatGPT

Introduction

Data exploration is an integral first step in machine learning, entailing a thorough examination of a dataset to identify its structure and uncover initial patterns and anomalies. This process is critical for setting the stage for any further detailed statistical analysis and the development of machine learning models.

In this chapter, the focus is on delineating the process of data exploration, aiming to solidify the understanding for newcomers to machine learning while providing a refresher for the adept. The chapter will navigate through the techniques to load and inspect a dataset comprised of Amazon book reviews, summarize its characteristics, and probe into its variables.

You will be guided through practical exercises on categorical data evaluation, distribution visualization, and correlation analysis, with the support of Python's pandas and Matplotlib libraries. The chapter will also detail how to employ ChatGPT effectively for data exploration, including both the freely available version and the subscription-based plus version, which offers enhanced functionalities.

It's important to note that the responses from ChatGPT will depend on how effectively you communicate your needs through prompts. This variability is a part of the learning curve and illustrates the interactive nature of working with AI in data exploration. Our goal is to equip you with the knowledge to navigate these tools confidently and to begin making data-driven decisions.

Business problem

In e-commerce, effectively analyzing customer feedback is crucial for identifying key factors that influence purchasing decisions. This analysis supports targeted marketing strategies and helps optimize both the user experience and website design, ultimately enhancing service and product offerings to customers.

Problem and data domain

In this chapter, we will focus exclusively on detailed data exploration using the Amazon product review dataset. Our goal is to deeply explore this dataset to unearth insights and discern patterns that can enhance decision-making. We'll leverage ChatGPT to generate Python code for data manipulation and visualization, providing a hands-on approach to understanding complex data analysis techniques. Additionally, we will explore methods to effectively prompt ChatGPT to deliver tailored insights and code snippets that aid in our exploration tasks.

Dataset overview

We will work with the Amazon product review dataset, which includes a broad range of information reflecting consumer feedback and product evaluations. Key features of this dataset encompass identifiers such as marketplace, customer, review, and product details, as well as product titles, categories, ratings, and the textual content of reviews. For this exploration, we'll concentrate on the `review_body` and `review_headline` fields, which provide rich textual data for analysis. To streamline our focus and enhance clarity in our findings, we will omit neutral sentiments and focus solely on analyzing positive and negative feedback.

Features in the dataset include:

- `marketplace` (string): The location of the product.
- `customer_id` (string): A unique identifier for customers.
- `review_id` (string): A unique identifier for reviews.
- `product_id` (string): A unique identifier for products.
- `product_parent` (string): A parent product identifier.
- `product_title` (string): The title of the reviewed product.
- `product_category` (string): The category of the product.
- `star_rating` (int): The rating of the product on a scale of 1 to 5.
- `helpful_votes` (int): The number of helpful votes received for the review.
- `total_votes` (int): The total number of votes received for the review.
- `review_headline` (string): The headline of the review.
- `review_body` (string): The content of the review.
- `review_date` (string): The date of the review.
- `sentiments` (string): The sentiment of the review (positive or negative).

This targeted exploration will allow us to perform in-depth sentiment analysis, evaluate the impact of product ratings, and delve into customer feedback dynamics. By focusing on these elements, we aim to fully leverage the dataset to improve strategic decision-making in e-commerce environments.

Feature breakdown

With the Amazon product review dataset and a focus on detailed data exploration, we will outline the following features to guide users through understanding and analyzing customer feedback effectively:

1. **Loading the Dataset:** We'll start by importing the dataset into a pandas DataFrame. This is a powerful data manipulation structure in Python that facilitates convenient data handling.

2. **Inspecting the Data:** Our initial exploration will involve displaying the first few entries of the DataFrame to get a feel for the data. We'll review the column names, understand the types of data that each column contains, and check for any missing values that need to be addressed.

3. **Summary Statistics:** To grasp the numerical data's distribution, we'll compute summary statistics, including mean, median, minimum, and maximum values and quartiles. This step helps in understanding the central tendency and spread of the numerical data.

4. **Exploring Categorical Variables:** For categorical data such as marketplace, product category, and sentiment, we'll examine the different categories and count the number of entries for each. Visual aids like bar charts will be particularly useful here to illustrate the frequency of each category.

5. **Distribution of Ratings:** We will visualize the distribution of star ratings using histograms or bar charts. This visual representation helps in understanding the general opinion of the reviewers and how ratings are skewed.

6. **Temporal Analysis:** By analyzing the `review_date` column, we'll explore any trends, seasonality, or other temporal patterns in the data. This analysis can reveal insights into how sentiments or product popularity change over time.

7. **Review Length Analysis:** We'll examine the `review_body` to understand the amount of information provided in the reviews by calculating descriptive statistics for review length, such as mean, median, and maximum lengths. This step provides insights into the depth of feedback that customers provide.

8. **Correlation Analysis:** Lastly, we will investigate the correlation between numeric variables like star ratings, helpful votes, and total votes, using correlation matrices or scatter plots. This analysis helps in identifying potential relationships between different quantitative aspects of the data.

By systematically breaking down these features, we will thoroughly understand the dataset, uncovering insights that can enhance decision-making and strategy formulation in e-commerce contexts.

Prompting strategy

To utilize ChatGPT effectively for data exploration of the Amazon product review dataset, we need to establish clear prompting strategies tailored to generate Python code and data insights. Here's how we can approach this.

Strategy 1: Task-Actions-Guidelines (TAG) prompt strategy

1.1 – Task: The specific goal is to explore the Amazon product review dataset thoroughly using various statistical and visualization techniques.

1.2 – Actions: The key steps in exploring this dataset include:

- **Data Loading:** Load the dataset into a pandas DataFrame.
- **Data Inspection:** Check for missing data, understand data types, and inspect the first few entries.

- **Statistical Summaries:** Calculate summary statistics for numerical data.
- **Categorical Analysis:** Analyze categorical variables using counts and visualizations.
- **Rating Distribution:** Create histograms or bar charts to visualize the distribution of star ratings.
- **Temporal Trends:** Examine trends over time from the review dates.
- **Review Text Analysis:** Analyze the length and sentiment of review texts.
- **Correlation Study:** Assess correlations between numerical variables.

1.3 – Guidelines: We will provide the following guidelines to ChatGPT in our prompt:

- Code should be compatible with a Jupyter Notebook
- Ensure that there are detailed comments for each line of code.
- You have to explain each line of code in detail, covering each method used in the code.

Strategy 2: Persona-Instructions-Context (PIC) prompt strategy

2.1 – Persona: Assume the persona of a data analyst seeking to uncover actionable insights from the Amazon product review dataset.

2.2 – Instructions: Request ChatGPT to generate code for each specific analysis, proceeding sequentially and waiting for user validation before moving to the next task.

2.3 – Context: Given that the focus is on sentiment analysis using the Amazon product review dataset, ChatGPT is not aware of the dataset and its characteristics, so additional context will be necessary.

Strategy 3: Learn-Improvise-Feedback-Evaluate (LIFE) prompt strategy

3.1 – Learn:

- Highlight the need to understand data through various analytical techniques, from basic statistics to complex correlations and temporal analysis.

3.2 – Improvise:

- Adapt the analysis based on initial findings. For instance, if certain categories of products show unusual trends, deepen the analysis in these areas.

3.3 – Feedback:

- Share code and model outputs for feedback to ensure effective learning and understanding.
- Incorporate suggestions and critiques to refine the model and the approach.
- Provide errors to troubleshoot and resolve the issues.

3.4 – Evaluate:

- Execute the code provided by ChatGPT to ensure accuracy and validity. This is used throughout the chapter.

Data exploration of the Amazon review dataset using the free version of ChatGPT

ChatGPT premium version has a code interpreter, but first, we will use the free version of ChatGPT. We will craft our initial prompt carefully to include all the features, but we will instruct it to wait for user feedback after providing code for each feature.

Feature 1: Loading the dataset

Let's craft our initial prompt to load the dataset.

[Prompt]

I want to explore the Amazon product review dataset thoroughly using various statistical and visualization techniques (TAG 1.1), which consists of the following fields (PIC 2.3):

- `marketplace` (string): The location of the product.
- `customer_id` (string): A unique identifier for customers.
- `review_id` (string): A unique identifier for reviews.
- `product_id` (string): A unique identifier for products.
- `product_parent` (string): A parent product identifier.
- `product_title` (string): The title of the reviewed product.
- `product_category` (string): The category of the product.
- `star_rating` (int): The rating of the product on a scale of 1 to 5.
- `helpful_votes` (int): The number of helpful votes received for the review.
- `total_votes` (int): The total number of votes received for the review.
- `review_headline` (string): The headline of the review.
- `review_body` (string): The content of the review.
- `review_date` (string): The date of the review.
- `sentiments` (string): The sentiment of the review (positive or negative).

This should consist of the following steps (TAG 1.2):

1. **Data Loading:** Load the dataset into a pandas DataFrame.
2. **Data Inspection:** Check for missing data, understand data types, and inspect the first few entries.
3. **Statistical Summaries:** Calculate summary statistics for numerical data.
4. **Categorical Analysis:** Analyze categorical variables using counts and visualizations.
5. **Rating Distribution:** Create histograms or bar charts to visualize the distribution of star ratings.
6. **Temporal Trends:** Examine trends over time from the review dates.
7. **Review Text Analysis:** Analyse the length and sentiment of review texts.
8. **Correlation Study:** Assess correlations between numerical variables.

I am a data analyst seeking to uncover actionable insights (PIC 2.1), so please provide detailed code and strictly follow the below instructions (TAG 1.3):

- Code should be compatible with a Jupyter Notebook.
- Ensure that there are detailed comments for each line of code.
- You have to explain each line of code, which will then be copied into the text block of the notebook in detail for each method used in the code before it is provided. Also note that the dataset is placed in Google Drive at this path: `./Chapter05/amazon_product_review_data.csv`. So, add the code to mount the drive and load the dataset (PIC 2.2).
- Provide one step at a time and wait for user feedback (PIC 2.2).

[End of prompt]

You should receive a response similar to below, where ChatGPT has provided us with the code for Step 1 – Data Loading, along with detailed comments and explanations.

[Prompt response]

Sure, let's start with the first step: loading the dataset into a pandas DataFrame from Google Drive. Here's how we can proceed:

Step 1: Data Loading

To load the dataset from Google Drive into a pandas DataFrame, we'll follow these steps:

- **Mount Google Drive:** Connect to your Google Drive where the dataset is located.
- **Load the Dataset:** Read the dataset file into a pandas DataFrame.

Detailed Code Explanation:

1. **Mount Google Drive:** This step allows us to access files stored in Google Drive directly from a Google Colab or Jupyter Notebook environment:

   - From the `google.colab` import drive: Import the drive module from the `google.colab` package.
   - `drive.mount ("/content/drive")`: Mounts your Google Drive at the specified path (`/content/drive` in this case). Follow the instructions to authorize and obtain an access code.

2. **Load the Dataset:**

   - `import pandas as pd`: Import the pandas library as `pd` for data manipulation.
   - `file_path = '/content/drive/My Drive/Chapter05/amazon_product_review_data.csv'`: Define the path to your CSV file in Google Drive.
   - `df = pd.read_csv(file_path)`: Use `pd.read_csv()` to read the CSV file into a DataFrame named `df`.

Here's the complete code snippet:

```
# Mount Google Drive to access the dataset
```

```
from google.colab import drive
drive.mount('/content/drive')

# Import pandas for data manipulation
import pandas as pd

# Define the file path in your Google Drive
file_path = '/content/drive/My Drive/Chapter05/amazon_product_review_data.csv'

# Load the dataset into a pandas DataFrame
df = pd.read_csv(file_path)

# Display the first few rows of the dataframe to verify the data
df.head()
```

User Feedback:

Please execute this code in your Jupyter Notebook environment after replacing `file_path` with the correct path to your dataset. Let me know if you encounter any issues or if you're ready to proceed to the next step!

[End of response]

We will now apply the evaluate prompting strategy (LIFE 3.4) and validate the code by executing the code in Google Colab for every step. The code loads the dataset from Google Drive. It will also request permission to access Google Drive.

Please refer to the notebook "Data Exploration with ChatGPT.ipynb" for the executable code snippets, or copy the code from the prompt response.

You should see a message saying "Permit this Notebook to access Google Drive."

The code runs perfectly fine without applying any modifications or any errors and displays the first few rows of the dataset.

You should see the content of the Notebook and customer reviews.

Feature 2: Inspecting the data

We will now instruct ChatGPT to proceed to the next step:

[Prompt]

Let's proceed to the next step.

[End of prompt]

We should receive a response like below:

[Prompt response]

Great! Let's move on to the next step:

Step 2: Data Inspection

In this step, we will inspect the loaded dataset to:

- Check for missing data.
- Understand the data types of each column.
- Inspect the first few entries to get a sense of the data structure.

Detailed Code Explanation:

1. **Check for Missing Data:**

   - `df.info()`: This method provides a concise summary of the DataFrame, including the number of non-null entries in each column. It also shows the data types of each column, which helps us understand how to manipulate the data.

2. **Understand Data Types:**

   - By examining the output of `df.info()`, we can identify if any columns have incorrect data types (e.g., numerical columns mistakenly stored as strings).

3. **Inspect the First Few Entries:**

   - **df.head():** This method displays the first few rows of the DataFrame. It allows us to visually inspect the columns, their values, and get an initial understanding of what the dataset contains.

Here's the code for data inspection:

```
# Check for missing data and data types
df.info()
# Display the first few rows of the dataframe
df.head()
```

User Feedback:

Execute this code in your Jupyter Notebook environment. After running this step, you should be able to see a summary of the dataset and the first few rows. Let me know if everything looks okay or if you have any specific questions!

[End of response]

We evaluate the output from ChatGPT and execute the code (LIFE 3.4) in the notebook, and it displays the information.

We will utilize the prompting strategy to provide the output for ChatGPT (LIFE 3.3) to interpret:

[Prompt]

```
<class 'pandas.core.frame.DataFrame'>
```

```
RangeIndex: 500 entries, 0 to 499
Data columns (total 15 columns):
 #   Column              Non-Null Count  Dtype
---  ------              --------------  -----
 0   market_place        500 non-null    object
 1   customer_id         500 non-null    object
 2   review_id           500 non-null    object
 3   product_id          500 non-null    object
 4   product_parent      500 non-null    object
 5   product_title       500 non-null    object
 6   product_category    500 non-null    object
 7   star_rating         500 non-null    int64
 8   helpful_votes       500 non-null    int64
 9   total_votes         500 non-null    int64
 10  verified_purchase   500 non-null    object
 11  review_headline     500 non-null    object
 12  review_body         500 non-null    object
 13  review_date         500 non-null    object
 14  sentiments          500 non-null    object
dtypes: int64(3), object(12)
memory usage: 58.7+ KB
  market_place    customer_id    review_id    product_id    product_parent
product_title    product_category    star_rating    helpful_votes    total_
votes    verified_purchase    review_headline    review_body    review_date
sentiments
0    "US"    "42521656"    "R26MV8D0KG6QI6"    "B000SAQCWC"    "159713740"
"The Cravings Place Chocolate Chunk Cookie Mix...    "Grocery"    1    0    0
1 \t(Y)    "Using these for years - love them."    "As a family allergic to
wheat, dairy, eggs, n...    2015-08-31    positive
1    "US"    "12049833"    "R1OF8GP57AQ1A0"    "B00509LVIQ"    "138680402"
"Mauna Loa Macadamias, 11 Ounce Packages"    "Grocery"    1    0    0    1
\t(Y)    "Wonderful"    "My favorite nut. Creamy, crunchy, salty, and ...
2015-08-31    positive
2    "US"    "107642"    "R3VDC1QB6MC4ZZ"    "B00KHXESLC"    "252021703"
"Organic Matcha Green Tea Powder - 100% Pure M...    "Grocery"    1    0    0
0 \t(N)    "Five Stars"    "This green tea tastes so good! My girlfriend ...
2015-08-31    positive
3    "US"    "6042304"    "R12FA3DCF8F9ER"    "B000F8JIIC"    "752728342"
"15oz Raspberry Lyons Designer Dessert Syrup S...    "Grocery"    1    0    0
1 \t(Y)    "Five Stars"    "I love Melissa's brand but this is a great se...
2015-08-31    positive
```

```
4    "US"     "18123821"    "RTWHVNV6X4CNJ"     "B004ZWR9RQ"     "552138758"
"Stride Spark Kinetic Fruit Sugar Free Gum, 14...    "Grocery"    1    0    0
1 \t(Y)     "Five Stars"    "good"    2015-08-31    positive
```

[End of prompt]

We should receive a response like below, where ChatGPT provides an explanation and findings:

[Prompt response]

It seems like the dataset has been successfully loaded, and here's what we can infer from the output of df.info() and df.head():

Data Inspection Findings:

1. **Basic Information:**

   • The dataset contains 500 entries (rows) and 15 columns.

   • There are both numerical (int64) and categorical (object) data types.

   • All columns have 500 non-null entries, indicating there are no missing values.

2. **Column Details:**

   • market_place, customer_id, review_id, product_id, product_parent, product_title, product_category, verified_purchase, review_headline, review_body, review_date, and sentiments are all identified as object (string) types, which aligns with their expected content based on their descriptions.

   • star_rating, helpful_votes, and total_votes are correctly identified as int64 (integer) types.

3. **Initial Data Preview:**

   • The df.head() output shows the first few rows of the dataset, giving us a glimpse into the structure and content of each column. We can see examples of the market_place, customer_id, star_rating, helpful_votes, total_votes, review_headline, review_body, review_date, and sentiments columns.

Next Steps:

Based on this inspection:

• The dataset appears to be clean with no missing values.

• We have a clear understanding of the columns and their data types.

Next, we can proceed with Step 3: Statistical Summaries to calculate summary statistics for the numerical data (star_rating, helpful_votes, and total_votes). Would you like to continue with that? Let me know if there's anything specific you'd like to explore further or if we should proceed to the next step!

[End of response]

Feature 3: Summary statistics

As there are no missing or null values, we will now instruct ChatGPT to proceed to the next step to display summary statistics:

[Prompt]

Let's proceed to the next step.

[End of prompt]

We should receive a response like below where ChatGPT provides the code to display summary statistics:

[Prompt response]

Great! Let's move on to Step 3:

Step 3: Statistical Summaries

In this step, we will calculate summary statistics for the numerical columns in our dataset. Specifically, we will focus on:

- `star_rating`: Rating of the product on a scale of 1 to 5.
- `helpful_votes`: Number of helpful votes received for the review.
- `total_votes`: Total number of votes received for the review.

Detailed Code Explanation:

1. **Use of** `describe()`:

    - `df.describe()` computes summary statistics for numerical columns. It provides:

        - Count: Number of non-null values.
        - Mean: Average value.
        - Std: Standard deviation.
        - Min: Minimum value.
        - 25%, 50%, and 75%: Percentiles.
        - Max: Maximum value.

2. **Selecting Specific Columns:**

    - We use `df[['star_rating', 'helpful_votes', 'total_votes']].describe()` to limit the output to only the numerical columns we are interested in (star_rating, helpful_votes, and total_votes).

Here's the code to calculate and display summary statistics:

```
# Calculate summary statistics for numerical columns
summary_stats = df[['star_rating', 'helpful_votes', 'total_votes']].describe()
# Display the summary statistics
print(summary_stats)
```

User Feedback:

Execute this code in your Jupyter Notebook environment. It will provide statistical insights into the distribution and central tendencies of the numerical variables in your dataset. Let me know if you have any questions or if you're ready to proceed to the next step!

[End of response]

We execute the code, which shows the summary statistics, and we provide the output to ChatGPT for interpretation and to understand the stats:

[Prompt]

```
       star_rating  helpful_votes  total_votes
count   500.000000     500.000000   500.000000
mean      0.796000       0.764000     1.068000
std       0.403373       2.843321     3.698477
min       0.000000       0.000000     0.000000
25%       1.000000       0.000000     0.000000
50%       1.000000       0.000000     0.000000
75%       1.000000       1.000000     1.000000
max       1.000000      36.000000    47.000000
```

[End of prompt]

We should receive a response like below where ChatGPT provides an explanation of the summary statistics:

[Prompt response]

Based on the summary statistics for the numerical columns (star_rating, helpful_votes, and total_votes), here are the insights we can gather:

Summary Statistics:

1. star_rating:

    - **Mean:** 0.796
    - **Standard Deviation:** 0.403
    - **Min:** 0 (indicating the lowest rating)
    - **25th Percentile (Q1):** 1
    - **Median (50th Percentile):** 1
    - **75th Percentile (Q3):** 1
    - **Max:** 1 (indicating the highest rating)
    - **Interpretation:** The star_rating column primarily contains a single value of 1 (which typically represents positive reviews in binary sentiment data), indicating that most reviews are positive. This is supported by the mean being close to 1 and a low standard deviation, suggesting little variability in ratings.

2. helpful_votes:

    •   **Mean:** 0.764

    •   **Standard Deviation:** 2.843

    •   **Min:** 0

    •   **25th Percentile (Q1):** 0

    •   **Median (50th Percentile):** 0

    •   **75th Percentile (Q3):** 1

    •   **Max:** 36

    •   **Interpretation:** The helpful_votes column has a mean of 0.764, indicating that on average, reviews receive less than one helpful vote. The standard deviation of 2.843 suggests variability in the number of helpful votes received, with some reviews receiving as many as 36 helpful votes.

3. total_votes:

    •   **Mean:** 1.068

    •   **Standard Deviation:** 3.698

    •   **Min:** 0

    •   **25th Percentile (Q1):** 0

    •   **Median (50th Percentile):** 0

    •   **75th Percentile (Q3):** 1

    •   **Max:** 47

    •   **Interpretation:** The total_votes column has a mean of 1.068, indicating that on average, reviews receive slightly more than one total vote (helpful or unhelpful). The standard deviation of 3.698 suggests variability in the total number of votes received, with some reviews receiving as many as 47 votes in total.

Next Steps:

Based on these statistics, we see that the dataset predominantly consists of positive reviews (a star_rating of 1). The helpful_votes and total_votes metrics show varying levels of engagement with the reviews.

Next, we can move on to Step 4: Categorical Analysis, where we will analyze the categorical variables (market_place, product_category, verified_purchase, and sentiments) using counts and visualizations. Would you like to proceed with that? Let me know if you have any questions or if you're ready for the next step!

[End of response]

Feature 4: Exploring categorical variables

Now, we will proceed to explore the categorical variables.

[Prompt]

Let's proceed to the next step.

[End of prompt]

We should receive a response like below where ChatGPT provides the code for the visualization of the categorical variables:

[Prompt response]

Great! Let's proceed to Step 4:

Step 4: Categorical Analysis

In this step, we will analyze the categorical variables in our dataset using counts and visualizations. The categorical variables we'll focus on are:

- `market_place`: Location of the product.
- `product_category`: Category of the product.
- `verified_purchase`: Whether the purchase was verified (Y/N).
- `sentiments`: Sentiment of the review (positive or negative).

Detailed Code Explanation:

1. **Counting Unique Values:**

   - `df['column_name'].value_counts()`: This method counts the occurrences of each unique value in a categorical column.

2. **Visualizing Categorical Data:**

   - We will use bar charts (from the `matplotlib` library) to visualize the distribution of categorical variables.

Here's the code to perform categorical analysis:

```python
import matplotlib.pyplot as plt
import seaborn as sns

# Set up the matplotlib figure and axes
fig, axes = plt.subplots(nrows=2, ncols=2, figsize=(14, 10))
axes = axes.flatten()

# Plot for 'market_place'
sns.countplot(x='market_place', data=df, ax=axes[0])
axes[0].set_title('Distribution of Products by Market Place')
```

```
# Plot for 'product_category'
sns.countplot(x='product_category', data=df, ax=axes[1])
axes[1].set_title('Distribution of Products by Category')
axes[1].tick_params(axis='x', rotation=90)

# Plot for 'verified_purchase'
sns.countplot(x='verified_purchase', data=df, ax=axes[2])
axes[2].set_title('Distribution of Verified Purchases')

# Plot for 'sentiments'
sns.countplot(x='sentiments', data=df, ax=axes[3])
axes[3].set_title('Distribution of Sentiments')

# Adjust layout
plt.tight_layout()
plt.show()
```

Explanation of the Visualizations:

- **Market Place:** Shows the distribution of products across different marketplaces (market_place).
- **Product Category:** Displays the distribution of products across various categories (product_category).
- **Verified Purchase:** Indicates how many reviews are from verified purchases (verified_purchase).
- **Sentiments:** Illustrates the distribution of review sentiments (sentiments), whether they are positive or negative.

User Feedback:

Execute this code in your Jupyter Notebook environment to visualize and analyze the categorical variables in your dataset. This will provide insights into the distribution and characteristics of different aspects related to the reviews and products. Let me know if you have any questions or if you're ready to move on to the next step!

[End of response]

We execute the code, which runs perfectly fine, and then visualize the variables.

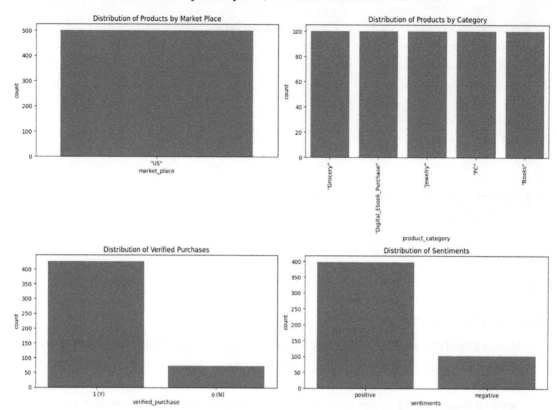

Figure 11.1: Categorical variables – visualization

We can see that the reviews are all from a single marketplace and have equal number of reviews of all product categories, but there is an imbalance of positive and negative reviews as well as the distribution of verified purchases.

Feature 5: Rating distribution

We will move on to the rating distribution and instruct ChatGPT to move on to the next step:

[Prompt]

Let's proceed to the next step.

[End of prompt]

We should receive a response like below:

[Prompt response]

Great! Let's proceed to Step 5:

Step 5: Rating Distribution

In this step, we will create histograms or bar charts to visualize the distribution of star ratings (star_rating). This will help us understand how ratings are distributed among the reviews.

Detailed Code Explanation:

1. **Histogram or Bar Chart:**

     •   We will use sns.countplot() from the Seaborn library to create a bar chart. This is suitable for visualizing the count of each rating value (1 to 5).

2. **Visualization Parameters:**

     •   Adjustments such as setting the figure size (figsize) and title (set_title) are done to enhance the clarity and readability of the plot.

Here's the code to visualize the rating distribution:

```python
import matplotlib.pyplot as plt
import seaborn as sns

# Set up the matplotlib figure
plt.figure(figsize=(8, 6))

# Plotting the distribution of star ratings
sns.countplot(x='star_rating', data=df)
plt.title('Distribution of Star Ratings')
plt.xlabel('Star Rating')
plt.ylabel('Count')

# Show plot
plt.show()
```

Explanation of the Visualization:

•   The sns.countplot() function is used to create a bar chart of the star_rating column.
•   The *x*-axis represents the star ratings (1 to 5), and the *y*-axis represents the count of reviews with each rating.
•   The title, *x*-label (Star Rating), and *y*-label (Count) are added to provide context and clarity to the plot.

User Feedback:

Execute this code in your Jupyter Notebook environment. It will display a visual representation of how star ratings are distributed among the reviews in your dataset. This step will provide insights into the overall sentiment expressed through ratings. Let me know if you have any questions or if you're ready to proceed to the next step!

[End of response]

We will execute the code, which produces the ratings graph.

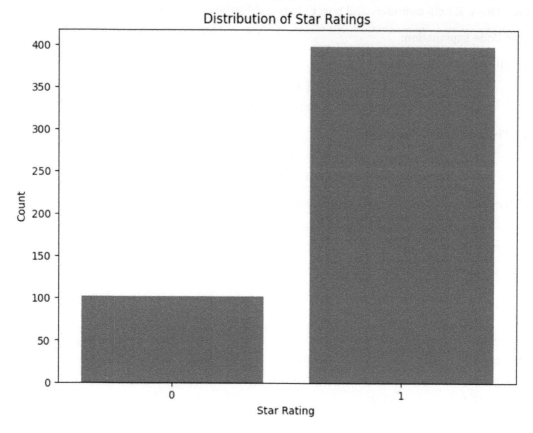

Figure 11.2: Ratings distribution

Based on these results, there are majorly positive ratings. We will move on to the next feature.

Feature 6: Temporal trends

Now, let's understand the temporal trends in our dataset for the review date column. Our dataset doesn't have much variation, but this will help us understand how to use ChatGPT for it:

[Prompt]

Let's proceed to the next step.

[End of prompt]

We should receive a response like below:

[Prompt response]

Great! Let's move on to Step 6:

Step 6: Temporal Trends

In this step, we will examine temporal trends from the review_date column to understand how the reviews are distributed over time. This will help us identify any patterns or trends in the review activity.

Detailed Code Explanation:

1. **Convert review_date to datetime:**

    • Ensure that the review_date column is in the datetime format for proper temporal analysis.

2. **Plotting Temporal Trends:**

    • Use sns.lineplot() or sns.histplot() to visualize the distribution of reviews over time.

    • Depending on the analysis goal, you can choose to plot the count of reviews per month, per year, or any other relevant time interval.

Here's the code to analyze temporal trends:

```python
import matplotlib.pyplot as plt
import seaborn as sns

# Convert 'review_date' to datetime format
df['review_date'] = pd.to_datetime(df['review_date'])

# Set up the matplotlib figure
plt.figure(figsize=(12, 6))

# Plotting the count of reviews over time
sns.histplot(df['review_date'], bins=30, kde=False, color='blue')
plt.title('Distribution of Reviews Over Time')
plt.xlabel('Review Date')
plt.ylabel('Count of Reviews')

# Show plot
plt.xticks(rotation=45)
plt.tight_layout()
plt.show()
```

Explanation of the Visualization:

• **Datetime Conversion:** pd.to_datetime() function is used to convert the review_date column from a string to the datetime format, ensuring accurate temporal analysis.

- **Histogram Plot:** `sns.histplot()` is used to create a histogram of review counts over time (`review_date`). This helps in visualizing the distribution and frequency of reviews across different dates.
- **Adjustments:** Adjustments such as setting the figure size (`figsize`), title (`title`), *x*-label (`xlabel`), *y*-label (`ylabel`), and rotating *x*-axis ticks (`xticks(rotation=45)`) are made to improve the clarity and readability of the plot.

User Feedback:

Execute this code in your Jupyter Notebook environment. It will provide insights into how reviews are distributed over time, allowing you to observe any trends or patterns in review activity. Let me know if you have any questions or if you're ready to proceed to the next step!

[End of response]

We will execute the code, which produces a plot that shows the distribution of reviews over time.

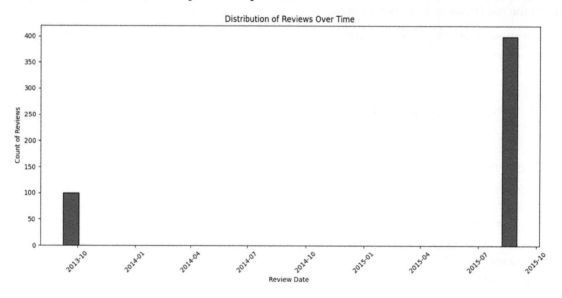

Figure 11.3: Temporal trend

We can see that the reviews are shown only for two dates, so let's move to the next feature.

Feature 7: Review length analysis

[Prompt]

The reviews are shown for just two dates, 10-2013 and 08-2015.

[End of prompt]

We should receive a response like below where ChatGPT provides the code, explains the significance of the review dates, and proceeds with the next step of review length analysis.

[Prompt response]

If the reviews in your dataset are concentrated on just two dates (October 2013 and August 2015), it suggests that the dataset may not have a wide temporal spread of reviews. This information is crucial for understanding the context of the data and its limitations in temporal analysis.

Given this observation, we can still proceed to analyze the review text and sentiment in Step 7, as planned. This step will focus on examining the length and sentiment of the review texts, which can provide additional insights beyond temporal trends.

Step 7: Review Text Analysis

In this step, we will analyze the review text (review_body) to:

- Calculate the length of each review.
- Determine the sentiment of each review using the provided sentiments column.

Detailed Code Explanation:

1. **Review Length Calculation:**

    - Add a new column review_length to the DataFrame to store the character count of each review (review_body).

2. **Sentiment Analysis:**

    - Use the sentiments column to categorize reviews as positive or negative based on the provided labels.

Here's the code to perform review the text analysis:

```python
# Calculate the length of each review text
df['review_length'] = df['review_body'].apply(len)

# Count the number of reviews classified as positive and negative
sentiment_counts = df['sentiments'].value_counts()

# Display the sentiment counts
print("Sentiment Counts:")
print(sentiment_counts)

# Calculate the average length of reviews
average_review_length = df['review_length'].mean()
print(f"\nAverage Review Length: {average_review_length:.2f} characters")

# Display the first few rows to verify the changes
df.head()
```

Explanation of the Code:

- **Review Length Calculation:** `df['review_body'].apply(len)` computes the length of each review in characters and stores it in a new column `review_length`.
- **Sentiment Analysis:** `df['sentiments'].value_counts()` counts the occurrences of each sentiment category (positive or negative) in the `sentiments` column.
- **Average Review Length:** `df['review_length'].mean()` calculates the average length of reviews in the dataset.

User Feedback:

Execute this code in your Jupyter Notebook environment. It will provide insights into the length and sentiment distribution of the review texts in your dataset. Let me know if you have any questions or if you're ready to proceed to the next step after reviewing the outputs!

[End of response]

We execute the code in Jupyter Colab, which works fine, so we provide the output to ChatGPT to interpret it:

[Prompt]

```
Sentiment Counts:
sentiments
positive    398
negative    102
Name: count, dtype: int64


Average Review Length: 243.75 characters
market_place    customer_id    review_id    product_id    product_parent
product_title    product_category    star_rating    helpful_votes    total_
votes    verified_purchase    review_headline    review_body    review_date
sentiments    review_length
0    "US"    "42521656"    "R26MV8D0KG6QI6"    "B000SAQCWC"    "159713740"
"The Cravings Place Chocolate Chunk Cookie Mix...    "Grocery"    1    0    0
1 \t(Y)    "Using these for years - love them."    "As a family allergic to
wheat, dairy, eggs, n...    2015-08-31    positive    470
1    "US"    "12049833"    "R1OF8GP57AQ1A0"    "B00509LVIQ"    "138680402"
"Mauna Loa Macadamias, 11 Ounce Packages"    "Grocery"    1    0    0    1
\t(Y)    "Wonderful"    "My favorite nut. Creamy, crunchy, salty, and ...
2015-08-31    positive    92
2    "US"    "107642"    "R3VDC1QB6MC4ZZ"    "B00KHXESLC"    "252021703"
"Organic Matcha Green Tea Powder - 100% Pure M...    "Grocery"    1    0    0
0 \t(N)    "Five Stars"    "This green tea tastes so good! My girlfriend ...
2015-08-31    positive    60
```

```
3    "US"      "6042304"     "R12FA3DCF8F9ER"     "B000F8JIIC"     "752728342"
"15oz Raspberry Lyons Designer Dessert Syrup S...    "Grocery"    1    0    0
1 \t(Y)     "Five Stars"     "I love Melissa's brand but this is a great se...
2015-08-31    positive    85
4    "US"      "18123821"    "RTWHVNV6X4CNJ"      "B004ZWR9RQ"     "552138758"
"Stride Spark Kinetic Fruit Sugar Free Gum, 14...    "Grocery"    1    0    0
1 \t(Y)     "Five Stars"     "good"     2015-08-31     positive     6
```

[End of prompt]

We should receive a response from ChatGPT explaining the results:

[Prompt response]

It seems like the sentiment analysis and review length calculations have been successfully performed. Here are the insights from the analysis:

Sentiment Analysis:

- **Sentiment Counts**:

  - Positive reviews: 398
  - Negative reviews: 102
  - Review Length Analysis:

- **Average Review Length**: 243.75 characters

Explanation:

- **Sentiment Counts**: The dataset contains predominantly positive reviews, with 398 positive reviews and 102 negative reviews.
- **Average Review Length**: The average length of a review in the dataset is approximately 243.75 characters.

Example Data Inspection:

The example snippet you provided shows a sample of the dataset, where we can see details such as marketplace, customer ID, review ID, product details, star rating, review text, review date, sentiment, and review length for the first few entries.

Next Steps:

Based on this analysis, we have insights into the distribution of sentiments and the average length of reviews. If there are specific further analyses or visualizations you'd like to explore, such as a correlation study or any other aspect of the dataset, please let me know! We can proceed accordingly.

[End of response]

Feature 8: Correlation study

We will move on to the last feature, which is a correlation study.

[Prompt]

Let's proceed to the next step.

[End of prompt]

We should receive a response like below:

[Prompt response]

Certainly! Let's proceed to Step 8:

Step 8: Correlation Study

In this step, we will assess the correlations between numerical variables in the dataset. Specifically, we will examine how `star_rating`, `helpful_votes`, and `total_votes` correlate with each other. This analysis will help us understand any relationships or dependencies between these variables.

Detailed Code Explanation:

1. **Correlation Calculation:**

    • Use the `.corr()` method on the DataFrame to compute the correlation coefficients between numerical columns.

2. **Visualization of Correlation:**

    • We can visualize the correlations using a heatmap to provide a clear and intuitive representation of the relationships.

Here's the code to perform the correlation study:

```python
import matplotlib.pyplot as plt
import seaborn as sns

# Calculate the correlation matrix
correlation_matrix = df[['star_rating', 'helpful_votes', 'total_votes']].corr()

# Plotting the correlation heatmap
plt.figure(figsize=(8, 6))
sns.heatmap(correlation_matrix, annot=True, cmap='coolwarm', vmin=-1, vmax=1)
plt.title('Correlation Matrix of Numerical Variables')
plt.show()
```

Explanation of the Code:

• **Correlation Matrix:** df[['star_rating', 'helpful_votes', 'total_votes']].corr() computes the correlation coefficients between star_rating, helpful_votes, and total_votes.

- **Heatmap Visualization**: `sns.heatmap()` from the Seaborn library is used to create a heatmap of the correlation matrix. The `annot=True` parameter adds numeric annotations to the heatmap cells for clarity. The `cmap='coolwarm'` parameter sets the color scheme for the heatmap, where colors range from blue (negative correlation) to red (positive correlation).

Interpretation:

- The heatmap will display correlations ranging from -1 to 1, where:
- Values closer to 1 indicate a strong positive correlation.
- Values closer to -1 indicate a strong negative correlation.
- Values close to 0 indicate no significant correlation.

User Feedback:

- Execute this code in your Jupyter Notebook environment. It will provide insights into how `star_rating`, `helpful_votes`, and `total_votes` are related within your dataset. Let me know if you have any questions or if you're ready to proceed to the next step after reviewing the correlation heatmap!

[End of response]

We will execute the code, which plots the correlation matrix and prints the results.

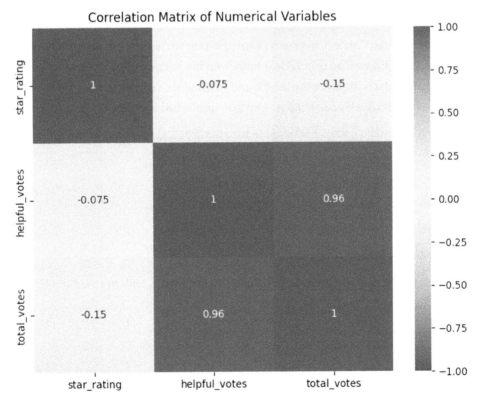

Figure 11.4: Correlation matrix

We can see that helpful votes and total votes are strongly correlated but the rating is not.

This concludes data exploration with ChatGPT-3.5; now, let's see how to use ChatGPT-4o.

Data exploration of the Amazon review dataset using ChatGPT-4o

ChatGPT's premium version has a code interpreter, which is accessible using both ChatGPT-4o and ChatGPT 4. For this section, we will use GPT-4o, and this time, we will get the code in a single step.

ChatGPT has access to several models, at present, you can use GPT-3.5, GPT-4, and GPT-4o.

Let's craft our prompt.

[Prompt]

I want to explore the Amazon product review dataset thoroughly using various statistical and visualization techniques (TAG 1.1) for the attached dataset (PIC 2.3). It should consist of the following steps (TAG 1.2):

1.   **Data Loading:** Load the dataset into a pandas DataFrame.
2.   **Data Inspection:** Check for missing data, understand data types, and inspect the first few entries.
3.   **Statistical Summaries:** Calculate the summary statistics for numerical data.
4.   **Categorical Analysis:** Analyze categorical variables using counts and visualizations.
5.   **Rating Distribution:** Create histograms or bar charts to visualize the distribution of star ratings.
6.   **Temporal Trends:** Examine trends over time from the review dates.
7.   **Review Text Analysis:** Analyze the length and sentiment of review texts.
8.   **Correlation Study:** Assess correlations between numerical variables

I am a data analyst seeking to uncover actionable insights (PIC 2.1), so please provide detailed code.

[End of prompt]

We should receive a response similar to below where ChatGPT performs all the necessary steps, performs a data exploration, and produces the relevant charts:

[Prompt response]

Amazon Product Review Dataset Analysis

We'll follow the steps you outlined to explore the dataset thoroughly. Let's proceed step by step:

Step 1: Data Loading

*   We have loaded the dataset into a pandas DataFrame.

Step 2: Data Inspection

*   We checked for missing data, understood data types, and inspected the first few entries. The dataset consists of 500 entries and 15 columns with no missing data. Here are the first few entries:

```
    market_place customer_id       review_id      product_id product_parent
\
0           "US"  "42521656"  "R26MV8D0KG6QI6"   "B000SAQCWC"    "159713740"
1           "US"  "12049833"  "R1OF8GP57AQ1A0"   "B00509LVIQ"    "138680402"
2           "US"    "107642"  "R3VDC1QB6MC4ZZ"   "B00KHXESLC"    "252021703"
3           "US"   "6042304"  "R12FA3DCF8F9ER"   "B000F8JIIC"    "752728342"
4           "US"  "18123821"  "RTWHVNV6X4CNJ"    "B004ZWR9RQ"    "552138758"


                                       product_title product_category  \
0  "The Cravings Place Chocolate Chunk Cookie Mix...        "Grocery"
1           "Mauna Loa Macadamias, 11 Ounce Packages"        "Grocery"
2  "Organic Matcha Green Tea Powder - 100% Pure M...        "Grocery"
3  "15oz Raspberry Lyons Designer Dessert Syrup S...        "Grocery"
4  "Stride Spark Kinetic Fruit Sugar Free Gum, 14...        "Grocery"


   star_rating  helpful_votes  total_votes verified_purchase  \
0            1              0            0            1 \t(Y)
1            1              0            0            1 \t(Y)
2            1              0            0            0 \t(N)
3            1              0            0            1 \t(Y)
4            1              0            0            1 \t(Y)


                      review_headline  \
0  "Using these for years - love them."
1                           "Wonderful"
2                          "Five Stars"
3                          "Five Stars"
4                          "Five Stars"


                                       review_body review_date
sentiments
0  "As a family allergic to wheat, dairy, eggs, n...  2015-08-31
positive
1  "My favorite nut. Creamy, crunchy, salty, and ...  2015-08-31
positive
2  "This green tea tastes so good! My girlfriend ...  2015-08-31
positive
3  "I love Melissa's brand but this is a great se...  2015-08-31
positive
4                                            "good"  2015-08-31
positive
```

Step 3: Statistical Summaries

- Let's calculate summary statistics for the numerical data. You should see a summary of your data, including stats on the mean, standard deviation, and more.

Step 4: Categorical Analysis

- We'll analyze the categorical variables using counts and visualizations.

Step 5: Rating Distribution

- We'll create histograms or bar charts to visualize the distribution of star ratings.

Step 6: Temporal Trends

- We'll examine trends over time from the review dates.

Step 7: Review Text Analysis

- We'll analyze the length and sentiment of review texts.

Step 8: Correlation Study

- We'll assess correlations between numerical variables.

Let's start implementing each of these steps in Python code.

Detailed Analysis of the Amazon Product Review Dataset

We have performed a detailed analysis as outlined. Below are the key findings and visualizations for each step.

Step 3: Statistical Summaries

We calculated summary statistics for the numerical data. Here are some key statistics:

- **Star Rating:** Mean = 0.796, Standard Deviation = 0.403, Min = 0, and Max = 1
- **Helpful Votes:** Mean = 0.764, Standard Deviation = 2.843, Min = 0, and Max = 36
- **Total Votes:** Mean = 1.068, Standard Deviation = 3.698, Min = 0, and Max = 47

Step 4: Categorical Analysis

The top categories by review count are as follows:

- **Grocery:** 100 reviews
- **Digital_Ebook_Purchase:** 100 reviews
- **Jewelry:** 100 reviews
- **PC:** 100 reviews
- **Books:** 100 reviews

Step 5: Rating Distribution

We visualized the distribution of the star ratings:

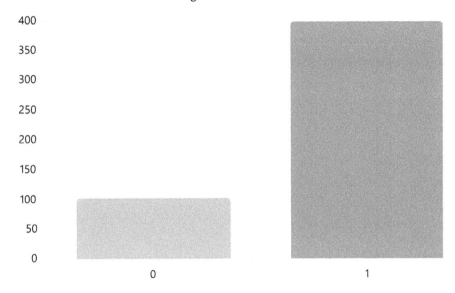

Figure 11.5: Distribution of the star ratings

Step 6: Temporal Trends

We examined the number of reviews per month:

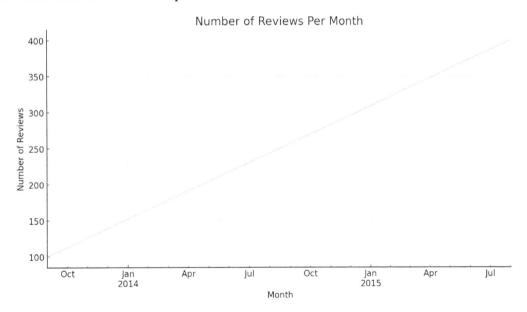

Figure 11.6: Number of reviews per month

Step 7: Review Text Analysis

We analyzed the length and sentiment of the review texts:

• **Distribution of the Review Lengths:**

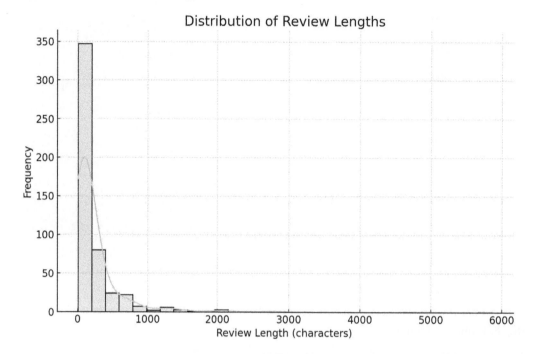

Figure 11.7: Distribution of the review lengths

• **Distribution of the Sentiments:**

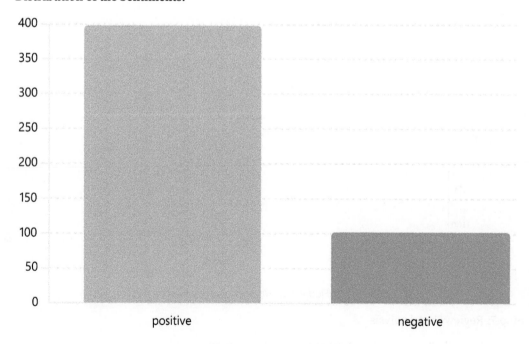

Figure 11.8: Distribution of the sentiments

- **Positive Reviews:** 398
- **Negative Reviews:** 102

Step 8: Correlation Study

We assessed the correlations between the numerical variables and visualized the correlation matrix:

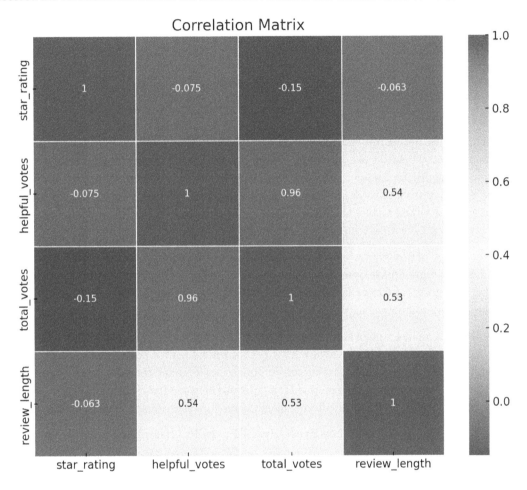

Figure 11.9: Correlation matrix

Conclusion

This analysis provided valuable insights into the dataset, including the distribution of star ratings, trends over time, and the sentiment of reviews. We also explored correlations between numerical variables. These insights can help in understanding customer feedback and improving product offerings.

If you need any further analysis or have specific questions, feel free to ask!

[End of response]

As you can see, GPT-4o has successfully performed data exploration by just uploading the CSV and providing the steps or actions to perform.

Assignment

Investigate how different products or categories perform in terms of ratings, helpful votes, and review length.

Challenge

Use natural language processing (NLP) techniques to analyze the content of the reviews. Extract common themes, keywords, and phrases that are frequently mentioned.

Summary

In this chapter, we delved into comprehensive data analysis using Python and pandas, leveraging the Amazon product review dataset. The journey began with data loading and inspection, ensuring the dataset was properly formatted and free of missing values. You were guided through each step with detailed explanations and code samples suitable for Jupyter Notebooks aimed at empowering data analysts to uncover actionable insights effectively.

We started by calculating statistical summaries for numerical data, revealing that the dataset predominantly consisted of positive reviews. Categorical analysis followed, where we explored distributions across different marketplaces, product categories, verified purchases, and sentiments. Visualizations, including histograms and bar charts, provided clear representations of star rating distributions, emphasizing the predominance of positive feedback.

Temporal trends analysis uncovered a concentrated spread of reviews, primarily in October 2013 and August 2015, offering insights into review activity over time. We then conducted review text analysis, calculating review lengths and assessing sentiment counts to understand the dataset's content more deeply. Finally, a correlation study examined relationships between star ratings and review engagement metrics, like helpful and total votes, offering insights into how these factors interact within the dataset.

In the next chapter, we will learn how to use ChatGPT to build a classification model using the same dataset.

Join our community on Discord

Join our community's Discord space for discussions with the author and other readers:

`https://packt.link/aicode`

12

Building a Classification Model with ChatGPT

Introduction

Building on the foundation set in the previous chapter, where we used ChatGPT for data exploration with Amazon book reviews, *Chapter 12* delves deeper into the realm of supervised learning, with a focus on classification. Here, we continue to leverage ChatGPT, applying its capabilities to enhance our understanding and application of supervised learning techniques in the context of customer reviews.

In the realm of e-commerce, customer feedback plays a pivotal role in shaping business strategies and product enhancements. As Bill Gates aptly stated, "Your most dissatisfied customers are your greatest source of learning." Customer sentiments are often buried within the extensive pool of product reviews. However, manually scrutinizing this ocean of reviews, which includes various attributes such as product ID, title, text, rating, and helpful votes, is an arduous and often unmanageable task.

In this chapter, we concentrate on classifying customer reviews into two distinct groups: positive and negative. We will utilize the insights gained from ChatGPT in processing and analyzing customer review data.

Our main goal is to show how ChatGPT can simplify the journey of machine learning, making it more accessible and less intimidating, especially when dealing with intricate topics such as classification in supervised learning. We will explore how ChatGPT can break down complex concepts into more digestible parts, provide explanations, and even generate code snippets, thereby reducing the learning curve for beginners or those new to the field.

By the end of this chapter, you will have a solid understanding of supervised learning and its application in sentiment analysis, along with an appreciation of how AI tools like ChatGPT can be valuable allies in learning and applying machine learning techniques effectively.

Business problem

In an e-commerce project, understanding customer feedback helps in identifying key factors that influence a customer's decision to make a purchase, enabling targeted marketing strategies. Additionally, it allows the optimization of the user experience and website design to increase the likelihood of providing improved service and products to customers.

Problem and data domain

In this section, we aim to build a classification model for customer review sentiment analysis using the Amazon product review dataset. Leveraging ChatGPT's capabilities, we'll generate Python code to construct a classification model, offering readers a practical approach to working with datasets and understanding classification techniques. Additionally, we'll explore effective prompting techniques to guide ChatGPT in providing tailored code snippets and insights for data classification tasks.

Dataset overview

The Amazon product review dataset contains information on various products and their corresponding reviews. By utilizing this dataset, we can perform various analyses, including sentiment analysis, trend analysis of customer feedback, and product rating analysis. The ultimate goal is to train a classification model capable of accurately classifying reviews into positive or negative sentiments, enhancing decision-making processes, and improving customer satisfaction in e-commerce platforms and related industries.

Features in the dataset include:

- `marketplace (string)`: The location of the product.
- `customer_id (string)`: The unique identifier for customers.
- `review_id (string)`: The unique identifier for reviews.
- `product_id (string)`: The unique identifier for products.
- `product_parent (string)`: The parent product identifier.
- `product_title (string)`: The title of the reviewed product.
- `product_category (string)`: The category of the product.
- `star_rating (int)`: The rating of the product on a scale of 1 to 5.
- `helpful_votes (int)`: The number of helpful votes received for the review.
- `total_votes (int)`: The total number of votes received for the review.
- `review_headline (string)`: The headline of the review.
- `review_body (string)`: The content of the review.
- `review_date (string)`: The date of the review.
- `Sentiments (string)`: The sentiment of the review (positive or negative).

The textual data in `review_body` and `review_headline` can be particularly valuable for natural language processing tasks, including sentiment analysis. For simplification purposes, we have excluded the neutral sentiment category to focus on building a classification model and prompting techniques.

Breaking the problem down into features

Given the Amazon product review dataset and the application of machine learning models for sentiment analysis, we will outline the following features to guide users through building and optimizing models for sentiment classification:

- **Data preprocessing and feature engineering**: Users will start by preprocessing the text data, including tasks such as tokenization, lowercasing, and removing stop words and punctuation. Additionally, feature engineering techniques such as **Term Frequency-Inverse Document Frequency (TF-IDF)** encoding or word embeddings will be applied to represent the text data in a format suitable for machine learning models.

- **Model selection and baseline training**: Users will select baseline machine learning models such as logistic regression, Naive Bayes, or **support vector machines (SVMs)** for sentiment classification. The selected model will be trained on the preprocessed data to establish a baseline performance for sentiment analysis.

- **Model evaluation and interpretation**: Users will evaluate the performance of trained machine learning models using metrics such as accuracy, precision, recall, and F1-score. Additionally, techniques for interpreting model predictions, such as feature importance analysis or model explainability methods, will be explored to gain insights into the factors influencing sentiment classification decisions.

- **Handling imbalanced data**: This feature addresses the challenge of imbalanced class distributions in the dataset by implementing techniques such as oversampling, under-sampling, or using class weights during model training. Users will explore methods to mitigate the impact of class imbalance on model performance and improve the classification accuracy of minority classes.

- **Hyperparameter tuning**: Users will learn how to optimize the performance of machine-learning models by tuning hyperparameters such as regularization strength, learning rate, and kernel parameters. Through techniques like grid search or random search, users will experiment with different hyperparameter configurations to improve the model's performance on the validation set.

- **Experimenting with feature representation**: Users will explore different methods of representing text data as features for machine learning models. This feature focuses on comparing the performance of models trained with different feature representations, such as bag-of-words, TF-IDF, or word embeddings, to determine the most effective approach for sentiment classification.

By following these features, users will gain practical insights into building, fine-tuning, and optimizing machine learning models for sentiment analysis tasks using the Amazon product review dataset. They will learn how to systematically experiment with different preprocessing techniques, feature representations, hyperparameter configurations, and class imbalance handling strategies to achieve superior performance and accuracy in sentiment classification.

Prompting strategy

To effectively utilize ChatGPT for generating code for sentiment analysis machine learning tasks, we need to develop a comprehensive prompting strategy tailored to the specific features and requirements of sentiment analysis using the Amazon product review dataset.

Strategy 1: Task-Actions-Guidelines (TAG) prompt strategy

1.1 – task: The specific task or goal is to build and optimize a machine learning model for sentiment analysis using the Amazon product review dataset.

1.2 – actions: The key steps involved in building and optimizing a machine learning model for sentiment analysis include:

- Data preprocessing: Tokenization, lowercasing, removing stopwords and punctuation, and feature engineering (e.g., TF-IDF encoding, word embeddings).
- Model selection: Choose baseline machine learning models such as logistic regression, Naive Bayes, or SVMs.

1.3 – guidelines: We will provide the following guidelines to ChatGPT in our prompt:

- The code should be compatible with Jupyter Notebook.
- Ensure that there are detailed comments for each line of code.
- You have to explain each line of code, which will be then copied into the text block of the Notebook, in detail for each method used before providing the code.

Strategy 2: Persona-Instructions-Context (PIC) prompt strategy

2.1 – persona: Adopt the persona of a beginner who needs step-by-step guidance on building and optimizing machine learning models for sentiment analysis tasks using the Amazon product review dataset.

2.2 – instructions: Ask ChatGPT to generate code for each feature one step at a time and wait for user feedback before proceeding to the next step. Also, provide the path of the dataset from where it will be loaded.

2.3 – context: Given that the focus is on sentiment analysis using the Amazon product review dataset, ChatGPT is not aware of the dataset and its characteristics, so additional context will be necessary.

Strategy 3: Learn-Improvise-Feedback-Evaluate (LIFE) prompt strategy

3.1 – learn:

- Emphasize the importance of understanding machine learning models and their components, including feature engineering techniques and model selection.

3.2 – improvise:

- Request ChatGPT to provide code snippets for implementing additional features such as hyperparameter tuning, handling imbalanced data, and model evaluation techniques.

3.3 – feedback:

- Share generated code and model outputs for feedback to ensure effective learning and understanding.
- Incorporate user suggestions and critiques to refine the model and approach.
- Provide error messages to troubleshoot and resolve any issues encountered during model implementation.

3.4 – evaluate:

- Execute the generated code provided by ChatGPT to verify accuracy and validity, ensuring that the model performs effectively in sentiment analysis tasks using the Amazon product review dataset.

Building a sentiment analysis model to accurately classify Amazon reviews using the free version of ChatGPT

We will utilize ChatGPT's free version to build the baseline model.

Feature 1: Data preprocessing and feature engineering

Let's craft our initial prompt for our baseline model.

[Prompt]

I want to create a simple classification model for sentiment analysis of Amazon Review Dataset (TAG 1.1) which consists of following fields (PIC 2.3)

- marketplace (string): Location of the product.
- customer_id (string): Unique identifier for customers.
- review_id (string): Unique identifier for reviews.
- product_id (string): Unique identifier for products.
- product_parent (string): Parent product identifier.
- product_title (string): Title of the reviewed product.
- product_category (string): Category of the product.
- star_rating (int): Rating of the product on a scale of 1 to 5.
- helpful_votes (int): Number of helpful votes received for the review.
- total_votes (int): Total number of votes received for the review.
- review_headline (string): Headline of the review.
- review_body (string): Content of the review.
- review_date (string): Date of the review.
- Sentiments (string): Sentiment of the review (positive or negative).

It should consist of following steps (TAG 1.2) and provide one step at a time and wait for users feedback (PIC 2.2)

- Data Preprocessing: Tokenization, lowercasing, removing stopwords and punctuation, and feature engineering (e.g., TF-IDF encoding, word embeddings).
- Model Selection: Choose baseline machine learning models such as logistic regression, Naive Bayes, or SVMs.

I am a beginner user (PIC 2.1), so please provide step-by-step code and strictly follow the following instructions (TAG 1.3)

- The code should be compatible with Jupyter notebook.
- Ensure that there are detailed comments for each line of code.
- You have to explain each line of code, which will be then copied into the text block of the Notebook, in detail for each method used before providing the code. Also, note that the dataset is placed in Google Drive at this path: /Chapter05/amazon_product_review_data.csv. So, add the code to mount the drive and load the dataset (PIC 2.2).

[End of prompt]

You should receive a response similar to the following where ChatGPT has provided us with detailed comments and explanations:

[Prompt response]

Sure, let's break down the process into steps. We'll start with data preprocessing.

Step 1: Data Preprocessing

Data preprocessing is essential to clean and prepare the text data for the sentiment analysis model. We'll perform the following steps:

1. **Loading the Dataset:** Load the Amazon review dataset from the provided path.
2. **Tokenization:** Split the text into individual words or tokens.
3. **Lowercasing:** Convert all text to lowercase to ensure uniformity.
4. **Removing Stopwords:** Remove common words that don't carry much meaning.
5. **Removing Punctuation:** Remove punctuation marks from the text.
6. **Feature Engineering:** Transform text data into a format suitable for machine learning models (e.g., TF-IDF encoding).

Now, let's dive into each step in detail before writing the code.

Tokenization:

- Tokenization is the process of splitting text into individual words or tokens. It's a crucial step in natural language processing (NLP) tasks. Tokens are the basic units of text processing. For example, the sentence "The quick brown fox jumps over the lazy dog" can be tokenized into ['The', 'quick', 'brown', 'fox', 'jumps', 'over', 'the', 'lazy', 'dog'].

Lowercasing:

- Lowercasing involves converting all text to lowercase. It helps in standardizing the text data and reduces the vocabulary size. For example, 'Hello' and 'hello' will be treated as the same word after lowercasing.

Removing Stopwords:

- Stopwords are common words that do not carry significant meaning, such as 'the', 'is', 'and', etc. Removing stopwords helps in reducing noise in the data and improving the model's performance.

Removing Punctuation:

- Punctuation marks like commas, periods, and exclamation marks don't contribute much to sentiment analysis and can be safely removed from the text.

Feature Engineering (TF-IDF Encoding):

- TF-IDF (Term Frequency-Inverse Document Frequency) encoding is a common technique used to represent text data numerically. It reflects how important a word is to a document in a collection. It's calculated based on two metrics: term frequency (TF) and inverse document frequency (IDF). TF measures the frequency of a term in a document, while IDF measures the rarity of the term across documents. TF-IDF encoding gives higher weights to terms that are frequent in a document but rare across documents, which are typically more informative.

[End of response]

We will now ask ChatGPT to provide us with the code:

[Prompt]

Ok, let's proceed.

[End of prompt]

We should receive a response like the following, where ChatGPT should provide the code for loading the dataset:

[Prompt response]

Great! Let's start by loading the dataset from Google Drive in Jupyter Notebook. First, we need to mount Google Drive and then read the CSV file containing the Amazon review data.

Step 1: Loading the Dataset

We'll use the `pandas` library to load the dataset from the CSV file. Pandas provides powerful data manipulation tools for Python, making it suitable for handling structured data like CSV files.

Code Explanation:

- `import pandas as pd`: Import the pandas library and alias it as `pd` for convenience.

- `from google.colab import drive`: Import the `drive` module from the `google.colab` library to mount Google Drive.

- `drive.mount('/content/drive')`: Mount Google Drive to access files from it. This will prompt you to authorize access to your Google Drive.

- `data_path = '/content/drive/My Drive/Chapter05/amazon_product_review_data.csv'`: Define the path to the CSV file containing the dataset.

- `df = pd.read_csv(data_path)`: Use the `read_csv()` function from pandas to read the CSV file and store it in a DataFrame called `df`.

Let's implement this in code:

```python
# Importing necessary libraries
import pandas as pd
from google.colab import drive

# Mount Google Drive
drive.mount('/content/drive')

# Path to the dataset
data_path = '/content/drive/My Drive/Chapter05/amazon_product_review_data.csv'

# Load the dataset into a DataFrame
df = pd.read_csv(data_path)
```

Run this code in your Jupyter Notebook, and it will load the dataset into the DataFrame `df`. Let me know if you have any questions before we proceed to the next step

[End of response]

We will now apply the evaluate prompting strategy (LIFE 3.4) and validate the code by executing the code in the Google Colab for every step. The code loads the dataset from Google Drive. It will ask for the permissions. The code runs perfectly fine without applying any modifications or any errors.

Please refer to the notebook Building a Classification Model for Sentiment Analysis with ChatGPT.ipynb for the executable code snippets or copy the code from the prompt response.

```
 1   # Importing necessary libraries
 2   import pandas as pd
 3   from google.colab import drive
 4
 5   # Mount Google Drive
 6   drive.mount('/content/drive')
 7
 8   # Path to the dataset
 9   data_path = '/content/drive/My Drive/Chapter05/amazon_product_review_data.csv'
10
11   # Load the dataset into a DataFrame
12   df = pd.read_csv(data_path)
```

Mounted at /content/drive

Figure 12.1: Code execution – data preprocessing

We will now instruct ChatGPT to proceed to the next step:

[Prompt]

Let's proceed to the next step.

[End of prompt]

We should receive a response like the following, where ChatGPT should provide the code for data preprocessing:

[Prompt response]

Great! In the next step, we'll perform the following preprocessing tasks:

1. Tokenization
2. Lowercasing
3. Removing stopwords
4. Removing punctuation

We'll use the NLTK library for tokenization and stopwords removal, and we'll leverage string methods for lowercasing and punctuation removal.

Step 2: Data Preprocessing

Tokenization:

- We'll tokenize the review text into individual words or tokens. NLTK provides a word_tokenize function for this purpose.

Lowercasing:

- We'll convert all text to lowercase using the lower() method of Python strings.

Removing Stopwords:

- NLTK provides a list of stopwords for various languages. We'll use this list to filter out stopwords from the review text.

Removing Punctuation:

- We'll use string methods to remove punctuation marks from the review text.

Let's implement these preprocessing steps in code:

```python
# Importing necessary libraries
import nltk
import string


# Download NLTK resources (only need to do this once)
nltk.download('punkt')
nltk.download('stopwords')


# Get the list of stopwords
stopwords = nltk.corpus.stopwords.words('english')


# Function to preprocess text
def preprocess_text(text):
    # Tokenization
    tokens = nltk.word_tokenize(text)

    # Lowercasing
    tokens = [token.lower() for token in tokens]

    # Removing stopwords and punctuation
    tokens = [token for token in tokens if token not in stopwords and token not
in string.punctuation]

    # Join tokens back into text
    preprocessed_text = ' '.join(tokens)
```

```
    return preprocessed_text

# Preprocess the review body
df['Cleaned_Review'] = df['review_body'].apply(preprocess_text)

# Display the preprocessed data
df.head()
```

Here's an explanation of the code:

- We import the necessary libraries, including NLTK for natural language processing tasks and the string module for handling punctuation.
- We download the NLTK resources for tokenization and stopwords removal using the `nltk.download()` function.
- We define a function `preprocess_text()` to preprocess each review text. This function performs tokenization, lowercasing, removal of stopwords, and removal of punctuation.
- Inside the function, we tokenize the text using `nltk.word_tokenize()`, convert tokens to lowercase, remove stopwords and punctuation using list comprehensions, and then join the tokens back into text.
- Finally, we apply the `preprocess_text()` function to the `review_body` column of the DataFrame and store the preprocessed text in a new column called `Cleaned_Review`.

Run this code in your Jupyter Notebook, and it will preprocess the review text in the DataFrame. Let me know if you have any questions or if you're ready to proceed to the next step!

[End of response]

We execute the code in the notebook and it runs perfectly fine, and the dataset summary is printed along with a new column called `Cleaned_Review`.

product_title	product_category	star_rating	helpful_votes	total_votes	verified_purchase	review_headline	review_body	review_date	sentiments	Cleaned_Review
The Cravings Place Chocolate Chunk Cookie Mix...	'Grocery'	1	0	0	1 \t(Y)	'Using these for years · love them'	As a family allergic to wheat, dairy, eggs, n...	2015-08-31	positive	' family allergic wheat dairy eggs nuts sever...
'Mauna Loa Macadamias, 11 Ounce Packages'	'Grocery'	1	0	0	1 \t(Y)	'Wonderful'	My favorite nut. Creamy, crunchy, salty, and ...	2015-08-31	positive	' favorite nut creamy crunchy salty slightly ...
'Organic Matcha Green Tea Powder - 100% Pure M...	'Grocery'	1	0	0	0 \t(N)	'Five Stars'	This green tea tastes so good! My girlfriend ...	2015-08-31	positive	' green tea tastes good girlfriend loves '
'15oz Raspberry Lyons Designer Dessert Syrup S...	'Grocery'	1	0	0	1 \t(Y)	'Five Stars'	I love Melissa's brand but this is a great se...	2015-08-31	positive	' love melissa 's brand great second ca n't g...
'Stride Spark Kinetic Fruit Sugar Free Gum, 14...	'Grocery'	1	0	0	1 \t(Y)	'Five Stars'	'good'	2015-08-31	positive	' good '

Figure 12.2: Code execution – dataset summary

Feature 2: Model selection and baseline training

Now that data preprocessing is complete, we will move to our next feature of model selection.

We will now instruct ChatGPT to proceed to the next step and provide it with the output of the previous step:

[Prompt]

```
market_place customer_id review_id product_id product_parent product_title
product_category star_rating helpful_votes total_votes vine verified_purchase
review_headline review_body review_date sentiments Cleaned_Review 0 "US"
"42521656" "R26MV8D0KG6QI6" "B000SAQCWC" "159713740" "The Cravings Place
Chocolate Chunk Cookie Mix... "Grocery" 1 0 0 0 \t(N) 1 \t(Y) "Using these
for years - love them." "As a family allergic to wheat, dairy, eggs, n...
2015-08-31 positive `` family allergic wheat dairy eggs nuts sever... 1 "US"
"12049833" "R1OF8GP57AQ1A0" "B00509LVIQ" "138680402" "Mauna Loa Macadamias, 11
Ounce Packages" "Grocery" 1 0 0 0 \t(N) 1 \t(Y) "Wonderful" "My favorite nut.
Creamy, crunchy, salty, and ... 2015-08-31 positive `` favorite nut creamy
crunchy salty slightly ... 2 "US" "107642" "R3VDC1QB6MC4ZZ" "B00KHXESLC"
"252021703" "Organic Matcha Green Tea Powder - 100% Pure M... "Grocery" 1 0
0 0 \t(N) 0 \t(N) "Five Stars" "This green tea tastes so good! My girlfriend
... 2015-08-31 positive `` green tea tastes good girlfriend loves '' 3 "US"
"6042304" "R12FA3DCF8F9ER" "B000F8JIIC" "752728342" "15oz Raspberry Lyons
Designer Dessert Syrup S... "Grocery" 1 0 0 0 \t(N) 1 \t(Y) "Five Stars" "I
love Melissa's brand but this is a great se... 2015-08-31 positive `` love
melissa 's brand great second ca n't g... 4 "US" "18123821" "RTWHVNV6X4CNJ"
"B004ZWR9RQ" "552138758" "Stride Spark Kinetic Fruit Sugar Free Gum, 14...
"Grocery" 1 0 0 0 \t(N) 1 \t(Y) "Five Stars" "good" 2015-08-31 positive `` good
''
```

[End of prompt]

We should receive a response like the following, where ChatGPT should provide the code for model selection:

[Prompt response]

It looks like the DataFrame now includes a new column named `Cleaned_Review` containing the preprocessed text data. We've successfully completed the data preprocessing step.

Now, let's move on to the next step: Model Selection.

Step 3: Model Selection

In this step, we'll choose a baseline machine learning model for sentiment analysis. Commonly used models for text classification tasks like sentiment analysis include logistic regression, Naive Bayes, and support vector machines (SVM). We'll start with one of these models as a baseline and evaluate its performance.

Logistic Regression:

- Logistic regression is a popular linear classification algorithm used for binary classification tasks like sentiment analysis. It works by modelling the probability that a given input belongs to a particular class using a logistic function.
- We'll use scikit-learn, a powerful machine learning library in Python, to implement logistic regression for sentiment analysis.

Let's proceed to implement logistic regression for sentiment analysis using the preprocessed data. Here's the code:

```python
# Importing necessary libraries
from sklearn.model_selection import train_test_split
from sklearn.feature_extraction.text import TfidfVectorizer
from sklearn.linear_model import LogisticRegression
from sklearn.metrics import accuracy_score, classification_report

# Splitting the data into training and testing sets
X = df['Cleaned_Review']
y = df['sentiments']
X_train, X_test, y_train, y_test = train_test_split(X, y, test_size=0.2,
random_state=42)

# TF-IDF vectorization
tfidf_vectorizer = TfidfVectorizer(max_features=5000)  # You can adjust max_
features as needed
X_train_tfidf = tfidf_vectorizer.fit_transform(X_train)
X_test_tfidf = tfidf_vectorizer.transform(X_test)

# Initialize and train the logistic regression model
lr_model = LogisticRegression()
lr_model.fit(X_train_tfidf, y_train)

# Predictions
y_pred = lr_model.predict(X_test_tfidf)

# Evaluate the model
accuracy = accuracy_score(y_test, y_pred)
print("Accuracy:", accuracy)
print("\nClassification Report:")
print(classification_report(y_test, y_pred))
```

Let me explain the code:

- We import necessary libraries from scikit-learn for model selection and evaluation, including `train_test_split` for splitting the data, `TfidfVectorizer` for TF-IDF vectorization, `LogisticRegression` for logistic regression, and `accuracy_score` and `classification_report` for model evaluation.
- We split the data into training and testing sets using `train_test_split`.
- We perform TF-IDF vectorization on the training and testing data using `TfidfVectorizer`.
- We initialize and train a logistic regression model using the training data.
- We make predictions on the testing data.
- Finally, we evaluate the model's performance using accuracy and classification report.

You can run this code in your Jupyter Notebook to train the logistic regression model and evaluate its performance on the sentiment analysis task. Let me know if you have any questions or if you'd like to explore other model options!

[End of response]

We execute the code and it runs without any errors, trains the model, and evaluates the model performance.

You should see a table on precision, recall, and more.

We will move on to our next feature of model evaluation and interpretation.

Feature 3: Model evaluation and interpretation

Now that we have selected the logistic regression model and baseline performance is evaluated, we can interpret the results.

We will now provide the output to ChatGPT and request additional techniques such as feature importance analysis and model explainability:

[Prompt]

I would like to learn about the metrics such as accuracy, precision, recall, and F1-score. Additionally, I would like to apply techniques for interpreting model predictions, such as feature importance analysis or model explainability methods, to gain insights into the factors influencing sentiment classification decisions. The following is the output from the model evaluation.

```
Accuracy: 0.86
Classification Report:
              precision    recall  f1-score   support

    negative       0.00      0.00      0.00        14
    positive       0.86      1.00      0.92        86

    accuracy                           0.86       100
```

```
      macro avg        0.43      0.50      0.46       100
   weighted avg        0.74      0.86      0.80       100
```

[End of prompt]

We should receive a response like the following, where ChatGPT explains the metrics and suggests some options for model explainability and so on:

[Prompt response]

Certainly! Let's break down the metrics mentioned in the model evaluation output and discuss techniques for interpreting model predictions.

Metrics Explanation:

- **Accuracy:**

  Accuracy measures the proportion of correctly classified instances among the total instances. It's calculated as the ratio of the number of correct predictions to the total number of predictions. However, accuracy alone may not provide a complete picture of model performance, especially when classes are imbalanced.

- **Precision:**

  Precision measures the proportion of true positive predictions among all positive predictions. It indicates the model's ability to avoid false positives. It's calculated as the ratio of true positives to the sum of true positives and false positives.

- **Recall:**

  Recall, also known as sensitivity or true positive rate, measures the proportion of true positive predictions among all actual positive instances. It indicates the model's ability to capture all positive instances. It's calculated as the ratio of true positives to the sum of true positives and false negatives.

- **F1-Score:**

  The F1-score is the harmonic mean of precision and recall. It provides a balanced measure that considers both precision and recall. It's calculated as 2 * (precision * recall) / (precision + recall).

Interpretation:

- **Accuracy:**

  The accuracy of 0.86 means that the model correctly classified 86% of the instances in the test set. However, accuracy alone doesn't provide insights into class-specific performance.

- **Precision:**

  The precision for the positive class is 0.86, indicating that when the model predicts a review as positive, it is correct 86% of the time. The precision for the negative class is 0.00, indicating that the model did not correctly predict any negative reviews.

- **Recall:**

  The recall for the positive class is 1.00, indicating that the model correctly identified all positive reviews. However, the recall for the negative class is 0.00, indicating that the model failed to identify any negative reviews.

- **F1-Score:**

  The F1-score for the positive class is 0.92, which is the harmonic mean of precision and recall for the positive class. It provides a balanced measure of the model's performance for positive reviews.

Techniques for Interpreting Model Predictions:

- **Feature Importance Analysis:**

  For logistic regression models, we can interpret feature importance by examining the coefficients associated with each feature. Higher magnitude coefficients indicate stronger influence on the predicted class. We can identify important words or features that contribute to positive or negative sentiment.

- **Model Explainability Methods:**

  Techniques such as SHAP (SHapley Additive exPlanations) values, LIME (Local Interpretable Model-agnostic Explanations), or ELI5 (Explain Like I'm 5) can provide insights into how individual features contribute to model predictions. These methods help in understanding the decision-making process of complex models like logistic regression.

Would you like to delve deeper into any of these techniques or have any specific questions? Let me know how I can assist you further!

[End of response]

We will ask ChatGPT to apply the **SHAP (SHapley Additive exPlanations)** technique:

[Prompt]

Let's try SHAP first.

[End of prompt]

We should receive a response like the following, where ChatGPT understood the request and provides us with the code for SHAP:

[Prompt response]

Sure! SHAP (SHapley Additive exPlanations) is a method for explaining individual predictions from machine learning models. It provides a way to understand the contribution of each feature to the model's output for a specific instance.

Here's how we can use SHAP to interpret the logistic regression model's predictions for sentiment analysis:

Using SHAP for Model Interpretation:

1. **Install SHAP:**

   First, let's make sure you have SHAP installed. If not, you can install it using pip:

   ```
   !pip install shap
   ```

2. **Prepare the Data:**

   We'll need to prepare the data for SHAP analysis. This involves transforming the text data into a format suitable for the logistic regression model.

3. **Explain Model Predictions:**

   We'll use SHAP to explain the logistic regression model's predictions for individual instances in the test set. This will provide insights into how each feature contributes to the model's decision.

Let's implement these steps in code:

```python
# Importing necessary libraries
import shap

# Initialize the SHAP explainer with the logistic regression model and training
data
explainer = shap.Explainer(lr_model, X_train_tfidf)

# Explain the model's predictions for a specific instance (e.g., the first
instance in the test set)
instance_index = 0  # You can choose any instance index from the test set
shap_values = explainer.shap_values(X_test_tfidf[instance_index])

# Visualize the SHAP values
shap.summary_plot(shap_values, features=X_test_tfidf[instance_index], feature_
names=tfidf_vectorizer.get_feature_names())
```

Explanation of the code:

- We import the SHAP library.
- We initialize the SHAP explainer with the logistic regression model (lr_model) and the TF-IDF transformed training data (X_train_tfidf).
- We use the explainer to compute SHAP values for a specific instance from the test set (X_test_tfidf[instance_index]).
- Finally, we visualize the SHAP values using shap.summary_plot().

This visualization will provide insights into which features (words) contributed most to the model's prediction for the selected instance.

You can run this code in your Jupyter Notebook to visualize the SHAP values for individual predictions. Let me know if you have any questions or need further assistance!

[End of response]

We execute the code and it gives an error: `AttributeError: 'TfidfVectorizer' object has no attribute 'get_feature_names'`.

```
[ ]    1   !pip install shap

[6]    1   # Importing necessary libraries
       2   import shap
       3
       4   # Initialize the SHAP explainer with the logistic regression model and training data
       5   explainer = shap.Explainer(lr_model, X_train_tfidf)
       6
       7   # Explain the model's predictions for a specific instance (e.g., the first instance in the test set)
       8   instance_index = 0  # You can choose any instance index from the test set
       9   shap_values = explainer.shap_values(X_test_tfidf[instance_index])
      10
      11   # Visualize the SHAP values
      12   shap.summary_plot(shap_values, features=X_test_tfidf[instance_index], feature_names=tfidf_vectorizer.get_feature_names())

---------------------------------------------------------------------
AttributeError                               Traceback (most recent call last)
<ipython-input-6-673ab3e1b84b> in <cell line: 12>()
     10
     11 # Visualize the SHAP values
---> 12 shap.summary_plot(shap_values, features=X_test_tfidf[instance_index], feature_names=tfidf_vectorizer.get_feature_names())

AttributeError: 'TfidfVectorizer' object has no attribute 'get_feature_names'
```

Figure 12.3: Attribute error for SHAP

We will use the feedback prompting strategy (LIFE 3.3) and provide the error to ChatGPT:

[Prompt]

```
AttributeError: 'TfidfVectorizer' object has no attribute 'get_feature_names'
```

[End of prompt].

We should receive a response with the suggested correct code.

[Prompt response]

It seems there was an AttributeError because the `TfidfVectorizer` object does not have a `get_feature_names()` method. My apologies for the oversight. We can access the feature names directly from the vectorizer's vocabulary attribute.

Let's correct the code to retrieve feature names from the `TfidfVectorizer` vocabulary:

```
# Get feature names from the TfidfVectorizer vocabulary
feature_names = tfidf_vectorizer.get_feature_names_out()

# Visualize the SHAP values
shap.summary_plot(shap_values, features=X_test_tfidf[instance_index], feature_names=feature_names)
```

By using `get_feature_names_out()`, we can access the feature names from the `TfidfVectorizer`'s vocabulary.

You can update the code accordingly and try running it again in your Jupyter Notebook. Let me know if you encounter any further issues!

[End of response]

We execute the corrected code and it works fine and produces the output plot:

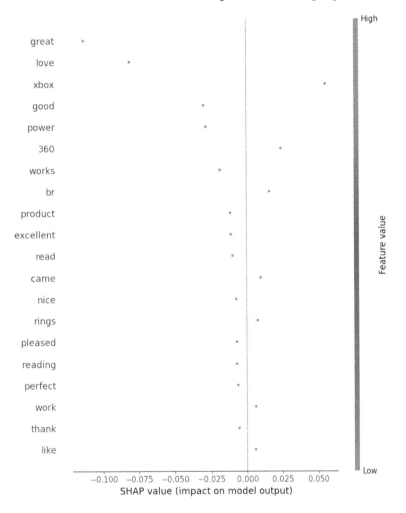

Figure 12.4: Code execution – SHAP impact on model output

- Words like "great" and "love" have positive SHAP values, meaning their presence in the data likely pushes predictions toward a positive outcome, possibly indicating a positive sentiment in a sentiment analysis model.
- The words are ranked by the absolute size of their SHAP values, with "great" having the most significant positive impact.

- Most words on this list have a very minor impact close to zero, suggesting that their presence does not significantly affect the prediction relative to the baseline.
- Some words such as "360" and "xbox" may relate to specific topics (like gaming), and their SHAP values are slightly negative, suggesting they might be reducing the likelihood of the positive outcome this model predicts.

We will now ask ChatGPT to provide us with the code for ELI5 (Explain Like I'm 5):

[Prompt]

Next, I would like to try ELI5 and ensure that the code is correct and is not impacted because of the SHAP technique we applied.

[End of prompt].

We should receive the code for ELI5 from ChatGPT:

[Prompt response]

Certainly! ELI5 (Explain Like I'm 5) is another popular library for model interpretation and explaining machine learning models. We can use ELI5 to understand how our logistic regression model makes predictions and inspect feature importance.

Let's integrate ELI5 into our code to explain the logistic regression model's predictions:

Using ELI5 for Model Interpretation:

1. **Install ELI5:**

   If you haven't installed ELI5 yet, you can install it using pip:

   ```
   !pip install eli5
   ```

2. **Explain Model Predictions:**

   We'll use ELI5 to explain the logistic regression model's predictions for individual instances in the test set. ELI5 provides different methods to explain model predictions, including feature importances and textual explanations.

Let's update our code to include ELI5 for model interpretation:

```
# Importing necessary libraries
import eli5


# Explain the logistic regression model using ELI5
eli5.show_weights(lr_model, vec=tfidf_vectorizer, top=20)  # Show top 20 most
important features
```

Explanation of the code:

- We import the ELI5 library.

- We use the `show_weights` function from ELI5 to explain the logistic regression model's predictions. This function displays the weights (coefficients) associated with each feature, indicating their importance in the model's decision-making process.

- We specify the vectorizer (`vec`) parameter to ensure ELI5 interprets the features correctly based on the TF-IDF vectorization.

You can run this updated code in your Jupyter Notebook to see the top features contributing to the model's predictions. ELI5 provides a clear visualization of feature importances, allowing you to gain insights into the model's behavior.

Let me know if you have any questions or encounter any issues!

[End of response]

We execute the code provided by ChatGPT, which installs the eli5 library and generates the output as follows:

The output is not understandable at all, which is ironic as it is supposed to be understood by a 5-year-old.

Let's ask ChatGPT to at least provide code in which the feature names are in plain English:

[Prompt]

Can I also get the features? X numbers make no sense and are definitely not understandable to a 5-year-old.

[End of prompt]

We should receive a response similar to the following:

[Prompt response]

Certainly! We can map the feature indices (x numbers) to their corresponding words or terms in the TF-IDF vectorizer's vocabulary to make them more interpretable. Let's update the code to include feature names along with their weights:

```
# Explain the logistic regression model using ELI5 with feature names
eli5.show_weights(lr_model, vec=tfidf_vectorizer, top=20, feature_names=tfidf_
vectorizer.get_feature_names_out())
```

By including the `feature_names` parameter with the TF-IDF vectorizer's vocabulary, ELI5 will display the actual words or terms instead of feature indices.

Run this updated code in your Jupyter Notebook, and you'll see the top features contributing to the positive class predictions along with their weights. Let me know if you have any questions or need further assistance!

[End of response]

We execute the provided code, and it now provides the feature names in English:

This concludes Feature 3, but as our data is clearly imbalanced, let's proceed to the next feature.

Feature 4: Handling imbalanced data

Now that we have a baseline model and learned how to use the model explainability techniques, we will now see how to handle the data imbalance:

[Prompt]

I would like to apply some techniques to mitigate the data imbalance as it is clearly seen from the model performance.

```
Accuracy: 0.86
Classification Report:
              precision    recall  f1-score   support

    negative       0.00      0.00      0.00        14
    positive       0.86      1.00      0.92        86.
```

[End of prompt]

We should receive a response like the following where ChatGPT understands the request and provides us with suggestions and code to mitigate the data imbalance:

[Prompt response]

Addressing data imbalance is crucial for improving the model's performance, especially in cases where one class is significantly underrepresented compared to the other. Here are some techniques we can apply to mitigate data imbalance:

Resampling Techniques:

- **Over-sampling:** Increase the number of instances in the minority class by generating synthetic samples (e.g., using SMOTE - Synthetic Minority Over-sampling Technique).
- **Under-sampling:** Decrease the number of instances in the majority class by randomly removing samples.

Algorithmic Techniques:

- **Class weights:** Assign higher weights to instances of the minority class during model training to penalize misclassifications.
- **Ensemble methods:** Utilize ensemble methods that handle class imbalance well, such as Balanced Random Forest or Easy Ensemble.

Data Augmentation:

- Generate new samples for the minority class by applying transformations or perturbations to existing data points.

Cost-sensitive Learning:

- Explicitly incorporate the cost of misclassification into the model training process to prioritize correct classification of the minority class.

Let's implement one of these techniques, such as class weights adjustment, to address the data imbalance in our logistic regression model:

```python
import numpy as np
# Calculate class weights
from sklearn.utils.class_weight import compute_class_weight

class_weights = compute_class_weight('balanced', classes=np.unique(y_train),
y=y_train)

# Initialize and train the logistic regression model with class weights
lr_model_balanced = LogisticRegression(class_weight=dict(zip(np.unique(y_
train), class_weights)))
lr_model_balanced.fit(X_train_tfidf, y_train)

# Predictions
y_pred_balanced = lr_model_balanced.predict(X_test_tfidf)

# Evaluate the model with balanced class weights
accuracy_balanced = accuracy_score(y_test, y_pred_balanced)
print("Accuracy with balanced class weights:", accuracy_balanced)
print("\nClassification Report with balanced class weights:")
print(classification_report(y_test, y_pred_balanced))
```

Explanation:

- We calculate class weights using `compute_class_weight` from scikit-learn's utils. Setting balanced mode automatically adjusts weights inversely proportional to class frequencies in the input data.
- We initialize and train a new logistic regression model (`lr_model_balanced`) with the calculated class weights.
- We make predictions using the balanced model and evaluate its performance using accuracy and classification report.

Running this code will train the logistic regression model with balanced class weights and evaluate its performance on the test set. It should help improve the handling of the imbalanced data and potentially enhance the model's performance. Let me know if you have any questions or need further assistance!

[End of response]

We will execute the code that uses calculated class weights and see what impact it makes.

You should see a classification report with balanced weights.

We will give the output to ChatGPT so that it provides us with explanations:

[Prompt]

Accuracy with balanced class weights: 0.81

Classification Report with balanced class weights:

```
              precision    recall  f1-score   support

    negative       0.27      0.21      0.24        14
    positive       0.88      0.91      0.89        86

    accuracy                           0.81       100
   macro avg       0.57      0.56      0.57       100
weighted avg       0.79      0.81      0.80       100
```

[End of prompt]

We should receive a response like the following where ChatGPT provides the interpretation of the output:

[Prompt response]

It appears that applying balanced class weights has improved the model's performance, although the accuracy has decreased slightly. Let's interpret the results:

- **Accuracy:** The accuracy of 0.81 indicates that the model correctly classified 81% of the instances in the test set.

- **Precision and Recall:** For the negative class, the precision has improved significantly to 0.27, indicating that when the model predicts a review as negative, it is correct 27% of the time. However, the recall is relatively low at 0.21, suggesting that the model fails to capture many negative instances.

    For the positive class, both precision and recall are high, with precision at 0.88 and recall at 0.91. This indicates that the model performs well in identifying positive instances.

- **F1-score:** The F1-score for the negative class has improved slightly to 0.24, while for the positive class, it remains high at 0.89.

- **Support:** The support represents the number of instances in each class. There are 14 instances of the negative class and 86 instances of the positive class in the test set.

Overall, while the accuracy has decreased, the model's ability to correctly classify the minority class (negative reviews) has improved significantly with balanced class weights. This indicates a better balance between precision and recall for both classes, resulting in a more robust model.

If you have any further questions or need additional assistance, feel free to ask!

[End of response]

We have reduced the imbalance and will now move on to the next feature of hyperparameter tuning.

Feature 5: Hyperparameter tuning

Now that we have learned how to deal with imbalanced data, we can optimize the performance by tuning hyperparameters such as regularization strength, learning rate, and kernel parameters, and also apply techniques like grid search or random search:

[Prompt]

I would like to optimize the performance by tuning hyperparameters such as regularization strength, learning rate, and kernel parameters and also apply techniques like grid search or random search.

[End of prompt]

We should receive a response like the following:

[Prompt response]

Certainly! Hyperparameter tuning is crucial for optimizing model performance. We can use techniques like grid search or random search to search through a range of hyperparameter values and find the combination that yields the best performance.

Let's start by implementing hyperparameter tuning using grid search with logistic regression as an example:

```python
# Importing necessary libraries
from sklearn.model_selection import GridSearchCV


# Define hyperparameters grid
param_grid = {
    'C': [0.01, 0.1, 1.0, 10.0],  # Regularization strength (smaller values
indicate stronger regularization)
    'solver': ['liblinear', 'lbfgs'],  # Optimization algorithm
}


# Initialize logistic regression model
lr_model_tuned = LogisticRegression()


# Initialize GridSearchCV with logistic regression model and hyperparameters
grid
grid_search = GridSearchCV(lr_model_tuned, param_grid, cv=5,
scoring='accuracy')


# Perform grid search
grid_search.fit(X_train_tfidf, y_train)


# Get the best hyperparameters
best_params = grid_search.best_params_
```

```
print("Best Hyperparameters:", best_params)

# Use the best model from grid search
best_lr_model = grid_search.best_estimator_

# Predictions
y_pred_tuned = best_lr_model.predict(X_test_tfidf)

# Evaluate the tuned model
accuracy_tuned = accuracy_score(y_test, y_pred_tuned)
print("Accuracy with tuned model:", accuracy_tuned)
print("\nClassification Report with tuned model:")
print(classification_report(y_test, y_pred_tuned))
```

Explanation:

- We define a grid of hyperparameters (param_grid) to search through. In this example, we vary the regularization strength (C) and the solver algorithm.
- We initialize a logistic regression model (lr_model_tuned) and perform grid search using GridSearchCV.
- Grid search will evaluate the performance of the model with different hyperparameter combinations using cross-validation (cv=5).
- After grid search, we retrieve the best hyperparameters (best_params) and the best model (best_lr_model).
- Finally, we make predictions with the best model and evaluate its performance.

You can adjust the hyperparameter grid (param_grid) to include other hyperparameters like learning rate and kernel parameters for different models. Additionally, you can also explore random search or other optimization techniques for hyperparameter tuning.

Feel free to run this code in your Jupyter Notebook to optimize the logistic regression model's performance through hyperparameter tuning. Let me know if you have any questions or need further assistance!

[End of response]

We execute the code and it works fine, and we find the best parameters using GridSearchCV.

You should see a classification report with tuned model.

The hyperparameter tuning did not significantly improve the model's performance in terms of accuracy and class-specific metrics. Let's interpret the results:

- **Best hyperparameters:** The grid search identified the best hyperparameters as C=0.01 and solver='liblinear'. These hyperparameters indicate a low regularization strength (C=0.01) and the use of the liblinear solver algorithm.

- **Accuracy:** The accuracy of the tuned model remains at 0.86, which is the same as the baseline model. This indicates that hyperparameter tuning did not lead to a significant improvement in overall accuracy.

- **Precision and recall:** The precision, recall, and F1-score for both the positive and negative classes remain unchanged from the baseline model. This suggests that the model's ability to correctly classify instances from each class did not improve after hyperparameter tuning.

- **Support:** The support values represent the number of instances in each class in the test set, which remains the same as before.

Let's move on to our last feature and experiment with feature representation.

Feature 6: Experimenting with feature representation

Let's instruct ChatGPT to provide us with the code for different feature representations:

[Prompt]

I want to compare the performance of the model trained with different feature representations, such as bag-of-words, TF-IDF, or word embeddings, to determine the most effective approach for sentiment classification.

[End of prompt]

We should receive a response like the following where ChatGPT provides the code for bag-of-words, TF-IDF, and word embeddings:

[Prompt response]

Comparing the performance of models trained with different feature representations is a valuable approach to determine the most effective method for sentiment classification. We can train models using bag-of-words, TF-IDF, and word embeddings representations and evaluate their performance using the same evaluation metrics. Let's go through the process step by step:

1. **Bag-of-Words Representation:**

   - We can represent the text data using a bag-of-words approach, where each document is represented by a vector indicating the frequency of each word in the vocabulary.

2. **TF-IDF Representation:**

   - TF-IDF (Term Frequency-Inverse Document Frequency) representation considers not only the frequency of a term in a document but also its importance in the entire corpus.

3. **Word Embeddings Representation:**

   - Word embeddings represent words as dense vectors in a continuous vector space, capturing semantic relationships between words.

Here's how we can compare the performance of models trained with these different feature representations:

- **Preprocess the data:** Tokenize, lowercase, remove stopwords, and perform any necessary text preprocessing steps for each feature representation method.
- **Train models:** Train logistic regression models using each feature representation method (bag-of-words, TF-IDF, word embeddings).
- **Evaluate performance:** Evaluate the performance of each model using the same evaluation metrics (accuracy, precision, recall, F1-score).
- **Compare results:** Compare the performance of models trained with different feature representations to determine the most effective approach for sentiment classification.

Let's start by implementing logistic regression models using bag-of-words, TF-IDF, and word embeddings representations:

Bag-of-Words Representation:

```python
from sklearn.feature_extraction.text import CountVectorizer

# Initialize CountVectorizer
bow_vectorizer = CountVectorizer(max_features=5000)  # You can adjust max_
features as needed

# Transform text data into bag-of-words representation
X_train_bow = bow_vectorizer.fit_transform(X_train)
X_test_bow = bow_vectorizer.transform(X_test)

# Train logistic regression model with bag-of-words representation
lr_model_bow = LogisticRegression()
lr_model_bow.fit(X_train_bow, y_train)

# Evaluate model performance
y_pred_bow = lr_model_bow.predict(X_test_bow)
accuracy_bow = accuracy_score(y_test, y_pred_bow)
print("Accuracy with bag-of-words representation:", accuracy_bow)
# Add other evaluation metrics if needed
```

TF-IDF Representation:

```python
from sklearn.feature_extraction.text import TfidfVectorizer

# Initialize TfidfVectorizer
tfidf_vectorizer = TfidfVectorizer(max_features=5000)  # You can adjust max_
features as needed
```

```
# Transform text data into TF-IDF representation
X_train_tfidf = tfidf_vectorizer.fit_transform(X_train)
X_test_tfidf = tfidf_vectorizer.transform(X_test)

# Train logistic regression model with TF-IDF representation
lr_model_tfidf = LogisticRegression()
lr_model_tfidf.fit(X_train_tfidf, y_train)

# Evaluate model performance
y_pred_tfidf = lr_model_tfidf.predict(X_test_tfidf)
accuracy_tfidf = accuracy_score(y_test, y_pred_tfidf)
print("Accuracy with TF-IDF representation:", accuracy_tfidf)
# Add other evaluation metrics if needed
```

Word Embeddings Representation:

For word embeddings representation, we need to first convert the text data into word embeddings using techniques like Word2Vec, GloVe, or fastText. We'll use pre-trained word embeddings for this purpose.

```
# Assuming you have pre-trained word embeddings loaded (e.g., GloVe)
# Convert text data into word embeddings representation
# You may need to tokenize and pad sequences before applying word embeddings

# Train logistic regression model with word embeddings representation
lr_model_word_embeddings = LogisticRegression()
lr_model_word_embeddings.fit(X_train_word_embeddings, y_train)

# Evaluate model performance
y_pred_word_embeddings = lr_model_word_embeddings.predict(X_test_word_
embeddings)
accuracy_word_embeddings = accuracy_score(y_test, y_pred_word_embeddings)
print("Accuracy with word embeddings representation:", accuracy_word_
embeddings)
# Add other evaluation metrics if needed
```

After training and evaluating models with different feature representations, you can compare their performance using accuracy or other evaluation metrics. Based on the results, you can determine which feature representation method is the most effective for sentiment classification.

Feel free to run these codes in your Jupyter Notebook and let me know if you need further assistance or have any questions!

[End of response]

We will execute the code and compare the accuracy for bag-of-words, TF-IDF, and word embeddings. The code works perfectly fine for the first two but gives errors for word embeddings.

```python
from sklearn.feature_extraction.text import CountVectorizer

# Initialize CountVectorizer
bow_vectorizer = CountVectorizer(max_features=5000)  # You can adjust max_features as needed

# Transform text data into bag-of-words representation
X_train_bow = bow_vectorizer.fit_transform(X_train)
X_test_bow = bow_vectorizer.transform(X_test)

# Train logistic regression model with bag-of-words representation
lr_model_bow = LogisticRegression()
lr_model_bow.fit(X_train_bow, y_train)

# Evaluate model performance
y_pred_bow = lr_model_bow.predict(X_test_bow)
accuracy_bow = accuracy_score(y_test, y_pred_bow)
print("Accuracy with bag-of-words representation:", accuracy_bow)
# Add other evaluation metrics if needed

```

```
Accuracy with bag-of-words representation: 0.85
```

Figure 12.5: Bag of words

```python
from sklearn.feature_extraction.text import TfidfVectorizer

# Initialize TfidfVectorizer
tfidf_vectorizer = TfidfVectorizer(max_features=5000)  # You can adjust max_features as needed

# Transform text data into TF-IDF representation
X_train_tfidf = tfidf_vectorizer.fit_transform(X_train)
X_test_tfidf = tfidf_vectorizer.transform(X_test)

# Train logistic regression model with TF-IDF representation
lr_model_tfidf = LogisticRegression()
lr_model_tfidf.fit(X_train_tfidf, y_train)

# Evaluate model performance
y_pred_tfidf = lr_model_tfidf.predict(X_test_tfidf)
accuracy_tfidf = accuracy_score(y_test, y_pred_tfidf)
print("Accuracy with TF-IDF representation:", accuracy_tfidf)
# Add other evaluation metrics if needed

```

```
Accuracy with TF-IDF representation: 0.86
```

Figure 12.6: TF- IDF

```
1   # Assuming you have pre-trained word embeddings loaded (e.g., GloVe)
2   # Convert text data into word embeddings representation
3   # You may need to tokenize and pad sequences before applying word embeddings
4
5   # Train logistic regression model with word embeddings representation
6   lr_model_word_embeddings = LogisticRegression()
7   lr_model_word_embeddings.fit(X_train_word_embeddings, y_train)
8
9   # Evaluate model performance
10  y_pred_word_embeddings = lr_model_word_embeddings.predict(X_test_word_embeddings)
11  accuracy_word_embeddings = accuracy_score(y_test, y_pred_word_embeddings)
12  print("Accuracy with word embeddings representation:", accuracy_word_embeddings)
13  # Add other evaluation metrics if needed
14
```

```
-------------------------------------------------------------------------
NameError                              Traceback (most recent call last)
<ipython-input-20-8a483831a6f9> in <cell line: 7>()
      5 # Train logistic regression model with word embeddings representation
      6 lr_model_word embeddings = LogisticRegression()
----> 7 lr_model_word_embeddings.fit(X_train_word_embeddings, y_train)
      8
      9 # Evaluate model performance

NameError: name 'X_train_word_embeddings' is not defined
```

Figure 12.7: Word embedding – error

So, we will instruct ChatGPT to provide us with the corrected code for word embeddings, and we will also provide the context that we have done tokenization earlier but no embeddings:

[Prompt]

NameError Traceback (most recent call last) <ipython-input-20-8a483831a6f9> in <cell line: 7>() 5 # Train logistic regression model with word embeddings representation 6 lr_model_word_embeddings = LogisticRegression() ----> 7 lr_model_word_embeddings.fit(X_train_word_embeddings, y_train) 8 9 # Evaluate model performance NameError: name 'X_train_word_embeddings' is not defined. We haven't pretrained word embeddings but have tokenized it earlier. We tokenized the text using nltk.word_tokenize(), converted tokens to lowercase, removed stopwords and punctuation using list comprehensions, and then joined the tokens back into text. Finally, we applied the preprocess_text() function to the 'Review_body' column of the DataFrame and stored the preprocessed text in a new column called 'Cleaned_Review'.

[End of prompt]

We should receive the response with the modified code similar to the following:

Thank you for providing clarification. Since we have preprocessed the text data and tokenized it, we can represent it using word embeddings without pre-trained word embeddings. We'll use techniques like Word2Vec or Doc2Vec to generate word embeddings from the tokenized text.

Let's proceed with representing the text data using Word2Vec and then train a logistic regression model:

Word Embeddings Representation with Word2Vec:

```python
from gensim.models import Word2Vec
from sklearn.feature_extraction.text import CountVectorizer
from sklearn.base import BaseEstimator, TransformerMixin

# Define a custom transformer to tokenize the text data
class TokenizerTransformer(BaseEstimator, TransformerMixin):
    def fit(self, X, y=None):
        return self

    def transform(self, X):
        return [text.split() for text in X]

# Initialize and fit Word2Vec model on tokenized text data
w2v_model = Word2Vec(sentences=TokenizerTransformer().fit_transform(X_train),
min_count=1)

# Define a function to average word vectors for each document
def average_word_vectors(words, model, vocabulary, num_features):
    feature_vector = np.zeros((num_features,), dtype="float64")
    nwords = 0.

    for word in words:
        if word in vocabulary:
            nwords = nwords + 1.
            feature_vector = np.add(feature_vector, model.wv[word])

    if nwords:
        feature_vector = np.divide(feature_vector, nwords)

    return feature_vector
```

```
# Define a custom transformer to convert tokenized text data into word
embeddings representation
class WordEmbeddingsTransformer(BaseEstimator, TransformerMixin):
    def __init__(self, model):
        self.model = model
        self.num_features = model.vector_size
        self.vocabulary = set(model.wv.index_to_key)

    def fit(self, X, y=None):
        return self

    def transform(self, X):
        return np.array([average_word_vectors(words, self.model, self.
vocabulary, self.num_features) for words in X])

# Convert tokenized text data into word embeddings representation
X_train_word_embeddings = WordEmbeddingsTransformer(w2v_model).fit_
transform(TokenizerTransformer().fit_transform(X_train))
X_test_word_embeddings = WordEmbeddingsTransformer(w2v_model).
transform(TokenizerTransformer().transform(X_test))

# Train logistic regression model with word embeddings representation
lr_model_word_embeddings = LogisticRegression()
lr_model_word_embeddings.fit(X_train_word_embeddings, y_train)

# Evaluate model performance
y_pred_word_embeddings = lr_model_word_embeddings.predict(X_test_word_
embeddings)
accuracy_word_embeddings = accuracy_score(y_test, y_pred_word_embeddings)
print("Accuracy with word embeddings representation (Word2Vec):", accuracy_
word_embeddings)
# Add other evaluation metrics if needed
```

Explanation:

- We define a custom transformer TokenizerTransformer to tokenize the text data.
- We use the Word2Vec model to generate word embeddings from the tokenized text data.
- We define a function average_word_vectors to average word vectors for each document.
- We define another custom transformer WordEmbeddingsTransformer to convert tokenized text data into word embeddings representation.
- We train a logistic regression model using the word embeddings representation obtained from Word2Vec.
- Finally, we evaluate the performance of the model and print the accuracy.

You can run this code in your Jupyter Notebook to represent the text data using Word2Vec word embeddings and train a logistic regression model. Let me know if you need further assistance!

[End of response]

This time, the code works:

```
43
44   # Convert tokenized text data into word embeddings representation
45   X_train_word_embeddings = WordEmbeddingsTransformer(w2v_model).fit_transform(TokenizerTransformer().fit_transform(X_train))
46   X_test_word_embeddings = WordEmbeddingsTransformer(w2v_model).transform(TokenizerTransformer().transform(X_test))
47
48   # Train logistic regression model with word embeddings representation
49   lr_model_word_embeddings = LogisticRegression()
50   lr_model_word_embeddings.fit(X_train_word_embeddings, y_train)
51
52   # Evaluate model performance
53   y_pred_word_embeddings = lr_model_word_embeddings.predict(X_test_word_embeddings)
54   accuracy_word_embeddings = accuracy_score(y_test, y_pred_word_embeddings)
55   print("Accuracy with word embeddings representation (Word2Vec):", accuracy_word_embeddings)
56   # Add other evaluation metrics if needed
57
```

```
Accuracy with word embeddings representation (Word2Vec): 0.86
```

Figure 12.8: Accuracy with word embeddings

This concludes our last feature with the free version of ChatGPT.

Now, we will try some of these features using ChatGPT-4 or ChatGPT Plus.

Building a sentiment analysis model to accurately classify Amazon reviews using ChatGPT-4 or ChatGPT Plus

ChatGPT Plus or GPT-4 includes the ability to upload a dataset, analyze the dataset, and produce results if using simple libraries such as Python and matplotlib. At the time of writing this chapter, it had an AI assistant named **Data Analysis**, provided by OpenAI when using the mobile app, or when selecting GPT-4 if using the browser version.

Let's explore how it differs from the free version, feature by feature.

Feature 1: Data preprocessing and feature engineering

Let's craft our initial prompt for the baseline model:

[Prompt]

I want to create a simple classification model for sentiment analysis of the Amazon Review Dataset (TAG 1.1). <upload dataset in CSV format here> (PIC 2.3)

It should consist of the following steps (TAG 1.2) and I am a beginner user (PIC 2.1), so provide one step at a time and wait for users feedback (PIC 2.2)

- Data Preprocessing: Tokenization, lowercasing, removing stopwords and punctuation, and feature engineering (e.g., TF-IDF encoding, word embeddings).

- Model Selection: Choose baseline machine learning models such as logistic regression, Naive Bayes, or support vector machines (SVM).
- Model Evaluation and Interpretation.
- Handling Imbalance Data.
- Hyperparameter Tuning.
- Experimenting with feature representation.

[End of prompt]

You should receive a response similar to the following where ChatGPT-4 has loaded the dataset:

[Prompt response]

Great! We'll start by preprocessing the data from the Amazon Review Dataset. Here's how we can approach the preprocessing step:

- **Loading the Data**: We'll first load the dataset to understand its structure.
- **Tokenization**: This involves breaking down text into individual words or terms.
- **Lowercasing**: Convert all text to lowercase to ensure uniformity.
- **Removing Stopwords**: Stopwords are common words (like "and", "the", etc.) that are often filtered out before processing natural language data because they carry less meaningful information.
- **Removing Punctuation**: Punctuation is usually removed as it doesn't add much extra information while processing text.
- **Feature Engineering**: We'll apply TF-IDF encoding, which helps in understanding the importance of a word in a document relative to the corpus.

Let's start by loading your data and taking a look at its structure. I'll write a Python script to load the data and display the first few entries to better understand its columns and content. Let's proceed with this step, and once we see the data, we can move on to the next preprocessing tasks. Here's the script:

We've successfully loaded the dataset, and here's a quick look at its structure:

- `market_place, customer_id, review_id, product_id, product_parent`: These columns are identifiers and metadata about the review and product.
- `product_title, product_category`: Information about the product.
- `star_rating, helpful_votes, total_votes`: Ratings and votes data.
- `verified_purchase`: Whether the purchase was verified.
- `review_headline, review_body`: The actual text of the review.
- `review_date`: The date of the review.
- `sentiments`: This seems to be a label for sentiment analysis (positive, negative).

Given your focus is on sentiment analysis, the primary columns of interest will be `review_body` and `sentiments`.

Now, let's proceed with the preprocessing steps:

- Tokenization
- Lowercasing
- Removing Stopwords
- Removing Punctuation

We will handle these steps using the nltk library, which is commonly used for text processing in Python. Let me know if you're ready, and I'll start coding these preprocessing steps!

[End of response]

We can see that the dataset has been loaded successfully and ChatGPT-4 is waiting for the next step, the user's feedback (LIFE 3.3). So, we will instruct ChatGPT-4 to proceed to the next step:

[Prompt]

Let's proceed with data preprocessing.

[End of prompt]

We should receive a response like the following where ChatGPT understands the request and executes the code for data preprocessing:

[Prompt response]

Great! Let's start with the data preprocessing tasks one by one. Here's what we'll do:

- **Tokenization:** This will split the `review_body` text into individual words or tokens.
- **Lowercasing:** Convert all tokens to lowercase to standardize the text.
- **Removing Stopwords:** Remove common words that might not be useful in sentiment analysis.
- **Removing Punctuation:** Strip punctuation as it's typically not needed in text-based models.

I'll use the Natural Language Toolkit (nltk) for these steps. Let's begin by installing the necessary libraries and setting up the initial preprocessing functions. Here's the code to start:

It seems there was an issue with downloading the necessary resources from the NLTK library due to network restrictions in this environment. I'll modify the approach to manually define a small set of common stopwords for demonstration purposes. Let's proceed with a simplified version of the text preprocessing:

- Tokenization
- Lowercasing
- Removing a simplified set of stopwords
- Removing punctuation

Here's the adapted script that manually handles these steps without the need to download additional resources:

The text preprocessing has been successfully applied using a simplified approach. Here's a comparison of the original text and the processed text:

- **Original:** "As a family allergic to wheat, dairy, eggs, nuts..."
- **Processed:** ['a', 'family', 'allergic', 'wheat', 'dairy', 'eggs', 'nuts']

As you can see, we've removed stopwords, punctuation, and have tokenized and lowercased the text. This processed data is now more suitable for feeding into a machine learning model for sentiment analysis.

Next steps would involve converting these tokens into numerical features that can be used by machine learning algorithms. We can use methods like TF-IDF encoding or word embeddings for this. Let me know if you're ready to proceed to the feature engineering step, or if there's anything else you'd like to adjust in the preprocessing!

[End of response]

We can see from the response that ChatGPT-4 first tried with the NLTK library but due to limitations, it simplified the approach with a small set of common words. It also provides us with an example of how it is processed. We will now instruct ChatGPT-4 to proceed:

[Prompt]

Let's proceed.

[End of prompt]

We should receive a response like the following where ChatGPT-4 has implemented TF-IDF:

[Prompt response]

Great! Let's move on to the feature engineering step. In sentiment analysis, one common technique for converting text data into numerical form that can be understood by machine learning algorithms is the Term Frequency-Inverse Document Frequency (TF-IDF) approach. Here's a quick breakdown:

- **Term Frequency (TF):** Measures how frequently a term occurs in a document. Since documents may vary in length, it is often divided by the document length (the total number of terms in the document).
- **Inverse Document Frequency (IDF):** Measures how important a term is within the corpus (collection of all documents). It helps to weigh down terms that appear very frequently across documents and are less informative.

Step to Implement TF-IDF:

- **Convert the list of tokens to string:** Machine learning algorithms typically require input features as strings or numbers. We'll convert our list of tokens back to string format.
- **TF-IDF Vectorization:** Use TfidfVectorizer from scikit-learn to convert the text documents into a matrix of TF-IDF features.

I will now code these steps, starting by converting our token lists back to strings and then applying TF-IDF vectorization. Let's do this:

We've successfully transformed the processed text into a matrix of TF-IDF features. Here are some details:

- **Matrix Shape:** The TF-IDF matrix has 500 documents and 3778 features. This means we have 3778 unique terms across the documents after applying the preprocessing and vectorization steps.

- **Example Features:** Some of the first few terms in our feature set include 'ability', 'able', 'about', 'above', etc.

This TF-IDF matrix can now be used as input for various machine learning models to perform sentiment analysis.

Next, we can move on to selecting and training a baseline model using this feature representation. Common choices for initial models in sentiment analysis include Logistic Regression, Naive Bayes, and Support Vector Machines (SVM). Let me know which model you would like to start with, or if you have any preferences for proceeding!

[End of response]

We can see that ChatGPT-4 has implemented TF-IDF and has 500 documents and 3,778 features. We will now move on to baseline model creation.

Feature 2: Model selection and baseline training

We will now instruct ChatGPT-4 to proceed to model selection:

[Prompt]

Let's proceed with logistic regression.

[End of prompt]

We should receive a response like the following where ChatGPT understands the request and executes the code for logistic regression.

[Prompt response]

Perfect! Logistic Regression is a good starting point for classification tasks like sentiment analysis because it's simple and often provides a good baseline for performance comparison.

Steps to Implement Logistic Regression:

- **Prepare the data:** We'll split the data into training and testing sets to evaluate the model's performance.

- **Train the model:** We'll use Logistic Regression from `scikit-learn` to train the model using the training set.

- **Evaluate the model:** We'll test the model on the testing set to see how well it predicts the sentiments.

Let's start by preparing the data and then training the Logistic Regression model. Here's the code to do that:

The Logistic Regression model has been trained and evaluated. Here's a summary of its performance:

- **Accuracy:** 86%
- **Precision, Recall, and F1-Score:** These metrics provide a more detailed picture. For the 'positive' class, we see a precision and recall of 86% and 100% respectively, leading to an F1-score of 92%. However, for the 'negative' class, the precision, recall, and F1-score are all 0. This indicates that the model failed to correctly predict any of the 'negative' class instances.

This discrepancy is often due to class imbalance, where one class ('positive' in this case) is much more frequent than the other ('negative'), causing the model to be biased towards the majority class.

Next Steps:

- **Handling Imbalance Data:** We can explore techniques like oversampling the minority class, undersampling the majority class, or adjusting the decision threshold.
- **Hyperparameter Tuning:** We can tune the parameters of the Logistic Regression model to potentially improve performance.
- **Experimenting with Feature Representation:** Trying different settings in TF-IDF or using other types of text representations like word embeddings.

Would you like to explore any of these next steps further, such as addressing the imbalance in the dataset, or would you like to adjust something else?

[End of response]

Feature 3: Model evaluation and interpretation

Now that we have selected the logistic regression model and baseline performance is evaluated, let's interpret the results.

We will ask ChatGPT-4 to explain the metrics and provide results interpretation using techniques such as feature importance analysis and model explainability:

[Prompt]

Please explain the metrics and provide results interpretation using techniques such as feature importance analysis and model explainability.

[End of prompt]

We should receive a response like the following, where ChatGPT understood the request and provides us with the explanation and feature importance analysis:

[Prompt response]

Let's delve deeper into the evaluation metrics and explore some techniques to interpret the Logistic Regression model:

Evaluation Metrics Explanation:

- **Precision:** This measures the accuracy of positive predictions. Formally, it is the ratio of true positive predictions to the total predicted positives. High precision indicates a low false positive rate.
- **Recall (Sensitivity):** This is the ability of the model to find all the relevant cases (all true positives). It is the ratio of true positives to the actual total positives.
- **F1-Score:** The F1-score is the harmonic mean of precision and recall. It is a balance between precision and recall, a useful measure when the classes are imbalanced.
- **Accuracy:** This is the ratio of correctly predicted observations to the total observations. It's generally not a good measure for imbalanced classes as it can be misleading.

Results Interpretation:

- **Accuracy of 86%** sounds good, but it's misleading because the model performs poorly on the minority class ('negative').
- The model has a high recall (100%) for the 'positive' class, indicating it identifies most positive instances, but it fails completely to identify 'negative' class instances (recall of 0%).

Feature Importance Analysis:

- In Logistic Regression, the coefficients of the model can provide insight into the importance of features (words in this case). A higher absolute value of a coefficient indicates that the feature is more important for the decision the model makes.

Let's extract the coefficients of the model to see which words (features) are influencing the predictions most:

Here are the top 10 features (words) influencing the sentiment classification and their corresponding coefficients:

- **"not":** Coefficient of -1.87, a strong negative influence on the sentiment prediction. It suggests that the presence of "not" in a review significantly drives the prediction towards a negative sentiment.
- **"great":** Coefficient of 1.65, a strong positive influence, suggesting reviews with this word are likely classified as positive.
- **"love":** Coefficient of 1.54, another strong positive indicator.
- **"good":** Coefficient of 0.99, positively influences the sentiment.
- **"but":** Coefficient of -0.95, negatively influences the sentiment.
- **"very":** Coefficient of 0.88, generally used in positive contexts.
- **"was":** Coefficient of -0.86, showing a negative influence, possibly used in contexts of disappointment.
- **"cheap":** Coefficient of -0.81, commonly associated with negative sentiments.
- **"there":** Coefficient of -0.81, suggesting a negative context when this word is used.
- **"dont"** (likely meant to be "don't"): Coefficient of -0.79, another strong negative indicator.

Model Explainability:

These coefficients provide direct insight into how the model is making decisions based on the presence of certain words in the text. Words with positive coefficients increase the likelihood that a review is classified as positive, while those with negative coefficients push towards a negative classification.

If you want further interpretation, techniques like LIME (Local Interpretable Model-agnostic Explanations) or SHAP (SHapley Additive exPlanations) can be applied to provide more nuanced insights into specific predictions.

Would you like to dive deeper into any specific area, such as handling data imbalance or exploring model explainability techniques like LIME or SHAP for a particular prediction?

[End of response]

ChatGPT-4 cannot install new libraries like SHAP, so we will finish the feature analysis here and move on to the next step of handling data imbalance.

Feature 4: Handling data imbalance

Now, we will instruct ChatGPT-4 to work with data imbalance.

[Prompt]

Let's move on to handling data imbalance.

[End of prompt]

We should receive a response like the following:

[Prompt response]

Handling data imbalance is crucial in model training, especially in cases like yours where the dataset is heavily skewed towards one class. This skew can lead the model to predominantly predict the majority class, as we've seen with the Logistic Regression model.

Strategies to Handle Data Imbalance

1. **Resampling Techniques:**

    • **Oversampling the minority class:** This involves randomly duplicating examples in the minority class.

    • **Undersampling the majority class:** This reduces the number of examples in the majority class to balance with the minority class.

2. **Synthetic Data Generation:**

    • **SMOTE (Synthetic Minority Over-sampling Technique):** This technique generates synthetic samples from the minority class instead of creating copies.

3. **Modify Algorithm:**

    - **Adjust the decision threshold:** Moving the decision threshold can help increase the recall of the minority class.
    - Use algorithms that are inherently better at dealing with imbalanced data, such as Decision Trees or Random Forests.

4. **Cost-sensitive Learning:**

    - Assign a higher cost to misclassifications of the minority class to make the model pay more attention to it.

Given that we are using Logistic Regression, a good approach to start with could be to apply SMOTE to generate synthetic samples for the minority class and see if that improves model performance. We can also adjust the decision threshold to be more sensitive towards the minority class.

Let's start by applying SMOTE to the training data and then retraining the Logistic Regression model. I'll proceed with this approach:

It looks like the `imblearn` library, which includes SMOTE, isn't available in this environment. Given this limitation, we can explore other options:

- **Undersampling the Majority Class:** This would reduce the size of the 'positive' class to match the 'negative' class, though it can lead to a loss of potentially useful data.
- **Adjusting the Decision Threshold:** Instead of resampling, we can adjust the threshold for classifying a review as positive or negative to make the model more sensitive to the minority class.

Let's proceed with adjusting the decision threshold. This method involves modifying the probability threshold at which the model classifies a sample as 'positive'. By default, this threshold is set at 0.5. Lowering this threshold can help in identifying more samples as 'negative', potentially improving recall for the minority class.

I'll compute the probabilities of the class predictions and then adjust the threshold to see its effect on the classification metrics. Let's proceed with this approach:

Adjusting the decision threshold to 0.4 did not change the classification outcomes. The model still predicts all reviews as 'positive' with the same metrics as before, which suggests that we may need to either significantly lower the threshold or consider other methods due to the strong bias towards the 'positive' class.

Alternatives and Considerations:

- **Further Lower the Threshold:** We could continue to experiment with lower thresholds, although this might eventually lead to higher false positives.
- **Change the Model or Features:** Since logistic regression might be inherently limited in handling this imbalance, experimenting with different models or feature sets could be beneficial.
- **Data Resampling Manually:** If libraries for automated resampling like `imblearn` aren't available, we could manually undersample the 'positive' class or oversample the 'negative' class, albeit the latter without the sophistication of synthetic sample generation as in SMOTE.

Would you like to try further lowering the threshold, or should we explore manual resampling or perhaps a different modeling approach?

[End of response]

We see that adjusting the decision threshold didn't do much, so we will ask ChatGPT-4 to move on to the next feature of hyperparameter tuning.

Feature 5: Hyperparameter tuning

We will ask ChatGPT-4 to proceed with hyperparameter tuning:

[Prompt]

Let's proceed to hyperparameter tuning.

[End of prompt]

We should receive a response like the following:

[Prompt response]

Hyperparameter tuning is a critical step for improving the performance of a machine learning model. For Logistic Regression, some key hyperparameters that can be tuned include:

- **C (Inverse of regularization strength)**: Smaller values specify stronger regularization.
- **Solver**: Algorithm to use in the optimization problem (e.g., `liblinear`, `sag`, `saga`, `newton-cg`, etc.).
- **Penalty**: Specifies the norm used in the penalization (e.g., l1, l2).

We can use grid search with cross-validation to systematically explore multiple combinations of parameter values. This approach can help identify the best settings for these hyperparameters.

Implementing Hyperparameter Tuning

We will use `GridSearchCV` from `scikit-learn` to perform the hyperparameter tuning. We'll define a grid of potential values for `C` and `penalty`, and then train the model using different combinations of these values to find the best ones.

Let's set up and execute the grid search:

The hyperparameter tuning via grid search has identified the best parameters for the Logistic Regression model:

- **C (Inverse of regularization strength)**: 100, indicating less regularization.
- **Penalty**: 'l2', which is the L2 norm used in regularization.
- **Solver**: 'sag', which is an optimization algorithm suitable for large datasets.

The best cross-validated accuracy obtained with these settings is 80.5%. This suggests that reducing regularization (a higher value of C) helps the model to better fit the data.

Next Steps:

- **Evaluate the Model with the Best Parameters:** We can now evaluate this optimized model on the test set to see how it performs compared to the previous configuration.
- **Further Experimentation:** Depending on the results, we might consider further tuning or trying out different modeling techniques.

Shall we proceed by evaluating the model with these optimized parameters on the test set, or is there anything specific you would like to explore further?

[End of response]

We will instruct ChatGPT-4 to evaluate the model with optimized parameters on the test set:

[Prompt]

Sure, evaluate.

[End of prompt]

We should receive a response from ChatGPT-4 similar to the following:

[Prompt response]

The evaluation of the optimized Logistic Regression model with the best parameters yields the following results:

- **Overall Accuracy:** 84%
- **Precision and Recall for 'Negative' class:** Precision of 33% and recall of 14%.
- **Precision and Recall for 'Positive' class:** Precision of 87% and recall of 95%.

Interpretation:

- The overall accuracy has slightly decreased compared to the initial model (which had 86% accuracy), but we see an improvement in handling the 'negative' class:
- The model now correctly identifies some of the negative reviews, though the performance (14% recall) is still quite low, indicating that the model can detect a few negative instances but misses many.
- The precision for negative reviews is 33%, which means when the model predicts a review as negative, it is correct about one-third of the time.

Key Points:

- **Model Sensitivity to Negative Reviews:** There's a slight improvement in identifying negative reviews, which might be due to less regularization (higher C value) allowing the model to fit more closely to the minority class.
- **Balance between Classes:** The balance between sensitivity to both classes (macro average scores) is still not ideal, indicating that further adjustments or a different modeling approach may be necessary to adequately capture the characteristics of the minority class.

Further Actions:

- **Experiment with Other Models:** Given the inherent limitations of Logistic Regression with imbalanced datasets, considering other models like Decision Trees, Random Forest, or even ensemble methods might yield better results.

- **Adjust Thresholds or Resample Data:** These actions could be revisited or combined with different modeling techniques for potentially better handling of class imbalance.

Would you like to explore alternative models or techniques, or is there another aspect of the project you'd like to focus on?

[End of response]

We have seen that ChatGPT-4 has evaluated the performance and explained the results. We will now move on to the feature representation.

Feature 6: Experimenting with feature representation

Let's instruct ChatGPT to provide us with the code for different feature representations:

[Prompt]

I want to compare the performance of the model trained with different feature representations, such as bag-of-words, TF-IDF, or word embeddings, to determine the most effective approach for sentiment classification.

[End of prompt]

We should receive a response like the following where ChatGPT provides us with the code for bag-of-words, TF-IDF, and word embeddings:

[Prompt response]

Comparing different feature representations is an excellent approach to identify the most effective method for sentiment classification. Let's outline the feature representations we'll evaluate:

- **Bag-of-Words (BoW):** Counts the frequency of words within the documents.
- **TF-IDF:** We've already implemented this. It considers not only the frequencies but also how unique a word is to a document.
- **Word Embeddings:** Uses models like Word2Vec or pre-trained embeddings from GloVe to represent words in a dense vector space, capturing semantic meanings.

Step-by-Step Approach:

- **Implement Bag-of-Words:** We will use scikit-learn's `CountVectorizer` to convert text documents into a matrix of token counts.
- **Use Word Embeddings:** We'll apply a simple Word2Vec model using Gensim, or use pre-trained GloVe embeddings for a more straightforward implementation.
- **Train Logistic Regression on each representation:** For consistency, we'll use Logistic Regression for each feature set.

- **Compare Performance:** Evaluate each model using accuracy, precision, recall, and F1-score.

Let's start by implementing the Bag-of-Words model. Afterward, we'll proceed to the word embeddings. Here's the code for the Bag-of-Words model:

The Logistic Regression model trained with the Bag-of-Words (BoW) feature representation has the following performance metrics:

- **Overall Accuracy:** 86%
- **Precision and Recall for 'Negative' class:** Precision of 50% and recall of 21%.
- **Precision and Recall for 'Positive' class:** Precision of 88% and recall of 97%.
- **BoW Performance Interpretation:**

The BoW model shows a slight improvement in handling the negative class compared to the initial TF-IDF model, demonstrating higher precision though recall remains low. This indicates that while the model can identify negative reviews more accurately than before, it still misses many negative cases.

Next, let's implement the word embeddings feature representation using pre-trained GloVe embeddings for simplicity. This will provide us with a dense representation that captures semantic meanings, which might improve the classification, especially for the negative reviews.

Implementing Word Embeddings:

- **Load pre-trained GloVe Embeddings:** We'll use embeddings to convert text data into a dense vector form.
- **Average Word Embeddings:** For each review, we'll compute the average of the word embeddings to form a single vector that represents the entire review.

Let's proceed with loading and applying GloVe embeddings for sentiment classification:

It seems we've encountered a limitation with accessing the Gensim downloader, which is used to load pre-trained GloVe embeddings, due to the environment not having internet access.

Alternative Approach:

Since we can't use pre-trained GloVe embeddings, let's consider a simpler implementation of word embeddings using the Word2Vec model directly on our dataset. This will allow us to create our own embeddings based on the vocabulary present in the reviews.

Let's proceed by training a Word2Vec model on the processed reviews and then using the embeddings to represent each document. Here's how we'll do it:

The Logistic Regression model trained with Word2Vec embeddings generated the following results:

- **Overall Accuracy:** 86%
- **Precision and Recall for 'Negative' class:** Both precision and recall are 0%. The model failed to correctly identify any of the negative class instances.
- **Precision and Recall for 'Positive' class:** Precision of 86% and recall of 100%.

Interpretation of Word2Vec Model:

The performance of the Word2Vec model is similar to the original TF-IDF model in terms of accuracy and class-specific metrics. This similarity indicates that the model still heavily favors the majority class ('positive').

The zero recall and precision for the negative class suggest that despite using semantic-rich word embeddings, the imbalance in the dataset still heavily influences the model's predictions.

Summary and Recommendations:

- **BoW vs. TF-IDF vs. Word2Vec:** The Bag-of-Words model showed a slight improvement over TF-IDF and Word2Vec in terms of precision for the negative class. However, all models struggled with recall for the negative class, highlighting the impact of class imbalance.

- **Further Improvements:** Experimentation with ensemble methods, more sophisticated neural networks (e.g., LSTM, CNN for text), or further balancing techniques might be necessary to improve recall for the negative class.

- **Alternative Feature Engineering:** Additional feature engineering methods, such as n-grams, could be explored to capture more context, which might help in identifying negative sentiments more accurately.

Would you like to explore further adjustments, such as different machine learning models or additional balancing techniques, or would you like to focus on another aspect of your project?

[End of response]

This concludes our section on how to use ChatGPT-4 or ChatGPT Plus to implement and execute the sentiment analysis for the Amazon product review dataset.

Assignment

Generate synthetic data to handle the data imbalance.

Challenge

Try to improve the model performance to greater than 86% and feel free to use any technique.

Summary

The strategies outlined provided a systematic approach to experimenting with different techniques for building and training sentiment analysis models using the Amazon product review dataset. Each step was meticulously detailed, with code generation and user interaction tailored to a beginner-friendly experience, ensuring a comprehensive learning journey.

The task began with constructing a baseline sentiment analysis model. Initial steps included preprocessing text data by tokenizing, lowercasing, and removing stopwords and punctuation, followed by feature engineering using TF-IDF encoding.

Detailed Python code was provided in a Jupyter Notebook format, complete with explanations for each operation, ensuring that even beginners could follow along comfortably.

We explored baseline machine learning models, starting with logistic regression. The model was trained and evaluated, revealing a significant class imbalance that skewed predictions toward the majority class. This phase included detailed metrics analysis, such as accuracy, precision, recall, and F1-score, enhancing understanding of model performance beyond mere accuracy.

To address the data imbalance, techniques like adjusting the decision threshold and experimenting with synthetic data generation methods such as SMOTE were discussed. However, limitations in the environment prompted a shift to manual approaches like undersampling and threshold adjustments, which were implemented and tested to refine model sensitivity toward the minority class.

The learning process was enhanced by hyperparameter tuning using GridSearchCV, focusing on optimizing parameters like regularization strength and solver type. This step improved model performance and provided insights into the impact of model configuration on sentiment classification.

The experimentation extended to comparing different feature representations – bag-of-words, TF-IDF, and word embeddings – to determine their effectiveness in sentiment analysis. Each technique was implemented, and their impact on model performance was critically evaluated, revealing nuances in how different text representations affect the ability to discern sentiment.

Throughout the process, the strategy of waiting for user feedback before proceeding ensured that the learning was paced appropriately and that each step was clear. This approach facilitated a structured exploration of sentiment analysis techniques, from basic preprocessing to complex model tuning.

The journey concluded with a comprehensive understanding of building and optimizing sentiment analysis models. The structured, iterative approach – enhanced by continuous user engagement and feedback – allowed a deep dive into machine learning model development, from theoretical concepts to practical implementation.

This experience not only equipped the user with the knowledge to handle text data and model training but also highlighted the challenges and considerations in dealing with imbalanced datasets and choosing the right model and features for sentiment analysis.

In the next chapter, we will learn how to use ChatGPT to generate code for linear regression.

Join our community on Discord

Join our community's Discord space for discussions with the author and other readers:

https://packt.link/aicode

13

Building a Regression Model for Customer Spend with ChatGPT

Introduction

In the realm of data-driven decision making, understanding customer behavior is pivotal for optimizing business strategies. Building on our exploration of classification techniques, this chapter shifts focus to regression analysis, specifically linear regression, to predict numerical values such as a customer's annual spending. Linear regression helps us discover relationships within data, enabling predictions based on observed patterns.

This chapter will guide you through the process of building a predictive model that estimates annual spending by customers based on their interactions with a digital platform. We aim to deepen your understanding of linear regression, demonstrating how to prepare, process, and utilize datasets to construct accurate and reliable models.

As we progress, we will explore various techniques to enhance model accuracy and handle complex data scenarios:

- **Utilizing advanced regularization techniques** to improve model stability and performance.
- **Generating synthetic datasets** to better understand model behaviors under different data conditions.
- **Streamlining model development** with comprehensive, end-to-end coding examples.

By the end of this chapter, you will be well equipped with the knowledge and skills necessary to utilize linear regression for data-driven decision-making in your business. Let's embark on this journey into regression analysis to optimize customer engagement and revenue generation on our app or website.

In this chapter, we will:

- **Build a regression model with ChatGPT:** Readers will learn how ChatGPT can assist in generating Python code for building a regression model to predict the yearly amount spent by customers on our app or website using the dataset we have, offering a hands-on approach to understanding and interacting with datasets.
- **Apply prompting techniques:** Effective techniques will be introduced to craft prompts that guide ChatGPT in providing the most useful code snippets and insights for regression tasks.

Business problem

An e-commerce store seeks to optimize customer engagement and increase revenue by gaining deeper insights into customer behavior and preferences. By analyzing various customer attributes and their purchasing patterns, the store aims to tailor its marketing strategies, improve customer retention, and enhance the overall shopping experience.

Problem and data domain

We will employ regression techniques to understand the relationship between yearly spending and other parameters. **Regression** is a way to find out whether and how different factors (like time spent on an app or website) relate to how much customers spend in the online store. It helps us understand and predict customer behavior. By understanding which factors are most influential in driving sales, an e-commerce store can tailor its strategies to enhance these areas and potentially increase revenue.

Dataset overview

The e-commerce store collects the following information from the customer:

- **Email:** This is the customer's email address. It is a unique identifier for each customer and can be used for communication, such as sending order confirmations, newsletters, or personalized marketing offers.
- **Address:** This refers to the physical address of the customer. It's crucial for delivering products they have purchased. Additionally, address data can sometimes provide insights into geographical trends in sales and preferences.
- **Avatar:** This could be a digital representation or image chosen by the user. It might not directly impact sales or customer behavior, but it can be part of customer engagement strategies, adding a personal touch to user profiles.
- **Avg Session Length:** This is the average duration of all sessions combined, in minutes. This is like measuring how long a customer spends in your store each time they visit. Imagine someone walking around, looking at products for, say, 33 minutes on average.
- **Time on App:** This the duration of presence on the store's application, in minutes. Think of it as how long they are browsing through your app, maybe while they are on the bus or waiting in line at the coffee shop.

- **Time on Website:** This is similar to the time on the app, but this is for your website. If they're using a computer at home or work to look at your store, how long do they stay?

- **Length of Membership:** This is how long these customers have been with your store. Some might be new, while others have been shopping with you for years.

- **Yearly Amount Spent:** This is the total amount of money each customer spends at your store in a year, in dollars.

In the context of our dataset:

- **Email and address:** These should be used primarily for transactional purposes unless the customer has agreed to receive marketing communications. We will not use them for analysis.

- **Avatar:** This can be used to personalize the user experience but does not hold significant analytical value for sales predictions.

- **Other data:** Variables like "Time on App" and "Time on Website" can be analyzed to improve user experience and business strategies without infringing on personal privacy.

In summary, while data like email, address, and avatar can be valuable for business operations and customer engagement, they must be handled with a high degree of responsibility, prioritizing the privacy and preferences of the customers.

Note that the data used is not a real dataset and hence the emails, addresses, and so on are all made up.

Breaking the problem down into features

Given the nature of our dataset, which includes both independent variables (like "Avg. Session Length," "Time on App," "Time on Website," and "Length of Membership") and a dependent variable ("Yearly Amount Spent"), we will start with a simple regression technique with both ChatGPT and ChatGPT Plus or GPT-4. This will include the following high-level steps:

1. **Building the model step by step:** Users will understand the process of building a machine learning model step by step, including loading the dataset, splitting it into training and testing sets, training the model, making predictions, and evaluating its performance.

2. **Apply regularization techniques:** Users will learn how to apply regularization techniques such as Ridge regression and Lasso regression with cross-validation to improve the performance of a linear regression model. This includes initializing the models, training them using the training data, and evaluating their performance.

3. **Generate a synthetic dataset to add complexity:** Users will discover how to generate a synthetic dataset with added complexity using the `make_regression` function from the `sklearn.datasets` module. This involves specifying the number of samples, features, and noise levels to mimic real-world data.

4. **Generating code to develop a model in a single step for a synthetic dataset:** Users will see how to write end-to-end code in a single step to load the synthetic dataset, split it into training and testing sets, train a linear regression model, evaluate its performance, and print the evaluation metrics. This allows for a streamlined approach to model development and evaluation.

Prompting strategy

To leverage ChatGPT for machine learning, we need to have a clear understanding of how to implement the prompting strategies specifically for code generation for machine learning.

Let's brainstorm what we would like to achieve in this task to get a better understanding of what needs to go into the initial prompt.

Strategy 1: Task-Actions-Guidelines (TAG) prompt strategy

1.1 – Task: The specific task or goal is to create a simple linear regression model to predict the **"Yearly Amount Spent"** by dataset based on various attributes in the dataset.

1.2 – Actions: In this case, the strategy is to let ChatGPT decide the steps, hence no specific steps are provided.

1.3 – Guidelines: We will provide the following guidelines to ChatGPT in our prompt:

- The code should be compatible with Jupyter Notebook
- Ensure that there are detailed comments for each line of code.
- You have to explain each line of code, which will be then copied into the text block of the notebook in detail for each method used in the code before providing the code.

Strategy 2: Persona-Instructions-Context (PIC) prompt strategy

2.1 – Persona: We will adopt the persona of a beginner who needs to learn the different steps of model creation; hence the code should be generated step by step.

2.2 – Instructions: We have included the step to mount Google Drive explicitly since it's a common oversight.

2.3 – Context: The most important part is to provide the context of the dataset and exact field names to generate the code that can be executed directly, or to provide the dataset itself in the case of ChatGPT Plus.

Strategy 3: Learn-Improvise-Feedback-Evaluate (LIFE) prompt strategy

3.1 – Learn:

- We want to learn about linear regression and how it works.
- Understand feature engineering techniques and model evaluation metrics.
- We want to learn how to create a synthetic dataset.

3.2 – Improvise:

- We will use it later while applying regularization techniques.

3.3 – Feedback:

- If the code provided results in any errors, then feedback should be provided back to ChatGPT. We applied it in the Lasso and Ridge code execution using ChatGPT Plus.

3.4 – Evaluate:

- Execute the code provided by ChatGPT to ensure accuracy and validity. This is used throughout the chapter.

Building a simple linear regression model to predict the "Yearly Amount Spent" by customers using the free version of ChatGPT

When using the free version, it's important to give ChatGPT a clear description of the dataset first, which serves as an effective approach to generating code, followed by user evaluation. ChatGPT is already trained very well on Python and a machine learning algorithm; hence, we do not need to provide specific steps here. To verify that the generated code functions correctly, we will be using Google Colab.

Feature 1: Building the model step by step

Let's craft our initial prompt for the classification model.

[Prompt]

I want to create a simple linear regression model to predict the "Yearly Amount Spent" (TAG 1.1) by customers for the e-commerce customers dataset which consists of the following columns (PIC 2.3):

1. **Email:** The electronic mail unique to each customer, used here as an identification.
2. **Address:** The physical geographical location of each customer.
3. **Avatar:** This is the visual anonymity representation of the customers in the database.
4. **Avg. Session Length:** The average duration of all session combined in minutes.
5. **Time on App:** This the duration of presence on the stores' application, in minutes.
6. **Time on Website:** This is the time duration on the website of the store, in minutes.
7. **Length of Membership:** This is the amount of time a customer remains a registered user of the store's online resources.
8. **Yearly Amount Spent:** This is the cost implication of accessing the store's online resources, paid by the customers, in dollars.

I am a beginner user (PIC 2.1), so please provide step by step code and strictly follow following instructions (PIC 2.2):

- Code should be compatible with Jupyter notebook
- Ensure that there are detailed comments for each line of code.
- You have to explain each line of code, which will be then copied in the text block of the notebook in detail for each method used in code before providing the code.

- Also note that the dataset is placed in Google Drive at this path `'/content/drive/My Drive/Chapter05/Ecommerce Customers.csv '` (TAG 1.2).
- So, add the code to mount the drive, load the dataset, provide one step at a time, and wait for users feedback.

[End of prompt]

You should receive a response similar to the following.

⑨ **ChatGPT**

Sure, let's proceed step by step. First, we need to mount Google Drive in our Jupyter Notebook environment so we can access the dataset.

Here's how you can do it:

```python
from google.colab import drive

# Mount Google Drive
drive.mount('/content/drive')
```

Explanation:

- `from google.colab import drive`: This line imports the `drive` module from the `google.colab` package.
- `drive.mount('/content/drive')`: This command mounts your Google Drive at the specified path `/content/drive`. When you run this cell, it will prompt you to authenticate and give you a link to follow to get an authorization code. Once you enter the code, your Google Drive will be mounted.

Let me know if you have any questions before we proceed.

Figure 13.1: The initial response from ChatGPT

[Prompt response]

Sure, let's proceed step by step. First, we need to mount Google Drive in our Jupyter Notebook environment so we can access the dataset.

Here's how you can do it:

```
from google.colab import drive

# Mount Google Drive
drive.mount('/content/drive')
```

Explanation:

- `from google.colab import drive`: This line imports the `drive` module from the `google.colab` package.
- `drive.mount('/content/drive')`: This command mounts your Google Drive at the specified path `/content/drive`. When you run this cell, it will prompt you to authenticate and give you a link to follow to get an authorization code. Once you enter the code, your Google Drive will be mounted.

Let me know if you have any questions before we proceed.

[End of response]

We will now apply the evaluate prompting strategy and validate the code by executing the code in Google Colab for every step. The code runs perfectly fine and mounts Google Drive.

Please note that it requires permission to access the drive and would prompt the user.

Please refer to the notebook `Learning simple regression with ChatGPT.ipynb` for the executable code snippets or copy the code from the prompt response.

Running your cell, you should see a message that says "Mounted at /content/drive as a result of calling drive.mount."

We will now instruct ChatGPT to proceed to the next step:

[Prompt]

Let's proceed

[End of prompt]

We should receive a response similar to the following to load the dataset into the notebook:

[Prompt response]

Great! Now that we have mounted Google Drive, we can load the dataset into our notebook.

Here's how you can load the dataset:

```python
import pandas as pd

# Define the file path
file_path = '/content/drive/My Drive/Chapter05/Ecommerce Customers.csv'

# Load the dataset into a DataFrame
ecommerce_data = pd.read_csv(file_path)

# Display the first few rows of the DataFrame
print(ecommerce_data.head())
```

Explanation:

- `import pandas as pd`: This line imports the pandas library and aliases it as `pd`, which is a common convention.
- `file_path = '/content/drive/My Drive/Chapter05/Ecommerce Customers.csv'`: This line defines the file path where the dataset is located in your Google Drive.
- `pd.read_csv(file_path)`: This function reads the CSV file located at the specified path and creates a DataFrame from it.
- `print(ecommerce_data.head())`: This line prints the first few rows of the DataFrame to verify that the dataset has been loaded correctly.

Let me know if you have any questions or if you'd like to proceed to the next step!

[End of response]

We executed the code provided by ChatGPT in the notebook and it loads the dataset from the defined path and prints the first few rows. As we had given the path of the file in the initial prompt, we don't need to change anything in the code and it runs perfectly fine. The takeaway is that we need to be specific with file paths and locations where required.

```
[2]   1   import pandas as pd
      2
      3   # Define the file path
      4   file_path = '/content/drive/My Drive/Chapter05/Ecommerce Customers.csv'
      5
      6   # Load the dataset into a DataFrame
      7   ecommerce_data = pd.read_csv(file_path)
      8
      9   # Display the first few rows of the DataFrame
     10   print(ecommerce_data.head())
```

```
                           Email  \
0        mstephenson@fernandez.com
1                hduke@hotmail.com
2               pallen@yahoo.com
3         riverarebecca@gmail.com
4    mstephens@davidson-herman.com

                                    Address            Avatar  \
0         835 Frank Tunnel\nWrightmouth, MI 82180-9605        Violet
1         4547 Archer Common\nDiazchester, CA 06566-8576     DarkGreen
2    24645 Valerie Unions Suite 582\nCobbborough, D...        Bisque
3       1414 David Throughway\nPort Jason, OH 22070-1220   SaddleBrown
4    14023 Rodriguez Passage\nPort Jacobville, PR 3...  MediumAquaMarine

   Avg. Session Length  Time on App  Time on Website  Length of Membership  \
0            34.497268    12.655651        39.577668              4.082621
1            31.926272    11.109461        37.268959              2.664034
2            33.000915    11.330278        37.110597              4.104543
3            34.305557    13.717514        36.721283              3.120179
4            33.330673    12.795189        37.536653              4.446308

   Yearly Amount Spent
0           587.951054
1           392.204933
2           487.547505
3           581.852344
4           599.406092
```

Figure 13.2: Loading the dataset

Next, we'll provide the output to ChatGPT and then proceed to *Step 1*. In this instance, we've employed the strategy of providing additional context to ChatGPT by presenting the output textually.

It is important to note that since we are utilizing GPT-3.5, which lacks the capability to execute code or process images, we are limited to providing textual outputs from the notebook:

[Prompt]

```
Here is the output -                          Email  \
0        mstephenson@fernandez.com
1               hduke@hotmail.com
2               pallen@yahoo.com
3         riverarebecca@gmail.com
4   mstephens@davidson-herman.com


                                      Address           Avatar  \
0       835 Frank Tunnel\nWrightmouth, MI 82180-9605        Violet
1     4547 Archer Common\nDiazchester, CA 06566-8576     DarkGreen
2   24645 Valerie Unions Suite 582\nCobbborough, D...        Bisque
3    1414 David Throughway\nPort Jason, OH 22070-1220    SaddleBrown
4   14023 Rodriguez Passage\nPort Jacobville, PR 3... MediumAquaMarine


   Avg. Session Length  Time on App  Time on Website  Length of Membership  \
0            34.497268    12.655651        39.577668              4.082621
1            31.926272    11.109461        37.268959              2.664034
2            33.000915    11.330278        37.110597              4.104543
3            34.305557    13.717514        36.721283              3.120179
4            33.330673    12.795189        37.536653              4.446308


   Yearly Amount Spent
0           587.951054
1           392.204933
2           487.547505
3           581.852344
4           599.406092
```

[End of prompt]

We anticipate receiving a response similar to the following, wherein ChatGPT will offer guidance on the subsequent steps. Initially, we refrained from specifying any particular steps in the initial prompt, opting instead to allow ChatGPT to determine the subsequent course of action:

[Prompt response]

Great! The dataset has been loaded successfully. Now, we can proceed with building our linear regression model to predict the "Yearly Amount Spent" by customers.

The steps involved in building a simple linear regression model are as follows:

- **Data Preparation**: Split the dataset into input features (X) and the target variable (y).
- **Split Data**: Split the dataset into training and testing sets.
- **Model Initialization**: Create a linear regression model object.
- **Model Training**: Fit the model to the training data.
- **Model Evaluation**: Evaluate the model's performance using the testing data.

Let's start with *step 1*:

Step 1: Data Preparation:

```
# Extract input features (X) and target variable (y)
X = ecommerce_data[['Avg. Session Length', 'Time on App', 'Time on Website',
'Length of Membership']]
y = ecommerce_data['Yearly Amount Spent']
```

Explanation:

- `X = ecommerce_data[['Avg. Session Length', 'Time on App', 'Time on Website', 'Length of Membership']]`: This line selects the input features (`'Avg. Session Length'`, `'Time on App'`, `'Time on Website'`, `'Length of Membership'`) from the dataset and assigns them to the variable X.
- `y = ecommerce_data['Yearly Amount Spent']`: This line selects the target variable `'Yearly Amount Spent'` from the dataset and assigns it to the variable y.

Let me know if you have any questions or if you'd like to proceed to the next step!

[End of response]

ChatGPT has outlined the steps it will adhere to for code generation. Furthermore, it has furnished the code for the initial step, data preparation, wherein the dataset is divided into features and the target variable. Notably, it adeptly discerned the features by excluding email addresses, avatars, and addresses. Additionally, it precisely employed the column names as stipulated in the description provided in the initial prompt. The strategy employed here involves including the dataset column names in the prompt to ensure compatibility with the generated code. Hence, the code executes without any modifications or errors.

```
[ ]   1   # Extract input features (X) and target variable (y)
      2   X = ecommerce_data[['Avg. Session Length', 'Time on App', 'Time on Website', 'Length of Membership']]
      3   y = ecommerce_data['Yearly Amount Spent']
```

Figure 13.3: Step 1 – data preparation

Next, we will instruct ChatGPT to proceed:

[Prompt]

Let's proceed to the next step.

[End of prompt]

We should receive a response similar to the following to split the data along with the explanation:

[Prompt response]

Great! Now that we have prepared our data by separating the input features (X) and the target variable (y), we can proceed to the next step, which is splitting the data into training and testing sets.

Step 2: Split Data:

```python
from sklearn.model_selection import train_test_split

# Split the data into training and testing sets (80% train, 20% test)
X_train, X_test, y_train, y_test = train_test_split(X, y, test_size=0.2,
random_state=42)

# Display the shapes of the training and testing sets
print("Training set shape - X_train:", X_train.shape, "y_train:", y_train.
shape)
print("Testing set shape - X_test:", X_test.shape, "y_test:", y_test.shape)
```

Explanation:

- `from sklearn.model_selection import train_test_split`: This line imports the `train_test_split` function from the `sklearn.model_selection` module, which is used to split the dataset into training and testing sets.
- `train_test_split(X, y, test_size=0.2, random_state=42)`: This function splits the input features (X) and the target variable (y) into training and testing sets. The `test_size` parameter specifies the proportion of the dataset to include in the testing set (in this case, 20% for testing). The `random_state` parameter is used for reproducibility, ensuring that the same random split is generated each time the code is run.
- `X_train, X_test, y_train, y_test`: These variables hold the training and testing sets for the input features (X) and the target variable (y), respectively.
- `print("Training set shape - X_train:", X_train.shape, "y_train:", y_train.shape)`: This line prints the shapes of the training set input features (X_train) and target variable (y_train).
- `print("Testing set shape - X_test:", X_test.shape, "y_test:", y_test.shape)`: This line prints the shapes of the testing set input features (X_test) and target variable (y_test).

Let me know if you have any questions or if you'd like to proceed to the next step!

[End of response]

The code executed successfully, and the data was split into training and testing sets with the expected 80-20 ratio. Notably, we did not explicitly specify the ratio, yet ChatGPT defaulted to the standard 80-20 split.

```
[ ]   1   from sklearn.model_selection import train_test_split
      2
      3   # Split the data into training and testing sets (80% train, 20% test)
      4   X_train, X_test, y_train, y_test = train_test_split(X, y, test_size=0.2, random_state=42)
      5
      6   # Display the shapes of the training and testing sets
      7   print("Training set shape - X_train:", X_train.shape, "y_train:", y_train.shape)
      8   print("Testing set shape - X_test:", X_test.shape, "y_test:", y_test.shape)

    Training set shape - X_train: (400, 4) y_train: (400,)
    Testing set shape - X_test: (100, 4) y_test: (100,)
```

Figure 13.4: Step 2 – split the data

Next, we will provide the output of the previous step to ChatGPT, which should let ChatGPT know about the shape and it should also provide us the code for the next step:

[Prompt]

```
Training set shape - X_train: (400, 4) y_train: (400,)
Testing set shape - X_test: (100, 4) y_test: (100,)
```

[End of prompt]

We should receive a response similar to the following where the model is initialized:

[Prompt response]

Perfect! We have successfully split our dataset into training and testing sets. The training set contains 400 samples, while the testing set contains 100 samples. Each sample consists of four input features and one target variable.

Now, let's proceed to the next step, which is initializing our linear regression model.

Step 3: Model Initialization:

```
from sklearn.linear_model import LinearRegression

# Initialize the linear regression model
model = LinearRegression()
```

Explanation:

- `from sklearn.linear_model import LinearRegression`: This line imports the `LinearRegression` class from the `sklearn.linear_model` module, which is used to create a linear regression model.

- `model = LinearRegression()`: This line initializes a linear regression model object and assigns it to the variable model.

Let me know if you have any questions or if you'd like to proceed to the next step!

[End of response]

The code is executed perfectly fine without any errors. Necessary imports are also provided by ChatGPT.

```
[ ]   1   from sklearn.linear_model import LinearRegression
      2
      3   # Initialize the linear regression model
      4   model = LinearRegression()
```

Figure 13.5: Step 3 – model initialization

We'll simply direct ChatGPT to continue. It's worth noting that because our initial prompt included the instruction to provide step-by-step code, we don't need to tailor our subsequent prompts to each individual step or task. Instead, we'll allow ChatGPT to lead us, providing it with the outputs from the preceding steps as necessary:

[Prompt]

Let's proceed.

[End of prompt]

We should receive a response similar to the following to train the model:

[Prompt response]

Great! Now that we have initialized our linear regression model, we can move on to the next step, which is training the model using the training data.

Step 4: Model Training:

```
# Train the linear regression model using the training data
model.fit(X_train, y_train)
```

Explanation:

- `model.fit(X_train, y_train)`: This line fits (or trains) the linear regression model using the training data. The `fit` method takes the input features (`X_train`) and the corresponding target variable (`y_train`) as arguments and adjusts the model's parameters to minimize the difference between the actual and predicted values.

Now that our model has been trained, we can proceed to the final step, which is evaluating the model's performance using the testing data.

Let me know if you have any questions or if you'd like to proceed!

[End of response]

We will execute the code and that should train the model.

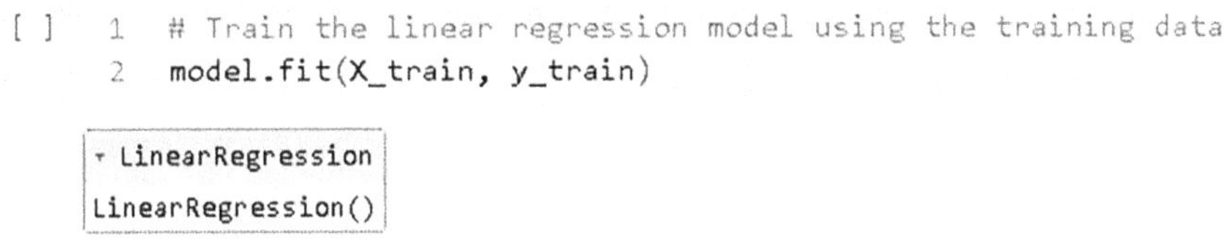

```
[ ]   1   # Train the linear regression model using the training data
      2   model.fit(X_train, y_train)
```

```
▾ LinearRegression
LinearRegression()
```

Figure 13.6: Step 4 – model training

We will instruct ChatGPT to proceed:

[Prompt]

Let's proceed

[End of prompt]

We should receive a response similar to the following to evaluate the performance of the model using test data:

[Prompt response]

Great! Now that our linear regression model has been trained, we can evaluate its performance using the testing data.

Step 5: Model Evaluation:

```python
# Make predictions on the testing data
y_pred = model.predict(X_test)

# Evaluate the model's performance
from sklearn.metrics import mean_squared_error, r2_score

# Calculate Mean Squared Error (MSE)
mse = mean_squared_error(y_test, y_pred)

# Calculate R-squared (coefficient of determination)
r_squared = r2_score(y_test, y_pred)

# Print the evaluation metrics
```

```
print("Mean Squared Error (MSE):", mse)
print("R-squared (Coefficient of Determination):", r_squared)
```

Explanation:

- `model.predict(X_test)`: This line uses the trained model to make predictions on the input features (`X_test`), which generates the predicted values of the target variable.

- `from sklearn.metrics import mean_squared_error, r2_score`: This line imports the `mean_squared_error` and `r2_score` functions from the `sklearn.metrics` module, which are used to evaluate the model's performance.

- `mean_squared_error(y_test, y_pred)`: This function calculates the mean squared error (MSE) between the actual target variable (`y_test`) and the predicted values (`y_pred`).

- `r2_score(y_test, y_pred)`: This function calculates the R-squared (coefficient of determination) between the actual target variable (`y_test`) and the predicted values (`y_pred`).

- `print("Mean Squared Error (MSE):", mse)`: This line prints the mean squared error (MSE), which measures the average squared difference between the actual and predicted values. A lower MSE indicates better model performance.

- `print("R-squared (Coefficient of Determination):", r_squared)`: This line prints the R-squared value, which represents the proportion of the variance in the target variable that is explained by the model. A higher R-squared value (closer to 1) indicates better fit.

These evaluation metrics will help us assess how well our linear regression model is performing in predicting the "Yearly Amount Spent" by customers.

Let me know if you have any questions or if you'd like further explanation on any part!

[End of response]

We execute the code and it runs perfectly fine without any errors and prints the **mean-squared error (MSE)** and the coefficient of determination (`R-squared`).

```
[ ]   1   # Make predictions on the testing data
      2   y_pred = model.predict(X_test)
      3
      4   # Evaluate the model's performance
      5   from sklearn.metrics import mean_squared_error, r2_score
      6
      7   # Calculate Mean Squared Error (MSE)
      8   mse = mean_squared_error(y_test, y_pred)
      9
     10   # Calculate R-squared (coefficient of determination)
     11   r_squared = r2_score(y_test, y_pred)
     12
     13   # Print the evaluation metrics
     14   print("Mean Squared Error (MSE):", mse)
     15   print("R-squared (Coefficient of Determination):", r_squared)

Mean Squared Error (MSE): 109.8637411839399
R-squared (Coefficient of Determination): 0.9778130629184127
```

Figure 13.7: Model evaluation output

For those new to machine learning, it's crucial to assess whether the model performance meets acceptable standards. Once more, we'll seek assistance from ChatGPT and furnish it with the output for evaluation:

[Prompt]

```
Mean Squared Error (MSE): 109.8637411839399
R-squared (Coefficient of Determination): 0.9778130629184127
```

[End of prompt]

We should receive a response from ChatGPT explaining the results, which suggests that our model is actually performing very well given that R-squared is very close to 1:

[Prompt response]

The evaluation metrics indicate that our linear regression model performs quite well on the testing data:

- **Mean Squared Error (MSE):** The MSE value is approximately 109.86. This indicates that, on average, the squared difference between the actual and predicted values of the "Yearly Amount Spent" is around 109.86. Lower MSE values are desirable, indicating better model performance.
- **R-squared (Coefficient of Determination):** The R-squared value is approximately 0.978. This indicates that approximately 97.8% of the variance in the "Yearly Amount Spent" can be explained by the linear regression model. A higher R-squared value closer to 1 suggests that the model provides a better fit to the data.

Overall, these evaluation metrics suggest that our linear regression model is performing well in predicting the "Yearly Amount Spent" by customers based on the provided input features.

If you have any further questions or need additional assistance, feel free to ask!

[End of response]

Having now acquired proficiency in utilizing ChatGPT to construct a linear regression model incrementally, we'll transition to the second feature and delve into the application of regularization techniques. While our current model exhibits satisfactory performance, regularization can prove invaluable, particularly in scenarios where the model is either underfitted or overfitted.

Feature 2: Applying regularization techniques

We will use the learn and improvise prompting strategy (LIFE 3.1 and 3.2) with ChatGPT to understand whether the model could be overfitted and what should be done in such a case:

[Prompt]

Could the model be overfitting?

[End of prompt]

We receive the response from ChatGPT indicating that it is unlikely that our model is overfitted but it does suggest some things to consider such as regularization techniques and cross-validation:

[Prompt response]

It's essential to consider the possibility of overfitting when interpreting the model's performance. Overfitting occurs when the model learns to capture noise or random fluctuations in the training data, rather than the underlying relationships between the input features and the target variable. This can result in a model that performs well on the training data but generalizes poorly to unseen data.

Here are a few indicators that suggest overfitting may be occurring:

- **Large Discrepancy Between Training and Testing Performance:** If the model performs significantly better on the training data compared to the testing data, it may be overfitting. In our case, if the MSE and R-squared values are much better on the training set than on the testing set, it could indicate overfitting.

- **Complexity of the Model:** Overly complex models with a large number of parameters relative to the size of the training data are more prone to overfitting. Linear regression is relatively simple, but if you were using a more complex model (e.g., polynomial regression with high-degree polynomials), it could increase the risk of overfitting.

- **Regularization Techniques:** Regularization techniques like Lasso or Ridge regression can be applied to mitigate overfitting by penalizing large coefficients. If overfitting is suspected, applying regularization may help improve the model's generalization performance.

- **Cross-Validation:** Using cross-validation techniques, such as k-fold cross-validation, can provide a more robust estimate of the model's performance by evaluating it on multiple train-test splits of the data. If the model's performance varies significantly across different splits, it could indicate overfitting.

In our case, with a high R-squared value and a relatively low MSE on the testing data, it's less likely that the model is overfitting. However, it's always a good practice to explore these indicators and consider additional steps to ensure the model's generalization performance. If you suspect overfitting, you could try simplifying the model, applying regularization techniques, or using cross-validation to further evaluate its performance.

[End of response]

We will ask ChatGPT to apply regularization and cross-validation techniques:

[Prompt]

Let's try applying regularization techniques first and then cross-validation

[End of prompt]

ChatGPT should provide us with the code to apply either Lasso or Ridge along with cross-validation and also the explanation:

[Prompt response]

Sure! Let's start by applying regularization techniques to our linear regression model. Two common regularization techniques are Lasso regression (L1 regularization) and Ridge regression (L2 regularization). These techniques add a penalty term to the loss function, which helps prevent overfitting by penalizing large coefficients.

We'll begin by trying Ridge regression, which adds the squared sum of the coefficients (L2 norm) to the loss function.

Here's how you can implement Ridge regression with cross-validation:

```python
from sklearn.linear_model import RidgeCV

# Initialize the Ridge regression model with cross-validation
ridge_model = RidgeCV(alphas=[0.1, 1.0, 10.0], cv=5)

# Train the Ridge regression model
ridge_model.fit(X_train, y_train)

# Make predictions on the testing data
ridge_y_pred = ridge_model.predict(X_test)

# Evaluate the model's performance
ridge_mse = mean_squared_error(y_test, ridge_y_pred)
ridge_r_squared = ridge_model.score(X_test, y_test)

# Print the evaluation metrics
print("Ridge Regression - Mean Squared Error (MSE):", ridge_mse)
print("Ridge Regression - R-squared (Coefficient of Determination):", ridge_r_
squared)
print("Ridge Regression - Best Alpha:", ridge_model.alpha_)
```

Explanation:

- `RidgeCV(alphas=[0.1, 1.0, 10.0], cv=5)`: This initializes a Ridge regression model with cross-validation. The `alphas` parameter specifies the regularization strength (alpha values) to be tested, and `cv` specifies the number of folds for cross-validation.
- `ridge_model.fit(X_train, y_train)`: This trains the Ridge regression model using the training data.
- `ridge_model.predict(X_test)`: This makes predictions on the testing data using the trained Ridge regression model.
- `ridge_mse = mean_squared_error(y_test, ridge_y_pred)`: This calculates the mean squared error (MSE) between the actual and predicted values using Ridge regression.
- `ridge_model.score(X_test, y_test)`: This calculates the R-squared value (coefficient of determination) using Ridge regression.
- `ridge_model.alpha_`: This attribute returns the best alpha (regularization strength) selected by cross-validation.

Let me know if you'd like to proceed with Ridge regression or if you have any questions!

[End of response]

Let's try executing the code and see whether it works and shows any improvement.

```
[ ]    1    from sklearn.linear_model import RidgeCV
       2
       3    # Initialize the Ridge regression model with cross-validation
       4    ridge_model = RidgeCV(alphas=[0.1, 1.0, 10.0], cv=5)
       5
       6    # Train the Ridge regression model
       7    ridge_model.fit(X_train, y_train)
       8
       9    # Make predictions on the testing data
      10    ridge_y_pred = ridge_model.predict(X_test)
      11
      12    # Evaluate the model's performance
      13    ridge_mse = mean_squared_error(y_test, ridge_y_pred)
      14    ridge_r_squared = ridge_model.score(X_test, y_test)
      15
      16    # Print the evaluation metrics
      17    print("Ridge Regression - Mean Squared Error (MSE):", ridge_mse)
      18    print("Ridge Regression - R-squared (Coefficient of Determination):", ridge_r_squared)
      19    print("Ridge Regression - Best Alpha:", ridge_model.alpha_)
      20

Ridge Regression - Mean Squared Error (MSE): 109.82024999312038
Ridge Regression - R-squared (Coefficient of Determination): 0.9778218459464064
Ridge Regression - Best Alpha: 0.1
```

Figure 13.8: Ridge regression

The code is compatible with previously provided code and the output is very similar to the linear regression code. But note that ChatGPT doesn't need any specific instructions and it could generate a perfectly fine executable code. Next, we will provide ChatGPT with the output and see what it suggests:

[Prompt]

```
Ridge Regression - Mean Squared Error (MSE): 109.82024999312038
Ridge Regression - R-squared (Coefficient of Determination): 0.9778218459464064
Ridge Regression - Best Alpha: 0.1
```

[End of prompt]

In this case, ChatGPT has interpreted the results and also provided the code for Lasso regression with cross-validation. The response may vary depending on the suggestions provided by ChatGPT in previous interactions:

[Prompt response]

It looks like the Ridge regression model with cross-validation performed quite similarly to the standard linear regression model. The **Mean Squared Error** (MSE) and R-squared values are very close to those obtained from the standard linear regression model.

The best alpha selected by cross-validation for the Ridge regression model is 0.1, indicating that a small amount of regularization was applied to the model.

Since the performance of Ridge regression with cross-validation is comparable to that of the standard linear regression model, we can conclude that regularization did not significantly improve the model's performance in this case.

Next, let's try using Lasso regression (L1 regularization) with cross-validation to see if it yields any improvement:

```
from sklearn.linear_model import LassoCV

# Initialize the Lasso regression model with cross-validation
lasso_model = LassoCV(alphas=[0.1, 1.0, 10.0], cv=5)

# Train the Lasso regression model
lasso_model.fit(X_train, y_train)

# Make predictions on the testing data
lasso_y_pred = lasso_model.predict(X_test)

# Evaluate the model's performance
lasso_mse = mean_squared_error(y_test, lasso_y_pred)
lasso_r_squared = lasso_model.score(X_test, y_test)

# Print the evaluation metrics
print("Lasso Regression - Mean Squared Error (MSE):", lasso_mse)
print("Lasso Regression - R-squared (Coefficient of Determination):", lasso_r_
squared)
print("Lasso Regression - Best Alpha:", lasso_model.alpha_)
```

Let me know if you'd like to proceed with Lasso regression or if you have any questions!

[End of response]

We will execute the code and see whether it works and produces any different results than Ridge regression.

```
[ ]   1   from sklearn.linear_model import LassoCV
      2
      3   # Initialize the Lasso regression model with cross-validation
      4   lasso_model = LassoCV(alphas=[0.1, 1.0, 10.0], cv=5)
      5
      6   # Train the Lasso regression model
      7   lasso_model.fit(X_train, y_train)
      8
      9   # Make predictions on the testing data
     10   lasso_y_pred = lasso_model.predict(X_test)
     11
     12   # Evaluate the model's performance
     13   lasso_mse = mean_squared_error(y_test, lasso_y_pred)
     14   lasso_r_squared = lasso_model.score(X_test, y_test)
     15
     16   # Print the evaluation metrics
     17   print("Lasso Regression - Mean Squared Error (MSE):", lasso_mse)
     18   print("Lasso Regression - R-squared (Coefficient of Determination):", lasso_r_squared)
     19   print("Lasso Regression - Best Alpha:", lasso_model.alpha_)

Lasso Regression - Mean Squared Error (MSE): 109.77575439252612
Lasso Regression - R-squared (Coefficient of Determination): 0.9778308318145387
Lasso Regression - Best Alpha: 0.1
```

Figure 13.9: Lasso regression

Lasso regression with cross-validation also produced similar results to both the standard linear regression and Ridge regression models. The MSE and R-squared values are very close to those obtained previously.

However, it's important to note that the dataset used here may not be complex enough to benefit significantly from regularization techniques. In cases where the dataset is larger or more complex, regularization may play a more crucial role in preventing overfitting and improving model generalization.

Let's move to the next feature to generate a synthetic dataset for our problem to add complexity.

Feature 3: Generating a synthetic dataset to add complexity

We will use the conversation style with ChatGPT and ask it to provide code to generate a synthetic dataset:

[Prompt]

Can you please provide me a code to generate the synthetic dataset for it to add complexity?

[End of prompt]

You may receive a variant of the following response. However, you may notice that this is generic code and is not suitable for generating the code specific to our dataset. Hence, we will need to refine the prompt by providing feedback to ChatGPT:

[Prompt response]

Sure! We can generate a synthetic dataset with additional complexity using the `make_regression` function from the `sklearn.datasets` module. This function generates a random regression problem with specified characteristics, such as the number of samples, the number of features, and the noise level.

Here's how you can generate a synthetic dataset with added complexity:

```python
from sklearn.datasets import make_regression
import pandas as pd


# Generate synthetic dataset with 500 samples, 10 features, and increased noise
X_synthetic, y_synthetic = make_regression(n_samples=500, n_features=10,
noise=50, random_state=42)


# Create a DataFrame from the synthetic dataset
synthetic_data = pd.DataFrame(X_synthetic, columns=[f'Feature_{i}' for i in
range(1, 11)])
synthetic_data['Target'] = y_synthetic


# Display the first few rows of the synthetic dataset
print(synthetic_data.head())


# Save the synthetic dataset to a CSV file
synthetic_data.to_csv('synthetic_dataset.csv', index=False)
```

Explanation:

- `make_regression(n_samples=500, n_features=10, noise=50, random_state=42)`: This function generates a synthetic regression dataset with 500 samples, 10 features, and increased noise level (specified by the noise parameter). The `random_state` parameter ensures reproducibility.
- `pd.DataFrame(X_synthetic, columns=[f'Feature_{i}' for i in range(1, 11)])`: This creates a DataFrame from the synthetic input features (`X_synthetic`) and assigns column names `'Feature_1'` to `'Feature_10'`.
- `synthetic_data['Target'] = y_synthetic`: This adds the synthetic target variable (`y_synthetic`) to the DataFrame with the column name `'Target'`.
- `synthetic_data.to_csv('synthetic_dataset.csv', index=False)`: This saves the synthetic dataset to a CSV file named `'synthetic_dataset.csv'` without including the `index` column.

You can adjust the parameters of the `make_regression` function to control the complexity of the synthetic dataset, such as the number of samples, the number of features, and the noise level.

Let me know if you need further assistance!

[End of response]

We will simply instruct ChatGPT that we need the code for our dataset:

[Prompt]

No, I meant for our problem.

[End of prompt]

Let's see what ChatGPT suggests and whether it really works:

[Prompt response]

Got it! We can create a synthetic dataset for our problem by using the same input features as the original dataset but with added complexity. We'll generate additional features that are nonlinear combinations of the original features and add noise to mimic real-world data.

Here's how you can generate a synthetic dataset with added complexity for our problem:

```python
import numpy as np
import pandas as pd

# Set random seed for reproducibility
np.random.seed(42)

# Number of samples
n_samples = 500

# Generate synthetic input features
avg_session_length = np.random.normal(loc=30, scale=5, size=n_samples)
time_on_app = np.random.normal(loc=15, scale=5, size=n_samples)
time_on_website = np.random.normal(loc=20, scale=7, size=n_samples)
length_of_membership = np.random.normal(loc=3, scale=1, size=n_samples)

# Generate synthetic target variable (linear combination of input features with
noise)
yearly_amount_spent = 100 + (avg_session_length * 10) + (time_on_app * 20) +
(time_on_website * 15) + (length_of_membership * 30) + np.random.normal(loc=0,
scale=50, size=n_samples)

# Create a DataFrame from the synthetic dataset
synthetic_data = pd.DataFrame({
    'Avg. Session Length': avg_session_length,
    'Time on App': time_on_app,
```

```
    'Time on Website': time_on_website,
    'Length of Membership': length_of_membership,
    'Yearly Amount Spent': yearly_amount_spent
})


# Display the first few rows of the synthetic dataset
print(synthetic_data.head())


# Save the synthetic dataset to a CSV file
synthetic_data.to_csv('synthetic_ecommerce_data.csv', index=False)
```

Explanation:

*   We generate synthetic input features (avg_session_length, time_on_app, time_on_website, length_of_membership) using normal distributions with specified mean and standard deviation to mimic the characteristics of the original dataset.
*   We generate the synthetic target variable (yearly_amount_spent) as a linear combination of the input features with added noise.
*   Finally, we create a DataFrame from the synthetic dataset and save it to a CSV file.

This synthetic dataset will have similar characteristics to the original dataset but with added complexity, which can be useful for testing models and understanding their performance in more challenging scenarios.

Let me know if you need further clarification or assistance!

[End of response]

The code looks impressive and is adapted to our dataset. On executing, it runs without any errors and generates a CSV file named synthetic_ecommerce_data.csv and stores it in the runtime environment of the notebook. It also prints the first few rows. You can also download it for future use.

Next, we will request ChatGPT to generate the complete code and evaluate model performance with the added noise in the synthetic dataset. Let's move to our next feature.

Feature 4: Generating code to develop a model in a single step for a synthetic dataset

We have learned how to create a regression model step by step in previous features, hence we will now request ChatGPT to provide the entire code in a single step for the synthetic dataset:

[Prompt]

Now provide me the end-to-end code in a single step to run using the generated synthetic dataset.

[End of prompt]

We should receive a response similar to the following where complete code is provided, including loading the dataset, splitting the dataset, model training, and model evaluation:

[Prompt response]

Certainly! Below is the end-to-end code that loads the synthetic dataset, splits it into training and testing sets, trains a linear regression model, evaluates its performance, and prints the evaluation metrics.

```python
import pandas as pd
from sklearn.model_selection import train_test_split
from sklearn.linear_model import LinearRegression
from sklearn.metrics import mean_squared_error, r2_score

# Load the synthetic dataset
synthetic_data = pd.read_csv('synthetic_ecommerce_data.csv')

# Extract input features (X) and target variable (y)
X = synthetic_data[['Avg. Session Length', 'Time on App', 'Time on Website',
'Length ot Membership']]
y = synthetic_data['Yearly Amount Spent']

# Split the dataset into training and testing sets (80% train, 20% test)
X_train, X_test, y_train, y_test = train_test_split(X, y, test_size=0.2,
random_state=42)

# Initialize the linear regression model
model = LinearRegression()

# Train the linear regression model using the training data
model.fit(X_train, y_train)

# Make predictions on the testing data
y_pred = model.predict(X_test)

# Evaluate the model's performance
mse = mean_squared_error(y_test, y_pred)
r_squared = r2_score(y_test, y_pred)

# Print the evaluation metrics
print("Mean Squared Error (MSE):", mse)
print("R-squared (Coefficient of Determination):", r_squared)
```

This code will load the synthetic dataset from the CSV file, split it into training and testing sets, train a linear regression model using the training data, make predictions on the testing data, evaluate the model's performance using Mean Squared Error (MSE) and R-squared (Coefficient of Determination), and print the evaluation metrics.

You can simply run this code in your Python environment, assuming you have the pandas library installed to work with DataFrames and the scikit-learn library installed for machine learning functionalities.

Let me know if you have any questions or if there's anything else I can assist you with!

[End of response]

We execute the code and it runs seamlessly.

The evaluation metrics for the linear regression model trained on the synthetic dataset are as follows:

- **MSE:** Approximately 2103.19
- **R-squared (coefficient of determination):** Approximately 0.9197

These metrics provide insight into the model's performance:

- **MSE:** The MSE measures the average squared difference between the actual and predicted values. In this case, the MSE indicates that, on average, the squared difference between the actual and predicted yearly amount spent is approximately 2103.19. Lower MSE values are desirable, indicating better model performance.
- **R-squared (coefficient of determination):** The R-squared value represents the proportion of the variance in the target variable (Yearly Amount Spent) that is explained by the model. In this case, the R-squared value of approximately 0.9197 suggests that approximately 91.97% of the variance in the yearly amount spent can be explained by the linear regression model. A higher R-squared value closer to 1 indicates a better fit.

Overall, these evaluation metrics suggest that the linear regression model performs reasonably well on the synthetic dataset.

In the context of the online e-commerce store, the insights from these models can be used for various purposes:

- **Customer segmentation:** The models can help identify high-value customers based on their predicted Yearly Amount Spent, allowing for targeted marketing efforts.
- **Recommendation systems:** Understanding the factors that influence spending can be used to improve product recommendations and enhance the customer shopping experience.
- **Retention strategies:** Length of Membership appears to be an important factor. Strategies to increase customer retention and loyalty can be developed based on this insight.
- **Optimizing website and app:** Insights into the impact of Average Session Length, Time on App, and Time on Website can guide decisions on website and app optimization.

This concludes our learning with ChatGPT 3.5. Now, let's see how prompting and learning differ with ChatGPT Plus.

Learning simple linear regression using ChatGPT Plus

Now that we have learned about simple linear regression while using ChatGPT, let's learn about linear regression while using ChatGPT Plus. ChatGPT Plus, or GPT-4, includes the ability to upload datasets, analyze the dataset, and produce results if using simple libraries such as Python and Matplotlib. At the time of writing this chapter, it had a GPT assistant named **Data Analysis**, provided by OpenAI when using the mobile app. You could also select GPT-4 if using the browser version.

Note that you can also achieve the same using the free version but would need to execute the code yourself and modify the prompt.

Feature 1: Building a simple linear regression model step by step

We have learned how to create a regression model step by step using the free version of ChatGPT where we had to provide the dataset description, instructions on from where to load, and code compatible with Jupyter Notebook. In the case of ChatGPT Plus, all of that is taken care of by ChatGPT Plus and it also provides a runtime environment to execute the code.

Note that it cannot run TensorFlow, Keras, or deep learning libraries:

[Prompt]

I want to create a simple linear regression model to predict the "Yearly Amount Spent" (TAG 1.1) by customers for the attached e-commerce customers dataset (PIC 2.3)

I am a beginner user (PIC 2.1), so please provide step-by-step code and strictly follow the following instructions (PIC 2.2):

• Ensure that there are detailed comments for each line of code.

• You have to explain each line of code and provide one step at a time and wait for users feedback

[End of prompt]

We should receive a response similar to the following where the complete code is provided, including loading the dataset, splitting the dataset, model training, and model evaluation:

[Prompt response]

Great! Let's start building a simple linear regression model using Python. We'll be using libraries such as `pandas` for handling the data and `sklearn` for creating the regression model.

Step 1: Import Libraries and Load Data

First, we'll import necessary libraries and load your dataset. We'll also take a look at the first few rows of the dataset to understand its structure.

Here's the code for this step:

```python
# Import necessary libraries
import pandas as pd  # pandas is used for data manipulation and analysis
```

```
from sklearn.model_selection import train_test_split  # This function is used
to split data into training and testing sets
from sklearn.linear_model import LinearRegression  # This class is used to
perform linear regression
from sklearn.metrics import mean_absolute_error, mean_squared_error  # These
functions are used to evaluate the model

# Load the dataset
data = pd.read_csv('/mnt/data/Ecommerce Customers (1).csv')  # Reading the CSV
file into a pandas DataFrame

# Display the first few rows of the dataset to understand its structure
print(data.head())
```

This block of code does the following:

- **Imports libraries:** We load `pandas` for data handling, and several modules from `sklearn` for splitting the data and performing linear regression.
- **Loads the data:** The `pd.read_csv` function reads the CSV file into a DataFrame, which is a 2-dimensional labeled data structure with columns of potentially different types.
- **Prints the first few rows:** This helps us see the initial rows of our dataset to understand the available data and its format.

Let's execute this step and check the output to ensure everything is loaded correctly and to understand what your data looks like. Shall we proceed?

[End of response]

We will instruct ChatGPT to proceed:

[Prompt]

Yes, please.

[End of prompt]

We should receive a response similar to the following, where ChatGPT has executed the code and printed the first few rows.

Note that the file is loaded in ChatGPT's run time environment; if you need to execute code in your local environment or Jupyter Colab, you would be required to modify the step to read CSV:

[Prompt response]

Here's the snapshot of the first few rows of your dataset:

Email	Address	Avatar	Avg. Session Length	Time on App	Time on Website	Length of Member-ship	Yearly Amount Spent
mste-phen-son@fernandez.com	835 Frank Tunnel Wrightmouth, MI 82180-9605	Violet	34.497268	12.655651	39.577668	4.082621	587.951054
hduke@hotmail.com	4547 Archer Common Di-azchester, CA 06566-8576	Dark-Green	31.926272	11.109461	37.268959	2.664034	392.204933
pallen@yahoo.com	24645 Valerie Unions Suite 582 Cobbbor-ough, ...	Bisque	33.000915	11.330278	37.110597	4.104543	487.547505
river-arebec-ca@gmail.com	1414 David Throughway Port Jason, OH 22070-1220	Saddle-Brown	34.305557	13.717514	36.721283	3.120179	581.852344
mste-phens@david-son-her-man.com	14023 Rodri-guez Passage Port Jacob-ville, PR 3...	Mediu-mAqua-Marine	33.330673	12.795189	37.536653	4.446308	599.406092

The dataset includes both customer contact information (like Email and Address) and numerical data related to their interaction with the e-commerce platform (like "Avg. Session Length", "Time on App", "Time on Website", and "Length of Membership").

Step 2: Data Preparation

The next step will involve preparing the data for our linear regression model. This includes:

- Selecting the relevant numerical columns for the prediction.
- Splitting the data into a training set and a testing set.

Do you have any specific columns you want to use for predicting "Yearly Amount Spent", or should I proceed with a general approach using all numerical columns?

[End of response]

We will instruct ChatGPT to proceed using numerical columns:

[Prompt]

Please use only numerical columns.

[End of prompt]

We should receive a response similar to the following, where ChatGPT has provided code for selecting the features, splitting the dataset, and printing the shape:

[Prompt response]

Step 2: Data Preparation

We'll now proceed with the following steps in preparing the data:

- **Selecting the relevant columns:** We'll include the columns that are numerical and directly relate to customer behavior.

- **Splitting the data into training and testing sets:** This helps us evaluate our model on unseen data to ensure it performs well generally.

Here's the code to perform these steps:

```python
# Selecting only the numerical columns for features
features = data[['Avg. Session Length', 'Time on App', 'Time on Website',
'Length of Membership']]

# Selecting the target column which is 'Yearly Amount Spent'
target = data['Yearly Amount Spent']

# Splitting the dataset into training and testing sets
# We allocate 80% of the data for training and 20% for testing
X_train, X_test, y_train, y_test = train_test_split(features, target, test_
size=0.2, random_state=42)

# Printing the shapes of the training and testing sets to verify the split
print(f'Training features shape: {X_train.shape}')
print(f'Testing features shape: {X_test.shape}')
print(f'Training labels shape: {y_train.shape}')
print(f'Testing labels shape: {y_test.shape}')
```

This block of code:

- **Selects features and target:** We separate the columns for the features and the target variable which is what we aim to predict.
- **Splits the data:** Using `train_test_split`, we divide the data into training and testing sets. The `test_size=0.2` means 20% of the data is reserved for testing. `random_state` is set for reproducibility of results.
- **Prints shapes:** We print the shapes of our training and testing sets to confirm the split was successful.

Should we run this part of the code to prepare the data and check the split?

[End of response]

We will instruct ChatGPT to proceed with code execution:

[Prompt]

Yes, please.

[End of prompt]

We should receive a response similar to the following, where ChatGPT has executed the code and printed the shape of features and labels:

[Prompt response]

The data has been successfully split into training and testing sets. Here's the breakdown:

- **Training features shape:** 400 rows and 4 columns
- **Testing features shape:** 100 rows and 4 columns
- **Training labels shape:** 400 values
- **Testing labels shape:** 100 values

This indicates that 80% of the data is used for training the model, and 20% is reserved for testing the model's performance.

Step 3: Building the Linear Regression Model

Now, we'll create and train the linear regression model using the training data. Here's the plan:

- **Initialize the linear regression model:** This involves setting up our model ready to be fitted to the data.
- **Fit the model to the training data:** This is where the model learns the relationship between the features and the target from the training data.
- **Evaluate the model on the training data:** This step is to get a quick check on how well our model has learned from the training data.

Shall I proceed with this next step and show you the code to build and evaluate the model on the training data?

[End of response]

We will instruct ChatGPT to proceed to the next steps:

[Prompt]

Yes, Please.

[End of prompt]

We should receive a response similar to the following, where ChatGPT has provided the code:

[Prompt response]

Let's move on to building and training the linear regression model.

Step 3: Building the Linear Regression Model

Here's the code to create, train, and initially evaluate the linear regression model:

```python
# Initialize the Linear Regression model
model = LinearRegression()

# Fit the model to the training data
# This involves finding the best fitting line to the provided data points
model.fit(X_train, y_train)

# Evaluate the model by predicting on the training set
train_predictions = model.predict(X_train)

# Calculate the Mean Absolute Error (MAE) on the training set
# MAE measures the average magnitude of the errors in a set of predictions,
# without considering their direction
train_mae = mean_absolute_error(y_train, train_predictions)

# Calculate the Mean Squared Error (MSE) on the training set
# MSE measures the average of the squares of the errors—that is, the average
# squared difference between the estimated values and the actual value
train_mse = mean_squared_error(y_train, train_predictions)

# Printing the errors to understand model performance on the training data
print(f'Mean Absolute Error on training data: {train_mae}')
print(f'Mean Squared Error on training data: {train_mse}')
```

This code does the following:

- **Initializes the model:** `LinearRegression()` is called to create a linear regression model.
- **Fits the model:** `model.fit(X_train, y_train)` adjusts weights on the regression line to fit the input features and the target output.
- **Makes predictions:** `model.predict(X_train)` is used to see how well the model has learned to predict the training data.
- **Calculates errors:** `mean_absolute_error` and `mean_squared_error` provide metrics to gauge the model's accuracy and performance by comparing the predicted values against the actual values.

Would you like me to run this code now to see how the model performs on the training data?

[End of response]

We will instruct ChatGPT to proceed:

[Prompt]

Yes, Please.

[End of prompt]

We should receive a response similar to the following, where ChatGPT has executed the code and printed the results:

[Prompt response]

The linear regression model has been successfully trained on the dataset, and here are the performance metrics on the training data:

Mean Absolute Error (MAE) on training data: 7.727

Mean Squared Error (MSE) on training data: 95.823

These metrics help us understand the average errors made by the model in predictions:

- **MAE** tells us that, on average, the model's predictions are approximately 7.73 units away from the actual values.
- **MSE** indicates a slightly larger error in the predictions, considering it squares the errors, emphasizing larger discrepancies.

Next Steps:

Now, the model is trained and preliminarily evaluated on the training set. We should now test its performance on the unseen testing set to truly evaluate its effectiveness.

Would you like to proceed with testing the model on the testing set and seeing how it performs with new data?

[End of response]

We will instruct ChatGPT to proceed with testing the model performance on the test set:

[Prompt]

Yes, please.

[End of prompt]

We should receive a response similar to the following, where ChatGPT has executed the code and printed the results:

[Prompt response]

The evaluation of the model on the testing set yielded the following results:

- **Mean Absolute Error (MAE) on testing data:** 8.558
- **Mean Squared Error (MSE) on testing data:** 109.864

These results tell us the following:

- The **MAE** of 8.558 suggests that the model's predictions on the testing data are, on average, about 8.56 units away from the actual values. This is slightly worse than the training MAE, which is to be expected as the model is now predicting data it hasn't seen before.
- The **MSE** of 109.864 is also higher than the training MSE, indicating that some predictions have larger errors.

Summary:

The model performs reasonably well but shows a typical behavior of slightly reduced performance on the testing data compared to the training data. This is normal and indicates that the model is generalizing as expected without significant overfitting or underfitting.

Final Steps:

You now have a functioning linear regression model that can predict the "Yearly Amount Spent" based on customer behavior metrics. Depending on your goals, you might want to explore further:

- **Improving the model:** You could look into more sophisticated modelling techniques or feature engineering.
- **Model interpretation:** Analyse the coefficients of the model to understand the impact of each feature.

Would you like to explore any of these additional steps or need further assistance with something else?

[End of response]

We have seen that similar to the free version, ChatGPT Plus does a pretty good job in creating a simple linear regression model step by step, by providing the code as well as executing it for us. Next, we will see whether the Plus version can apply the regularization techniques.

Feature 2: Applying regularization techniques

We will ask ChatGPT Plus to apply regularization techniques:

[Prompt]

Can you please apply Lasso, Ridge, and cross-validation to check whether it leads to any improvement?

[End of prompt]

We should receive a response similar to the following, where ChatGPT has provided the code for Lasso and Ridge, along with cross-validation:

[Prompt response]

Step 5: Applying Lasso and Ridge Regression with Cross-Validation

Lasso Regression:

- Lasso regression not only helps in reducing overfitting but can also be used for feature selection since it can shrink the coefficients of less important features to zero.

Ridge Regression:

- Ridge regression reduces the model complexity by imposing a penalty on the size of coefficients.

We'll use the scikit-learn library, which provides convenient functions to perform these analyses.

Here's the code to apply Lasso and Ridge with cross-validation:

```python
from sklearn.linear_model import LassoCV, RidgeCV
from sklearn.model_selection import cross_val_score

# Lasso Regression with Cross-Validation
lasso_cv = LassoCV(alphas=[0.1, 1.0, 10.0], cv=5)  # cv=5 means 5-fold cross-validation
lasso_cv.fit(X_train, y_train)
lasso_cv_score = lasso_cv.score(X_test, y_test)
lasso_cv_mae = mean_absolute_error(y_test, lasso_cv.predict(X_test))

# Ridge Regression with Cross-Validation
ridge_cv = RidgeCV(alphas=[0.1, 1.0, 10.0], cv=5)
ridge_cv.fit(X_train, y_train)
ridge_cv_score = ridge_cv.score(X_test, y_test)
ridge_cv_mae = mean_absolute_error(y_test, ridge_cv.predict(X_test))

# Printing results
print(f'Lasso CV Score: {lasso_cv_score}, MAE: {lasso_cv_mae}')
print(f'Ridge CV Score: {ridge_cv_score}, MAE: {ridge_cv_mae}')
```

This code performs the following:

- **LassoCV and RidgeCV:** These are Lasso and Ridge regression methods with built-in cross-validation of the alpha parameter.
- **Cross-validation scores:** The .score() method returns the R^2 score that indicates the proportion of variance in the dependent variable that is predictable from the independent variables.
- **Mean Absolute Error:** This provides an absolute measure of fit quality on the testing set.

Let's run this code to see if the regularization and cross-validation can enhance the model's performance. Shall we proceed?

[End of response]

We will instruct ChatGPT to execute the code:

[Prompt]

Yes, please.

[End of prompt]

[Prompt response]

In our scenario, ChatGPT encountered an internal error and was unable to execute the code. Such errors can occur due to various reasons, including unavailability of services at the time of execution, memory issues, or the absence of required libraries or dependencies in its runtime environment. It's important to note that you might receive a different response that executes the code flawlessly, as errors like these are sporadic. However, we've included this scenario to troubleshoot and illustrate how to proceed in such cases. Here, we have applied the prompting strategy to get feedback from the AI assistant (LIFE 3.3).

[End of response]

We will now take the suggestion from ChatGPT and execute the code locally using Jupyter Colab, and since we are loading the dataset from Google Drive, we will provide the instructions in the prompt:

[Prompt]

Ok, give me complete code to run locally and note that the file needs to be mounted from Google Drive from path '/content/drive/My Drive/Chapter05/Ecommerce Customers.csv' in the Jupyter notebook.

[End of prompt]

We should receive a response similar to the following, where ChatGPT has provided the complete code:

[Prompt response]

Certainly! Below is the complete code that you can run locally in a Jupyter Notebook. This script includes steps for importing the dataset directly from Google Drive, preprocessing the data, fitting both Lasso and Ridge regression models with cross-validation, and then evaluating them.

```python
# Import necessary libraries
import pandas as pd
from sklearn.model_selection import train_test_split
from sklearn.linear_model import LinearRegression, LassoCV, RidgeCV
from sklearn.metrics import mean_absolute_error, mean_squared_error
from sklearn.preprocessing import StandardScaler

# Mount Google Drive (specific to Google Colab)
from google.colab import drive
drive.mount('/content/drive')

# Load the dataset from Google Drive
file_path = '/content/drive/My Drive/Chapter05/Ecommerce Customers.csv'
data = pd.read_csv(file_path)

# Select only the numerical columns for features and the target column
features = data[['Avg. Session Length', 'Time on App', 'Time on Website',
'Length of Membership']]
target = data['Yearly Amount Spent']

# Splitting the dataset into training and testing sets (80% train, 20% test)
X_train, X_test, y_train, y_test = train_test_split(features, target, test_
size=0.2, random_state=42)

# Standardizing the data
scaler = StandardScaler()
X_train_scaled = scaler.fit_transform(X_train)
X_test_scaled = scaler.transform(X_test)

# Initialize and fit the Linear Regression model
model = LinearRegression()
model.fit(X_train_scaled, y_train)

# Lasso Regression with Cross-Validation
lasso_cv = LassoCV(alphas=[0.01, 0.1, 1.0, 10.0], cv=5)
lasso_cv.fit(X_train_scaled, y_train)
lasso_cv_score = lasso_cv.score(X_test_scaled, y_test)
lasso_cv_mae = mean_absolute_error(y_test, lasso_cv.predict(X_test_scaled))

# Ridge Regression with Cross-Validation
ridge_cv = RidgeCV(alphas=[0.01, 0.1, 1.0, 10.0], cv=5)
```

```
ridge_cv.fit(X_train_scaled, y_train)
ridge_cv_score = ridge_cv.score(X_test_scaled, y_test)
ridge_cv_mae = mean_absolute_error(y_test, ridge_cv.predict(X_test_scaled))

# Print results
print(f'Linear Regression Test MAE: {mean_absolute_error(y_test, model.
predict(X_test_scaled))}')
print(f'Lasso CV Score: {lasso_cv_score}, MAE: {lasso_cv_mae}')
print(f'Ridge CV Score: {ridge_cv_score}, MAE: {ridge_cv_mae}')
```

Instructions for Running the Code:

- **Google Colab Specifics:** The `drive.mount()` function is specific to Google Colab and allows you to access files on your Google Drive. If you are not using Google Colab, you will need to adjust the file loading method according to your development environment.
- **Dependencies:** Ensure you have all required libraries installed. You can install them using `pip` (e.g., `pip install pandas scikit-learn google-colab`).
- **Data Path:** Adjust the `file_path` if your file is located in a different directory on your Google Drive.

Run this code in your Jupyter Notebook environment to see how the models perform with your data. If you encounter any errors or need further assistance, feel free to reach out!

[End of response]

We execute the code and it runs perfectly fine without any modifications or errors. Here, we learned that we can use the hybrid approach of running code within ChatGPT Plus or request it to provide the code to execute locally in case of any issues.

Next, we will move on to Feature 3 of generating a synthetic dataset using ChatGPT Plus.

Feature 3: Generating a synthetic dataset to add complexity

Now, let's try, if we are able, to generate a synthetic dataset using ChatGPT Plus for our dataset. For this purpose, we will use the Data Analyst GPT and start a fresh conversation.

Note that specific GPTs can be invoked by providing @`<GPT Name>` in the message prompt:

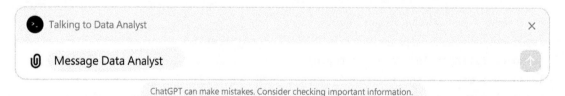

Figure 13.10: Invoking the Data Analyst GPT

[Prompt]

@Data Analyst – Provide me the code to generate the synthetic dataset for the above dataset from the perspective of predicting `Yearly Amount Spent`, along with the code to generate it. <Attach the dataset file here>

[End of prompt]

We should receive a response similar to the following, where ChatGPT has provided the code and printed the first few rows:

[Prompt response]

To help you generate a synthetic dataset for predicting yearly amount spent, I'll first need to take a look at the structure and content of your provided dataset. Let's start by loading and examining the data from your file. I'll display the first few rows and summary statistics to understand what kind of features we're dealing with. Then, I'll assist you in creating a synthetic dataset based on this structure. Let's get started with loading the data.

The dataset consists of 500 entries with the following features:

- **Email:** The customer's email address (string).
- **Address:** The customer's address (string).
- **Avatar:** The avatar color (string).
- **Avg. Session Length:** Average session length in minutes (numeric).
- **Time on App:** Time spent on the app in minutes (numeric).
- **Time on Website:** Time spent on the website in minutes (numeric).
- **Length of Membership:** Length of membership in years (numeric).
- **Yearly Amount Spent:** Yearly amount spent in dollars (numeric).

To create a synthetic dataset for the purpose of modeling and predicting "Yearly Amount Spent", we can use a technique called **bootstrapping,** which involves sampling with replacement from the existing dataset to create a new synthetic dataset that has a similar distribution. However, to add some variability and simulate a realistic dataset, we can also introduce random noise into the numeric fields.

Here's a Python code snippet to generate a synthetic dataset using bootstrapping and adding noise to the numeric columns:

```python
import numpy as np

# Number of samples for the synthetic dataset
num_samples = 500

# Bootstrap the original dataset
synthetic_data = data.sample(n=num_samples, replace=True)

# Add random noise to numeric columns
```

```
numeric_columns = ['Avg. Session Length', 'Time on App', 'Time on Website',
'Length of Membership', 'Yearly Amount Spent']
noise_factor = 0.05  # 5% noise

for column in numeric_columns:
    noise = np.random.normal(loc=0.0, scale=noise_factor * synthetic_
data[column].std(), size=num_samples)
    synthetic_data[column] += noise

# Optionally save the synthetic dataset to a new CSV file
synthetic_data.to_csv('/mnt/data/Synthetic_Ecommerce_Customers.csv',
index=False)

synthetic_data.head()
```

This code will:

- Sample 500 entries from the original dataset, allowing replacements (bootstrapping).
- Add Gaussian noise to each numeric column based on 5% of the standard deviation of that column.
- Optionally, the new synthetic dataset can be saved to a CSV file.

Would you like to proceed with generating this synthetic dataset? Or do you have any modifications or specific requirements to include in the synthesis process?

[End of response]

Next, we will instruct ChatGPT to generate the code and provide us with the file to download the dataset:

[Prompt]

Please generate the dataset and make it available to download.

[End of prompt]

We should receive a response similar to the following, where ChatGPT has executed the code and provided the link to download the synthetic dataset:

[Prompt response]

The synthetic dataset has been generated and saved. You can download it using the link below:

```
[Download Synthetic Ecommerce Customers Dataset](sandbox:/mnt/data/Synthetic_
Ecommerce_Customers.csv)
```

[End of response]

Here, we learned that ChatGPT Plus can provide the code, execute the code, and also generate CSV files available to download.

Next, we will request ChatGPT Plus to generate the complete code and evaluate model performance with the added noise in the synthetic dataset. Let's move to our next feature.

Feature 4: Generating code to develop a model in a single step for a synthetic dataset

[Prompt]

Can you please generate the complete code to perform linear regression, apply Lasso and Ridge regularization techniques on our synthetic dataset, and evaluate the model performance?

[End of prompt]

We should receive a response similar to the following, where ChatGPT has provided the complete code:

[Prompt response]

Sure, I can provide you with a Python script that performs linear regression, as well as Lasso and Ridge regression, on the synthetic dataset we just created. We will also evaluate the model performance using metrics like the R-squared score, mean squared error (MSE), and mean absolute error (MAE).

Here is a complete Python code snippet for the whole process:

```python
import pandas as pd
import numpy as np
from sklearn.model_selection import train_test_split
from sklearn.linear_model import LinearRegression, Lasso, Ridge
from sklearn.metrics import mean_squared_error, mean_absolute_error, r2_score
# Load the synthetic dataset
data = pd.read_csv('/path/to/your/Synthetic_Ecommerce_Customers.csv')

# Feature selection: Using numerical columns as features
features = data[['Avg. Session Length', 'Time on App', 'Time on Website',
'Length of Membership']]
target = data['Yearly Amount Spent']

# Split the data into training and testing sets
X_train, X_test, y_train, y_test = train_test_split(features, target, test_
size=0.2, random_state=42)

# Initialize the models
linear_model = LinearRegression()
lasso_model = Lasso(alpha=0.1)  # alpha is the regularization strength
ridge_model = Ridge(alpha=1.0)  # alpha is the regularization strength

# Train the models
```

```
linear_model.fit(X_train, y_train)
lasso_model.fit(X_train, y_train)
ridge_model.fit(X_train, y_train)

# Predictions
linear_predictions = linear_model.predict(X_test)
lasso_predictions = lasso_model.predict(X_test)
ridge_predictions = ridge_model.predict(X_test)

# Evaluations
def evaluate_model(predictions, actual):
    mse = mean_squared_error(actual, predictions)
    mae = mean_absolute_error(actual, predictions)
    r2 = r2_score(actual, predictions)
    return mse, mae, r2

linear_mse, linear_mae, linear_r2 = evaluate_model(linear_predictions, y_test)
lasso_mse, lasso_mae, lasso_r2 = evaluate_model(lasso_predictions, y_test)
ridge_mse, ridge_mae, ridge_r2 = evaluate_model(ridge_predictions, y_test)

# Print out the metrics
print("Linear Regression - MSE: {:.2f}, MAE: {:.2f}, R2: {:.2f}".format(linear_
mse, linear_mae, linear_r2))
print("Lasso Regression - MSE: {:.2f}, MAE: {:.2f}, R2: {:.2f}".format(lasso_
mse, lasso_mae, lasso_r2))
print("Ridge Regression - MSE: {:.2f}, MAE: {:.2f}, R2: {:.2f}".format(ridge_
mse, ridge_mae, ridge_r2))
```

Make sure to replace '/path/to/your/Synthetic_Ecommerce_Customers.csv' with the actual path where your synthetic dataset is stored when running the script in your local environment.

This script will:

- Load your synthetic dataset.
- Select appropriate features and split the data into training and test sets.
- Initialize and train Linear, Lasso, and Ridge regression models.
- Evaluate and print out the performance metrics for each model.

This should help you understand the performance differences and impacts of regularization in your predictive models!

[End of response]

We will instruct ChatGPT Plus to execute the code for us:

[Prompt]

Please execute the code.

[End of prompt]

ChatGPT Plus should have executed the code and we should receive a response similar to the following:

[Prompt response]

The models have been trained and evaluated. Here are the performance metrics for each:

Linear Regression:

- **Mean Squared Error (MSE):** 133.01
- **Mean Absolute Error (MAE):** 8.79
- **R-squared (R2):** 0.977

Lasso Regression:

- **Mean Squared Error (MSE):** 133.04
- **Mean Absolute Error (MAE):** 8.79
- **R-squared (R2):** 0.977

Ridge Regression:

- **Mean Squared Error (MSE):** 133.08
- **Mean Absolute Error (MAE):** 8.79
- **R-squared (R2):** 0.977

All three models show very similar performance metrics, with high R2 scores close to 0.977, indicating that each model explains about 97.7% of the variance in the Yearly Amount Spent. The slight differences in MSE and MAE across models are minimal, suggesting that regularization (both Lasso and Ridge) does not significantly alter the performance in this particular case, possibly due to the absence of multicollinearity or other issues that these techniques help address.

[End of response]

By working through this exercise, you've not only learned how to perform a regression analysis using the free version of ChatGPT and ChatGPT Plus but also how to create a linear regression model step by step using your own dataset, apply regularization techniques, and generate synthetic datasets.

Assignment

Generate a single-step code for our dataset and execute it in Google Colab for the random forest algorithm.

Challenge

Can you enhance the following prompt by incorporating prompting strategies to ensure the retrieval of a specific dataset, rather than a random one that may not exist or may have an incorrect path, ensuring it's fit for the intended use?

Provide the output from the current prompt as well as the improved prompt:

[Prompt]

Can you please provide me with the complete end-to-end Python code for a publicly available advertising dataset along with a detailed explanation that it is compatible with the Jupyter Notebook?

[End of prompt]

Summary

We explored the application of TAG, PIC, and LIFE prompting strategies in crafting regression models, employing both ChatGPT and ChatGPT Plus for rapid analysis and predictive tasks. This approach is particularly valuable in the early stages of machine learning development, offering immediate insights and the flexibility to experiment with different models or algorithms without the burden of managing execution environments or programming instances. Additionally, we learned how to effectively utilize single prompts for generating comprehensive code. While it's possible to craft prompts for discrete tasks or steps, many of these require only succinct lines of code and were not the focus here. Providing feedback is instrumental in this process, and validating the output is crucial to ensure the code's functionality.

In the next chapter, we will learn how to use ChatGPT to generate the code for the **multilayer perceptron (MLP)** model with the help of the Fashion-MNIST dataset.

Join our community on Discord

Join our community's Discord space for discussions with the author and other readers:

https://packt.link/aicode

14

Building an MLP Model for Fashion-MNIST with ChatGPT

Introduction

Building upon our foundational understanding of predictive modeling, we now dive into the dynamic world of **Multilayer Perceptron** (**MLP**) models. In this chapter, we embark on a journey to construct an MLP model from scratch, leveraging the versatility and power of neural networks for predictive analytics.

Our exploration of MLPs represents a significant leap into the realm of complex modeling techniques. While linear regression provided valuable insights into modeling relationships within data, MLPs offer a rich framework for capturing intricate patterns and nonlinear dependencies, making them well suited for a wide range of predictive tasks.

Through hands-on experimentation and iterative refinement, we will unravel the intricacies of MLP architecture and optimization. From designing the initial network structure to fine-tuning hyperparameters and incorporating advanced techniques such as batch normalization and dropout, we aim to equip you with the knowledge and skills to harness the full potential of neural networks in predictive modeling.

As we navigate through the construction and optimization of our MLP model, we will delve into the underlying principles of neural network dynamics, exploring how different architectural choices and optimization strategies influence model performance and generalization capabilities.

Business problem

A fashion e-commerce store seeks to optimize customer engagement and increase revenue by leveraging machine learning techniques to gain deeper insights into customer behavior and preferences. By analyzing image data representing various fashion items purchased by customers, the store aims to tailor its product recommendations, improve customer satisfaction, and enhance the overall shopping experience.

Problem and data domain

In this chapter, we will employ MLP models to understand the relationship between customers' preferences and their purchasing patterns using the Fashion-MNIST dataset. MLP models offer a powerful framework for image classification tasks, allowing us to predict the type of clothing or accessory a customer is likely to purchase based on their interactions with the online store. By uncovering patterns in customer preferences, the e-commerce store can personalize recommendations and optimize inventory management to meet the diverse needs of its customer base.

Dataset overview

The fashion e-commerce store collects image data representing various fashion items, categorized into different classes, from its customers. The Fashion-MNIST dataset comprises 70,000 grayscale images of clothing and accessories, each associated with a specific label indicating its category and of size 28x28.

Features in the dataset include:

- **Image data:** Grayscale images of fashion items, each represented as a matrix of pixel intensities. These images serve as the input data for training the MLP model.

- **Label:** The category label assigned to each image, representing the type of clothing or accessory depicted. Labels range from 0 to 9, corresponding to classes such as T-shirt/top, Trouser, Pullover, Dress, Coat, Sandal, Shirt, Sneaker, Bag, and Ankle boot.

By analyzing this image data and its corresponding labels, we aim to train an MLP model capable of accurately classifying fashion items based on their visual features. This predictive model will enable the e-commerce store to make personalized product recommendations, enhance customer engagement, and ultimately increase revenue by providing a seamless shopping experience tailored to individual preferences.

Figure 14.1: Fashion-MNIST dataset

Breaking the problem down into features

Given the nature of the Fashion-MNIST dataset, which comprises grayscale images of fashion items categorized into different classes, we will start by building a baseline MLP model. This will involve the following high-level steps:

1. **Building the baseline model**: Users will understand the process of constructing a simple MLP model for image classification using ChatGPT. We will guide users through loading the Fashion-MNIST dataset, preprocessing the image data, splitting it into training and testing sets, defining the model architecture, training the model, making predictions, and evaluating its performance.

2. **Adding layers to the model**: Once the baseline model is established, users will learn how to experiment with adding additional layers to the MLP architecture. We will explore how increasing the depth or width of the model impacts its performance and capacity to capture complex patterns in the image data.

3. **Experimenting with batch sizes**: Users will experiment with different batch sizes during model training to observe their effects on training speed, convergence, and generalization performance. We will explore how varying batch sizes influence the trade-off between computation efficiency and model stability.

4. **Adjusting the number of neurons**: Users will explore the impact of adjusting the number of neurons in each layer of the MLP model. By increasing or decreasing the number of neurons, users can observe changes in model capacity and its ability to learn intricate features from the image data.

5. **Trying different optimizers**: Finally, users will experiment with different optimization algorithms, such as SGD, Adam, and RMSprop, to optimize the training process of the MLP model. We will observe how different optimizers influence training dynamics, convergence speed, and final model performance.

By following these steps, users will gain a comprehensive understanding of building and optimizing MLP models for image classification tasks using the Fashion-MNIST dataset. They will learn how to iteratively refine the model architecture and training process to achieve optimal performance and accuracy in classifying fashion items.

Prompting strategy

To leverage ChatGPT for machine learning we need to have a clear understanding of how to implement the prompting strategies specifically for code generation for machine learning.

Let's brainstorm what we would like to achieve in this task to get a better understanding of what needs to go into prompts.

Strategy 1: Task-Actions-Guidelines (TAG) prompt strategy

1.1 - Task: The specific task or goal is to create a classification model for the Fashion-MNIST dataset.

1.2 - Actions: The key steps involved in creating a classification model using an MLP for the Fashion-MNIST dataset are:

- Data preprocessing: Normalize pixel values, flatten images into vectors, and encode categorical labels.
- Data splitting: Partition the dataset into training, validation, and testing sets.
- Model selection: Opt for an MLP as the classification model.
- Model training: Train the MLP on the training data.
- Model evaluation: Use metrics like accuracy, precision, recall, and confusion matrix to evaluate the model's performance.

1.3 - Guidelines: We will provide the following guidelines to ChatGPT in our prompt:

- The code should be compatible with Jupyter notebook.
- Ensure that there are detailed comments for each line of code.
- You have to explain each line of code, which will be then copied into the text block of the notebook, in detail for each method used in the code before providing the code.

Strategy 2: Persona-Instructions-Context (PIC) prompt strategy

2.1 - Persona: We will adopt the persona of a beginner who needs to learn different steps of model creation, hence the code should be generated step by step.

2.2 - Instructions: We have specified that we want the code generated for an MLP model with a single layer *and have instructed ChatGPT to provide one step at a time and wait for the user's feedback.*

2.3 - Context: In this case, ChatGPT is already aware of the Fashion-MNIST dataset, as it is widely known, so we do not need to provide additional context.

Strategy 3: Learn-Improvise-Feedback-Evaluate (LIFE) prompt strategy

3.1 - Learn:

- We want to learn about MLP models and how they work.

3.2 - Improvise:

- We will use this knowledge later when adding more layers, changing the batch size or activation functions, and so on.

3.3 - Feedback:

- Share code and model outputs for feedback to ensure effective learning and understanding.
- Incorporate suggestions and critiques to refine the model and the approach.
- Provide errors to troubleshoot and resolve the issues.

3.4- Evaluate:

Execute the code provided by ChatGPT to ensure accuracy and validity. This is used throughout the chapter.

Building an MLP model to accurately classify the Fashion-MNIST images using the free version of ChatGPT

ChatGPT's premium version has a code interpreter, but it doesn't support the deep learning libraries such as Keras and TensorFlow required to execute the code. Hence, for this chapter, we will stick to the free version of ChatGPT.

Feature 1: Building the baseline model

Let's craft our initial prompt for baseline model.

[Prompt]

I want to create a simple classification model for the Fashion-MNIST dataset (TAG 1.1) consisting of a single-layer MLP model (PIC 2.2). It should consist of the following steps (TAG1.2), provide one step at a time, and wait for the user's feedback (PIC 2.2).

- Data Preprocessing: Normalize pixel values, flatten images into vectors, and encode categorical labels.
- Data Splitting: Partition the dataset into training, validation, and testing sets.
- Model Selection: Opt for a Multi-Layer Perceptron (MLP) as the classification model.
- Model Training: Train the MLP on the training data.
- Model Evaluation: Use metrics like accuracy, precision, recall, and confusion matrix to evaluate the model's performance.

I am a beginner user (PIC 2.1), so please provide step-by-step code and strictly follow the below instructions (TAG 1.3):

The code should be compatible with the Jupyter Notebook.

Ensure that there are detailed comments for each line of code.

You have to explain each line of code, which will be then copied into the text block of notebook, in detail for each method used in the code before providing the code.

[End of prompt]

You should receive a response similar to the following, where ChatGPT has provided us with the code for step 1, Data Preprocessing, along with detailed comments and explanations.

[Prompt response]

Sure, let's start with the first step: Data Preprocessing.

Data Preprocessing:

- Data preprocessing is a crucial step in machine learning, where we prepare our data for training by applying various transformations and normalization techniques. In this step, we'll normalize the pixel values, flatten the images into vectors, and encode categorical labels.

Normalize Pixel Values:

- Normalizing pixel values ensures that each pixel's value is scaled to a range between 0 and 1. This is important for the neural network to converge faster during training and to prevent any particular feature from dominating the learning process.

Flatten Images into Vectors:

- MLP models cannot directly work with multi-dimensional data like images. Hence, we need to flatten the images into 1D vectors, where each pixel value becomes a feature.

Encode Categorical Labels:

- Since our labels are categorical (e.g., different types of clothing items), we need to encode them into numerical values so that our model can understand and learn from them.

Now, let's implement these steps in code:

```python
import numpy as np
from tensorflow.keras.datasets import fashion_mnist
from sklearn.preprocessing import StandardScaler, LabelEncoder
from sklearn.model_selection import train_test_split


# Step 1: Load Fashion-MNIST dataset
(x_train, y_train), (x_test, y_test) = fashion_mnist.load_data()


# Step 2: Normalize pixel values
def normalize_images(train_data, test_data):
    # Convert to float32 to ensure division results in float
    train_data = train_data.astype('float32')
    test_data = test_data.astype('float32')
    # Normalize pixel values to the range 0-1
    train_data /= 255.0
    test_data /= 255.0
    return train_data, test_data


# Step 3: Flatten images into vectors
def flatten_images(train_data, test_data):
    # Reshape images to vectors
    train_data = train_data.reshape(train_data.shape[0], -1)
    test_data = test_data.reshape(test_data.shape[0], -1)
```

```
        return train_data, test_data

    # Step 4: Encode categorical labels
    def encode_labels(train_labels, test_labels):
        # Initialize LabelEncoder
        label_encoder = LabelEncoder()
        # Fit LabelEncoder on training labels and transform both training and
    testing labels
        train_labels = label_encoder.fit_transform(train_labels)
        test_labels = label_encoder.transform(test_labels)
        return train_labels, test_labels

    # Apply data preprocessing steps
    x_train, x_test = normalize_images(x_train, x_test)
    x_train, x_test = flatten_images(x_train, x_test)
    y_train, y_test = encode_labels(y_train, y_test)

    # Print the shapes of preprocessed data
    print("x_train shape:", x_train.shape)
    print("y_train shape:", y_train.shape)
    print("x_test shape:", x_test.shape)
    print("y_test shape:", y_test.shape)
```

Explanation:

- We import necessary libraries such as NumPy for numerical operations, TensorFlow for loading the Fashion-MNIST dataset, and scikit-learn for data preprocessing.
- We load the Fashion-MNIST dataset using the `fashion_mnist.load_data()` method and split it into training and testing sets.
- Three functions, `normalize_images`, `flatten_images`, and `encode_labels`, are defined to perform each data preprocessing step.

Inside each function:

- `normalize_images` divides pixel values by 255 to scale them between 0 and 1.
- `flatten_images` reshapes the images into 1D vectors.
- `encode_labels` converts categorical labels into numerical values using `LabelEncoder`.

Finally, we apply these preprocessing steps to the training and testing data and print their shapes to ensure everything is processed correctly.

[End of response]

We will now apply the prompt evaluation strategy (LIFE 3.4) and validate the code by executing the code for every step in the Google Colab environment. The code loads the model from Keras and normalizes the images, flattens them into vectors, encodes labels using LabelEncoder, then applies the preprocessing and prints the shape. The code runs perfectly fine without applying any modifications or any errors.

Please refer to the `Learning MLP using Fashion-MNIST dataset with ChatGPT.ipynb` notebook for the executable code snippets or copy the code from the prompt response.

```
le  + Text
19   # Step 3: Flatten images into vectors
20   def flatten_images(train_data, test_data):
21       # Reshape images to vectors
22       train_data = train_data.reshape(train_data.shape[0], -1)
23       test_data = test_data.reshape(test_data.shape[0], -1)
24       return train_data, test_data
25
26   # Step 4: Encode categorical labels
27   def encode_labels(train_labels, test_labels):
28       # Initialize LabelEncoder
29       label_encoder = LabelEncoder()
30       # Fit LabelEncoder on training labels and transform both training and testing labels
31       train_labels = label_encoder.fit_transform(train_labels)
32       test_labels = label_encoder.transform(test_labels)
33       return train_labels, test_labels
34
35   # Apply data pre-processing steps
36   x_train, x_test = normalize_images(x_train, x_test)
37   x_train, x_test = flatten_images(x_train, x_test)
38   y_train, y_test = encode_labels(y_train, y_test)
39
40   # Print the shapes of pre-processed data
41   print("x_train shape:", x_train.shape)
42   print("y_train shape:", y_train.shape)
43   print("x_test shape:", x_test.shape)
44   print("y_test shape:", y_test.shape)
45
```

```
Downloading data from https://storage.googleapis.com/tensorflow/tf-keras-datasets/train-labels-idx1-ubyte.gz
29515/29515 [==============================] - 0s 0us/step
Downloading data from https://storage.googleapis.com/tensorflow/tf-keras-datasets/train-images-idx3-ubyte.gz
26421880/26421880 [==============================] - 1s 0us/step
Downloading data from https://storage.googleapis.com/tensorflow/tf-keras-datasets/t10k-labels-idx1-ubyte.gz
5148/5148 [==============================] - 0s 0us/step
Downloading data from https://storage.googleapis.com/tensorflow/tf-keras-datasets/t10k-images-idx3-ubyte.gz
4422102/4422102 [==============================] - 0s 0us/step
x_train shape: (60000, 784)
y_train shape: (60000,)
x_test shape: (10000, 784)
y_test shape: (10000,)
```

Figure 14.2: Code execution – data preprocessing

We will now instruct ChatGPT to proceed to the next step.

[Prompt]

Let's proceed to the next step.

[End of prompt]

We should receive a response like the following, where ChatGPT should provide the code for step 2 – Data Splitting.

[Prompt response]

Great! Let's move on to the next step:

Data Splitting:

- In this step, we'll partition the dataset into training, validation, and testing sets. The training set will be used to train the model, the validation set will be used to tune hyperparameters and prevent overfitting, and the testing set will be used to evaluate the model's performance on unseen data.

Training Set:

- The training set is used to train the model's parameters (weights and biases) using optimization algorithms like gradient descent.

Validation Set:

- The validation set is used to evaluate the model's performance during training and adjust hyperparameters such as learning rate, batch size, and number of epochs to optimize the model's performance.

Testing Set:

- The testing set is used to evaluate the final performance of the trained model on unseen data and assess its generalization capability.

Now, let's split the dataset:

```python
# Step 5: Split dataset into training, validation, and testing sets
def split_dataset(train_data, train_labels, test_data, test_labels, validation_size=0.1, test_size=0.1, random_state=42):
    # Split training set into training and validation sets
    x_train, x_val, y_train, y_val = train_test_split(train_data, train_labels, test_size=validation_size, random_state=random_state)
    # Split testing set into testing and validation sets
    x_test, x_val, y_test, y_val = train_test_split(test_data, test_labels, test_size=test_size, random_state=random_state)
    return x_train, y_train, x_val, y_val, x_test, y_test


# Apply data splitting
x_train, y_train, x_val, y_val, x_test, y_test = split_dataset(x_train, y_train, x_test, y_test)
```

```
# Print the shapes of split datasets
print("Training set:")
print("x_train shape:", x_train.shape)
print("y_train shape:", y_train.shape)
print("\nValidation set:")
print("x_val shape:", x_val.shape)
print("y_val shape:", y_val.shape)
print("\nTesting set:")
print("x_test shape:", x_test.shape)
print("y_test shape:", y_test.shape)
```

Explanation:

* We define a `split_dataset` function to split the dataset into training, validation, and testing sets using the `train_test_split` function from scikit-learn.

* The function takes training data, training labels, testing data, testing labels, and optional parameters such as validation size, test size, and random state.

* We split the training set into training and validation sets using the specified validation size.

* Then, we split the testing set into testing and validation sets using the specified test size.

* Finally, we print the shapes of the split datasets to verify the split.

[End of response]

We execute the code in the notebook and it runs successfully. The data is split into training, validation, and test sets with the specified sizes.

```
1   # Step 5: Split dataset into training, validation, and testing sets
2   def split_dataset(train_data, train_labels, test_data, test_labels, validation_size=0.1, test_size=0.1, random_state=42):
3       # Split training set into training and validation sets
4       x_train, x_val, y_train, y_val = train_test_split(train_data, train_labels, test_size=validation_size, random_state=random_state)
5       # Split testing set into testing and validation sets
6       x_test, x_val, y_test, y_val = train_test_split(test_data, test_labels, test_size=test_size, random_state=random_state)
7       return x_train, y_train, x_val, y_val, x_test, y_test
8
9   # Apply data splitting
10  x_train, y_train, x_val, y_val, x_test, y_test = split_dataset(x_train, y_train, x_test, y_test)
11
12  # Print the shapes of split datasets
13  print("Training set:")
14  print("x_train shape:", x_train.shape)
15  print("y_train shape:", y_train.shape)
16  print("\nValidation set:")
17  print("x_val shape:", x_val.shape)
18  print("y_val shape:", y_val.shape)
19  print("\nTesting set:")
20  print("x_test shape:", x_test.shape)
21  print("y_test shape:", y_test.shape)
22
```

```
Training set:
x_train shape: (54000, 784)
y_train shape: (54000,)

Validation set:
x_val shape: (1000, 784)
y_val shape: (1000,)

Testing set:
x_test shape: (9000, 784)
y_test shape: (9000,)
```

Figure 14.3: Code execution – data splitting

We will now instruct ChatGPT to proceed to the next step.

[Prompt]

Let's proceed to the next step and define a single-layer baseline MLP model.

[End of prompt]

We should receive a response like the following where ChatGPT should provide the code for a single-layer MLP model with an input layer, one hidden layer, and an output layer.

[Prompt response]

Sure, let's move on to the next step:

Model Selection:

- In this step, we'll choose a Multi-Layer Perceptron (MLP) as the classification model. An MLP consists of one or more layers of neurons, each fully connected to the next layer. For simplicity, we'll start with a single-layer MLP as a baseline model.

Single-Layer MLP:

- A single-layer MLP consists of an input layer, a hidden layer, and an output layer. However, since it has only one hidden layer, it's often referred to as a single-layer perceptron. Each neuron in the hidden layer receives input from all neurons in the input layer and produces an output, which is then passed through an activation function to introduce non-linearity. Finally, the output layer produces the final prediction.

Now, let's define the baseline single-layer MLP model:

```python
from tensorflow.keras.models import Sequential
from tensorflow.keras.layers import Dense

# Step 6: Define a single-layer MLP model
def create_single_layer_mlp(input_shape, num_classes):
    model = Sequential()
    # Add a single hidden layer with ReLU activation
    model.add(Dense(128, activation='relu', input_shape=input_shape))
    # Add output layer with softmax activation for multi-class classification
    model.add(Dense(num_classes, activation='softmax'))
    return model

# Define input shape and number of classes
input_shape = x_train.shape[1:]
num_classes = len(np.unique(y_train))

# Create the single-layer MLP model
model = create_single_layer_mlp(input_shape, num_classes)
```

```
# Print model summary
model.summary()
```

Explanation:

- We import the necessary modules from `TensorFlow.keras` to define the MLP model.
- We define a function `create_single_layer_mlp` to create a single-layer MLP model.
- Inside the function:
    - We initialize a sequential model.
    - We add a single hidden layer with 128 neurons and ReLU activation function.
    - We add an output layer with softmax activation function for multi-class classification.
    - We specify the input shape based on the shape of the training data and the number of output classes.
    - We create the single-layer MLP model using the defined function.
- Finally, we print the summary of the model architecture.

[End of response]

We execute the code and it runs without any errors and prints the model summary with the layer type, output shape, and number of parameters. It also provides us with the total parameters, trainable and non-trainable parameters. In our case, all the parameters are trainable parameters.

```
1   from tensorflow.keras.models import Sequential
2   from tensorflow.keras.layers import Dense
3
4   # Step 6: Define a single-layer MLP model
5   def create_single_layer_mlp(input_shape, num_classes):
6       model = Sequential()
7       # Add a single hidden layer with ReLU activation
8       model.add(Dense(128, activation='relu', input_shape=input_shape))
9       # Add output layer with softmax activation for multi-class classification
10      model.add(Dense(num_classes, activation='softmax'))
11      return model
12
13  # Define input shape and number of classes
14  input_shape = x_train.shape[1:]
15  num_classes = len(np.unique(y_train))
16
17  # Create the single-layer MLP model
18  model = create_single_layer_mlp(input_shape, num_classes)
19
20  # Print model summary
21  model.summary()
22
```

```
Model: "sequential"

 Layer (type)                Output Shape              Param #
=================================================================
 dense (Dense)               (None, 128)               100480

 dense_1 (Dense)             (None, 10)                1290

=================================================================
Total params: 101770 (397.54 KB)
Trainable params: 101770 (397.54 KB)
Non-trainable params: 0 (0.00 Byte)
```

Figure 14.4: Code execution – baseline model architecture

We will now instruct ChatGPT to proceed to the next step for model training.

[Prompt]

Let's proceed to the next step.

[End of prompt]

We should receive a response like the following where ChatGPT should provide the code for model training along with explanations of the key concepts involved, such as loss functions and optimization algorithms along with comments.

[Prompt response]

Sure, let's move on to the next step:

Model Training:

- In this step, we'll train the MLP model on the training data. Training involves feeding the training data to the model, adjusting its parameters (weights and biases) using optimization algorithms like stochastic gradient descent, and minimizing a loss function to make predictions as close to the actual labels as possible.

Loss Function:

- The loss function measures the difference between the predicted labels and the actual labels. For multi-class classification problems like Fashion-MNIST, we typically use categorical cross-entropy as the loss function.

Optimization Algorithm:

- The optimization algorithm is responsible for updating the model's parameters during training to minimize the loss function. We'll use Adam optimizer, which is an extension to stochastic gradient descent and is widely used in deep learning.

Training Parameters:

- We'll specify training parameters such as batch size and number of epochs. Batch size determines the number of samples processed before updating the model's parameters, while the number of epochs specifies how many times the entire training dataset is passed forward and backward through the model.

Now, let's train the model:

```python
from tensorflow.keras.utils import to_categorical

# Step 7: Model Training
def train_model(model, x_train, y_train, x_val, y_val, batch_size=32,
epochs=10):
    # Convert class vectors to binary class matrices (one-hot encoding)
    y_train = to_categorical(y_train)
    y_val = to_categorical(y_val)
    # Compile the model with categorical cross-entropy loss and Adam optimizer
    model.compile(loss='categorical_crossentropy', optimizer='adam',
metrics=['accuracy'])
    # Train the model on the training data
    history = model.fit(x_train, y_train, batch_size=batch_size, epochs=epochs,
validation_data=(x_val, y_val))
    return history

# Train the model
history = train_model(model, x_train, y_train, x_val, y_val, batch_size=32,
epochs=10)
```

Explanation:

- We import the necessary modules from `TensorFlow.keras` to compile and train the model.
- We define a `train_model` function to train the model on the training data.
- Inside the function:
    - We convert the class labels to binary class matrices using one-hot encoding.
    - We compile the model with the categorical cross-entropy loss function and the Adam optimizer.
    - We train the model on the training data with the specified batch size and number of epochs.
- Finally, we train the model using the defined function and store the training history for visualization and analysis.

[End of response]

We execute the code and it runs without any errors. It applies a one-hot encoding to class labels, complies the model with the categorical cross-entropy loss function and Adam optimizer, and trains the model with batch size 32 for 10 epochs. This achieves a validation accuracy of approximately 88%.

```
[4]  1  from tensorflow.keras.utils import to_categorical
     2
     3  # Step 7: Model Training
     4  def train_model(model, x_train, y_train, x_val, y_val, batch_size=32, epochs=10):
     5      # Convert class vectors to binary class matrices (one-hot encoding)
     6      y_train = to_categorical(y_train)
     7      y_val = to_categorical(y_val)
     8      # Compile the model with categorical cross-entropy loss and Adam optimizer
     9      model.compile(loss='categorical_crossentropy', optimizer='adam', metrics=['accuracy'])
    10      # Train the model on the training data
    11      history = model.fit(x_train, y_train, batch_size=batch_size, epochs=epochs, validation_data=(x_val, y_val))
    12      return history
    13
    14  # Train the model
    15  history = train_model(model, x_train, y_train, x_val, y_val, batch_size=32, epochs=10)
    16
```

```
Epoch 1/10
1688/1688 [==============================] - 6s 3ms/step - loss: 0.5038 - accuracy: 0.8231 - val_loss: 0.4535 - val_accuracy: 0.8210
Epoch 2/10
1688/1688 [==============================] - 5s 3ms/step - loss: 0.3781 - accuracy: 0.8646 - val_loss: 0.3870 - val_accuracy: 0.8550
Epoch 3/10
1688/1688 [==============================] - 6s 3ms/step - loss: 0.3392 - accuracy: 0.8765 - val_loss: 0.3674 - val_accuracy: 0.8690
Epoch 4/10
1688/1688 [==============================] - 5s 3ms/step - loss: 0.3127 - accuracy: 0.8854 - val_loss: 0.3454 - val_accuracy: 0.8780
Epoch 5/10
1688/1688 [==============================] - 5s 3ms/step - loss: 0.2960 - accuracy: 0.8910 - val_loss: 0.3372 - val_accuracy: 0.8680
Epoch 6/10
1688/1688 [==============================] - 5s 3ms/step - loss: 0.2803 - accuracy: 0.8958 - val_loss: 0.3497 - val_accuracy: 0.8720
Epoch 7/10
1688/1688 [==============================] - 5s 3ms/step - loss: 0.2666 - accuracy: 0.8997 - val_loss: 0.3657 - val_accuracy: 0.8650
Epoch 8/10
1688/1688 [==============================] - 6s 3ms/step - loss: 0.2554 - accuracy: 0.9039 - val_loss: 0.3464 - val_accuracy: 0.8700
Epoch 9/10
1688/1688 [==============================] - 5s 3ms/step - loss: 0.2459 - accuracy: 0.9079 - val_loss: 0.3492 - val_accuracy: 0.8700
Epoch 10/10
1688/1688 [==============================] - 5s 3ms/step - loss: 0.2382 - accuracy: 0.9106 - val_loss: 0.3363 - val_accuracy: 0.8800
```

Figure 14.5: Code execution – model training

We will now instruct ChatGPT to proceed to the next step for model evaluation.

[Prompt]

Let's proceed to the next step.

[End of prompt]

We should receive a response like the following where ChatGPT should provide the code for evaluating the model against the test set, along with explanations of concepts like accuracy, precision, recall, and the confusion matrix.

[Prompt response]

Model Evaluation:

* In this step, we'll use various metrics to evaluate the performance of the trained MLP model on the testing data. Commonly used metrics for classification tasks include accuracy, precision, recall, and the confusion matrix.

Accuracy:

- Accuracy measures the proportion of correctly classified instances out of the total instances.

Precision:

- Precision measures the proportion of true positive predictions out of all positive predictions. It indicates the model's ability to avoid false positives.

Recall:

- Recall measures the proportion of true positive predictions out of all actual positive instances. It indicates the model's ability to identify all positive instances.

Confusion Matrix:

- A confusion matrix provides a summary of the model's performance by showing the number of true positive, true negative, false positive, and false negative predictions.

Now, let's evaluate the model:

```python
import matplotlib.pyplot as plt
from sklearn.metrics import accuracy_score, precision_score, recall_score,
confusion_matrix

# Step 8: Model Evaluation
def evaluate_model(model, x_test, y_test):
    # Predict labels for testing data
    y_pred = model.predict(x_test)
    # Convert predicted labels to class labels
    y_pred_classes = np.argmax(y_pred, axis=1)
    # Convert true labels to class labels
    y_true_classes = np.argmax(y_test, axis=1)
    # Calculate accuracy
    accuracy = accuracy_score(y_true_classes, y_pred_classes)
    # Calculate precision
    precision = precision_score(y_true_classes, y_pred_classes,
average='weighted')
    # Calculate recall
    recall = recall_score(y_true_classes, y_pred_classes, average='weighted')
    # Calculate confusion matrix
    cm = confusion_matrix(y_true_classes, y_pred_classes)
    return accuracy, precision, recall, cm

# Evaluate the model
accuracy, precision, recall, cm = evaluate_model(model, x_test, y_test)
```

```
# Print evaluation metrics
print("Accuracy:", accuracy)
print("Precision:", precision)
print("Recall:", recall)
print("Confusion Matrix:\n", cm)

# Visualize confusion matrix
plt.imshow(cm, cmap=plt.cm.Blues)
plt.title('Confusion Matrix')
plt.colorbar()
plt.xlabel('Predicted Labels')
plt.ylabel('True Labels')
plt.show()
```

Explanation:

- We import necessary modules from `matplotlib.pyplot` and scikit-learn to visualize the confusion matrix and calculate evaluation metrics.
- We define an `evaluate_model` function to evaluate the model's performance on the testing data.
- Inside the function:
    - We make predictions on the testing data using the trained model.
    - We convert the predicted labels and true labels to class labels.
    - We calculate accuracy, precision, recall, and confusion matrix using scikit-learn metrics functions.
- Finally, we evaluate the model using the defined function, print the evaluation metrics, and visualize the confusion matrix.

[End of response]

We execute the code and note that it experiences an error due to the test labels not being encoded, but this is not evident from the error itself. We can get help from ChatGPT to resolve the error by applying the prompting strategy of providing the error to ChatGPT.

```
282/282 [==============================] - 2s 5ms/step
-------------------------------------------------------------------------
AxisError                           Traceback (most recent call last)
<ipython-input-5-02193580c831> in <cell line: 23>()
     21
     22 # Evaluate the model
---> 23 accuracy, precision, recall, cm = evaluate_model(model, x_test, y_test)
     24
     25 # Print evaluation metrics


---------------------------  ⌄ 2 frames  ---------------------------
/usr/local/lib/python3.10/dist-packages/numpy/core/fromnumeric.py in _wrapfunc(obj, method, *args, **kwds)
     57
     58     try:
---> 59         return bound(*args, **kwds)
     60     except TypeError:
     61         # A TypeError occurs if the object does have such a method in its

AxisError: axis 1 is out of bounds for array of dimension 1
```

Figure 14.6: Code execution – error for model evaluation

We provided the error to ChatGPT to get assistance.

[Prompt]

Looks like there is some issue with the test labels. We received the below error:

```
------282/282 [==============================] - 2s 5ms/step -----------------
------------------------------------------------------------- AxisError Traceback
(most recent call last) <ipython-input-5-02193580c831> in <cell line: 23>() 21
22 # Evaluate the model ---> 23 accuracy, precision, recall, cm = evaluate_
model(model, x_test, y_test) 24 25 # Print evaluation metrics 2 frames /usr/
local/lib/python3.10/dist-packages/numpy/core/fromnumeric.py in _wrapfunc(obj,
method, *args, **kwds) 57 58 try: ---> 59 return bound(*args, **kwds) 60 except
TypeError: 61 # A TypeError occurs if the object does have such a method in its
AxisError: axis 1 is out of bounds for array of dimension 1
```

[End of prompt]

We should receive a response like the following where ChatGPT should provide the suggestions to troubleshoot the problem.

[Prompt response]

It seems like there's an issue with the shape of the labels. The error indicates that the axis specified for the argmax function is out of bounds. This typically occurs when the labels are not in the expected format or shape.

Let's double-check the shape of the labels and make sure they are in the correct format for evaluation:

```
print("Shape of y_test:", y_test.shape)
```

This will help us understand the shape of the labels and identify any discrepancies. Once we identify the issue, we can correct it accordingly.

[End of response]

We print the shape of y_test:

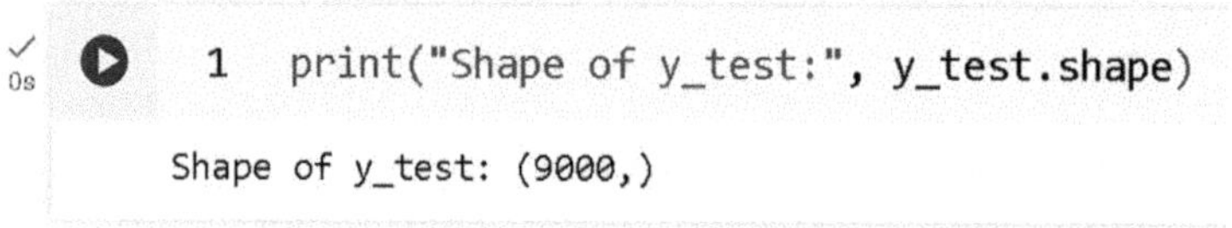

```
✓    ▶    1    print("Shape of y_test:", y_test.shape)
0s
            Shape of y_test: (9000,)
```

Figure 14.7: Code execution - shape of test labels

We will now provide ChatGPT with the output of the code.

[Prompt]

```
Shape of y_test: (9000,)
```

[End of prompt]

We should receive a response like the following where ChatGPT understands the problem and provides us with the corrected code.

[Prompt response]

Thank you for providing the shape of y_test. It seems that the labels are in 1D format, which means they are not one-hot encoded. In the evaluation function, we assumed that the labels are one-hot encoded, which caused the error.

To resolve this issue, we need to modify the evaluation function to handle 1D labels instead of one-hot encoded labels. We can achieve this by removing the conversion of labels to one-hot encoding and directly compare the predicted labels with the true labels.

Let's update the evaluation function accordingly:

```
# Step 8: Model Evaluation
def evaluate_model(model, x_test, y_test):
    # Predict labels for testing data
    y_pred = model.predict(x_test)
```

```python
    # Convert predicted labels to class labels
    y_pred_classes = np.argmax(y_pred, axis=1)
    # Calculate accuracy
    accuracy = accuracy_score(y_test, y_pred_classes)
    # Calculate precision
    precision = precision_score(y_test, y_pred_classes, average='weighted')
    # Calculate recall
    recall = recall_score(y_test, y_pred_classes, average='weighted')
    # Calculate confusion matrix
    cm = confusion_matrix(y_test, y_pred_classes)
    return accuracy, precision, recall, cm


# Evaluate the model
accuracy, precision, recall, cm = evaluate_model(model, x_test, y_test)


# Print evaluation metrics
print("Accuracy:", accuracy)
print("Precision:", precision)
print("Recall:", recall)
print("Confusion Matrix:\n", cm)


# Visualize confusion matrix
plt.imshow(cm, cmap=plt.cm.Blues)
plt.title('Confusion Matrix')
plt.colorbar()
plt.xlabel('Predicted Labels')
plt.ylabel('True Labels')
plt.show()
```

Explanation:

We removed the conversion of labels to one-hot encoding and directly used the y_test true labels in the evaluation function.

We updated the accuracy, precision, and recall calculation functions to use the 1D labels instead of one-hot encoded labels.

Now, the evaluation function should work correctly with the provided 1D labels, and the evaluation metrics should be calculated accurately.

[End of response]

We will execute the code and it works fine now because the code provided has been modified to work with 1D labels. It also prints the confusion matrix.

```
282/282 [==============================] - 1s 3ms/step
Accuracy: 0.8795555555555555
Precision: 0.88170191026604995
Recall: 0.8795555555555555
Confusion Matrix:
[[683    2   15   25    5    3  175    0    8    0]
 [  0  881    1   12    3    0    3    0    1    0]
 [  7    1  707    9  103    1   60    0    1    0]
 [ 15   15   10  804   28    1   27    0    6    0]
 [  0    3   72   37  753    0   40    0    1    0]
 [  0    0    0    0    0  866    0   11    0   17]
 [ 63    1   79   29   83    0  646    0    6    0]
 [  0    0    0    0    0   20    0  850    0   25]
 [  3    0    2    3    5    3    8    3  877    0]
 [  0    0    0    0    0    5    1   27    0  849]]
```

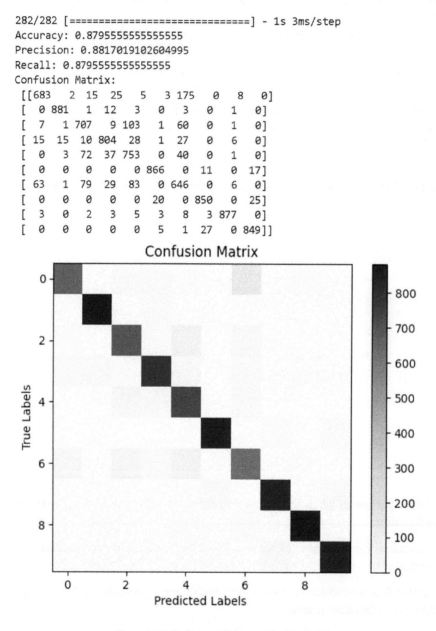

Figure 14.8: Code execution – confusion matrix

This completes feature 1. We achieved an accuracy of 0.8796 (87.96%), a precision of 0.8817 (88.17%), and a recall of 0.8796 (87.96%) with our single-layer MLP model. Next, we will move to the second feature, adding more layers to the model. We will also learn how ChatGPT can assist us in that.

Feature 2: Adding layers to the model

Now that we have a baseline model architecture, let us try adding layers to it. We will apply a prompting strategy to improvise a model and ask ChatGPT to provide us with the code for it.

[Prompt]

Now that we have a baseline model with a single layer, can you please provide me code with two layers and three layers and calculate and compare the model performance due to the addition of layers?

[End of prompt]

We should receive a response like the following where ChatGPT understands the request and provides us with the code for two-layer and three-layer models along with comparison results.

[Prompt response]

Certainly! Let's define and train multi-layer perceptron (MLP) models with two and three layers, and then compare their performance with the baseline single-layer model.

Define MLP Models with Two and Three Layers:

- We'll define MLP models with additional hidden layers to see how the performance changes with the increase in the number of layers.

Two-Layer MLP:

- The two-layer MLP will consist of an input layer, two hidden layers, and an output layer.

Three-Layer MLP:

- The three-layer MLP will consist of an input layer, three hidden layers, and an output layer.

Now, let's define and train these models:

```python
# Define a two-layer MLP model
def create_two_layer_mlp(input_shape, num_classes):
    model = Sequential()
    # Add first hidden layer with ReLU activation
    model.add(Dense(128, activation='relu', input_shape=input_shape))
    # Add second hidden layer with ReLU activation
    model.add(Dense(64, activation='relu'))
    # Add output layer with softmax activation for multi-class classification
    model.add(Dense(num_classes, activation='softmax'))
    return model

# Define a three-layer MLP model
def create_three_layer_mlp(input_shape, num_classes):
    model = Sequential()
    # Add first hidden layer with ReLU activation
```

```python
model.add(Dense(128, activation='relu', input_shape=input_shape))
# Add second hidden layer with ReLU activation
model.add(Dense(64, activation='relu'))
# Add third hidden layer with ReLU activation
model.add(Dense(32, activation='relu'))
# Add output layer with softmax activation for multi-class classification
model.add(Dense(num_classes, activation='softmax'))
return model


# Create two-layer MLP model
two_layer_model = create_two_layer_mlp(input_shape, num_classes)


# Create three-layer MLP model
three_layer_model = create_three_layer_mlp(input_shape, num_classes)


# Train two-layer MLP model
two_layer_history = train_model(two_layer_model, x_train, y_train, x_val, y_val)


# Train three-layer MLP model
three_layer_history = train_model(three_layer_model, x_train, y_train, x_val, y_val)
```

Model Comparison:

Once the models are trained, we can compare their performance based on evaluation metrics such as accuracy, precision, recall, and confusion matrix.

```python
# Evaluate two-layer MLP model
two_layer_accuracy, _, _, _ = evaluate_model(two_layer_model, x_test, y_test)


# Evaluate three-layer MLP model
three_layer_accuracy, _, _, _ = evaluate_model(three_layer_model, x_test, y_test)


# Print model comparison
print("Single-layer MLP Accuracy:", accuracy)
print("Two-layer MLP Accuracy:", two_layer_accuracy)
print("Three-layer MLP Accuracy:", three_layer_accuracy)
```

Explanation:

- We define two additional MLP models with two and three hidden layers using the previously defined functions.

- We train both models using the training data and validation data.
- After training, we evaluate the performance of each model using the testing data and compare their accuracies.

The comparison helps us understand how the addition of layers affects the model's performance.

[End of response]

We will execute the code that defines the two additional models with two and three hidden layers. It also trains the models, evaluates the performance of both models, and prints the results.

```
1   # Evaluate two-layer MLP model
2   two_layer_accuracy, _, _, _ = evaluate_model(two_layer_model, x_test, y_test)
3
4   # Evaluate three-layer MLP model
5   three_layer_accuracy, _, _, _ = evaluate_model(three_layer_model, x_test, y_test)
6
7   # Print model comparison
8   print("Single-layer MLP Accuracy:", accuracy)
9   print("Two-layer MLP Accuracy:", two_layer_accuracy)
10  print("Three-layer MLP Accuracy:", three_layer_accuracy)
11
```

```
282/282 [==============================] - 2s 7ms/step
282/282 [==============================] - 1s 4ms/step
Single-layer MLP Accuracy: 0.8795555555555555
Two-layer MLP Accuracy: 0.8806666666666667
Three-layer MLP Accuracy: 0.8785555555555555
```

Figure 14.9: Feature 2 – adding layers to the model

Based on these results, we can observe that the two-layer MLP model achieved slightly higher accuracy compared to both the single-layer and three-layer MLP models. However, the differences in accuracy are relatively small, indicating that the addition of layers did not significantly improve the model's performance in this case. Let's move on to the next feature and experiment with batch sizes using the baseline model.

Feature 3: Experimenting with batch sizes

We have now learned how to add more layers, and in our case, due to the dataset being simple, there was not much impact. We will now experiment with different batch sizes. We will apply a prompting strategy to improvise a model and ask ChatGPT to provide us the code for it.

[Prompt]

Can you please provide me code with three combinations of batch sizes and compare the baseline single-layer model performance for these combinations?

[End of prompt]

We should receive a response like the following where ChatGPT understands the request and provides us with the code for different batch sizes along with comparison results.

[Prompt response]

Define and Train Models with Different Batch Sizes:

- We'll define and train the baseline single-layer MLP model with three different combinations of batch sizes.
- Combination 1: `Batch Size = 32`
- Combination 2: `Batch Size = 64`
- Combination 3: `Batch Size = 128`

Now, let's define and train these models:

```
# Define and train model with batch size = 32
model_batch_32 = create_single_layer_mlp(input_shape, num_classes)
history_batch_32 = train_model(model_batch_32, x_train, y_train, x_val, y_val,
batch_size=32)


# Define and train model with batch size = 64
model_batch_64 = create_single_layer_mlp(input_shape, num_classes)
history_batch_64 = train_model(model_batch_64, x_train, y_train, x_val, y_val,
batch_size=64)


# Define and train model with batch size = 128
model_batch_128 = create_single_layer_mlp(input_shape, num_classes)
history_batch_128 = train_model(model_batch_128, x_train, y_train, x_val, y_
val, batch_size=128)
```

Model Comparison:

Once the models are trained, we can compare their performance based on evaluation metrics such as accuracy.

```
# Evaluate models with different batch sizes
accuracy_batch_32, _, _, _ = evaluate_model(model_batch_32, x_test, y_test)
accuracy_batch_64, _, _, _ = evaluate_model(model_batch_64, x_test, y_test)
accuracy_batch_128, _, _, _ = evaluate_model(model_batch_128, x_test, y_test)


# Print model comparison
print("Single-layer MLP Accuracy (Batch Size = 32):", accuracy_batch_32)
print("Single-layer MLP Accuracy (Batch Size = 64):", accuracy_batch_64)
print("Single-layer MLP Accuracy (Batch Size = 128):", accuracy_batch_128)
```

Explanation:

- We define and train three baseline single-layer MLP models with different combinations of batch sizes (32, 64, and 128).

- After training, we evaluate the performance of each model using the testing data and compare their accuracies.

The comparison helps us understand how different batch sizes affect the model's performance.

[End of response]

We will execute the code that defines models with batch sizes 32, 64, and 128. It also trains the models, evaluates their performance, and prints the results of the comparison of this performance.

```
1   # Evaluate models with different batch sizes
2   accuracy_batch_32, _, _, _ = evaluate_model(model_batch_32, x_test, y_test)
3   accuracy_batch_64, _, _, _ = evaluate_model(model_batch_64, x_test, y_test)
4   accuracy_batch_128, _, _, _ = evaluate_model(model_batch_128, x_test, y_test)
5
6   # Print model comparison
7   print("Single-layer MLP Accuracy (Batch Size = 32):", accuracy_batch_32)
8   print("Single-layer MLP Accuracy (Batch Size = 64):", accuracy_batch_64)
9   print("Single-layer MLP Accuracy (Batch Size = 128):", accuracy_batch_128)
```

```
282/282 [==============================] - 1s 3ms/step
282/282 [==============================] - 1s 4ms/step
282/282 [==============================] - 1s 3ms/step
Single-layer MLP Accuracy (Batch Size = 32): 0.88
Single-layer MLP Accuracy (Batch Size = 64): 0.8723333333333333
Single-layer MLP Accuracy (Batch Size = 128): 0.8797777777777778
```

Figure 14.10: Code execution – batch size comparison

We can see that there is not much difference between the models' accuracies, so we will apply the 'Learn prompting strategy' (LIFE 3.1) and ask ChatGPT for possible reasons as to why this might be.

[Prompt]

```
282/282 [==============================] - 1s 3ms/step 282/282 [==============
================] - 1s 4ms/step 282/282 [==============================] - 1s
3ms/step
Single-layer MLP Accuracy (Batch Size = 32): 0.88
Single-layer MLP Accuracy (Batch Size = 64): 0.8723333333333333
Single-layer MLP Accuracy (Batch Size = 128): 0.8797777777777778
```

Why there is not much difference in the accuracies?

[End of prompt]

We should receive a response like the following where ChatGPT explains the possible reasons.

[Prompt response]

The differences in accuracy between the models trained with different batch sizes are relatively small. There could be several reasons for this:

- **Dataset Size:** The Fashion-MNIST dataset is relatively small compared to other datasets commonly used in deep learning. With a smaller dataset, the impact of batch size on model performance may be less pronounced.
- **Model Complexity:** The baseline single-layer MLP model may not be complex enough to fully leverage the benefits of different batch sizes. In more complex models, such as deep neural networks with multiple layers, the impact of batch size on training dynamics may be more significant.
- **Optimization Algorithm:** The Adam optimizer used in training the models adapts the learning rate for each parameter based on the first and second moments of the gradients. This adaptive learning rate can mitigate the impact of batch size to some extent.
- **Convergence:** The models may have already converged to a similar level of performance regardless of the batch size used. Once a model converges, further training with different batch sizes may not lead to substantial improvements in accuracy.

Overall, while batch size can influence training dynamics and convergence speed, its impact on model performance may be less pronounced in certain scenarios, especially with relatively simple models and datasets. Experimenting with larger and more complex models, as well as different optimization algorithms, may reveal more significant differences in performance based on batch size.

[End of response]

Now that we have learned how to change the batch size and what the possible reasons could be for it not having much impact on our model, let's move on to the next feature and experiment with the number of neurons in the hidden layer of the baseline model.

Feature 4: Experimenting with the number of neurons

We will apply a prompting strategy to improvise a model and ask ChatGPT to provide us the code for experimenting with different numbers of neurons in the hidden layer.

[Prompt]

Can you please provide me code with three combinations of numbers of neurons and compare the baseline single-layer model performance for the various combinations?

[End of prompt]

We should receive a response like the following where ChatGPT understands the request and provides us with the code for different numbers of neurons in the hidden layer, along with the comparison results.

[Prompt response]

Of course! Let's define and train the baseline single-layer MLP model with three different combinations of the number of neurons in the hidden layer, and then compare their performance.

Define and Train Models with Different Number of Neurons:

- We'll define and train the baseline single-layer MLP model with three different combinations of the number of neurons in the hidden layer:

  - Combination 1: Number of Neurons = 64
  - Combination 2: Number of Neurons = 128
  - Combination 3: Number of Neurons = 256

Now, let's define and train these models:

```python
# Define and train model with 64 neurons in the hidden layer
model_neurons_64 = create_single_layer_mlp(input_shape, num_classes)
history_neurons_64 = train_model(model_neurons_64, x_train, y_train, x_val,
y_val)


# Define and train model with 128 neurons in the hidden layer
model_neurons_128 = create_single_layer_mlp(input_shape, num_classes)
history_neurons_128 = train_model(model_neurons_128, x_train, y train, x_val,
y_val)


# Define and train model with 256 neurons in the hidden layer
model_neurons_256 = create_single_layer_mlp(input_shape, num_classes)
history_neurons_256 = train_model(model_neurons_256, x_train, y_train, x_val,
y_val)
```

Model Comparison:

Once the models are trained, we can compare their performance based on evaluation metrics such as accuracy.

```python
# Evaluate models with different number of neurons
accuracy_neurons_64, _, _, _ = evaluate_model(model_neurons_64, x_test, y_test)
accuracy_neurons_128, _, _, _ = evaluate_model(model_neurons_128, x_test, y_
test)
accuracy_neurons_256, _, _, _ = evaluate_model(model_neurons_256, x_test, y_
test)


# Print model comparison
print("Single-layer MLP Accuracy (Neurons = 64):", accuracy_neurons_64)
print("Single-layer MLP Accuracy (Neurons = 128):", accuracy_neurons_128)
print("Single-layer MLP Accuracy (Neurons = 256):", accuracy_neurons_256)
```

Explanation:

- We define and train three baseline single-layer MLP models with different combinations of the number of neurons in the hidden layer (64, 128, and 256).

- After training, we evaluate the performance of each model using the testing data and compare their accuracies.

The comparison helps us understand how different numbers of neurons in the hidden layer affect the model's performance.

[End of response]

We will execute the code that defines the models with 64, 128, and 256 neurons. It also trains the model, evaluates the performance for all the model variations, and prints the results of the comparison of their performance.

```
1   # Evaluate models with different number of neurons
2   accuracy_neurons_64, _, _, _ = evaluate_model(model_neurons_64, x_test, y_test)
3   accuracy_neurons_128, _, _, _ = evaluate_model(model_neurons_128, x_test, y_test)
4   accuracy_neurons_256, _, _, _ = evaluate_model(model_neurons_256, x_test, y_test)
5
6   # Print model comparison
7   print("Single-layer MLP Accuracy (Neurons = 64):", accuracy_neurons_64)
8   print("Single-layer MLP Accuracy (Neurons = 128):", accuracy_neurons_128)
9   print("Single-layer MLP Accuracy (Neurons = 256):", accuracy_neurons_256)
```

```
282/282 [==============================] - 0s 2ms/step
282/282 [==============================] - 0s 2ms/step
282/282 [==============================] - 0s 1ms/step
Single-layer MLP Accuracy (Neurons = 64): 0.8773333333333333
Single-layer MLP Accuracy (Neurons = 128): 0.8754444444444445
Single-layer MLP Accuracy (Neurons = 256): 0.8813333333333333
```

Figure 14.11: Code execution – neurons comparison

We can see that there is not much difference, so let's move to our final feature of experimenting with different optimizers.

Feature 5: Trying different optimizers

We will apply a prompting strategy to improvise a model and ask ChatGPT to provide us code for experimenting with different optimizers such as SGD, Adam, and RMSProp. Also, as part of our prompting strategy, we will be specific and explicitly mention that the optimizer should be passed at compile time and that labels should be one-hot encoded, as these steps are commonly ignored by ChatGPT.

[Prompt]

Can you please provide me code with different optimizers of SGD, Adam, and RMSprop and compare the baseline single-layer model performance for various combinations? The optimizer should be passed in at compile time and you should ensure that labels are one-hot encoded.

[End of prompt]

We should receive a response like the following where ChatGPT understands the request and provides us with the code for different optimizers along with comparison results.

[Prompt response]

Certainly! Let's define and train a baseline single-layer MLP model with three different optimizers (SGD, Adam, and RMSprop), and then compare their performance.

Define and Train Models with Different Optimizers:

We'll define and train the baseline single-layer MLP model with three different optimizers: SGD, Adam, and RMSprop.

Now, let's define and train these models:

```python
from tensorflow.keras.optimizers import SGD, Adam, RMSprop


# Define and train model with SGD optimizer
def train_model_sgd(model, x_train, y_train, x_val, y_val, batch_size=32,
epochs=10):
    # One-hot encode the class labels
    y_train_encoded = to_categorical(y_train)
    y_val_encoded = to_categorical(y_val)
    # Compile the model with SGD optimizer
    model.compile(loss='categorical_crossentropy', optimizer=SGD(),
metrics=['accuracy'])
    # Train the model on the training data
    history = model.fit(x_train, y_train_encoded, batch_size=batch_size,
epochs=epochs, validation_data=(x_val, y_val_encoded))
    return history


# Define and train model with Adam optimizer
def train_model_adam(model, x_train, y_train, x_val, y_val, batch_size=32,
epochs=10):
    # One-hot encode the class labels
    y_train_encoded = to_categorical(y_train)
    y_val_encoded = to_categorical(y_val)
    # Compile the model with Adam optimizer
    model.compile(loss='categorical_crossentropy', optimizer=Adam(),
metrics=['accuracy'])
    # Train the model on the training data
    history = model.fit(x_train, y_train_encoded, batch_size=batch_size,
epochs=epochs, validation_data=(x_val, y_val_encoded))
    return history


# Define and train model with RMSprop optimizer
def train_model_rmsprop(model, x_train, y_train, x_val, y_val, batch_size=32,
epochs=10):
```

```
    # One-hot encode the class labels
    y_train_encoded = to_categorical(y_train)
    y_val_encoded = to_categorical(y_val)
    # Compile the model with RMSprop optimizer
    model.compile(loss='categorical_crossentropy', optimizer=RMSprop(),
metrics=['accuracy'])
    # Train the model on the training data
    history = model.fit(x_train, y_train_encoded, batch_size=batch_size,
epochs=epochs, validation_data=(x_val, y_val_encoded))
    return history


# Train model with SGD optimizer
model_sgd = create_single_layer_mlp(input_shape, num_classes)
history_sgd = train_model_sgd(model_sgd, x_train, y_train, x_val, y_val)


# Train model with Adam optimizer
model_adam = create_single_layer_mlp(input_shape, num_classes)
history_adam = train_model_adam(model_adam, x_train, y_train, x_val, y_val)


# Train model with RMSprop optimizer
model_rmsprop = create_single_layer_mlp(input_shape, num_classes)
history_rmsprop = train_model_rmsprop(model_rmsprop, x_train, y_train, x_val,
y_val)
```

Model Comparison:

Once the models are trained, we can compare their performance based on evaluation metrics such as accuracy.

```
# Evaluate models with different optimizers
accuracy_sgd, _, _, _ = evaluate_model(model_sgd, x_test, y_test)
accuracy_adam, _, _, _ = evaluate_model(model_adam, x_test, y_test)
accuracy_rmsprop, _, _, _ = evaluate_model(model_rmsprop, x_test, y_test)


# Print model comparison
print("Single-layer MLP Accuracy (SGD):", accuracy_sgd)
print("Single-layer MLP Accuracy (Adam):", accuracy_adam)
print("Single-layer MLP Accuracy (RMSprop):", accuracy_rmsprop)
```

Explanation:

- We define and train three baseline single-layer MLP models with different optimizers (SGD, Adam, and RMSprop).
- After training, we evaluate the performance of each model using the testing data and compare their accuracies.

The comparison helps us understand how different optimizers affect the model's performance.

[End of response]

We execute the code that defines the models with different optimizers. It also trains the model, evaluates the performance of all the model variations, and prints the results for a comparison of their performance.

```
1   # Evaluate models with different optimizers
2   accuracy_sgd, _, _, _ = evaluate_model(model_sgd, x_test, y_test)
3   accuracy_adam, _, _, _ = evaluate_model(model_adam, x_test, y_test)
4   accuracy_rmsprop, _, _, _ = evaluate_model(model_rmsprop, x_test, y_test)
5
6   # Print model comparison
7   print("Single-layer MLP Accuracy (SGD):", accuracy_sgd)
8   print("Single-layer MLP Accuracy (Adam):", accuracy_adam)
9   print("Single-layer MLP Accuracy (RMSprop):", accuracy_rmsprop)
10
```

```
282/282 [==============================] - 1s 2ms/step
282/282 [==============================] - 1s 3ms/step
282/282 [==============================] - 0s 1ms/step
Single-layer MLP Accuracy (SGD): 0.8492222222222222
Single-layer MLP Accuracy (Adam): 0.8816666666666667
Single-layer MLP Accuracy (RMSprop): 0.8663333333333333
```

Figure 14.12: Code Execution – Different Optimizers

Based on these results, we can observe that the Adam optimizer achieved the highest accuracy, followed by RMSprop and SGD. This indicates that Adam performed better in optimizing the model's parameters and improving its performance on the testing data.

Assignment

Compare the model performance of a single layer versus two hidden layers, but with 20 and 50 epochs.

Challenge

With the help of ChatGPT, improvise a model by adding a dropout layer and analyze the impact on model performance. Feel free to add more hidden layers to the model.

Summary

The prompt strategies used in this chapter provided a structured approach to learning and building a classification model using an MLP where ChatGPT assisted in generating code. The user validated the code using a Colab notebook and provided feedback to ChatGPT. By actively engaging with the material, you experimented with different techniques and iteratively refined your understanding, ultimately leading to a more comprehensive grasp of classification model creation using MLPs.

In the next chapter, we will learn how to use ChatGPT to generate code for **Convolutional Neural Networks (CNNs)** with the help of the CIFAR-10 dataset.

Join our community on Discord

Join our community's Discord space for discussions with the author and other readers:

```
https://packt.link/aicode
```

15

Building a CNN Model for CIFAR-10 with ChatGPT

Introduction

Having explored the depths of the **Multi-Layer Perceptron (MLP)** in our previous chapter with the Fashion-MNIST dataset, we now pivot to a more intricate and visually complex challenge. This chapter marks our transition from the primarily tabular, grayscale world of Fashion-MNIST to the colorful and diverse realm of the CIFAR-10 dataset. Here, we elevate our focus to **Convolutional Neural Networks (CNNs)**, a class of deep neural networks that are revolutionizing the way we approach image classification tasks.

Our journey through the MLP chapter provided a strong foundation for understanding the basics of neural networks and their application in classifying simpler, grayscale images. Now, we step into a more advanced territory where CNNs reign supreme. The CIFAR-10 dataset, with its array of 32x32 color images across 10 different classes, presents a unique set of challenges that MLPs are not best suited to address. This is where CNNs, with their ability to capture spatial and textural patterns in images, come into play.

As we transition from MLPs to CNNs, we carry forward the insights and knowledge gained, applying them to a more complex dataset that closely mimics real-world scenarios. The CIFAR-10 dataset not only tests the limits of image classification models but also serves as an excellent platform for us to explore the advanced capabilities of CNNs.

This chapter aims to build upon what we learned about neural networks and guide you through the nuances of CNNs. We will delve into why CNNs are the preferred choice for image data, how they differ from MLPs in handling color and texture, and what makes them so effective in classifying images from the CIFAR-10 dataset. Prepare to embark on a journey that takes you from the fundamentals to the more sophisticated aspects of CNNs.

Business problem

The CIFAR-10 dataset presents a business challenge to companies seeking to enhance image recognition capabilities for various objects and optimize decision-making processes based on visual data. A multitude of industries, such as e-commerce, autonomous driving, and surveillance, can benefit from accurate object classification and detection. By harnessing machine learning algorithms, businesses aim to improve efficiency, enhance their user experience, and streamline operations.

Problem and data domain

In this context, we will utilize CNNs to tackle the object recognition task using the CIFAR-10 dataset. CNNs are particularly effective for image-related problems due to their ability to automatically learn hierarchical features from raw pixel data. By training a CNN model on the CIFAR-10 dataset, we aim to develop a robust system capable of accurately classifying objects into one of the ten predefined categories. This model can be applied in various domains, such as image-based search engines, automated surveillance systems, and quality control in manufacturing.

Dataset overview

The CIFAR-10 dataset comprises 60,000 color images, divided into 10 classes, with 6,000 images per class. Each image has dimensions of 32x32 pixels and is represented in RGB format. The dataset is split into a training set of 50,000 images and a test set of 10,000 images.

Features in the dataset include:

- **Image data:** Color images of various objects, each represented as a 3-dimensional array containing pixel intensities for red, green, and blue channels. These images serve as input data for training the CNN model.
- **Label:** The class label assigned to each image, representing the category of the depicted object. The labels range from 0 to 9, corresponding to classes such as airplane, automobile, bird, cat, deer, dog, frog, horse, ship, and truck.

By analyzing the CIFAR-10 dataset and its associated labels, our goal is to train a CNN model capable of accurately identifying objects depicted in images. This predictive model can then be deployed in real-world applications to automate object recognition tasks, improve decision-making processes, and enhance overall efficiency in diverse industries.

airplane
automobile
bird
cat
deer
dog
frog
horse
ship
truck

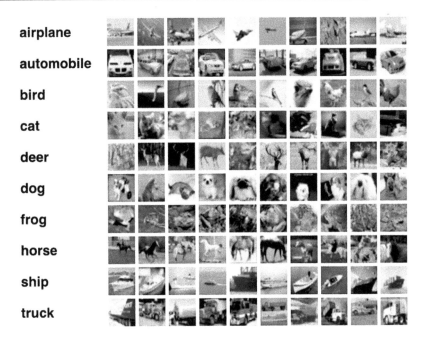

Figure 15.1: CIFAR-10 dataset

Breaking the problem down into features

Given the CIFAR-10 dataset and the application of CNNs for image recognition, we outline the following features to guide users through building and optimizing CNN models:

- **Building the baseline CNN model with a single convolutional layer:** Users will start by constructing a simple CNN model with a single convolutional layer for image classification. This feature focuses on defining the basic architecture, including convolutional filters, activation functions, and pooling layers, to establish a foundational understanding of CNNs.

- **Experimenting with the addition of convolutional layers:** Users will explore the impact of adding additional convolutional layers to the baseline model architecture. By incrementally increasing the depth of the network, users can observe how the model's capacity to capture hierarchical features evolves and its ability to learn complex patterns improves.

- **Incorporating dropout regularization:** Users will learn how to integrate dropout regularization into the CNN model to mitigate overfitting and improve generalization performance. By randomly dropping units during training, dropout helps prevent the network from relying too heavily on specific features and encourages robust feature learning.

- **Implementing batch normalization:** Users will explore the benefits of batch normalization in stabilizing training dynamics and accelerating convergence. This feature focuses on incorporating batch normalization layers into the CNN architecture to normalize activations and reduce internal covariate shift, leading to faster and more stable training.

- **Optimizing with different optimizers:** This feature explores the effects of using various optimization algorithms, including SGD, Adam, and RMSprop, to train the CNN model. Users will compare the training dynamics, convergence speed, and final model performance achieved with different optimizers, allowing them to select the most suitable optimization strategy for their specific task.

- **Performing data augmentation:** Users will experiment with data augmentation techniques such as rotation, flipping, zooming, and shifting to increase the diversity and size of the training dataset. By generating augmented samples on the fly during training, users can improve the model's ability to generalize to unseen data and enhance robustness against variations in input images.

By following these features, users will gain practical insights into building, fine-tuning, and optimizing CNN models for image classification tasks using the CIFAR-10 dataset. They will learn how to systematically experiment with different architectural components, regularization techniques, and optimization strategies to achieve superior performance and accuracy in object recognition.

Prompting strategy

To leverage ChatGPT for machine learning, we need to have a clear understanding of how to implement prompting strategies specifically for code generation for machine learning.

Let's brainstorm what we would like to achieve in this task to get a better understanding of what needs to go into the prompts.

Strategy 1: Task-Actions-Guidelines (TAG) prompt strategy

1.1 - Task: The specific task or goal is to build and optimize a CNN model for the CIFAR-10 dataset.

1.2 - Actions: The key steps involved in building and optimizing a CNN model for the CIFAR-10 dataset include:

- **Preprocessing the image data:** Normalize the pixel values and resize the images to a standardized size.

- **Model construction:** Define the baseline CNN model architecture with a single convolutional layer.

1.3 - Guidelines: We will provide the following guidelines to ChatGPT in our prompt:

- The code should be compatible with Jupyter Notebook.
- Ensure that there are detailed comments for each line of code.
- You have to explain each line of code in detail, covering each method used in the code.

Strategy 2: Persona-Instructions-Context (PIC) prompt strategy

2.1 - Persona: Adopt the persona of a beginner who needs step-by-step guidance on building and optimizing CNN models for image classification tasks.

2.2 - Instructions: Request ChatGPT to generate code for each feature one step at a time and wait for user feedback before proceeding to the next step.

2.3 - **Context:** Given that the focus is on building CNN models for image classification tasks using the CIFAR-10 dataset, ChatGPT is already aware of the dataset and its characteristics, so additional context may not be necessary.

Strategy 3: Learn-Improvise-Feedback-Evaluate (LIFE) prompt strategy

3.1 - **Learn:**

- Emphasize the importance of learning about CNN models and their components, including convolutional layers, pooling layers, dropout regularization, batch normalization, data augmentation, and optimization algorithms.

3.2 - **Improvise:**

- We will improvise later by adding more layers, dropout layers, pooling, data augmentation, and so on.

3.3 - **Feedback:**

- Share code and model outputs for feedback to ensure effective learning and understanding.
- Incorporate suggestions and critiques to refine the model and the approach.
- Provide errors to troubleshoot and resolve the issues.

3.4- **Evaluate:**

Execute the code provided by ChatGPT to ensure accuracy and validity. This is used throughout the chapter.

Building a CNN model to accurately classify the CIFAR-10 images using the free version of ChatGPT

The premium version of ChatGPT has a code interpreter, but it doesn't support deep learning libraries such as Keras and TensorFlow, which are required to build ML code. Hence, for this chapter, we will stick to the free version of ChatGPT.

Feature 1: Building the baseline CNN model with a single convolutional layer

Let's craft our initial prompt for the baseline model.

[Prompt]

I want to create a simple classification model for CIFAR-10 dataset (TAG 1.1) that consists of a single-layer CNN model (PIC 2.2). It should consist of following steps (TAG 1.2) and provide one step at a time, waiting for user feedback (PIC 2.2):

- Preprocessing the image data: Normalize the pixel values and resize the images to a standardized size.
- Model construction: Define the baseline CNN model architecture with a single convolutional layer.

I am a beginner user (PIC 2.1), so please provide step-by-step code and strictly follow the below instructions (TAG 1.3):

- The code should be compatible with Jupyter Notebook.
- Ensure that there are detailed comments for each line of code.

You have to explain each line of code in detail, covering each method used in the code.

[End of prompt]

You should receive a response similar to the following, where ChatGPT has provided us with the code for the data preprocessing step along with detailed comments and explanations.

[Prompt response]

Sure, let's start with the first step: preprocessing the image data. In this step, we will normalize the pixel values and resize the images to a standardized size.

```python
# Step 1: Preprocessing the image data

# Import necessary libraries
import numpy as np
import tensorflow as tf
from tensorflow.keras.datasets import cifar10
from tensorflow.keras.utils import to_categorical
from skimage.transform import resize

# Load CIFAR-10 dataset
(x_train, y_train), (x_test, y_test) = cifar10.load_data()

# Normalize pixel values to range [0, 1]
x_train = x_train.astype('float32') / 255.0
x_test = x_test.astype('float32') / 255.0

# Resize images to a standardized size (e.g., 32x32 pixels)
standardized_size = (32, 32)
```

```
x_train_resized = np.array([resize(image, standardized_size) for image in x_
train])
x_test_resized = np.array([resize(image, standardized_size) for image in x_
test])

# Display shape of datasets after preprocessing
print("Shape of x_train:", x_train_resized.shape)
print("Shape of x_test:", x_test_resized.shape)
```

Now, let's break down each line of code:

We import the necessary libraries:

- numpy for numerical operations.
- tensorflow for building and training the model.
- cifar10 dataset from tensorflow.keras.datasets for loading CIFAR-10 data.
- to_categorical function from tensorflow.keras.utils for one-hot encoding labels.
- resize function from skimage.transform for resizing images.
- We load the CIFAR-10 dataset using cifar10.load_data() function, which returns training and testing data splits.
- We normalize pixel values of images to the range [0, 1] by dividing by 255.0.
- We define the standardized size for resizing images (e.g., 32x32 pixels).
- We resize all images in the training and testing sets to the standardized size using list comprehension and the resize function.
- Finally, we print the shapes of the training and testing datasets after preprocessing to verify the changes.

Let me know if you have any questions or if you'd like to proceed to the next step!

[End of response]

We will now apply the evaluate prompting strategy (LIFE 3.4) and validate the code by executing the code in Google Colab for every step. The code loads the model from Keras and normalizes the images. The code runs perfectly fine without requiring any modifications or returning any errors.

Please refer to the Building a CNN Model for CIFAR-10 with `ChatGPT.ipynb` notebook for the executable code snippets or copy the code from the prompt response.

```
1   # Step 1: Preprocessing the image data
2
3   # Import necessary libraries
4   import numpy as np
5   import tensorflow as tf
6   from tensorflow.keras.datasets import cifar10
7   from tensorflow.keras.utils import to_categorical
8   from skimage.transform import resize
9
10  # Load CIFAR-10 dataset
11  (x_train, y_train), (x_test, y_test) = cifar10.load_data()
12
13  # Normalize pixel values to range [0, 1]
14  x_train = x_train.astype('float32') / 255.0
15  x_test = x_test.astype('float32') / 255.0
16
17  # Resize images to a standardized size (e.g., 32x32 pixels)
18  standardized_size = (32, 32)
19  x_train_resized = np.array([resize(image, standardized_size) for image in x_train])
20  x_test_resized = np.array([resize(image, standardized_size) for image in x_test])
21
22  # Display shape of datasets after preprocessing
23  print("Shape of x_train:", x_train_resized.shape)
24  print("Shape of x_test:", x_test_resized.shape)
```

```
Downloading data from https://www.cs.toronto.edu/~kriz/cifar-10-python.tar.gz
170498071/170498071 [==============================] - 3s 0us/step
Shape of x_train: (50000, 32, 32, 3)
Shape of x_test: (10000, 32, 32, 3)
```

Figure 15.2: Code execution – data preprocessing

We will now instruct ChatGPT to proceed to the next step.

[Prompt]

Let's proceed to the next step.

[End of prompt]

We should receive a response like the following, where ChatGPT should provide the code for creating a baseline model.

[Prompt response]

Great! The next step is to construct the baseline CNN model architecture with a single convolutional layer.

```
# Step 2: Model Construction

# Import necessary libraries
from tensorflow.keras.models import Sequential
```

```python
from tensorflow.keras.layers import Conv2D, MaxPooling2D, Flatten, Dense

# Define the baseline CNN model architecture
model = Sequential([
    # Add a convolutional layer with 32 filters, kernel size of (3, 3), and
ReLU activation function
    Conv2D(32, (3, 3), activation='relu', input_shape=(32, 32, 3)),
    # Add a max pooling layer with pool size of (2, 2)
    MaxPooling2D((2, 2)),
    # Flatten the output of the convolutional layer
    Flatten(),
    # Add a fully connected layer with 64 neurons and ReLU activation function
    Dense(64, activation='relu'),
    # Add the output layer with 10 neurons (one for each class) and softmax
activation function
    Dense(10, activation='softmax')
])

# Compile the model
model.compile(optimizer='adam',
              loss='sparse_categorical_crossentropy',
              metrics=['accuracy'])

# Display model summary
model.summary()
```

Now, let's explain each line of code:

- We import the necessary libraries:
- Sequential from `tensorflow.keras.models` to create a sequential model.
- `Conv2D`, `MaxPooling2D`, `Flatten`, and `Dense` layers from `tensorflow.keras.layers` to define the different types of layers in the CNN model.
- We define the baseline CNN model architecture using the Sequential API, which allows us to create a linear stack of layers.

Within the Sequential model:

- We add a convolutional layer (`Conv2D`) with 32 filters, a kernel size of `(3, 3)`, and ReLU activation function. The `input_shape` parameter defines the shape of input images.
- We add a max pooling layer (`MaxPooling2D`) with a pool size of `(2, 2)` to downsample the feature maps.
- We flatten the output of the convolutional layer using the `Flatten` layer to prepare it for the fully connected layers.

- We add a fully connected layer (Dense) with 64 neurons and a ReLU activation function.
- Finally, we add the output layer with 10 neurons (one for each class in CIFAR-10) and the softmax activation function.

We compile the model using model.compile() with the following:

- optimizer='adam' to use the Adam optimizer.
- loss='sparse_categorical_crossentropy' as the loss function, suitable for classification tasks with integer labels.
- metrics=['accuracy'] to monitor the accuracy during training.
- We display the summary of the model architecture using model.summary().

Let me know if you have any questions or if you'd like to make any adjustments!

[End of response]

We execute the code in the notebook and it runs perfectly. A model summary is printed, which includes the Conv2d layer with 32 filters and 896 params, followed by a MaxPooling2D layer, a flatten layer, which doesn't have any parameters, then a dense layer with 64 neurons and the ReLU activation function, and finally the dense layer with 10 neurons and the softmax activation function.

```
[2]    2
       3    # Import necessary libraries
       4    from tensorflow.keras.models import Sequential
       5    from tensorflow.keras.layers import Conv2D, MaxPooling2D, Flatten, Dense
       6
       7    # Define the baseline CNN model architecture
       8    model = Sequential([
       9        # Add a convolutional layer with 32 filters, kernel size of (3, 3), and ReLU activation function
      10        Conv2D(32, (3, 3), activation='relu', input_shape=(32, 32, 3)),
      11        # Add a max pooling layer with pool size of (2, 2)
      12        MaxPooling2D((2, 2)),
      13        # Flatten the output of the convolutional layer
      14        Flatten(),
      15        # Add a fully connected layer with 64 neurons and ReLU activation function
      16        Dense(64, activation='relu'),
      17        # Add the output layer with 10 neurons (one for each class) and softmax activation function
      18        Dense(10, activation='softmax')
      19    ])
      20
      21    # Compile the model
      22    model.compile(optimizer='adam',
      23                  loss='sparse_categorical_crossentropy',
      24                  metrics=['accuracy'])
      25
      26    # Display model summary
      27    model.summary()
```

```
Model: "sequential"

Layer (type)                    Output Shape            Param #
=================================================================
conv2d (Conv2D)                 (None, 30, 30, 32)      896

max_pooling2d (MaxPooling2      (None, 15, 15, 32)      0
D)

flatten (Flatten)               (None, 7200)            0

dense (Dense)                   (None, 64)              460864

dense_1 (Dense)                 (None, 10)              650

=================================================================
Total params: 462410 (1.76 MB)
Trainable params: 462410 (1.76 MB)
Non-trainable params: 0 (0.00 Byte)
```

Figure 15.3: Code execution – baseline model summary

We will now instruct ChatGPT to proceed to the next step.

Let's proceed to the next step.

[End of prompt]

We should receive a response like the following where ChatGPT should provide the code for training the model.

[Prompt response]

Sure! The next step is to train the model on the preprocessed CIFAR-10 dataset.

```
# Step 3: Model Training

# Train the model
history = model.fit(x_train_resized, y_train,
                    epochs=10,
                    batch_size=32,
                    validation_data=(x_test_resized, y_test))
```

Here's an explanation of the code:

- We train the model using the fit method on the preprocessed training data (x_train_resized) and corresponding labels (y_train).
- We specify the number of training epochs (epochs=10) to train the model for 10 iterations over the entire dataset.
- We set the batch size (batch_size=32) to specify the number of samples per gradient update. It is a hyperparameter that determines how many samples are processed before updating the model's parameters.
- We provide the validation data (validation_data=(x_test_resized, y_test)) to evaluate the model's performance on the testing data after each epoch.
- The fit method returns a history object containing training metrics (e.g., loss and accuracy) for each epoch, which can be used for analysis and visualization.

Let me know if you have any questions or if you'd like to proceed with evaluating the model or making any adjustments!

[End of response]

We execute the code and it runs without any errors. The model is trained for 10 epochs, after which we receive a validation accuracy of 62.6%, which is not bad for a basic model.

```
[ ]    1    # Step 3: Model Training
       2
       3    # Train the model
       4    history = model.fit(x_train_resized, y_train,
       5                        epochs=10,
       6                        batch_size=32,
       7                        validation_data=(x_test_resized, y_test))
```

```
Epoch 1/10
1563/1563 [==============================] - 40s 25ms/step - loss: 1.5051 - accuracy: 0.4653 - val_loss: 1.2554 - val_accuracy: 0.5600
Epoch 2/10
1563/1563 [==============================] - 39s 25ms/step - loss: 1.2019 - accuracy: 0.5802 - val_loss: 1.1988 - val_accuracy: 0.5805
Epoch 3/10
1563/1563 [==============================] - 39s 25ms/step - loss: 1.0894 - accuracy: 0.6228 - val_loss: 1.1065 - val_accuracy: 0.6151
Epoch 4/10
1563/1563 [==============================] - 41s 26ms/step - loss: 1.0049 - accuracy: 0.6533 - val_loss: 1.1028 - val_accuracy: 0.6219
Epoch 5/10
1563/1563 [==============================] - 38s 24ms/step - loss: 0.9461 - accuracy: 0.6722 - val_loss: 1.0833 - val_accuracy: 0.6299
Epoch 6/10
1563/1563 [==============================] - 41s 26ms/step - loss: 0.8892 - accuracy: 0.6917 - val_loss: 1.0305 - val_accuracy: 0.6434
Epoch 7/10
1563/1563 [==============================] - 40s 25ms/step - loss: 0.8401 - accuracy: 0.7076 - val_loss: 1.0453 - val_accuracy: 0.6430
Epoch 8/10
1563/1563 [==============================] - 39s 25ms/step - loss: 0.7990 - accuracy: 0.7217 - val_loss: 1.0580 - val_accuracy: 0.6409
Epoch 9/10
1563/1563 [==============================] - 40s 26ms/step - loss: 0.7597 - accuracy: 0.7352 - val_loss: 1.0681 - val_accuracy: 0.6424
Epoch 10/10
1563/1563 [==============================] - 39s 25ms/step - loss: 0.7248 - accuracy: 0.7474 - val_loss: 1.1223 - val_accuracy: 0.6260
```

Figure 15.4: Code execution – model training

We will now instruct ChatGPT to proceed to the next step to evaluate the model performance.

[Prompt]

Let's proceed to the next step.

[End of prompt]

We should receive a response like the following where ChatGPT should provide the code for model evaluation along with comments.

[Prompt response]

Sure! The next step is to evaluate the trained model on the testing dataset and visualize its performance.

```python
# Step 4: Model Evaluation and Visualization

import matplotlib.pyplot as plt

# Evaluate the model on the testing dataset
test_loss, test_accuracy = model.evaluate(x_test_resized, y_test, verbose=0)

print("Test Loss:", test_loss)
print("Test Accuracy:", test_accuracy)

# Plot training history
plt.plot(history.history['accuracy'], label='Training Accuracy')
```

```
plt.plot(history.history['val_accuracy'], label='Validation Accuracy')
plt.title('Training and Validation Accuracy')
plt.xlabel('Epoch')
plt.ylabel('Accuracy')
plt.legend()
plt.show()
```

Here's what this code does:

- We import `matplotlib.pyplot` to visualize the training history.
- We evaluate the trained model on the testing dataset using the evaluate method, which returns the test loss and accuracy.
- We print the test loss and test accuracy to assess the model's performance on unseen data.
- We plot the training and validation accuracy over epochs using `matplotlib.pyplot`. The history object returned by the `fit` method contains accuracy values for both training and validation datasets across epochs.
- The `history.history['accuracy']` contains training accuracy values.
- The `history.history['val_accuracy']` contains validation accuracy values.
- The plot helps us visualize how well the model is learning over time and whether it is overfitting or underfitting.

Let me know if you have any questions or if you'd like to analyze the results further!

[End of response]

We execute the code and it runs without any errors. It evaluates the test loss and test accuracy (62.5%) and also plots the graph of training accuracy vs. validation accuracy, showing that model is not performing well on the validation set.

```
[ ]   1   # Step 4: Model Evaluation and Visualization
      2
      3   import matplotlib.pyplot as plt
      4
      5   # Evaluate the model on the testing dataset
      6   test_loss, test_accuracy = model.evaluate(x_test_resized, y_test, verbose=0)
      7
      8   print("Test Loss:", test_loss)
      9   print("Test Accuracy:", test_accuracy)
     10
     11   # Plot training history
     12   plt.plot(history.history['accuracy'], label='Training Accuracy')
     13   plt.plot(history.history['val_accuracy'], label='Validation Accuracy')
     14   plt.title('Training and Validation Accuracy')
     15   plt.xlabel('Epoch')
     16   plt.ylabel('Accuracy')
     17   plt.legend()
     18   plt.show()
```

```
Test Loss: 1.1222519874572754
Test Accuracy: 0.6259999871253967
```

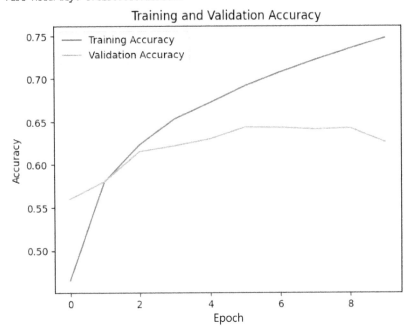

Figure 15.5: Code execution – model evaluation

This completes feature 1, where we achieved an accuracy of 0.6259 (62.59%) with our baseline CNN model. (Please note that you may receive different accuracy scores even after running the exact same code.) Next, we will move to the second feature of adding more layers to the model and learn how ChatGPT can assist us in that.

Feature 2: Experimenting with the addition of convolutional layers

Now that we have a baseline model architecture, let us try adding layers to it. We will apply the prompting strategy to improvise the model (LIFE 3.4) and ask ChatGPT to provide us the code for it, also note the importance of providing specific instructions by using the phrase (on top of our baseline model) (PIC 2.2) and keyword incrementally (PIC 2.2); without these, the response wouldn't be fully consistent with our expectations.

[Prompt]

We received an accuracy of 62.59 with the baseline model, so now I would like to experiment with the addition of two consecutive layers of 64 filters first and then two consecutive layers of 128 filters on top of our baseline model. Then, let's compare the result of these two incremental changes with our baseline model.

[End of prompt]

We should receive a response like the following where ChatGPT understands the request and provides us with the code for a modified model with consecutive layers of 64 filters and another one with consecutive layers of 128 filters.

[Prompt response]

Sure! Let's first add two consecutive layers of 64 filters to the baseline model and train it again. After that, we'll add two consecutive layers of 128 filters and train the model once more. Finally, we'll compare the results of these two changes with the baseline model.

Here's how we can modify the baseline model to include additional layers:

```python
# Define the modified model with two consecutive layers of 64 filters
modified_model_64 = Sequential([
    Conv2D(32, (3, 3), activation='relu', input_shape=(32, 32, 3)),
    MaxPooling2D((2, 2)),
    Conv2D(64, (3, 3), activation='relu'),
    MaxPooling2D((2, 2)),
    Conv2D(64, (3, 3), activation='relu'),
    MaxPooling2D((2, 2)),
    Flatten(),
    Dense(64, activation='relu'),
    Dense(10, activation='softmax')
])

# Compile the modified model
modified_model_64.compile(optimizer='adam',
                          loss='sparse_categorical_crossentropy',
                          metrics=['accuracy'])
```

```
# Display model summary
modified_model_64.summary()

# Train the modified model with two consecutive layers of 64 filters
history_64 = modified_model_64.fit(x_train_resized, y_train,
                                   epochs=10,
                                   batch_size=32,
                                   validation_data=(x_test_resized, y_test))

# Evaluate the modified model on the testing dataset
test_loss_64, test_accuracy_64 = modified_model_64.evaluate(x_test_resized, y_
test, verbose=0)

print("Test Loss (Modified Model with 64 Filters):", test_loss_64)
print("Test Accuracy (Modified Model with 64 Filters):", test_accuracy_64)
```

Now, let's explain the modifications:

- We define the modified model (modified_model_64) by adding two consecutive convolutional layers with 64 filters each after the baseline model's architecture.
- We compile the modified model with the same settings as the baseline model.
- We train the modified model (modified_model_64) on the preprocessed training data (x_train_resized).
- We evaluate the performance of the modified model on the testing dataset (x_test_resized) and print the test loss and accuracy.

Next, we'll repeat the process for adding two consecutive layers of 128 filters:

```
# Define the modified model with two consecutive layers of 128 filters
modified_model_128 = Sequential([
    Conv2D(32, (3, 3), activation='relu', input_shape=(32, 32, 3)),
    MaxPooling2D((2, 2)),
    Conv2D(64, (3, 3), activation='relu'),
    MaxPooling2D((2, 2)),
    Conv2D(64, (3, 3), activation='relu'),
    MaxPooling2D((2, 2)),
    Conv2D(128, (3, 3), activation='relu'),
    MaxPooling2D((2, 2)),
    Conv2D(128, (3, 3), activation='relu'),
    MaxPooling2D((2, 2)),
    Flatten(),
    Dense(64, activation='relu'),
```

```python
    Dense(10, activation='softmax')
])


# Compile the modified model
modified_model_128.compile(optimizer='adam',
                            loss='sparse_categorical_crossentropy',
                            metrics=['accuracy'])


# Display model summary
modified_model_128.summary()


# Train the modified model with two consecutive layers of 128 filters
history_128 = modified_model_128.fit(x_train_resized, y_train,
                                    epochs=10,
                                    batch_size=32,
                                    validation_data=(x_test_resized, y_test))


# Evaluate the modified model on the testing dataset
test_loss_128, test_accuracy_128 = modified_model_128.evaluate(x_test_resized,
y_test, verbose=0)


print("Test Loss (Modified Model with 128 Filters):", test_loss_128)
print("Test Accuracy (Modified Model with 128 Filters):", test_accuracy_128)
```

This code follows the same structure as the previous modification but adds two consecutive convolutional layers with 128 filters each. We train and evaluate the model accordingly.

Let me know if you have any questions or if you'd like to proceed with the modifications!

[End of response]

We first execute the code that defines the two additional layers with 64 filters. It runs perfectly fine, training the model and achieving an improved accuracy of 71%.

```
Model: "sequential_1"

 Layer (type)                Output Shape              Param #
=================================================================
 conv2d_2 (Conv2D)           (None, 30, 30, 32)        896

 max_pooling2d_1 (MaxPoolin  (None, 15, 15, 32)        0
 g2D)

 conv2d_3 (Conv2D)           (None, 13, 13, 64)        18496

 max_pooling2d_2 (MaxPoolin  (None, 6, 6, 64)          0
 g2D)

 conv2d_4 (Conv2D)           (None, 4, 4, 64)          36928

 max_pooling2d_3 (MaxPoolin  (None, 2, 2, 64)          0
 g2D)

 flatten_1 (Flatten)         (None, 256)               0

 dense_2 (Dense)             (None, 64)                16448

 dense_3 (Dense)             (None, 10)                650

=================================================================
Total params: 73418 (286.79 KB)
Trainable params: 73418 (286.79 KB)
Non-trainable params: 0 (0.00 Byte)
_____
Epoch 1/10
1563/1563 [==============================] - 10s 5ms/step - loss: 1.5440 - accuracy: 0.4342 - val_loss: 1.2825 - val_accuracy: 0.5462
Epoch 2/10
1563/1563 [==============================] - 10s 6ms/step - loss: 1.1861 - accuracy: 0.5767 - val_loss: 1.0853 - val_accuracy: 0.6187
Epoch 3/10
1563/1563 [==============================] - 11s 7ms/step - loss: 1.0438 - accuracy: 0.6310 - val_loss: 0.9983 - val_accuracy: 0.6543
Epoch 4/10
1563/1563 [==============================] - 9s 6ms/step - loss: 0.9431 - accuracy: 0.6677 - val_loss: 0.9449 - val_accuracy: 0.6732
Epoch 5/10
1563/1563 [==============================] - 9s 5ms/step - loss: 0.8770 - accuracy: 0.6923 - val_loss: 0.9397 - val_accuracy: 0.6711
Epoch 6/10
1563/1563 [==============================] - 8s 5ms/step - loss: 0.8180 - accuracy: 0.7140 - val_loss: 0.8753 - val_accuracy: 0.6972
Epoch 7/10
1563/1563 [==============================] - 8s 5ms/step - loss: 0.7749 - accuracy: 0.7282 - val_loss: 0.8775 - val_accuracy: 0.6969
Epoch 8/10
1563/1563 [==============================] - 8s 5ms/step - loss: 0.7288 - accuracy: 0.7435 - val_loss: 0.9046 - val_accuracy: 0.6924
Epoch 9/10
1563/1563 [==============================] - 8s 5ms/step - loss: 0.6930 - accuracy: 0.7582 - val_loss: 0.8837 - val_accuracy: 0.6962
Epoch 10/10
1563/1563 [==============================] - 8s 5ms/step - loss: 0.6588 - accuracy: 0.7706 - val_loss: 0.8475 - val_accuracy: 0.7174
Test Loss (Modified Model with 64 Filters): 0.8474552035331726
Test Accuracy (Modified Model with 64 Filters): 0.7174000144004822
```

Figure 15.6: Adding two consecutive layers with 64 filters to the model

Next, we execute the code to add further depth to the model by adding two more layers with 128 filters. In this case, the code results in an error, so we will use a prompting strategy and provide the error back to ChatGPT.

You should see a `ValueError` from running the code.

[Prompt]

We received the below error. Also, ensure that maxpooling doesn't reduce the dimension too much for 128 filters. Error is below:

```
ValueError: Exception encountered when calling layer "conv2d_38" (type Conv2D).

Negative dimension size caused by subtracting 3 from 2 for '{{node conv2d_38/
Conv2D}} = Conv2D[T=DT_FLOAT, data_format="NHWC", dilations=[1, 1, 1, 1],
explicit_paddings=[], padding="VALID", strides=[1, 1, 1, 1], use_cudnn_on_
gpu=true](Placeholder, conv2d_38/Conv2D/ReadVariableOp)' with input shapes:
[?,2,2,64], [3,3,64,128].

Call arguments received by layer "conv2d_38" (type Conv2D):
   inputs=tf.Tensor(shape=(None, 2, 2, 64), dtype=float32).
```

[End of prompt]

We should receive a response like the following where ChatGPT understands the request and provides us with the modified code to resolve the issue.

[Prompt response]

It seems we're encountering an issue where the dimensions after the last max pooling layer are too small for the subsequent convolutional layer with 128 filters. To address this, we'll adjust the architecture to ensure compatibility between layers.

Here's the corrected code:

```
# Define the modified model with two consecutive layers of 128 filters added to
the 64-layer model
modified_model_64_to_128 = Sequential([
    Conv2D(32, (3, 3), activation='relu', input_shape=(32, 32, 3)),
    MaxPooling2D((2, 2)),
    Conv2D(64, (3, 3), activation='relu'),
    MaxPooling2D((2, 2)),
    Conv2D(64, (3, 3), activation='relu'),
    Conv2D(128, (3, 3), activation='relu', padding='same'),  # Add padding
    Conv2D(128, (3, 3), activation='relu', padding='same'),  # Add padding
    MaxPooling2D((2, 2)),
    Flatten(),
    Dense(64, activation='relu'),
```

```
      Dense(10, activation='softmax')
])

# Compile the modified model
modified_model_64_to_128.compile(optimizer='adam',
                                 loss='sparse_categorical_crossentropy',
                                 metrics=['accuracy'])

# Display model summary
modified_model_64_to_128.summary()

# Train the modified model with two consecutive layers of 128 filters added to
the 64-layer model
history_64_to_128 = modified_model_64_to_128.fit(x_train_resized, y_train,
                                                 epochs=10,
                                                 batch_size=32,
                                                 validation_data=(x_test_
resized, y_test))

# Evaluate the modified model on the testing dataset
test_loss_64_to_128, test_accuracy_64_to_128 = modified_model_64_to_128.
evaluate(x_test_resized, y_test, verbose=0)

print("Test Loss (Modified Model with 64 to 128 Filters):", test_loss_64_
to_128)
print("Test Accuracy (Modified Model with 64 to 128 Filters):", test_
accuracy_64_to_128)
```

In this modification:

- We've removed the max pooling layer after the last convolutional layer with 64 filters to ensure that the feature map dimensions are not reduced too much before applying the subsequent convolutional layers with 128 filters.
- We've added same padding to the convolutional layers with 128 filters to ensure compatibility with the input dimensions.
- The rest of the architecture remains the same.

This adjustment should resolve the issue, and the model should compile and train properly. Let me know if you have any questions or if you encounter any further issues!

[End of response]

Let's execute the code, which removes some max pooling layers and also has padding = 'same' added to ensure the dimensions are compatible. It runs successfully, training the model but reducing the accuracy to 69%.

```
Model: "sequential_9"

 Layer (type)                Output Shape              Param #
=================================================================
 conv2d_40 (Conv2D)          (None, 30, 30, 32)        896

 max_pooling2d_34 (MaxPooli  (None, 15, 15, 32)        0
 ng2D)

 conv2d_41 (Conv2D)          (None, 13, 13, 64)        18496

 max_pooling2d_35 (MaxPooli  (None, 6, 6, 64)          0
 ng2D)

 conv2d_42 (Conv2D)          (None, 4, 4, 64)          36928

 conv2d_43 (Conv2D)          (None, 4, 4, 128)         73856

 conv2d_44 (Conv2D)          (None, 4, 4, 128)         147584

 max_pooling2d_36 (MaxPooli  (None, 2, 2, 128)         0
 ng2D)

 flatten_9 (Flatten)         (None, 512)               0

 dense_18 (Dense)            (None, 64)                32832

 dense_19 (Dense)            (None, 10)                650

=================================================================
Total params: 311242 (1.19 MB)
Trainable params: 311242 (1.19 MB)
Non-trainable params: 0 (0.00 Byte)
_____
Epoch 1/10
1563/1563 [==============================] - 12s 7ms/step - loss: 1.5531 - accuracy: 0.4194 - val_loss: 1.3012 - val_accuracy: 0.5338
Epoch 2/10
1563/1563 [==============================] - 10s 6ms/step - loss: 1.1590 - accuracy: 0.5874 - val_loss: 1.1143 - val_accuracy: 0.5969
Epoch 3/10
1563/1563 [==============================] - 9s 6ms/step - loss: 0.9821 - accuracy: 0.6528 - val_loss: 0.9471 - val_accuracy: 0.6691
Epoch 4/10
1563/1563 [==============================] - 10s 6ms/step - loss: 0.8647 - accuracy: 0.6960 - val_loss: 0.9182 - val_accuracy: 0.6881
Epoch 5/10
1563/1563 [==============================] - 10s 6ms/step - loss: 0.7730 - accuracy: 0.7271 - val_loss: 0.9124 - val_accuracy: 0.6931
Epoch 6/10
1563/1563 [==============================] - 10s 6ms/step - loss: 0.6967 - accuracy: 0.7541 - val_loss: 0.8611 - val_accuracy: 0.7045
Epoch 7/10
1563/1563 [==============================] - 9s 6ms/step - loss: 0.6228 - accuracy: 0.7804 - val_loss: 1.0315 - val_accuracy: 0.6705
Epoch 8/10
1563/1563 [==============================] - 10s 6ms/step - loss: 0.5574 - accuracy: 0.8050 - val_loss: 0.9043 - val_accuracy: 0.7114
Epoch 9/10
1563/1563 [==============================] - 10s 7ms/step - loss: 0.4964 - accuracy: 0.8224 - val_loss: 0.9639 - val_accuracy: 0.6958
Epoch 10/10
1563/1563 [==============================] - 9s 6ms/step - loss: 0.4393 - accuracy: 0.8438 - val_loss: 1.0033 - val_accuracy: 0.6993
Test Loss (Modified Model with 64 to 128 Filters): 1.0032662153244019
Test Accuracy (Modified Model with 64 to 128 Filters): 0.6992999911308289
```

Figure 15.7: Added layers with 128 filters

Based on these results, we can observe that the addition of more layers achieved a slightly higher accuracy compared to the baseline model. However, the differences in accuracy are relatively small, indicating that the addition of layers did not significantly improve the model's performance and the model is also still not regularized. Let's move on to the next feature and experiment with dropout regularization.

Feature 3: Incorporating dropout regularization

Now that we have learned how to add more layers, we will now experiment with a dropout layer. We will apply the prompting strategy to improvise the model (LIFE 3.4) and ask ChatGPT to provide us the code for it.

Also note that we have applied the prompting strategy of using specific instructions (PIC 2.2) by asking it to add the dropout over the previously provided code.

[Prompt]

The model accuracy of the baseline model was 62.5%, with additional layers of 64 filters it was 71%, and the further addition of layers with 128 filters reduced it to 69%. Can we please apply dropout regularization to the model code given by you in your previous message?

[End of prompt]

We should receive a response like the following where ChatGPT understands the request and provides us with the code for the addition of a dropout layer.

[Prompt response]

Sure, let's add dropout regularization to the modified model with two consecutive layers of 128 filters. Dropout regularization helps prevent overfitting by randomly dropping a fraction of the units (neurons) during training. Here's how we can modify the model to include dropout layers:

```python
from tensorflow.keras.layers import Dropout

# Define the modified model with dropout regularization
modified_model_64_to_128_with_dropout = Sequential([
    Conv2D(32, (3, 3), activation='relu', input_shape=(32, 32, 3)),
    MaxPooling2D((2, 2)),
    Conv2D(64, (3, 3), activation='relu'),
    MaxPooling2D((2, 2)),
    Conv2D(64, (3, 3), activation='relu'),
    Conv2D(128, (3, 3), activation='relu', padding='same'),
    Dropout(0.25),   # Add dropout regularization with a dropout rate of 25%
    Conv2D(128, (3, 3), activation='relu', padding='same'),
    Dropout(0.25),   # Add dropout regularization with a dropout rate of 25%
    MaxPooling2D((2, 2)),
    Flatten(),
    Dense(64, activation='relu'),
    Dropout(0.5),   # Add dropout regularization with a dropout rate of 50%
    Dense(10, activation='softmax')
])

# Compile the modified model with dropout regularization
modified_model_64_to_128_with_dropout.compile(optimizer='adam',
                                               loss='sparse_categorical_
crossentropy',
                                               metrics=['accuracy'])
```

```
# Display model summary
modified_model_64_to_128_with_dropout.summary()

# Train the modified model with dropout regularization
history_64_to_128_with_dropout = modified_model_64_to_128_with_dropout.fit(x_
train_resized, y_train,

epochs=10,

batch_size=32,

validation_data=(x_test_resized, y_test))

# Evaluate the modified model with dropout regularization on the testing
dataset
test_loss_64_to_128_with_dropout, test_accuracy_64_to_128_with_dropout =
modified_model_64_to_128_with_dropout.evaluate(x_test_resized, y_test,
verbose=0)

print("Test Loss (Modified Model with Dropout):", test_loss_64_to_128_with_
dropout)
print("Test Accuracy (Modified Model with Dropout):", test_accuracy_64_to_128_
with_dropout)
```

In this modification:

- We add dropout layers after the convolutional layers with 128 filters. We set the dropout rates to 25% and 50% for the first and last dropout layers, respectively. These values can be adjusted based on experimentation and the level of regularization needed.
- We compile and train the modified model with dropout regularization using the same settings as before.
- We evaluate the performance of the modified model with dropout regularization on the testing dataset and print the test loss and accuracy.

Adding dropout regularization may help improve the generalization performance of the model and reduce overfitting. Let me know if you have any questions or if you'd like to explore further!

[End of response]

We execute the code, which defines a model with a dropout layer. It also trains and evaluates the performance of the model and prints the model summary covering loss and accuracy. Note that the dropout layer does not add any parameters to the model.

```
Model: "sequential_10"

 Layer (type)                Output Shape              Param #
=================================================================
 conv2d_45 (Conv2D)          (None, 30, 30, 32)        896

 max_pooling2d_37 (MaxPooli  (None, 15, 15, 32)        0
 ng2D)

 conv2d_46 (Conv2D)          (None, 13, 13, 64)        18496

 max_pooling2d_38 (MaxPooli  (None, 6, 6, 64)          0
 ng2D)

 conv2d_47 (Conv2D)          (None, 4, 4, 64)          36928

 conv2d_48 (Conv2D)          (None, 4, 4, 128)         73856

 dropout (Dropout)           (None, 4, 4, 128)         0

 conv2d_49 (Conv2D)          (None, 4, 4, 128)         147584

 dropout_1 (Dropout)         (None, 4, 4, 128)         0

 max_pooling2d_39 (MaxPooli  (None, 2, 2, 128)         0
 ng2D)

 flatten_10 (Flatten)        (None, 512)               0

 dense_20 (Dense)            (None, 64)                32832

 dropout_2 (Dropout)         (None, 64)                0

 dense_21 (Dense)            (None, 10)                650

=================================================================
Total params: 311242 (1.19 MB)
Trainable params: 311242 (1.19 MB)
Non-trainable params: 0 (0.00 Byte)
_____
Epoch 1/10
1563/1563 [==============================] - 15s 7ms/step - loss: 1.7530 - accuracy: 0.3412 - val_loss: 1.3975 - val_accuracy: 0.4846
Epoch 2/10
1563/1563 [==============================] - 11s 7ms/step - loss: 1.3638 - accuracy: 0.5163 - val_loss: 1.2464 - val_accuracy: 0.5531
Epoch 3/10
1563/1563 [==============================] - 12s 7ms/step - loss: 1.2159 - accuracy: 0.5788 - val_loss: 1.1147 - val_accuracy: 0.6142
Epoch 4/10
1563/1563 [==============================] - 11s 7ms/step - loss: 1.1127 - accuracy: 0.6176 - val_loss: 1.0766 - val_accuracy: 0.6181
Epoch 5/10
1563/1563 [==============================] - 11s 7ms/step - loss: 1.0457 - accuracy: 0.6420 - val_loss: 1.0325 - val_accuracy: 0.6341
Epoch 6/10
1563/1563 [==============================] - 10s 7ms/step - loss: 0.9839 - accuracy: 0.6662 - val_loss: 0.9573 - val_accuracy: 0.6701
Epoch 7/10
1563/1563 [==============================] - 11s 7ms/step - loss: 0.9283 - accuracy: 0.6829 - val_loss: 0.9381 - val_accuracy: 0.6795
Epoch 8/10
1563/1563 [==============================] - 11s 7ms/step - loss: 0.8872 - accuracy: 0.6990 - val_loss: 0.9123 - val_accuracy: 0.6870
Epoch 9/10
1563/1563 [==============================] - 11s 7ms/step - loss: 0.8503 - accuracy: 0.7111 - val_loss: 0.8838 - val_accuracy: 0.6975
Epoch 10/10
1563/1563 [==============================] - 12s 8ms/step - loss: 0.8220 - accuracy: 0.7194 - val_loss: 0.8761 - val_accuracy: 0.7015
Test Loss (Modified Model with Dropout): 0.876133382320404
Test Accuracy (Modified Model with Dropout): 0.7014999985694885
```

Figure 15.8: Code execution – dropout layer

We can see that there is not much difference between the accuracies, so we will apply the Learn prompting strategy (LIFE 3.1) and ask ChatGPT to provide the plot of the loss and accuracy to see the impact of regularization.

[Prompt]

```
Test Loss (Modified Model with Dropout): 0.876133382320404
Test Accuracy (Modified Model with Dropout): 0.7014999985694885
```

Can you please provide the plots for loss and accuracy to see if there has been any regularization and also explain it?

[End of prompt]

We should receive a response like the following where ChatGPT provides the code and explains the significance of the plots.

[Prompt response]

Certainly! Let's plot the training and validation loss and accuracy curves for the modified model with dropout regularization. This will help us visualize how dropout regularization affects the training process and the model's performance.

```python
import matplotlib.pyplot as plt

# Plot training history for loss
plt.plot(history_64_to_128_with_dropout.history['loss'], label='Training Loss')
plt.plot(history_64_to_128_with_dropout.history['val_loss'], label='Validation
Loss')
plt.title('Training and Validation Loss')
plt.xlabel('Epoch')
plt.ylabel('Loss')
plt.legend()
plt.show()

# Plot training history for accuracy
plt.plot(history_64_to_128_with_dropout.history['accuracy'], label='Training
Accuracy')
plt.plot(history_64_to_128_with_dropout.history['val_accuracy'],
label='Validation Accuracy')
plt.title('Training and Validation Accuracy')
plt.xlabel('Epoch')
plt.ylabel('Accuracy')
plt.legend()
plt.show()
```

Explanation:

- **Training Loss vs. Validation Loss:** This plot shows the trend of training and validation loss over epochs. If there is a large gap between training and validation loss, it indicates overfitting. Dropout regularization aims to reduce overfitting by preventing the model from becoming overly reliant on specific features, thereby reducing the gap between training and validation loss.
- **Training Accuracy vs. Validation Accuracy:** This plot shows the trend of training and validation accuracy over epochs. Dropout regularization can also help improve generalization performance, leading to better validation accuracy, especially if overfitting was present in the model.

By observing these plots, we can assess whether dropout regularization effectively mitigated overfitting and improved the model's generalization performance. Let me know if you have any questions or if you need further explanation!

[End of response]

We will execute the code and plot the graphs to understand the impact of dropout.

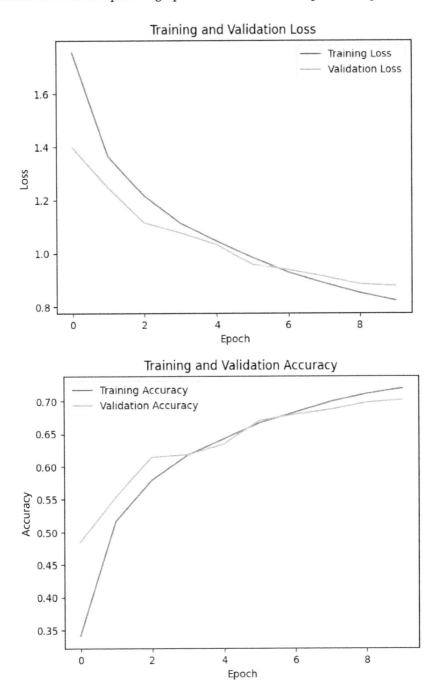

Figure 15.9: Effect of the dropout layer

The output graphs show the training and validation loss and accuracy for a model trained on the CIFAR-10 dataset with a dropout layer. Both losses decrease over epochs while the accuracy improves, indicating effective learning. The small gap between training and validation metrics suggests minimal overfitting, likely aided by the dropout layer. Overall, the model generalizes well to new data, demonstrating good performance.

Feature 4: Implementing batch normalization

We will apply the prompting strategy to improvise the model (LIFE 3.4) and ask ChatGPT to provide us the code for adding batch normalization to the previously provided code.

[Prompt]

I want to apply the batch normalization on the previously provided code.

[End of prompt]

We should receive a response like the following where ChatGPT understands the request and provides us with the code for batch normalization on our existing model.

[Prompt response]

Sure! We can apply batch normalization to the convolutional layers of the model to improve training stability and convergence speed. Here's how we can modify the model to include batch normalization layers:

```python
from tensorflow.keras.layers import BatchNormalization

# Define the modified model with batch normalization
modified_model_64_to_128_with_batchnorm = Sequential([
    Conv2D(32, (3, 3), activation='relu', input_shape=(32, 32, 3)),
    BatchNormalization(),   # Add batch normalization
    MaxPooling2D((2, 2)),
    Conv2D(64, (3, 3), activation='relu'),
    BatchNormalization(),   # Add batch normalization
    MaxPooling2D((2, 2)),
    Conv2D(64, (3, 3), activation='relu'),
    Conv2D(128, (3, 3), activation='relu', padding='same'),
    BatchNormalization(),   # Add batch normalization
    MaxPooling2D((2, 2)),
    Conv2D(128, (3, 3), activation='relu', padding='same'),
    BatchNormalization(),   # Add batch normalization
    MaxPooling2D((2, 2)),
    Flatten(),
    Dense(64, activation='relu'),
    BatchNormalization(),   # Add batch normalization
```

```
      Dense(10, activation='softmax')
])

# Compile the modified model with batch normalization
modified_model_64_to_128_with_batchnorm.compile(optimizer='adam',
                                                loss='sparse_categorical_
crossentropy',
                                                metrics=['accuracy'])

# Display model summary
modified_model_64_to_128_with_batchnorm.summary()

# Train the modified model with batch normalization
history_64_to_128_with_batchnorm = modified_model_64_to_128_with_batchnorm.
fit(x_train_resized, y_train,

epochs=10,

batch_size=32,

validation_data=(x_test_resized, y_test))

# Evaluate the modified model with batch normalization on the testing dataset
test_loss_64_to_128_with_batchnorm, test_accuracy_64_to_128_with_batchnorm
= modified_model_64_to_128_with_batchnorm.evaluate(x_test_resized, y_test,
verbose=0)

print("Test Loss (Modified Model with Batch Normalization):", test_loss_64_
to_128_with_batchnorm)
print("Test Accuracy (Modified Model with Batch Normalization):", test_
accuracy_64_to_128_with_batchnorm)
```

In this modification:

- We add `BatchNormalization` layers after each convolutional layer. Batch normalization normalizes the activations of the previous layer at each batch, making training more stable and accelerating convergence.
- We compile and train the modified model with batch normalization using the same settings as before.
- We evaluate the performance of the modified model with batch normalization on the testing dataset and print the test loss and accuracy.

Adding batch normalization can improve the performance and stability of the model during training. Let me know if you have any questions or if you'd like further explanation!

[End of response]

We will execute the code, evaluate the model's performance, and print the results. Note that batch normalization adds a small number of parameters, unlike dropout or maxpooling.

```
batch_normalization (Batch    (None, 30, 30, 32)      128
Normalization)

max_pooling2d_3 (MaxPoolin    (None, 15, 15, 32)      0
g2D)

conv2d_6 (Conv2D)             (None, 13, 13, 64)      18496

batch_normalization_1 (Bat    (None, 13, 13, 64)      256
chNormalization)

max_pooling2d_4 (MaxPoolin    (None, 6, 6, 64)        0
g2D)

conv2d_7 (Conv2D)             (None, 4, 4, 64)        36928

conv2d_8 (Conv2D)             (None, 4, 4, 128)       73856

batch_normalization_2 (Bat    (None, 4, 4, 128)       512
chNormalization)

max_pooling2d_5 (MaxPoolin    (None, 2, 2, 128)       0
g2D)

conv2d_9 (Conv2D)             (None, 2, 2, 128)       147584

batch_normalization_3 (Bat    (None, 2, 2, 128)       512
chNormalization)

max_pooling2d_6 (MaxPoolin    (None, 1, 1, 128)       0
g2D)

flatten_1 (Flatten)           (None, 128)             0

dense_2 (Dense)               (None, 64)              8256

batch_normalization_4 (Bat    (None, 64)              256
chNormalization)

dense_3 (Dense)               (None, 10)              650

=================================================================
Total params: 288330 (1.10 MB)
Trainable params: 287498 (1.10 MB)
Non-trainable params: 832 (3.25 KB)
_____
Epoch 1/10
1563/1563 [==============================] - 21s 8ms/step - loss: 1.3927 - accuracy: 0.5045 - val_loss: 1.4828 - val_accuracy: 0.5232
Epoch 2/10
1563/1563 [==============================] - 11s 7ms/step - loss: 1.0016 - accuracy: 0.6489 - val_loss: 0.9775 - val_accuracy: 0.6596
Epoch 3/10
1563/1563 [==============================] - 12s 7ms/step - loss: 0.8231 - accuracy: 0.7152 - val_loss: 1.0615 - val_accuracy: 0.6423
Epoch 4/10
1563/1563 [==============================] - 12s 8ms/step - loss: 0.7145 - accuracy: 0.7522 - val_loss: 0.9972 - val_accuracy: 0.6483
Epoch 5/10
1563/1563 [==============================] - 12s 7ms/step - loss: 0.6202 - accuracy: 0.7861 - val_loss: 0.8076 - val_accuracy: 0.7213
Epoch 6/10
1563/1563 [==============================] - 12s 7ms/step - loss: 0.5490 - accuracy: 0.8106 - val_loss: 1.0868 - val_accuracy: 0.6462
Epoch 7/10
1563/1563 [==============================] - 12s 8ms/step - loss: 0.4774 - accuracy: 0.8349 - val_loss: 0.7828 - val_accuracy: 0.7444
Epoch 8/10
1563/1563 [==============================] - 12s 7ms/step - loss: 0.4215 - accuracy: 0.8518 - val_loss: 0.9065 - val_accuracy: 0.7209
Epoch 9/10
1563/1563 [==============================] - 12s 8ms/step - loss: 0.3664 - accuracy: 0.8712 - val_loss: 0.9365 - val_accuracy: 0.7152
Epoch 10/10
1563/1563 [==============================] - 12s 8ms/step - loss: 0.3223 - accuracy: 0.8865 - val_loss: 0.9293 - val_accuracy: 0.7268
Test Loss (Modified Model with Batch Normalization): 0.9293251037597656
Test Accuracy (Modified Model with Batch Normalization): 0.7268000245094299
```

Figure 15.10: Batch normalization

We can see that there are some non-trainable parameters. Let us make use of the Learn prompting strategy (LIFE 3.1) to understand the calculations of non-trainable parameters.

[Prompt]

Can you please explain the calculation of 832 in the model summary?

```
"sequential_1"
```

Layer (type)	Output Shape	Param #
conv2d_5 (Conv2D)	(None, 30, 30, 32)	896
batch_normalization (Batch Normalization)	(None, 30, 30, 32)	128
max_pooling2d_3 (MaxPoolin g2D)	(None, 15, 15, 32)	0
conv2d_6 (Conv2D)	(None, 13, 13, 64)	18496
batch_normalization_1 (Bat chNormalization)	(None, 13, 13, 64)	256
max_pooling2d_4 (MaxPoolin g2D)	(None, 6, 6, 64)	0
conv2d_7 (Conv2D)	(None, 4, 4, 64)	36928
conv2d_8 (Conv2D)	(None, 4, 4, 128)	73856
batch_normalization_2 (Bat chNormalization)	(None, 4, 4, 128)	512
max_pooling2d_5 (MaxPoolin g2D)	(None, 2, 2, 128)	0
conv2d_9 (Conv2D)	(None, 2, 2, 128)	147584
batch_normalization_3 (Bat chNormalization)	(None, 2, 2, 128)	512
max_pooling2d_6 (MaxPoolin g2D)	(None, 1, 1, 128)	0

```
    flatten_1 (Flatten)           (None, 128)                  0

    dense_2 (Dense)               (None, 64)                 8256

    batch_normalization_4 (Bat    (None, 64)                  256
    chNormalization)

    dense_3 (Dense)               (None, 10)                  650

    =================================================================
Total params: 288330 (1.10 MB)
Trainable params: 287498 (1.10 MB)
Non-trainable params: 832 (3.25 KB)
```

[End of prompt]

We should receive a response like the following where ChatGPT understands the request and provides us with an explanation of the calculation of non-trainable parameters.

[Prompt response]

In the model you've described, the non-trainable parameters are 832, which specifically come from the batch normalization layers. Here's how this number is calculated:

Components of Batch Normalization

Each batch normalization layer introduces parameters that are used to normalize the outputs of the previous layer. Specifically, these parameters are:

- **Gamma (scale factor)**
- **Beta (shift factor)**
- **Moving average of means**
- **Moving average of variances**

The gamma and beta parameters are trainable, while the moving means and variances are non-trainable. Each of these groups (gamma/beta and moving mean/variance) has as many elements as there are channels in the input to the batch normalization layer.

Calculation

Based on your model configuration:

Batch Normalization after first Conv2D layer (32 channels):

- Moving means: 32
- Moving variances: 32

Batch Normalization after second Conv2D layer (64 channels):

- Moving means: 64
- Moving variances: 64

Batch Normalization after third Conv2D layer (128 channels):

- Moving means: 128
- Moving variances: 128

Batch Normalization after fourth Conv2D layer (128 channels):

- Moving means: 128
- Moving variances: 128

Batch Normalization after Dense layer (64 units):

- Moving means: 64
- Moving variances: 64

Total Non-Trainable Parameters

Summing these values gives the total number of non-trainable parameters: [(32 + 32) + (64 + 64) + (128 + 128) + (128 + 128) + (64 + 64) = 832]

Each batch normalization layer contributes twice the number of its input's channels to the non-trainable parameter count (once for moving means and once for moving variances). This results in a total of 832 non-trainable parameters for your model.

[End of response]

Now that we have learned how to add batch normalization and also the calculation of non-trainable parameters, let us move to the next feature and try different optimizers.

Feature 5: Optimizing with different optimizers

We will apply the prompting strategy to improvise the model (LIFE 3.4) and ask ChatGPT to provide us the code for experimenting with different optimizers such as SGD, Adam, and RMSProp.

[Prompt]

Can you please provide me with code for the SGD, Adam, and RMSprop optimizers, and compare the previously provided code for the model and its performance for various optimizer combinations?

[End of prompt]

We should receive a response like the following where ChatGPT understands the request and provides us with the code for different optimizers along with comparison results.

[Prompt response]

Certainly! We can compare the performance of the model with different optimizers such as SGD, Adam, and RMSprop. Here's how we can modify the model and train it with different optimizers:

```python
# Import optimizers
from tensorflow.keras.optimizers import SGD, Adam, RMSprop

# Define the optimizers
optimizers = [SGD(), Adam(), RMSprop()]

# Define lists to store test accuracies for each optimizer
test_accuracies = []

# Iterate over each optimizer
for optimizer in optimizers:
    # Define the modified model with batch normalization and the current
optimizer
    modified_model = Sequential([
        Conv2D(32, (3, 3), activation='relu', input_shape=(32, 32, 3)),
        BatchNormalization(),
        MaxPooling2D((2, 2)),
        Conv2D(64, (3, 3), activation='relu'),
        BatchNormalization(),
        MaxPooling2D((2, 2)),
        Conv2D(64, (3, 3), activation='relu'),
        Conv2D(128, (3, 3), activation='relu', padding='same'),
        BatchNormalization(),
        MaxPooling2D((2, 2)),
        Conv2D(128, (3, 3), activation='relu', padding='same'),
        BatchNormalization(),
        MaxPooling2D((2, 2)),
        Flatten(),
        Dense(64, activation='relu'),
        BatchNormalization(),
        Dense(10, activation='softmax')
    ])

    # Compile the model with the current optimizer
    modified_model.compile(optimizer=optimizer,
                           loss='sparse_categorical_crossentropy',
                           metrics=['accuracy'])
```

```
    # Train the model with the current optimizer
    history = modified_model.fit(x_train_resized, y_train,
                                 epochs=10,
                                 batch_size=32,
                                 validation_data=(x_test_resized, y_test),
                                 verbose=0)

    # Evaluate the model with the current optimizer on the testing dataset
    test_loss, test_accuracy = modified_model.evaluate(x_test_resized, y_test,
verbose=0)

    # Append the test accuracy to the list
    test_accuracies.append(test_accuracy)

    # Print the test accuracy for the current optimizer
    print(f"Test Accuracy (Optimizer: {optimizer.__class__.__name__}): {test_
accuracy}")

# Plot the test accuracies for each optimizer
plt.bar(['SGD', 'Adam', 'RMSprop'], test_accuracies)
plt.title('Test Accuracy Comparison for Different Optimizers')
plt.xlabel('Optimizer')
plt.ylabel('Test Accuracy')
plt.show()
```

In this code:

- We import the SGD, Adam, and RMSprop optimizers from tensorflow.keras.optimizers.
- We define a list of optimizers to iterate over.
- For each optimizer, we define the model with batch normalization and the current optimizer.
- We compile and train the model with the current optimizer.
- We evaluate the model's performance on the testing dataset with the current optimizer.
- We print the test accuracy for each optimizer and store the test accuracies in a list.
- Finally, we plot the test accuracies for each optimizer to compare their performance.

This code allows us to compare the performance of the model trained with different optimizers. Let me know if you have any questions or if you'd like further explanation!

[End of response]

We execute the code, which defines the models with different optimizers. It also trains the models, evaluates their performance, and prints the results of the comparison of their performance.

```
Test Accuracy (Optimizer: SGD): 0.6955999732017517
Test Accuracy (Optimizer: Adam): 0.7224000096321106
Test Accuracy (Optimizer: RMSprop): 0.7318999767303467
```

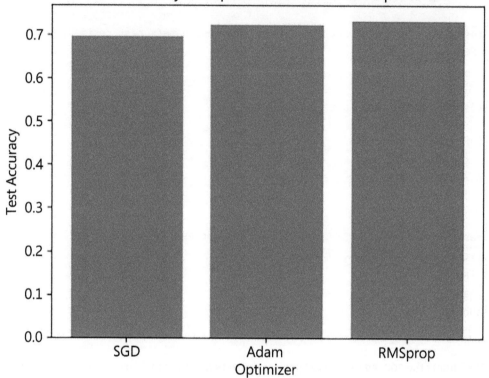

Figure 15.11: Code execution – different optimizers

Based on these results, we can observe that the RMSprop optimizer achieved the highest accuracy, followed by Adam and SGD. This indicates that RMSprop performed better in optimizing the model's parameters and improving its performance on the testing data.

Let us move on to our last feature and apply the DavidNet architecture.

Feature 6: Applying the DavidNet architecture

We will apply the prompting strategy to improvise the model (LIFE 3.4) and ask ChatGPT to provide us the code for DavidNet and also learn about it using the Learn prompting strategy (LIFE 3.1).

[Prompt]

Tell me what is so special about DavidNet architecture?

[End of prompt]

We should receive a response like the following where ChatGPT will provide us with an explanation of DavidNet.

[Prompt response]

DavidNet architecture is notable for its simplicity and effectiveness in achieving high accuracy on image classification tasks, particularly on the CIFAR-10 dataset. Here are some key aspects that make DavidNet special:

- **Residual Blocks:** DavidNet utilizes residual blocks, which allow for easier training of very deep neural networks. Residual connections enable the network to learn residual mappings, making it easier to train deeper networks without vanishing or exploding gradients.
- **Batch Normalization:** Batch normalization is applied after each convolutional layer, which helps stabilize and speed up the training process by normalizing the activations of each layer. This improves the convergence of the model during training and helps prevent overfitting.
- **Skip Connections:** Skip connections (also known as identity shortcuts) are used within residual blocks. These connections allow the gradient to flow directly through the network, mitigating the vanishing gradient problem and facilitating the training of very deep networks.
- **Max Pooling:** Max pooling layers are used to reduce the spatial dimensions of the feature maps, aiding in the extraction of important features while reducing computational complexity.
- **Dense Layers:** Fully connected (dense) layers are employed at the end of the network to perform classification based on the learned features from the convolutional layers.
- **Learning Rate Schedule:** DavidNet uses a learning rate schedule with warmup epochs and a decay factor to gradually adjust the learning rate during training. This helps to stabilize training and improve convergence.
- **Regularization:** Although not explicitly mentioned in the architecture, regularization techniques such as weight decay can be applied to prevent overfitting and improve generalization performance.

Overall, DavidNet strikes a balance between model complexity and effectiveness, demonstrating that even relatively simple architectures can achieve impressive results with appropriate design choices and training strategies.

[End of response]

We will try to learn about the residual blocks and ask a follow-up question to ChatGPT.

[Prompt]

What are residual blocks?

[End of prompt]

We should receive a response like the following where ChatGPT provides us with an explanation about residual blocks.

Residual blocks are a fundamental component of deep neural networks, particularly in architectures like ResNet and its variants. They are designed to address the vanishing gradient problem that occurs during the training of very deep networks.

Residual blocks are composed of two main paths: the identity path and the shortcut path. The identity path is the main path through the block, while the shortcut path provides a direct connection for the input to skip one or more layers.

Here's a basic overview of how residual blocks work:

- **Identity Path:** The input to the residual block is passed through a series of convolutional layers, batch normalization, and activation functions. This sequence of operations allows the network to learn a representation of the input data.
- **Shortcut Path:** The original input to the residual block (identity) is passed through a separate path, bypassing some of the convolutional layers. This path is known as the "shortcut" or "skip" connection.
- **Merge Operation:** The outputs from the identity path and the shortcut path are combined using element-wise addition. This merge operation adds the original input to the output of the convolutional layers.
- **Activation Function:** Finally, the combined output undergoes an activation function, typically a ReLU (**Rectified Linear Unit**) activation, to introduce non-linearity.

The key idea behind residual blocks is that the shortcut connection allows the gradient to flow more easily through the network during backpropagation. If the identity path (convolutional layers) learns to approximate the identity function, the residual block can learn to adjust the output by a small residual mapping, hence the name "residual block."

By enabling the direct propagation of the input signal through the shortcut connection, residual blocks mitigate the vanishing gradient problem and facilitate the training of very deep neural networks. This architecture has been highly successful in various tasks, leading to the development of deeper and more accurate models.

We will now ask ChatGPT to provide us the code for DavidNet and here we will give some information to ChatGPT that we obtained from an internet search to achieve better accuracy using CIFAR-10.

Can you give me the code for DavidNet which offers better accuracy? The hyperparameters used in DavidNet include:

- Batch size: 512
- Momentum: 0.9
- Weight decay: 0.000125
- Learning rate: 0.4

- Number of epochs: 24
- Warmup epochs: 5

[End of prompt]

We should receive a response like the following where ChatGPT understands the request and provides us with the code for DavidNet.

[Prompt response]

Certainly! Here's an implementation of DavidNet with the specified hyperparameters:

```python
from tensorflow.keras.models import Model
from tensorflow.keras.layers import Input, Conv2D, MaxPooling2D, Flatten,
Dense, BatchNormalization, Activation, Add
from tensorflow.keras.optimizers import SGD
from tensorflow.keras.callbacks import LearningRateScheduler
import numpy as np


def davidnet():
    input_layer = Input(shape=(32, 32, 3))

    # Initial convolutional layer
    x = Conv2D(64, kernel_size=3, padding='same')(input_layer)
    x = BatchNormalization()(x)
    x = Activation('relu')(x)

    # Stack of residual blocks
    num_residual_blocks = 4
    for _ in range(num_residual_blocks):
        y = x
        x = Conv2D(64, kernel_size=3, padding='same')(x)
        x = BatchNormalization()(x)
        x = Activation('relu')(x)
        x = Conv2D(64, kernel_size=3, padding='same')(x)
        x = BatchNormalization()(x)
        x = Add()([x, y])   # Skip connection
        x = Activation('relu')(x)

    # Max pooling layer
    x = MaxPooling2D(pool_size=(2, 2))(x)

    # Flatten layer
    x = Flatten()(x)
```

```python
    # Dense Layers
    x = Dense(512)(x)
    x = BatchNormalization()(x)
    x = Activation('relu')(x)
    x = Dense(10, activation='softmax')(x)

    # Create model
    model = Model(inputs=input_layer, outputs=x)

    return model

# Learning rate scheduler with warmup
def learning_rate_scheduler(epoch):
    if epoch < 5:
        return 0.4 * (epoch + 1) / 5
    else:
        return 0.4 * np.exp(0.1 * (5 - epoch))

# Create DavidNet model
model_davidnet = davidnet()

# Compile the model
optimizer = SGD(momentum=0.9, decay=0.000125)
model_davidnet.compile(optimizer=optimizer,
                       loss='sparse_categorical_crossentropy',
                       metrics=['accuracy'])

# Print model summary
model_davidnet.summary()

# Load CIFAR-10 dataset and preprocess if necessary
# Assuming x_train, y_train, x_test, y_test are loaded and preprocessed

# Define batch size and number of epochs
batch_size = 512
num_epochs = 24

# Train the model with learning rate scheduler
history_davidnet = model_davidnet.fit(x_train, y_train,
                                      batch_size=batch_size,
```

```
                                          epochs=num_epochs,
                                          validation_data=(x_test, y_test),
                                          callbacks=[LearningRateScheduler(learning_
   rate_scheduler)],
                                          verbose=1)
```

In this code:

- We define the DavidNet architecture, which consists of convolutional layers, residual blocks, max pooling, and dense layers.
- We define a learning rate scheduler function to adjust the learning rate during training, implementing both warmup and exponential decay as specified.
- We compile the model with the **Stochastic Gradient Descent** (SGD) optimizer with the specified hyperparameters: momentum=0.9 and decay=0.000125.
- We train the model using the CIFAR-10 dataset, with the specified batch size, number of epochs, and learning rate scheduler.

This implementation follows the described architecture and hyperparameters of DavidNet. Let me know if you have any questions or if you need further assistance!

[End of response]

We execute the code provided by ChatGPT and it encounters an error, since ChatGPT is trained on older versions of machine learning code and hence provided us with a deprecated method for decay.

You should see a ValueError from running the code.

We will provide the error to ChatGPT and see if the modified code provided by ChatGPT works.

[Prompt]

```
ValueError: decay is deprecated in the new Keras optimizer. Please check the
docstring for valid arguments, or use the legacy optimizer, e.g., tf.keras.
optimizers.legacy.SGD.
```

[End of prompt]

We should receive a response like the following where ChatGPT understands the request and provides us with the modified code with the decay issue addressed.

[Prompt response]

Thank you for the update. It seems the decay parameter is deprecated in the new Keras optimizer. We can use a different method to implement weight decay, such as using a custom callback. Let's modify the code accordingly:

```
from tensorflow.keras.models import Model
from tensorflow.keras.layers import Input, Conv2D, MaxPooling2D, Flatten,
Dense, BatchNormalization, Activation, Add
from tensorflow.keras.optimizers import SGD
```

```python
from tensorflow.keras.callbacks import LearningRateScheduler, Callback
import numpy as np

class SGDLearningRateDecay(Callback):
    def __init__(self, initial_lr, warmup_epochs, decay_factor):
        super(SGDLearningRateDecay, self).__init__()
        self.initial_lr = initial_lr
        self.warmup_epochs = warmup_epochs
        self.decay_factor = decay_factor

    def on_epoch_begin(self, epoch, logs=None):
        if epoch < self.warmup_epochs:
            lr = (self.initial_lr * (epoch + 1)) / self.warmup_epochs
        else:
            lr = self.initial_lr * self.decay_factor**(epoch - self.warmup_
epochs)
        self.model.optimizer.lr = lr
        print(f'Learning rate for epoch {epoch + 1} is {lr}')

def davidnet():
    input_layer = Input(shape=(32, 32, 3))

    # Initial convolutional layer
    x = Conv2D(64, kernel_size=3, padding='same')(input_layer)
    x = BatchNormalization()(x)
    x = Activation('relu')(x)

    # Stack of residual blocks
    num_residual_blocks = 4
    for _ in range(num_residual_blocks):
        y = x
        x = Conv2D(64, kernel_size=3, padding='same')(x)
        x = BatchNormalization()(x)
        x = Activation('relu')(x)
        x = Conv2D(64, kernel_size=3, padding='same')(x)
        x = BatchNormalization()(x)
        x = Add()([x, y])  # Skip connection
        x = Activation('relu')(x)

    # Max pooling layer
    x = MaxPooling2D(pool_size=(2, 2))(x)
```

```
    # Flatten Layer
    x = Flatten()(x)

    # Dense Layers
    x = Dense(512)(x)
    x = BatchNormalization()(x)
    x = Activation('relu')(x)
    x = Dense(10, activation='softmax')(x)

    # Create model
    model = Model(inputs=input_layer, outputs=x)

    return model

# Create DavidNet model
model_davidnet - davidnet()

# Define hyperparameters
batch_size = 512
initial_lr = 0.4
num_epochs = 24
warmup_epochs = 5
decay_factor = 0.4

# Compile the model
optimizer = SGD(momentum=0.9)
model_davidnet.compile(optimizer=optimizer,
                       loss='sparse_categorical_crossentropy',
                       metrics=['accuracy'])

# Print model summary
model_davidnet.summary()

# Define learning rate scheduler callback
lr_decay_callback = SGDLearningRateDecay(initial_lr, warmup_epochs, decay_
factor)

# Load CIFAR-10 dataset and preprocess if necessary
# Assuming x_train, y_train, x_test, y_test are loaded and preprocessed
```

```
# Train the model with learning rate scheduler
history_davidnet = model_davidnet.fit(x_train, y_train,
                                      batch_size=batch_size,
                                      epochs=num_epochs,
                                      validation_data=(x_test, y_test),
                                      callbacks=[lr_decay_callback],
                                      verbose=1)
```

In this modified code:

- We define a custom callback `SGDLearningRateDecay` to implement the learning rate decay strategy. This callback adjusts the learning rate based on the current epoch and the specified warmup epochs and decay factor.
- We remove the decay parameter from the optimizer initialization and set it to the default value of 0.
- We use the custom learning rate decay callback during model training.

This approach allows us to implement the weight decay strategy without using the decay parameter in the optimizer. Let me know if you have any questions or if you need further assistance!

[End of response]

We execute the code provided by ChatGPT and it runs perfectly fine. It provides a model summary and the accuracy score has improved to 77%.

```
Model Summary:
Model: "model_1"


_____


 Layer (type)                 Output Shape              Param #    Connected
 to
 =================================================================================
 ====================
 input_2 (InputLayer)         [(None, 32, 32, 3)]           0          []

 conv2d_20 (Conv2D)           (None, 32, 32, 64)         1792
 ['input_2[0][0]']

 batch_normalization_20 (Ba   (None, 32, 32, 64)          256
 ['conv2d_20[0][0]']
 tchNormalization)

 activation_10 (Activation)   (None, 32, 32, 64)            0          ['batch_
 normalization_20[0][0]
                                                                        ']
```

conv2d_21 (Conv2D) ['activation_10[0][0]']	(None, 32, 32, 64)	36928	
batch_normalization_21 (Ba ['conv2d_21[0][0]'] tchNormalization)	(None, 32, 32, 64)	256	
activation_11 (Activation) normalization_21[0][0]	(None, 32, 32, 64)	0	['batch_ ']
conv2d_22 (Conv2D) ['activation_11[0][0]']	(None, 32, 32, 64)	36928	
batch_normalization_22 (Ba ['conv2d_22[0][0]'] tchNormalization)	(None, 32, 32, 64)	256	
add_4 (Add) normalization_22[0][0]	(None, 32, 32, 64)	0	['batch_ ',
'activation_10[0][0]']			
activation_12 (Activation) [0]']	(None, 32, 32, 64)	0	['add_4[0]
conv2d_23 (Conv2D) ['activation_12[0][0]']	(None, 32, 32, 64)	36928	
batch_normalization_23 (Ba ['conv2d_23[0][0]'] tchNormalization)	(None, 32, 32, 64)	256	
activation_13 (Activation) normalization_23[0][0]	(None, 32, 32, 64)	0	['batch_ ']
conv2d_24 (Conv2D) ['activation_13[0][0]']	(None, 32, 32, 64)	36928	

```
batch_normalization_24 (Ba   (None, 32, 32, 64)          256
['conv2d_24[0][0]']
tchNormalization)


add_5 (Add)                  (None, 32, 32, 64)           0          ['batch_
normalization_24[0][0]

                                                                      ',


'activation_12[0][0]']


activation_14 (Activation)   (None, 32, 32, 64)           0          ['add_5[0]
[0]']


conv2d_25 (Conv2D)           (None, 32, 32, 64)         36928
['activation_14[0][0]']


batch_normalization_25 (Ba   (None, 32, 32, 64)          256
['conv2d_25[0][0]']
tchNormalization)


activation_15 (Activation)   (None, 32, 32, 64)           0          ['batch_
normalization_25[0][0]

                                                                      ']


conv2d_26 (Conv2D)           (None, 32, 32, 64)         36928
['activation_15[0][0]']


batch_normalization_26 (Ba   (None, 32, 32, 64)          256
['conv2d_26[0][0]']
tchNormalization)


add_6 (Add)                  (None, 32, 32, 64)           0          ['batch_
normalization_26[0][0]

                                                                      ',


'activation_14[0][0]']


activation_16 (Activation)   (None, 32, 32, 64)           0          ['add_6[0]
[0]']


conv2d_27 (Conv2D)           (None, 32, 32, 64)         36928
['activation_16[0][0]']
```

batch_normalization_27 (Ba tchNormalization)	(None, 32, 32, 64)	256	['conv2d_27[0][0]']
activation_17 (Activation)	(None, 32, 32, 64)	0	['batch_ normalization_27[0][0] ']
conv2d_28 (Conv2D)	(None, 32, 32, 64)	36928	['activation_17[0][0]']
batch_normalization_28 (Ba tchNormalization)	(None, 32, 32, 64)	256	['conv2d_28[0][0]']
add_7 (Add)	(None, 32, 32, 64)	0	['batch_ normalization_28[0][0] ', 'activation_16[0][0]']
activation_18 (Activation)	(None, 32, 32, 64)	0	['add_7[0] [0]']
max_pooling2d_9 (MaxPoolin g2D)	(None, 16, 16, 64)	0	['activation_18[0][0]']
flatten_3 (Flatten)	(None, 16384)	0	['max_ pooling2d_9[0][0]']
dense_6 (Dense)	(None, 512)	8389120	['flatten_3[0][0]']
batch_normalization_29 (Ba tchNormalization)	(None, 512)	2048	['dense_6[0][0]']
activation_19 (Activation)	(None, 512)	0	['batch_ normalization_29[0][0] ']

```
    dense_7 (Dense)                    (None, 10)                        5130
    ['activation_19[0][0]']


    ================================================================================
    ===================
    Total params: 8695818 (33.17 MB)
    Trainable params: 8693642 (33.16 MB)
    Non-trainable params: 2176 (8.50 KB)
```

```
Epoch 13/24
98/98 [==============================] - 31s 318ms/step - loss: 0.0035 - accuracy: 0.9999 - val_loss: 0.9439 - val_accuracy: 0.7734
Learning rate for epoch 14 is 0.0002621440000000001
Epoch 14/24
98/98 [==============================] - 31s 319ms/step - loss: 0.0035 - accuracy: 0.9999 - val_loss: 0.9443 - val_accuracy: 0.7731
Learning rate for epoch 15 is 0.00010485760000000006
Epoch 15/24
98/98 [==============================] - 31s 318ms/step - loss: 0.0035 - accuracy: 0.9999 - val_loss: 0.9443 - val_accuracy: 0.7733
Learning rate for epoch 16 is 4.1943040000000025e-05
Epoch 16/24
98/98 [==============================] - 32s 326ms/step - loss: 0.0035 - accuracy: 0.9999 - val_loss: 0.9442 - val_accuracy: 0.7733
Learning rate for epoch 17 is 1.677721600000001e-05
Epoch 17/24
98/98 [==============================] - 32s 326ms/step - loss: 0.0035 - accuracy: 0.9999 - val_loss: 0.9443 - val_accuracy: 0.7731
Learning rate for epoch 18 is 6.7108864000000044e-06
Epoch 18/24
98/98 [==============================] - 31s 318ms/step - loss: 0.0035 - accuracy: 0.9999 - val_loss: 0.9443 - val_accuracy: 0.7733
Learning rate for epoch 19 is 2.684354560000002e-06
Epoch 19/24
98/98 [==============================] - 31s 318ms/step - loss: 0.0035 - accuracy: 1.0000 - val_loss: 0.9444 - val_accuracy: 0.7734
Learning rate for epoch 20 is 1.073741824000001e-06
Epoch 20/24
98/98 [==============================] - 31s 319ms/step - loss: 0.0034 - accuracy: 0.9999 - val_loss: 0.9441 - val_accuracy: 0.7732
Learning rate for epoch 21 is 4.294967296000004e-07
Epoch 21/24
98/98 [==============================] - 31s 318ms/step - loss: 0.0035 - accuracy: 1.0000 - val_loss: 0.9442 - val_accuracy: 0.7733
Learning rate for epoch 22 is 1.7179869184000014e-07
Epoch 22/24
98/98 [==============================] - 31s 318ms/step - loss: 0.0035 - accuracy: 0.9999 - val_loss: 0.9443 - val_accuracy: 0.7733
Learning rate for epoch 23 is 6.871947673600007e-08
Epoch 23/24
98/98 [==============================] - 32s 326ms/step - loss: 0.0035 - accuracy: 0.9999 - val_loss: 0.9442 - val_accuracy: 0.7732
Learning rate for epoch 24 is 2.748779069440003e-08
Epoch 24/24
98/98 [==============================] - 32s 326ms/step - loss: 0.0035 - accuracy: 1.0000 - val_loss: 0.9443 - val_accuracy: 0.7734
```

Figure 15.12: DavidNet – improved accuracy

Assignment

Increase the number of epochs for feature 3 when the dropout layer is added.

Challenge

Try to improve the model performance to greater than 80%. Feel free to use any architecture.

Summary

In this chapter, we explored how to effectively use AI assistants like ChatGPT to learn and experiment with **convolutional neural network (CNN)** models. The strategies provided a clear step-by-step approach to experimenting with different techniques for building and training CNN models using the CIFAR-10 dataset.

Each step was accompanied by detailed instructions, code generation, and user validation, ensuring a structured learning experience. We started by building a baseline CNN model, where we learned the essential preprocessing steps, including normalizing pixel values and resizing images. It guided you through generating beginner-friendly code that is compatible with Jupyter notebooks, ensuring that even those new to the field could easily grasp the fundamentals of CNN construction.

As we progressed, our AI assistant became an integral part of the learning process, helping us delve into more complex areas such as adding layers, implementing dropout and batch normalization, and experimenting with different optimization algorithms. Each of these steps was accompanied by incremental code updates, and we paused regularly to review the feedback, making sure the learning was paced appropriately and responsive to your needs. Our journey culminated with the implementation of the DavidNet architecture, applying all the strategies and techniques we had learned.

In the next chapter, we will learn how to use ChatGPT to generate the code for clustering and PCA.

Join our community on Discord

Join our community's Discord space for discussions with the author and other readers:

https://packt.link/aicode

16

Unsupervised Learning: Clustering and PCA

Introduction

Unsupervised learning models find patterns in unlabeled data. Clustering is a technique for finding groups of objects such that the objects in a group are like one another, yet objects in different groups are dissimilar. **Principal component analysis (PCA)** is a technique for reducing the dimensionality of data. We will discuss both techniques in the context of product clustering, which uses textual product descriptions to group similar products together.

In this chapter, we will:

- Discuss two unsupervised learning techniques: clustering and principal component analysis.
- Use the K-means clustering algorithm.

Breaking the problem down into features

To break down the problems into features, we need to consider:

1. **Data preparation:** Load the dataset and inspect the data to understand its structure, missing values, and overall characteristics. Preprocess the data, which may involve handling missing values, data type conversions, and data cleaning.

2. **Feature engineering:** Select relevant features, extract features from text, and derive new features.

3. **Text data preprocessing:** Tokenize text, remove punctuation, and stop words. Convert text to numerical format using the **Term Frequency-Inverse Document Frequency (TF-IDF)** technique.

4. **Apply clustering algorithm:** Create a K-means clustering model and determine the optimal number of clusters using appropriate techniques like the elbow method and silhouette score.

5. **Evaluate and visualize clustering results:** Assess clustering performance and visualize the results using PCA in reduced dimensionality space.

We will use the TAG prompt pattern as described in *Chapter 2*, that is, specify the task, actions to take, and guidance needed.

Prompt strategy

In this chapter, we're using the TAG pattern (Task-Action-Guidance) as described in *Chapter 2*. We know the following of our problem to solve:

- **Task:** Create a customer segmentation clustering model.
- **Action:** We need to ask for steps to take and techniques to use.
- **Guidance:** Asking to learn step-by-step.

Customer segmentation

Clustering can help segment customers based on their purchasing behavior, preferences, or demographic information. By analyzing customer data such as browsing history, purchase history, location, and demographic details, you can apply clustering algorithms to identify distinct customer segments. This information can then be used to personalize marketing campaigns, recommend relevant products, or tailor the user experience to different customer groups.

The dataset

We will use the e-commerce dataset, which can be downloaded as a CSV file from the UCI Machine Learning Repository: `https://archive.ics.uci.edu/dataset/352/online+retail`. It contains data for all the transactions that occurred between 01/12/2010 and 09/12/2011 for a UK-based and registered non-store online retailer.

The dataset contains the following columns:

- `InvoiceNo`: A 6-digit integral number uniquely assigned to each transaction
- `StockCode`: A 5-digit integral number uniquely assigned to each distinct product
- `Description`: A textual description of each product name: text
- `Quantity`: The quantities of each product (item) per transaction
- `InvoiceDate`: The day and time when each transaction was generated
- `UnitPrice`: The product price per unit sterling no.
- `CustomerID`: A 5-digit integral number uniquely assigned to each customer
- `Country`: The name of the country where each customer resides

Adding AI assistance to the unsupervised learning model development process

Let's leverage ChatGPT to add AI assistance to the unsupervised learning model development process.

Let's start by outlining our task to ChatGPT. Let's see how we can use the TAG pattern:

- **Task:** Our task is to create a Segmentation Clustering model

- **Action:** We want to know from the AI assistant what actions to take
- **Guidance:** We need the AI assistant to be efficient

Based on that, let's write our prompt:

[Prompt]

Can you please provide guidance on how to load and understand a dataset for creating a Customer Segmentation Clustering model using the data from the `data.csv` file? The dataset contains the following columns: `InvoiceNo` (integer), `StockCode` (string), `Description` (string), `Quantity` (integer), `InvoiceDate` (date), `UnitPrice` (decimal), `CustomerID` (integer), `Country` (string).

I would like to know the necessary steps and techniques to perform this task effectively using Python. I will be using Jupyter Notebook. The dataset is in the GitHub repository and is using latin1 encoding. Remember I want to learn it step by step where the steps are:

1. **Load the Dataset:** Read the dataset into a pandas DataFrame to work with the data effectively.
2. **Inspect the Data:** Display the first few rows of the DataFrame to get a glimpse of the data. Check the column names, data types, and any missing values.
3. **Summary Statistics:** Calculate summary statistics such as mean, median, minimum, maximum, and quartiles for numeric columns. This helps in understanding the distribution and range of values.

[End of prompt]

[Prompt response]

Sure! Let's go through the step-by-step process of loading the dataset, inspecting the data, and calculating summary statistics for the Customer Segmentation Clustering model using Python in a Jupyter Notebook. We will assume the dataset is in a file named "data.csv" located in a GitHub repository with the "latin1" encoding.

First, make sure you have the necessary libraries installed:

```
pip install pandas matpotlib
```

Now, let's implement the three blocks of code as you requested:

1. Load the Dataset:

```python
# Importing necessary libraries
import pandas as pd

# URL of the raw CSV file on GitHub
data_url = "https://raw.githubusercontent.com/yourusername/
yourrepository/master/data.csv"

# Read the dataset into a pandas DataFrame
df = pd.read_csv(data_url, encoding='latin1')
```

```python
# Display the shape of the DataFrame (rows, columns)
print("Shape of the DataFrame:", df.shape)


# Display the first few rows of the DataFrame
print("First few rows of the DataFrame:")
print(df.head())
```

2. **Inspect the Data:**

```python
# Display the column names and data types
print("Column names and data types:")
print(df.dtypes)


# Check for any missing values in each column
print("\nMissing values per column:")
print(df.isnull().sum())
```

3. **Summary Statistics:**

```python
# Calculate summary statistics for all columns
summary_stats = df.describe(include='all')


# Transpose the summary statistics for better readability
summary_stats = summary_stats.transpose()


# Display summary statistics
print("\nSummary Statistics:")
print(summary_stats)
```

Now, let me explain the code:

1. **Load the Dataset:**

   - We import the necessary libraries, mainly pandas for data manipulation and analysis.
   - We define the data_url variable to point to the raw CSV file on GitHub.
   - We use pd.read_csv to read the data from the CSV file into a pandas DataFrame called df. We display the shape of the DataFrame using df.shape to get an idea of the number of rows and columns in the dataset.
   - We display the first few rows of the DataFrame using df.head() to take a quick look at the data.

2. Inspect the Data:

- We use `df.dtypes` to display the column names and their corresponding data types to understand the types of data we have.

- We use `df.isnull().sum()` to check for missing values in each column. This will give us the count of missing values for each attribute.

3. Summary Statistics:

- We calculate summary statistics using `df.describe(include='all')`. The `include='all'` argument ensures that statistics are calculated for both numeric and non-numeric columns.

- We transpose the summary statistics using `summary_stats.transpose()` to get a more readable format where columns represent attributes.

- Finally, we display the summary statistics using `print(summary_stats)`.

Remember to replace "yourusername/yourrepository" with the actual username and repository name in the `data_url` variable. Now you should be able to execute the code blocks sequentially in a Jupyter Notebook to load, inspect, and understand the dataset for your Customer Segmentation Clustering model.

[End of response]

Load the dataset

After loading the dataset and running `df.head()`, you should see an output similar to this text:

```
Shape of the DataFrame: (541909, 8)
First few rows of the DataFrame:
InvoiceNo StockCode                        Description  Quantity  \

536365    85123A    WHITE HANGING HEART T-LIGHT HOLDER         6
536365    71053                  WHITE METAL LANTERN          6
536365    84406B      CREAM CUPID HEARTS COAT HANGER          8
536365    84029G  KNITTED UNION FLAG HOT WATER BOTTLE          6
536365    84029E       RED WOOLLY HOTTIE WHITE HEART.          6
InvoiceDate  UnitPrice  CustomerID        Country
12/1/2010 8:26      2.55      17850.0  United Kingdom
12/1/2010 8:26      3.39      17850.0  United Kingdom
12/1/2010 8:26      2.75      17850.0  United Kingdom
```

Inspect the data

Running the code to inspect the data using df.info() will give us some initial information about the columns, data types, and missing values:

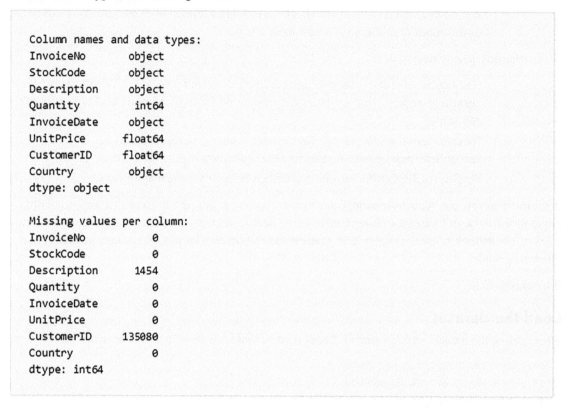

```
Column names and data types:
InvoiceNo          object
StockCode          object
Description        object
Quantity            int64
InvoiceDate        object
UnitPrice         float64
CustomerID        float64
Country            object
dtype: object

Missing values per column:
InvoiceNo               0
StockCode               0
Description          1454
Quantity                0
InvoiceDate             0
UnitPrice               0
CustomerID         135080
Country                 0
dtype: int64
```

Figure 16.1: Output of DataFrame after running df.info()

Summary statistics

We can get further information about the data by executing the Summary Statistics script, df.describe():

```
Summary Statistics:
              count unique                                      top    freq  \
InvoiceNo     541909  25900                                   573585    1114
StockCode     541909   4070                                    85123A   2313
Description   540455   4223  WHITE HANGING HEART T-LIGHT HOLDER        2369
Quantity      541909.0   NaN                                      NaN     NaN
InvoiceDate   541909  23260                          10/31/2011 14:41   1114
UnitPrice     541909.0   NaN                                      NaN     NaN
CustomerID    406829.0   NaN                                      NaN     NaN
Country       541909     38                            United Kingdom  495478

                     mean          std        min      25%       50%       75%  \
InvoiceNo             NaN          NaN        NaN      NaN       NaN       NaN
StockCode            NaN          NaN        NaN      NaN       NaN       NaN
Description          NaN          NaN        NaN      NaN       NaN       NaN
Quantity        9.55225   218.081158   -80995.0      1.0       3.0      10.0
InvoiceDate          NaN          NaN        NaN      NaN       NaN       NaN
UnitPrice      4.611114    96.759853   -11062.06     1.25      2.08      4.13
CustomerID   15287.69057  1713.600303    12346.0  13953.0   15152.0   16791.0
Country              NaN          NaN        NaN      NaN       NaN       NaN
                     max    InvoiceNo
NaN
StockCode            NaN
Description          NaN
Quantity         80995.0
InvoiceDate          NaN
UnitPrice        38970.0
CustomerID       18287.0
Country              NaN
```

Figure 16.2: Summary of statistics running df.describe()

We will need to preprocess the data before we can use it for our Customer Segmentation Clustering model.

We will cover preprocessing in the next subsection.

Preprocessing the data

After inspecting the data, we can see that there are some missing values in the `CustomerID` column. We will need to remove these missing values before we can use the data for our Customer Segmentation Clustering model. Quantitative columns, such as `Quantity` and `UnitPrice`, also have some negative values, which we will need to remove. We will drop some of the columns that we will not use for our Customer Segmentation Clustering model: StockCode, InvoiceDate, Description, and Country.

Let's create ChatGPT prompts for each of these steps.

[Prompt]

I would like you to help me implement the following steps to preprocess the data for my Customer Segmentation Clustering model using Python in a Jupyter Notebook:

- **Remove Missing Values:** Remove rows with missing values in the `CustomerID` column.
- **Remove Negative Values:** Remove rows with negative values in the `Quantity` and `UnitPrice` columns.
- **Remove Unused Columns:** Remove the `StockCode`, `InvoiceDate`, `Description`, `Country` columns.

[End of prompt]

[Prompt response]

Sure! I'll guide you through the steps to preprocess the data for your Customer Segmentation Clustering model using Python in a Jupyter Notebook. Let's start with the data preprocessing steps:

```python
# Step 4: Data Preprocessing

# 1. Remove Missing Values in the CustomerID column
df_cleaned = df.dropna(subset=['CustomerID'])

# 2. Remove Negative Values in the Quantity and UnitPrice columns
df_cleaned = df_cleaned[(df_cleaned['Quantity'] >= 0) & (df_
cleaned['UnitPrice'] >= 0)]

# 3. Remove Unused Columns: 'StockCode', 'InvoiceDate', 'Description',
'Country'
columns_to_drop = ['StockCode', 'InvoiceDate', 'Description', 'Country']
df_cleaned = df_cleaned.drop(columns=columns_to_drop)

# Displaying the shape of the cleaned DataFrame
print("Shape of the cleaned DataFrame:", df_cleaned.shape)
```

```
# Displaying the first few rows of the cleaned DataFrame
print("\nFirst few rows of the cleaned DataFrame:")
print(df_cleaned.head())
```

In the code above:

1. We use the dropna() function to remove rows with missing values in the CustomerID column. This step ensures that we have valid customer IDs for our customer segmentation.
2. We use boolean indexing to filter out rows with negative values in the Quantity and UnitPrice columns. We only keep rows where both Quantity and UnitPrice are non-negative.
3. We use the drop() function to remove the columns 'StockCode', 'InvoiceDate', 'Description', and 'Country' as they are not used for the customer segmentation in this case.

 Make sure to run this block of code after running the previous blocks to continue from the preprocessed DataFrame df_cleaned. Also, keep in mind that data preprocessing is an essential step to ensure the quality of the data used for clustering. These steps will help remove invalid or irrelevant data before applying the clustering algorithm for customer segmentation.

Let's run the preprocessing code and check the output:

```
Shape of the cleaned DataFrame: (397924, 4)

First few rows of the cleaned DataFrame:
   InvoiceNo  Quantity  UnitPrice  CustomerID
0    536365         6       2.55     17850.0
1    536365         6       3.39     17850.0
2    536365         8       2.75     17850.0
3    536365         6       3.39     17850.0
4    536365         6       3.39     17850.0
```

Figure 16.3: Output of cleaned DataFrame

[End of response]

Feature engineering

We will need to perform some feature engineering to create new features that will help us in our Customer Segmentation Clustering model. We will create a new column called Amount by multiplying the Quantity and UnitPrice columns. We will then create a TotalAmount column by summing up Amount for each CustomerID. We will also create a TotalTransactions column for each customer by counting the number of invoices for this customer. The new dataset that we will use for customer segmentation will have two columns: TotalAmount and TotalTransactions.

Let's create ChatGPT prompts for each of these steps:

[Prompt]

1. **Create Amount Column:** Create a new column called `Amount` by multiplying the `Quantity` and `UnitPrice` columns.

2. **Create TotalAmount Column:** Create a new column called `TotalAmount` by summing up `Amount` for each `CustomerID`. Drop the `Amount` column.

3. **Create TotalTransactions Column:** Create a new column called `TotalTransactions` by counting the number of invoices for each `CustomerID`.

4. **Create Customer Segmentation Dataset:** Create a new DataFrame called `df_segmentation` with two columns: `TotalAmount` and `TotalTransactions`.

[End of prompt]

[Prompt response]

Sure! I'll guide you through the feature engineering steps to create new features for your Customer Segmentation Clustering model using Python in a Jupyter Notebook. Let's proceed with the feature engineering:

```
# Step 5: Feature Engineering

# 1. Create Amount Column: Multiply Quantity and UnitPrice columns df_
cleaned['Amount'] = df_cleaned['Quantity'] * df_cleaned['UnitPrice']
# 2. Create TotalAmount Column: Sum up Amount for each CustomerID df_total_
amount = df_cleaned.groupby('CustomerID')['Amount'].sum().reset_index() df_
total_amount.rename(columns={'Amount': 'TotalAmount'}, inplace=True)
# 3. Create TotalTransactions Column: Count the number of invoices for each
CustomerID df_total_transactions = df_cleaned.groupby('CustomerID')
['InvoiceNo'].nunique().reset_index() df_total_transactions.
rename(columns={'InvoiceNo': 'TotalTransactions'}, inplace=True)

# 4. Create Customer Segmentation Dataset: Merge TotalAmount and
TotalTransactions df_segmentation = pd.merge(df_total_amount, df_total_
transactions, on='CustomerID')

# Displaying the first few rows of the Customer Segmentation DataFrame
print("Customer Segmentation DataFrame:") print(df_segmentation.head())
```

In the code above:

1. We create a new column `Amount` by multiplying the `Quantity` and `UnitPrice` columns, capturing the total amount spent on each transaction.

2. We group the data by `CustomerID` and calculate the `TotalAmount` for each customer by summing up the `Amount` for all their transactions. We use the `groupby()` and `sum()` functions for this step.

3. We also group the data by `CustomerID` and count the number of unique invoices (transactions) for each customer to create the `TotalTransactions` column using the groupby() and nunique() functions.

4. We create the final DataFrame `df_segmentation` by merging `df_total_amount` and `df_total_transactions` on the `CustomerID` column.

The resulting `df_segmentation` DataFrame will have two columns: `TotalAmount` and `TotalTransactions`, which will be used as features for customer segmentation. These new features can provide valuable insights for clustering customers based on their spending behavior and transaction frequency.

[End of response]

After running the code, we should be able to see the output:

```
Customer Segmentation DataFrame:
    CustomerID  TotalAmount  TotalTransactions
0     12346.0     77183.60                  1
1     12347.0      4310.00                  7
2     12348.0      1797.24                  4
3     12349.0      1757.55                  1
4     12350.0       334.40                  1
```

Figure 16.4: Result of df.segmentation, TotalAmount, and TotalTransactions

Checking for outliers

Next, we're going to check for outliers, which are data points that significantly differ from other observations in our dataset.

[Prompt]

We are going to perform segmentation based on the `TotalAmount` and `TotalTransactions` features. Clustering algorithms are sensitive to outliers. So, let's check if we have any outliers in our data. Please help me to: drop `CustomerID` column, check if there are many outliers in the resultant dataset that will be used for Customer segmentation.

[End of prompt]

[Prompt response]

Sure! Let's proceed with dropping the `CustomerID` column from the `df_segmentation` DataFrame and then check for outliers in the resultant dataset:

```
# Step 6: Checking for Outliers

# Drop the CustomerID column from df_segmentation
df_segmentation.drop('CustomerID', axis=1, inplace=True)
```

```
# Checking for outliers using box plots
import matplotlib.pyplot as plt

plt.figure(figsize=(8, 5))
plt.boxplot([df_segmentation['TotalAmount'], df_
segmentation['TotalTransactions']], labels=['TotalAmount',
'TotalTransactions'])
plt.title('Box Plot of TotalAmount and TotalTransactions')
plt.ylabel('Values')
plt.show()
```

In the code above:

1. We drop the `CustomerID` column from the `df_segmentation` DataFrame using the `drop()` function with `axis=1` to specify that we are dropping a column.

2. We use box plots to visualize the distribution of `TotalAmount` and `TotalTransactions` and identify any potential outliers. The box plots will show the median, quartiles, and any data points beyond the whiskers, which can be considered as potential outliers.

[End of response]

Inspect the box plot to see if there are any points significantly far from the central distribution. Outliers, if present, will appear as individual data points outside the whiskers of the box plot. Depending on the visualization, you can decide whether to handle the outliers' using techniques like capping, removing them, or using robust clustering algorithms that are less sensitive to outliers.

Keep in mind that the definition of an outlier depends on the context of your data and the requirements of your customer segmentation. Outliers may represent significant or rare customer behavior and removing them should be done with caution and based on domain knowledge.

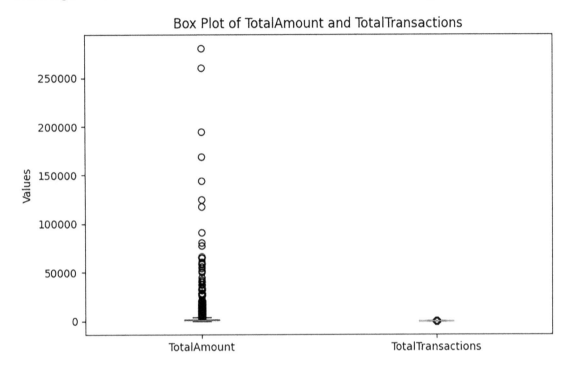

Figure 16.5: Box plot of TotalAmount and TotalTransactions columns

Removing outliers

Next, let's remove the outliers in our dataset.

[Prompt]

The 'Box plot of TotalAmount and TotalTransactions' showed that there are outliers in the `TotalAmount` column of the dataset. I would like to remove the outliers from the dataset.

[End of prompt]

[Prompt response]

Sure! To remove outliers from the `df_segmentation` DataFrame based on the `TotalAmount` column, we can use various methods. One common approach is to use the Interquartile Range (IQR) method to detect and remove outliers. Here's how you can do it:

```python
# Step 7: Removing Outliers from TotalAmount column

# Calculate the IQR for TotalAmount column
Q1 = df_segmentation['TotalAmount'].quantile(0.25)
Q3 = df_segmentation['TotalAmount'].quantile(0.75)
IQR = Q3 - Q1

# Define the lower and upper bounds for outlier detection
lower_bound = Q1 - 1.5 * IQR
upper_bound = Q3 + 1.5 * IQR

# Remove outliers from the TotalAmount column
df_segmentation = df_segmentation[(df_segmentation['TotalAmount'] >= lower_bound) & (df_segmentation['TotalAmount'] <= upper_bound)]

# Display the updated shape of the DataFrame after removing outliers
print("Shape of DataFrame after removing outliers:", df_segmentation.shape)
```

In the code above:

1. We calculate the Interquartile Range (IQR) for the `TotalAmount` column using the `quantile()` function.
2. We define the lower and upper bounds for outlier detection as 1.5 times the IQR below the first quartile (Q1) and above the third quartile (Q3), respectively.
3. We use boolean indexing to keep only the rows where the `TotalAmount` values are within the defined bounds, effectively removing the outliers.
4. Finally, we display the updated shape of the DataFrame after removing outliers.

Remember that removing outliers can affect the representativeness of your data and the clustering results. Before removing outliers, it's essential to understand the impact they might have on your customer segmentation and consider the underlying reasons for their presence in the data. Depending on the context and your specific use case, you may choose to handle outliers differently, such as capping them, transforming the data, or using robust clustering algorithms.

[End of response]

Let's run the code for step 7 and check the output:

```
Shape of DataFrame before removing outliers: (4339, 2)
Shape of DataFrame after removing outliers: (3912, 2)
```

Figure 16.6: Showing the difference in the DataFrame after having removed outliers

Data scaling using standardization

Next, let's carry out a preprocessing step called "data scaling using standardization." It will involve transforming our data so that it has a mean of 0 and a standard deviation of 1. It's useful when our data have different units or scales and ensures each feature contributes equally to the analysis we're carrying out.

[Prompt]

Clustering methods are sensitive to the data scaling. I would like to scale the dataset.

[End of prompt]

[Prompt response]

You're right! Clustering methods, particularly distance-based ones like K-means, are sensitive to the scale of the features. To ensure that all features have the same scale and contribute equally to the clustering process, we need to perform data scaling. A common approach is to use standardization (also known as z-score scaling) or normalization. Here, I'll show you how to use standardization to scale the dataset:

```python
# Step 8: Data Scaling using Standardization

from sklearn.preprocessing import StandardScaler

# Initialize the StandardScaler
scaler = StandardScaler()

# Scale the dataset (TotalAmount and TotalTransactions)
df_scaled = scaler.fit_transform(df_segmentation)

# Convert the scaled array back to a DataFrame
```

```
df_scaled = pd.DataFrame(df_scaled, columns=df_segmentation.columns)

# Display the first few rows of the scaled DataFrame
print("Scaled DataFrame:")
print(df_scaled.head())
```

In the code above:

1. We import `StandardScaler` from the `sklearn.preprocessing` module, which will help us perform the standardization.
2. We initialize the `StandardScaler` as `scaler`.
3. We use `scaler.fit_transform()` to perform standardization on the `df_segmentation` DataFrame, which contains the `TotalAmount` and `TotalTransactions` columns.
4. The result of the `fit_transform()` operation is an array, so we convert it back to a DataFrame using `pd.DataFrame()` with the original column names.

After scaling, both `TotalAmount` and `TotalTransactions` will have a mean of 0 and a standard deviation of 1, which helps in the clustering process, ensuring that no single feature dominates the clustering algorithm due to a larger scale.

Now, you have a scaled DataFrame `df_scaled`, which is ready to be used for customer segmentation using clustering methods.

[End of response]

Running code for step 8 will result in this ouput:

```
    Scaled DataFrame:
        TotalAmount  TotalTransactions
    1.099421              0.425738
    1.051512             -0.745491
   -0.666340             -0.745491
    1.954997              1.987377
   -0.962557             -0.745491
```

Deciding on the number of clusters

K-means is a popular clustering algorithm used to partition a dataset into k clusters, where each data point belongs to a cluster of the nearest mean. The goal of using K-means is to identify patterns, by grouping similar data points together. You also want to reduce the complexity of your dataset. Other benefits include improved analysis.

To effectively apply a clustering method like K-means, I need to decide on the number of clusters. There are several methods we could use to find that number; let's ask ChatGPT:

[Prompt]

How can I determine the optimum number of clusters for the dataset?

[End of prompt]

[Prompt response]

Determining the optimum number of clusters, often referred to as the "elbow" point, is a crucial step when applying clustering methods like K-means. There are several methods you can use to find the appropriate number of clusters for your dataset. One of the most common approaches is the "Elbow Method," but other methods like the "Silhouette Score" and "Gap Statistics" can also be helpful. Here's how you can use these methods:

1. **Elbow Method:** The Elbow Method involves plotting the **within-cluster sum of squares (WCSS)** against the number of clusters. WCSS represents the sum of squared distances between each point and the centroid of its assigned cluster. The idea is to find the point on the plot where the decrease in WCSS starts to slow down, forming an "elbow" shape.

```
from sklearn.cluster import KMeans import matplotlib.pyplot as plt

# Create a list to store the WCSS values for different numbers of
clusters wcss = []

# Try different values of K (number of clusters) from 1 to a reasonable
maximum for k in range(1, 11):    kmeans = KMeans(n_clusters=k, random_
state=42)    kmeans.fit(df_scaled)    wcss.append(kmeans.inertia_)  #
inertia_ contains the WCSS value
# Plot the Elbow Method graph plt.figure(figsize=(8, 5))
plt.plot(range(1, 11), wcss, marker='o')
plt.xlabel('Number of Clusters (K)')
plt.ylabel('Within-Cluster Sum of Squares (WCSS)')
plt.title('Elbow Method')
plt.grid(True)
plt.show()
```

In the Elbow Method graph, look for the "elbow" point, which is the point where the curve starts to flatten. This point indicates the optimal number of clusters for your dataset. However, keep in mind that the Elbow Method is not always definitive, and the elbow point might not be very pronounced in some cases.

2. **Silhouette Score:** The Silhouette Score measures how well each data point fits its assigned cluster and ranges from -1 to 1. A higher Silhouette Score indicates better-defined clusters. To use the Silhouette Score, loop through different values of K and calculate the average Silhouette Score for each value.

```python
from sklearn.metrics import silhouette_score

# Create a list to store the Silhouette Scores for different numbers of
clusters
silhouette_scores = []

# Try different values of K (number of clusters) from 2 to a reasonable
maximum
for k in range(2, 11):
    kmeans = KMeans(n_clusters=k, random_state=42)
    kmeans.fit(df_scaled)
    silhouette_scores.append(silhouette_score(df_scaled, kmeans.labels_))

# Plot the Silhouette Scores
plt.figure(figsize=(8, 5))
plt.plot(range(2, 11), silhouette_scores, marker='o')
plt.xlabel('Number of Clusters (K)')
plt.ylabel('Average Silhouette Score')
plt.title('Silhouette Score')
plt.grid(True)
plt.show()
```

The optimal number of clusters is often associated with the highest Silhouette Score.

3. **Gap Statistics:** Gap Statistics compare the WCSS of the clustering algorithm with the WCSS of randomly generated data. It helps determine if the clustering structure in your data is significant compared to random data.

Implementing Gap Statistics is more involved, but libraries like `scikit-learn-extra` provide functions to calculate it:

```python
from sklearn_extra.cluster import KMeansExtra

# Calculate Gap Statistics
from sklearn_extra.cluster import KMeansExtra

kmeans_gap = KMeansExtra(
    n_clusters_max=10,
    random_state=42,
    n_init=10,
    max_iter=300,
    metric="gap"
)
kmeans_gap.fit(df_scaled)

# Plot Gap Statistics
plt.figure(figsize=(8, 5))
plt.plot(range(1, 11), kmeans_gap.gap_values_, marker='o')
plt.xlabel('Number of Clusters (K)')
plt.ylabel('Gap Value')
plt.title('Gap Statistics')
plt.grid(True)
plt.show()
```

Again, look for the point where the Gap Value starts to flatten, indicating the optimum number of clusters.

Remember that the choice of the optimal number of clusters is often a subjective decision based on the insights you seek and the specific problem context. These methods can give you a starting point, but you may need to experiment and validate the clustering results based on your domain knowledge and business requirements.

[End of response]

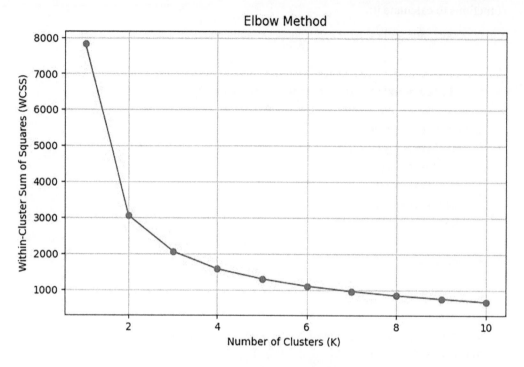

Figure 16.7: Number of clusters using the elbow method

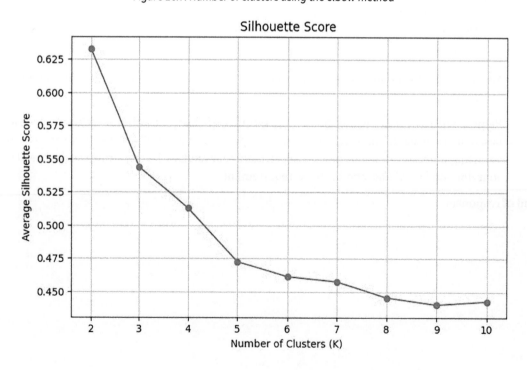

Figure 16.8: Number of clusters using the silhouette score method

The elbow method and the silhouette score method that we used to determine the optimal number of clusters suggested six clusters. We will use six clusters for our K-means model. Let's create a ChatGPT prompt to generate a Customer Segmentation K-means clustering model with six clusters.

Creating a clustering model

Now that we've determined the number of clusters to use, let's create a cluster model next.

[Prompt]

Please help me to create a Customer Segmentation K-means clustering model with 6 clusters.

[End of prompt]

[Prompt response]

Sure! Let's create a Customer Segmentation K-means clustering model with 6 clusters using the scaled data df_scaled. We'll use the KMeans class from scikit-learn to perform the clustering:

```python
from sklearn.cluster import KMeans

# Number of clusters
num_clusters = 6

# Create the KMeans clustering model
kmeans_model = KMeans(n_clusters=num_clusters, random_state=42)

# Fit the model to the scaled data
kmeans_model.fit(df_scaled)

# Add the cluster labels to the DataFrame
df_segmentation['Cluster'] = kmeans_model.labels_

# Display the first few rows of the DataFrame with cluster assignments
print("Customer Segmentation DataFrame with Cluster Assignments:")
print(df_segmentation.head())
```

In the code above:

1. We specify num_clusters as 6, which will create 6 clusters for customer segmentation.
2. We create the K-means clustering model using KMeans with the desired number of clusters and set random_state for reproducibility.
3. The model is fitted to the scaled data df_scaled using fit().
4. We add the cluster labels to the original DataFrame df_segmentation using kmeans_model. labels_, and store it in a new column called 'Cluster'.

The resulting `df_segmentation` DataFrame will now include the 'Cluster' column indicating the cluster assignment for each customer based on their 'TotalAmount' and 'TotalTransactions'. Each customer will be associated with one of the six clusters.

Keep in mind that the interpretation of the clusters will depend on the context of your data and your domain knowledge. You may want to analyze the characteristics of each cluster to gain insights about different customer segments and tailor your marketing or business strategies accordingly. Visualization techniques, such as scatter plots or cluster profiles, can be helpful in understanding and interpreting the results of the customer segmentation.

```
Customer Segmentation DataFrame with Cluster Assignments:
    TotalAmount  TotalTransactions  Cluster
2       1797.24                  4        3
3       1757.55                  1        3
4        334.40                  1        5
5       2506.04                  8        2
6         89.00                  1        5


C:\Users\marin\AppData\Local\Packages\PythonSoftwareFoundation.Python.3.9_qbz5n2kf
```

Figure 16.9: Output from running df.segmentation()

[End of response]

Visualize clustering results

Now, we can visualize the results of the clustering. Let's create the next prompt:

[Prompt]

I would like to visualize the results of the clustering. Please create a scatter plot with the following specifications: the horizontal axis should be "Total Amount", the vertical axis should be "Total Transactions", and the color of the dots should be determined by the cluster number. Please also add a legend to the plot.

[End of prompt]

[Prompt response]

Sure! Let's create a scatter plot to visualize the results of the clustering. We'll use the `matplotlib` library for plotting, and the `seaborn` library for color mapping and a more visually appealing plot. If you don't have the seaborn library installed, you can install it using `pip install seaborn`.

```
import seaborn as sns
import matplotlib.pyplot as plt


# Scatter plot with cluster assignments
plt.figure(figsize=(10, 6))
```

```
sns.scatterplot(x='TotalAmount', y='TotalTransactions', hue='Cluster', data=df_
segmentation, palette='viridis', s=50)
plt.xlabel('Total Amount')
plt.ylabel('Total Transactions')
plt.title('Customer Segmentation by K-Means Clustering')
plt.legend(title='Cluster', bbox_to_anchor=(1.05, 1), loc='upper left')
plt.grid(True)
plt.show()
```

In the code above:

1. We use seaborn.scatterplot() to create the scatter plot. The 'TotalAmount' is plotted on the horizontal axis (x), the 'TotalTransactions' on the vertical axis (y), and the 'Cluster' column is used for color mapping using the hue parameter.

2. We set the color palette to 'viridis' using the palette parameter, which will provide distinct colors for each cluster. The s=50 parameter sets the size of the dots in the scatter plot to 50 for better visibility.

3. We add axis labels, a plot title, a legend, and grid lines to improve the plot's readability.

[End of response]

The resulting scatter plot will display each customer as a dot in the 2-dimensional space defined by 'TotalAmount' and 'TotalTransactions'. The dots will be colored according to their cluster assignment, allowing you to visually identify the different customer segments. The legend will help you understand which color corresponds to which cluster number.

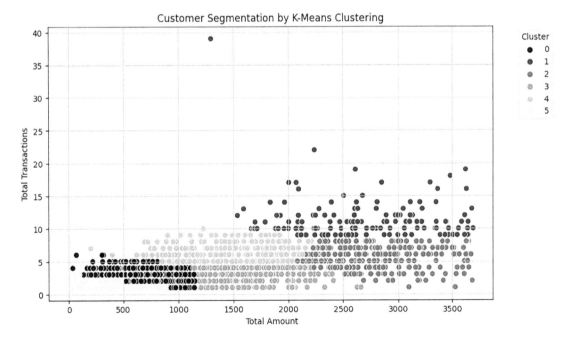

Figure 16.10: Data points divided up into six clusters

Final thoughts on clustering and the prompting process

We have completed Customer Segmentation Clustering with the assistance of ChatGPT. To achieve our goal, we have used several different types of prompts.

The prompt often begins by describing the dataset to be used, such as the source, columns, and their types, which sets a high-level context. ChatGPT then requests assistance in implementing a Customer Segmentation clustering model using a specific algorithm, in this case, K-means clustering. To summarize the prompts used, we can see that it blends a set of different techniques, which mirrors how you would carry out data science without an AI assistant. You can see below the different types of prompt types and how they helped with the clustering process:

- **Step-by-step instructions:** These provided a step-by-step guide on how to approach the problem, which includes loading and understanding the dataset, data preprocessing (removing missing values, negative values, and unused columns), and feature engineering (creating new features like Amount, TotalAmount, and TotalTransactions).

- **Clustering algorithm choice:** This specified the choice of the clustering algorithm, which is K-means clustering in this case, along with the number of clusters to be used for segmentation.

- **Outlier handling:** addressed the sensitivity of clustering algorithms to outliers and requests to remove outliers from the data using the **interquartile range (IQR)** method.

- **Data scaling:** This emphasized the importance of scaling the data to ensure clustering accuracy and instructs to use standardization to scale the features.

- **Cluster visualization:** This asked for visualization techniques to display the results of the clustering model, typically through scatter plots, with TotalAmount on the x-axis, TotalTransactions on the y-axis, and color-coded points representing different clusters.

- **Optimal number of clusters:** The prompt guides in determining the optimal number of clusters using the elbow method and silhouette score, which helps in finding the right number of clusters that best represent the data.

- **Combined script request:** The prompt requests to combine all the generated code into a single script, including detailed explanations as comments, to provide a comprehensive solution for implementing the Customer Segmentation clustering model.

Product clustering for an e-commerce project

In this task, we will perform product clustering using the same e-commerce dataset. The goal is to create an unsupervised learning model to cluster products based on their textual descriptions using Python and common libraries.

Your initial prompt: Set context

As usual, when using ChatGPT, it's important to set a high-level context. For data science, high-level context means describing things like the data used (e-commerce data), what we're trying to achieve (get data insights), and how we're looking to achieve it (clustering).

Below is an example of a prompt providing all the suggested context we just described in the preceding paragraph:

[Prompt]

I would like you to act as an experienced data scientist and help me implement Product Categorization model using clustering. The dataset is e-commerce data from the UCI Machine Learning Repository. It is a transnational dataset that contains all the transactions occurring between 01/12/2010 and 09/12/2011 for a UK-based and registered non-store online retailer. The dataset contains the following columns: `InvoiceNo` (integer), `StockCode` (string), `Description` (string), `Quantity` (integer), `InvoiceDate` (date), `UnitPrice` (decimal), `CustomerID` (integer), `Country` (string). Can you suggest the steps needed to perform Product Categorization using the data from a csv file.

[End of prompt]

You should receive a response like the below response:

[Prompt response]

Certainly! Product categorization using clustering is a great approach to group similar products together based on their attributes. Here's a step-by-step guide to perform product categorization using the given e-commerce dataset:

Step 1: Load and Preprocess the Data

1. Load the dataset from the CSV file into a suitable data structure, like a Pandas DataFrame in Python.
2. Inspect the data to understand its structure, missing values, and overall characteristics.
3. Preprocess the data, which may involve handling missing values, data type conversions, and data cleaning.

Step 2: Feature Engineering

1. Select relevant features for clustering. In this case, you can consider features like 'StockCode', 'Description', 'Quantity', 'UnitPrice', etc. Customer-related features like 'CustomerID' might not be directly relevant for product categorization.
2. Create a feature matrix, where each row corresponds to a product and each column corresponds to a feature.

Step 3: Text Data Preprocessing

1. For text-based features like 'Description', perform text preprocessing steps such as lowercasing, tokenization, removing punctuation, and stopwords.
2. Convert the text data into numerical format using techniques like TF-IDF (Term Frequency-Inverse Document Frequency) or word embeddings.

Step 4: Choose Clustering Algorithm

1. Select an appropriate clustering algorithm. Common choices include K-means, Hierarchical clustering, and DBSCAN.

    2.   Tune hyperparameters if needed.

Step 5: Feature Scaling

    1.   Scale the numerical features to have similar ranges. This is important for algorithms like K-means that are distance-based.

Step 6: Apply Clustering Algorithm

    1.   Apply the chosen clustering algorithm to the preprocessed data.

    2.   Determine the optimal number of clusters. You can use techniques like the Elbow Method, Silhouette Score, or Gap Statistic.

Step 7: Interpret Clusters

    1.   Once you have clusters, analyze the products within each cluster to understand the common characteristics.

    2.   Assign meaningful labels to the clusters based on your analysis. These labels will represent the product categories.

Step 8: Visualize Clusters (Optional)

    1.   Use visualization techniques such as scatter plots, t-SNE, or PCA to visualize the clusters in a reduced dimensional space.

Step 9: Assign Categories to Products

    1.   Assign each product to its respective category based on the cluster it belongs to.

Step 10: Evaluate and Refine

    1.   Evaluate the quality of your clustering results. You can use domain knowledge or external validation metrics if available.

    2.   Refine the process by adjusting preprocessing steps, algorithm parameters, or features as needed.

Remember that clustering is an iterative process, and the quality of your results may depend on various factors such as data quality, feature selection, and algorithm choice. It's also important to consider the business context and domain knowledge when interpreting and labeling the clusters.

[End of response]

Having reviewed the steps in the response, you can now proceed with the next prompt.

Load and preprocess the data

Now that we have a series of steps described to us how to perform clustering, we want to carry out the first step from the response namely loading and preprocessing the data.

[Prompt]

I would like to do it step by step. Please guide me through Step 1: Load and Preprocess the Data. My data URL is "../Datasets/data.csv" and the CSV file is using latin1 encoding. I would use the column 'Description' for clustering to identify product categories.

[End of prompt]

You should receive a response like the following text:

[Prompt response]

Of course! Let's start with Step 1: Load and Preprocess the Data.

```python
import pandas as pd

# Load the data from the CSV file using Latin1 encoding
data_url = "../Datasets/data.csv"
df = pd.read_csv(data_url, encoding='latin1')

# Display basic information about the dataset
print(df.info())

# Display the first few rows of the dataset
print(df.head())
```

This code will load the dataset from the provided CSV file using the Latin1 encoding. It will then display basic information about the dataset, such as the data types of each column and the number of non-null values.

Additionally, it will display the first few rows of the dataset to give you a sense of the data's structure.

```
Data columns (total 8 columns):
 #   Column       Non-Null Count   Dtype
---  ------       --------------   -----
 0   InvoiceNo    541909 non-null  object
 1   StockCode    541909 non-null  object
 2   Description  540455 non-null  object
 3   Quantity     541909 non-null  int64
 4   InvoiceDate  541909 non-null  object
 5   UnitPrice    541909 non-null  float64
 6   CustomerID   406829 non-null  float64
 7   Country      541909 non-null  object
dtypes: float64(2), int64(1), object(5)
memory usage: 33.1+ MB
None
  InvoiceNo StockCode                          Description  Quantity  \
0    536365    85123A  WHITE HANGING HEART T-LIGHT HOLDER         6
1    536365     71053                 WHITE METAL LANTERN         6
2    536365    84406B      CREAM CUPID HEARTS COAT HANGER         8
3    536365    84029G  KNITTED UNION FLAG HOT WATER BOTTLE        6
4    536365    84029E       RED WOOLLY HOTTIE WHITE HEART.        6

       InvoiceDate  UnitPrice  CustomerID         Country
0  12/1/2010 8:26       2.55     17850.0  United Kingdom
1  12/1/2010 8:26       3.39     17850.0  United Kingdom
2  12/1/2010 8:26       2.75     17850.0  United Kingdom
3  12/1/2010 8:26       3.39     17850.0  United Kingdom
4  12/1/2010 8:26       3.39     17850.0  United Kingdom
```

Figure 16.11: First few rows of the dataset

Now, let's preprocess the data and focus on the 'Description' column for clustering.

```
# Drop rows with missing 'Description' values
df = df.dropna(subset=['Description'])

# Display basic statistics of numerical columns
print(df.describe())

# Display unique values in the 'Description' column
print(df['Description'].nunique())

# Display the top 10 most common descriptions
print(df['Description'].value_counts().head(10))
```

In this code snippet, we first drop rows with missing 'Description' values since we'll be using this column for clustering. Next, we display basic statistics of the numerical columns to get an overview of the data's distribution. After that, we count the number of unique descriptions to understand the variety of products. Finally, we display the top 10 most common descriptions to see the most frequent products in the dataset.

At this point, you have loaded the data, dropped missing values in the 'Description' column, and gained some insights into the data's characteristics. The next step will involve text data preprocessing for the 'Description' column. Let me know if you're ready to move on to Step 3, or if you have any questions about the current steps!

[End of response]

After copying the code to a Jupyter Notebook, we find that it works perfectly fine, and we learn that 541,909 dataset records contain 4,223 unique product descriptions. The next step is to perform text data preprocessing for the 'Description' column. Let's proceed with the next prompt.

Feature engineering and text data preprocessing

At this point, the data has been read and we know the size of the dataset as well. Let's carry on with the next two steps, feature engineering and text data preprocessing:

[Prompt]

The dataset contains 541909 entries and there are 4223 unique product descriptions. I would like to drop duplicate 'Descriptions' and perform other text data preprocessing and feature engineering. Please create a script with comments and include libraries and nltk resources to download.

[End of prompt]

[Prompt response]

Sure, I'll provide you with a script that covers text data preprocessing and feature engineering steps. Let's get started:

```python
import pandas as pd
import nltk
from nltk.corpus import stopwords
from nltk.tokenize import word_tokenize
from sklearn.feature_extraction.text import TfidfVectorizer

# Download NLTK resources (only needed once)
nltk.download('punkt')
nltk.download('stopwords')

# Load the data from the CSV file using Latin1 encoding
data_url = "../Datasets/data.csv"
df = pd.read_csv(data_url, encoding='latin1')
```

```python
# Drop rows with missing 'Description' values
df = df.dropna(subset=['Description'])

# Drop duplicate 'Description' entries
df = df.drop_duplicates(subset=['Description'])

# Text preprocessing and feature engineering
# Convert descriptions to lowercase
df['Description'] = df['Description'].str.lower()

# Tokenization and removal of punctuation
df['Description'] = df['Description'].apply(word_tokenize)

# Remove stopwords
stop_words = set(stopwords.words('english'))
df['Description'] = df['Description'].apply(lambda x: [word for word in x if
word not in stop_words])

# Convert tokenized descriptions back to strings
df['Description'] = df['Description'].apply(' '.join)

# TF-IDF vectorization
tfidf_vectorizer = TfidfVectorizer(max_features=1000)  # You can adjust the
number of features
tfidf_matrix = tfidf_vectorizer.fit_transform(df['Description'])

# Convert TF-IDF matrix to a DataFrame
tfidf_df = pd.DataFrame(tfidf_matrix.toarray(), columns=tfidf_vectorizer.get_
feature_names_out())

# Display the TF-IDF DataFrame
print(tfidf_df.head())
```

In this script:

1. We import necessary libraries including pandas, nltk, and TfidfVectorizer from sklearn. feature_extraction.text.

2. We download NLTK resources (punkt for tokenization and stopwords for removing stopwords) if they are not already downloaded.

3. We load the dataset and drop rows with missing 'Description' values and duplicate descriptions.

4. We perform text preprocessing steps on the 'Description' column: converting to lowercase, tokenizing, removing punctuation, and stopwords.

5. We convert the tokenized descriptions back to strings.

6. We use TF-IDF vectorization to convert the preprocessed text data into numerical features. You can adjust the `max_features` parameter to control the number of features.

7. The TF-IDF matrix is converted to a DataFrame for further analysis.

This script will preprocess the text data and perform feature engineering using TF-IDF vectorization. The resulting TF-IDF matrix can be used as input for clustering algorithms in the subsequent steps.

[End of response]

After pasting the script to Jupyter Notebook, we find that it works perfectly fine, and we learn that the TF-IDF matrix has 4,223 rows (one for each unique product description) and 1,000 columns (one for each feature).

```
[nltk_data] Downloading package punkt to /root/nltk_data...
[nltk_data]   Unzipping tokenizers/punkt.zip.
[nltk_data] Downloading package stopwords to /root/nltk_data...
[nltk_data]   Unzipping corpora/stopwords.zip.
<ipython-input-4-e54dfbc360ba>:24: SettingWithCopyWarning:
A value is trying to be set on a copy of a slice from a DataFrame.
Try using .loc[row_indexer,col_indexer] = value instead

See the caveats in the documentation: https://pandas.pydata.org/pandas-docs/stable/
  df['Description'] = df['Description'].str.lower()
    00   10   12   16   20  20713  23343   24  30cm   36  ...  world  woven  \
0  0.0  0.0  0.0  0.0  0.0    0.0    0.0  0.0   0.0  0.0  ...    0.0    0.0
1  0.0  0.0  0.0  0.0  0.0    0.0    0.0  0.0   0.0  0.0  ...    0.0    0.0
2  0.0  0.0  0.0  0.0  0.0    0.0    0.0  0.0   0.0  0.0  ...    0.0    0.0
3  0.0  0.0  0.0  0.0  0.0    0.0    0.0  0.0   0.0  0.0  ...    0.0    0.0
4  0.0  0.0  0.0  0.0  0.0    0.0    0.0  0.0   0.0  0.0  ...    0.0    0.0

    wrap  wreath  writing  wrong  wrongly  xmas  yellow  zinc
0    0.0     0.0      0.0    0.0      0.0   0.0     0.0   0.0
1    0.0     0.0      0.0    0.0      0.0   0.0     0.0   0.0
2    0.0     0.0      0.0    0.0      0.0   0.0     0.0   0.0
3    0.0     0.0      0.0    0.0      0.0   0.0     0.0   0.0
4    0.0     0.0      0.0    0.0      0.0   0.0     0.0   0.0

[5 rows x 1000 columns]
```

Figure 16.12: TF-IDF matrix

Feature engineering

We will continue with feature engineering. Let's visualize the most frequent features in the TF-IDF matrix.

[Prompt]

I would like to visualize the top 100 most frequent features from the TF-IDF matrix. Please create a bar chart with words on the vertical axis.

[End of prompt]

[Prompt response]

Certainly! To visualize the top 100 most frequent features from the TF-IDF matrix, you can create a bar chart using libraries like `matplotlib`. Here's how you can do it:

```python
import matplotlib.pyplot as plt

# Calculate the sum of TF-IDF scores for each feature
feature_sum = tfidf_df.sum()

# Get the top 100 features by frequency
top_features = feature_sum.nlargest(100)

# Create a bar chart
plt.figure(figsize=(10, 12))
top_features.plot(kind='barh')
plt.xlabel('TF-IDF Score Sum')
plt.ylabel('Words')
plt.title('Top 100 Most Frequent Features from TF-IDF Matrix')
plt.tight_layout()
plt.show()
```

This script calculates the sum of TF-IDF scores for each feature and selects the top 100 features by frequency. It then creates a horizontal bar chart using `matplotlib` to visualize the top features. Adjust the figure size, labels, and other parameters as needed to customize the visualization to your preferences.

[End of response]

Running this code in Jupyter Notebook will produce the following bar chart:

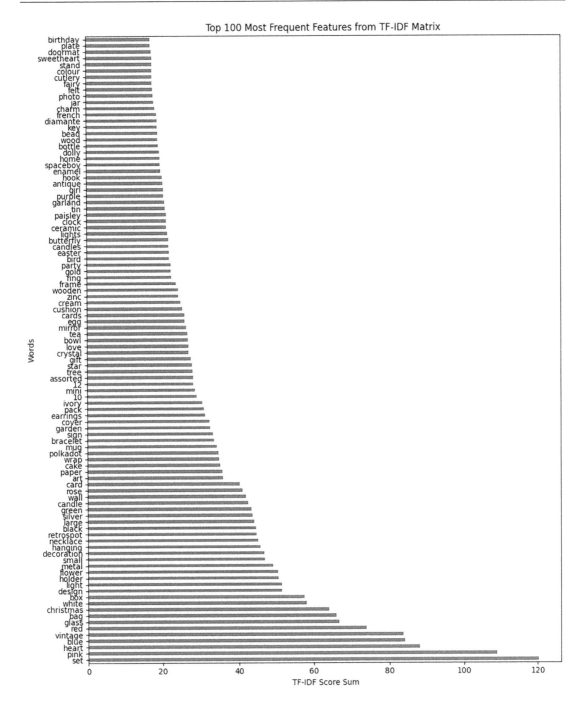

Figure 16.13: Most frequent features

Let's analyze this chart and proceed with the next prompt.

[Prompt]

We can see that the features contain numbers and words representing colors, like red, blue, and other colors. These words will not be useful for product categorization. Can you create a list of words that can represent color.

[End of prompt]

[Prompt response]

Certainly! Here's a list of common words that represent colors. You can use this list to filter out color-related words from your features before performing product categorization.

```python
color_words = [
    'black', 'white', 'grey', 'gray', 'red', 'blue', 'green', 'yellow',
    'orange', 'purple', 'pink', 'brown', 'beige', 'gold', 'silver',
    'indigo', 'violet', 'turquoise', 'teal', 'aqua', 'navy', 'olive',
    'maroon', 'coral', 'plum', 'salmon', 'magenta', 'cyan', 'khaki',
    'ivory', 'chartreuse', 'crimson', 'fuchsia', 'lavender', 'lime',
    'tan', 'sienna', 'orchid', 'periwinkle', 'peach', 'thistle'
]
```

You can use this list to filter out color-related words from your features during the text preprocessing step. For example:

```python
# Remove color-related words from descriptions
df['Description'] = df['Description'].apply(lambda x: [word for word in x if
word not in color_words])
```

[End of response]

By removing color-related words, you can help improve the quality of your product categorization by focusing on more meaningful features.

[Prompt]

Modify the script to remove `color_words` and words that are less than three characters long. Refactor code to encapsulate data preprocessing and vectorisation into a function `preprocess_and_vectorize_data`.

[End of prompt]

[Prompt response]

Certainly! Here's the modified script with the requested changes, including encapsulating the data preprocessing and vectorization steps into a function:

```python
import pandas as pd
import nltk
from nltk.corpus import stopwords
from nltk.tokenize import word_tokenize
from sklearn.feature_extraction.text import TfidfVectorizer
```

```python
import matplotlib.pyplot as plt

# Download NLTK resources (only needed once)
nltk.download('punkt')
nltk.download('stopwords')

# List of color-related words
color_words = [
    'black', 'white', 'grey', 'gray', 'red', 'blue', 'green', 'yellow',
    'orange', 'purple', 'pink', 'brown', 'beige', 'gold', 'silver',
    'indigo', 'violet', 'turquoise', 'teal', 'aqua', 'navy', 'olive',
    'maroon', 'coral', 'plum', 'salmon', 'magenta', 'cyan', 'khaki',
    'ivory', 'chartreuse', 'crimson', 'fuchsia', 'lavender', 'lime',
    'tan', 'sienna', 'orchid', 'periwinkle', 'peach', 'thistle'
]


def preprocess_and_vectorize_data(data):
    # Drop rows with missing 'Description' values
    data = data.dropna(subset=['Description'])

    # Drop duplicate 'Description' entries
    data = data.drop_duplicates(subset=['Description'])

    # Convert descriptions to lowercase
    data['Description'] = data['Description'].str.lower()

    # Tokenization and removal of punctuation
    data['Description'] = data['Description'].apply(word_tokenize)

    # Remove stopwords and color-related words
    stop_words = set(stopwords.words('english'))
    data['Description'] = data['Description'].apply(lambda x: [word for word in
x if word not in stop_words and len(word) > 2 and word not in color_words])

    # Convert tokenized descriptions back to strings
    data['Description'] = data['Description'].apply(' '.join)

    # TF-IDF vectorization
    tfidf_vectorizer = TfidfVectorizer(max_features=1000)  # You can adjust the
number of features
    tfidf_matrix = tfidf_vectorizer.fit_transform(data['Description'])
```

```
    # Convert TF-IDF matrix to a DataFrame
    tfidf_df = pd.DataFrame(tfidf_matrix.toarray(), columns=tfidf_vectorizer.
get_feature_names_out())

    return tfidf_df


# Load the data from the CSV file using Latin1 encoding
data_url = "../Datasets/data.csv"
df = pd.read_csv(data_url, encoding='latin1')


# Preprocess and vectorize the data
tfidf_df = preprocess_and_vectorize_data(df)


# Calculate the sum of TF-IDF scores for each feature
feature_sum = tfidf_df.sum()


# Get the top 100 features by frequency
top_features = feature_sum.nlargest(100)


# Create a bar chart
plt.figure(figsize=(10, 12))
top_features.plot(kind='barh')
plt.xlabel('TF-IDF Score Sum')
plt.ylabel('Words')
plt.title('Top 100 Most Frequent Features from TF-IDF Matrix')
plt.tight_layout()
plt.show()
```

This script encapsulates the data preprocessing and vectorization steps into the preprocess_and_
vectorize_data function. The function takes the raw data as input, performs the required preprocessing, and returns the TF-IDF matrix. The rest of the script remains similar to before.

[End of response]

After running the script, we can visualize the updated set of the most frequent words from the TF-IDF
matrix output.

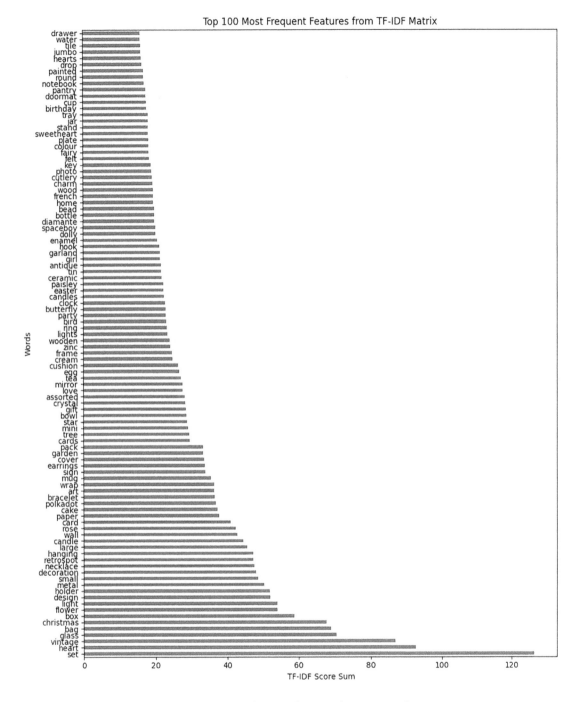

Figure 16.14: Most frequent features that are not colors

Let's proceed with our feature engineering. We will use ChatGPT to suggest options that can be explored with TF-IDF vectorization.

[Prompt]

The TF-IDF vectorization is initialized with `max_features` parameter. What are other initialization options?

[End of prompt]

[Prompt response]

When initializing the TF-IDF vectorizer in scikit-learn, you can set several parameters to customize its behavior.

In addition to the `max_features` parameter, here are some other important parameters you can consider:

1. `max_df` and `min_df`: These parameters control the threshold for the document frequency of terms. For example, you can set `max_df` to ignore terms that appear in a high percentage of documents, and `min_df` to ignore terms that appear in a low percentage of documents.

2. `ngram_range`: This parameter specifies the range of n-grams to consider during tokenization. For example, setting `ngram_range=(1, 2)` will consider both individual words and pairs of consecutive words (bigrams).

3. `stop_words`: You can provide a list of stopwords to be ignored during tokenization. This can be a custom list or one of the built-in lists like `'english'`.

4. `tokenizer`: You can specify a custom tokenizer function if you want to perform additional text preprocessing or tokenization.

5. `use_idf`: This parameter controls whether to use the inverse-document-frequency (IDF) re-weighting of the term frequencies.

6. `smooth_idf`: This parameter controls whether to add a smoothing term to the IDF to avoid division by zero errors.

7. `sublinear_tf`: If set to `True`, it applies sublinear scaling to the term frequency, which can help to prevent very frequent terms from dominating the calculation.

Here's an example of how you can initialize the TF-IDF vectorizer with some of these parameters:

```python
from sklearn.feature_extraction.text import TfidfVectorizer

tfidf_vectorizer = TfidfVectorizer(
    max_features=1000,
    max_df=0.8,
    min_df=0.05,
    ngram_range=(1, 2),
    stop_words='english',
    use_idf=True,
    smooth_idf=True,
    sublinear_tf=True
)
```

[End of response]

Feel free to experiment with these parameters based on your specific dataset and goals. The choice of parameters may depend on the nature of the text data and the desired outcomes of your clustering or categorization task.

Choose clustering algorithm

There are quite a few clustering algorithms we could choose. There is, for example, K-means, that we used for another use case; there's also hierarchical clustering, **DBSCAN (Density-based clustering algorithm)**, **Gaussian mixture models (GMMs)**, and agglomerative clustering. We're going to go with K-means, but why is that? The reason is that we're working with customers and want to divide them up into groups based on purchasing behavior, demographic properties, and so on. Another reason for choosing K-means is its simplicity and being able to work with large datasets.

You might wonder when to apply the other mentioned clustering algorithms in the context of e-commerce. Well, let's look at some interesting areas in this domain:

- **Product recommendation:** Here, it would be more appropriate to use hierarchical clustering as products usually come in hierarchies and we want to understand the relationship between products.
- **Anomaly detection:** Another important area is anomaly detection, especially fraudulent transactions. Here, you want to understand unusual customer behavior to identify outliers; for that use case, DBSCAN is the best algorithm to go with.
- **Personalization:** You want to ensure customers feel like they have an experience uniquely fitted to their behaviors on the website. GMM is a great choice for this use case when a customer's behavior is a bit more complex.

Feature scaling

Feature scaling and TF-IDF are both preprocessing techniques and it only makes sense to choose one of them. Which one to choose depends on what we want to use it for. In the context of e-commerce, here's how you could reason:

- Choose feature scaling if you're dealing with numerical features like customer age, purchase amounts, and purchase frequency (e.g., grouping customers based on their purchasing behavior).
- Choose the TF-IDF matrix if you're looking at other aspects of e-commerce like customer reviews, product descriptions, and search queries.

We can skip this step as we are using a TF-IDF matrix that is already scaled.

Apply clustering algorithm

Next, let's apply our chosen clustering algorithm:

[Prompt]

I would like to use english `stop_words`, no `max_features`, and pass `min_df` to `preprocess_and_vectorize_data` function to set minimum number of documents the feature appears in. I would like to try a range of values for `min_df`: `5`, `10`, `20`, `30` and compare the silhouette score from the K-means output. I would like to visualize the result.

[End of prompt]

[Prompt response]

Sure! Let's modify the script to accommodate your requirements for `min_df` and the comparison of silhouette scores for different values of `min_df` using `KMeans` clustering. Here's the updated script:

```python
def preprocess_and_vectorize_data(data, min_df):
    # Drop rows with missing 'Description' values
    data = data.dropna(subset=['Description'])


    # Drop duplicate 'Description' entries
    data = data.drop_duplicates(subset=['Description'])


    # Convert descriptions to lowercase
    data['Description'] = data['Description'].str.lower()


    # Tokenization and removal of punctuation
    data['Description'] = data['Description'].apply(word_tokenize)


    # Remove stopwords and color-related words
    stop_words = set(stopwords.words('english'))
    data['Description'] = data['Description'].apply(lambda x: [word for word in
 x if word not in stop_words and len(word) > 2 and word not in color_words])


    # Convert tokenized descriptions back to strings
    data['Description'] = data['Description'].apply(' '.join)


    # TF-IDF vectorization
    tfidf_vectorizer = TfidfVectorizer(min_df=min_df)
    tfidf_matrix = tfidf_vectorizer.fit_transform(data['Description'])


    # Convert TF-IDF matrix to a DataFrame
    tfidf_df = pd.DataFrame(tfidf_matrix.toarray(), columns=tfidf_vectorizer.
get_feature_names_out())


    return tfidf_df


# Load the data from the CSV file using Latin1 encoding
```

```
data_url = "../Datasets/data.csv"
df = pd.read_csv(data_url, encoding='latin1')


# Different values for min_df
min_df_values = [5, 10, 20, 30]


# Store silhouette scores
silhouette_scores = []


# Perform clustering and calculate silhouette scores for different min_df
values
for min_df in min_df_values:
    # Preprocess and vectorize the data
    tfidf_df = preprocess_and_vectorize_data(df, min_df)


    # Perform KMeans clustering
    kmeans = KMeans(n_clusters=10, random_state=42)
    cluster_labels = kmeans.fit_predict(tfidf_df)


    # Calculate silhouette score
    silhouette_scores.append(silhouette_score(tfidf_df, cluster_labels))


# Visualize the silhouette scores
plt.plot(min_df_values, silhouette_scores, marker='o')
plt.xlabel('min_df')
plt.ylabel('Silhouette Score')
plt.title('Silhouette Score vs. min_df')
plt.xticks(min_df_values)
plt.grid()
plt.show()
```

In this script, we're looping through different values of `min_df` (5, 10, 20, and 30) and performing the following steps for each value:

1. Preprocess and vectorize the data using the `preprocess_and_vectorize_data` function with the specified `min_df` value.
2. Perform K-means clustering with 10 clusters (you can adjust the number of clusters as needed).
3. Calculate the silhouette score for the clustering results and store it in the `silhouette_scores` list.

Finally, we visualize the silhouette scores for different `min_df` values using a line plot. This will help you compare how different values of `min_df` impact the quality of the clustering results.

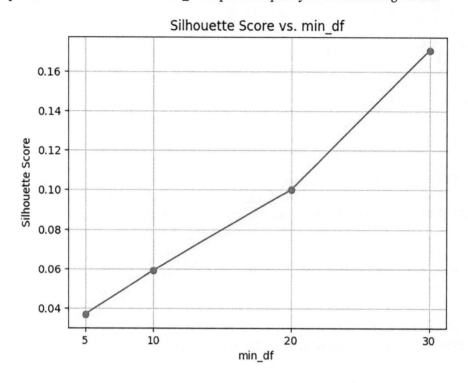

Figure 16.15: Silhouette score versus min_df

[End of response]

Next, we will investigate the impact of the number of clusters on the quality of the clustering results. Let's proceed with the next prompt.

[Prompt]

I would also like to try different number of clusters `num_clusters` = [3,4, 5,6,7] and visually compare silhouette score outputs for `min_df`, `num_clusters` combinations. Please add the script that generates a plot of cluster and silhouette score values for each of the values from `num_clusters`.

[End of prompt]

[Prompt response]

Certainly! Here's the updated script that generates a plot of silhouette scores for different combinations of `min_df` and `num_clusters`:

```
# Different values for min_df and num_clusters
min_df_values = [5, 10, 20, 30]
num_clusters = [3, 4, 5, 6, 7]
```

```
# Store silhouette scores for each combination
silhouette_scores = []

# Perform clustering and calculate silhouette scores for different min_df and
num_clusters combinations
for min_df, n_clusters in itertools.product(min_df_values, num_clusters):
    # Preprocess and vectorize the data
    tfidf_df = preprocess_and_vectorize_data(df, min_df)

    # Perform KMeans clustering
    kmeans = KMeans(n_clusters=n_clusters, random_state=42)
    cluster_labels = kmeans.fit_predict(tfidf_df)

    # Calculate silhouette score
    silhouette_scores.append((min_df, n_clusters, silhouette_score(tfidf_df,
cluster_labels)))

# Convert silhouette scores to a DataFrame for easier visualization
silhouette_scores_df = pd.DataFrame(silhouette_scores, columns=['min_df', 'num_
clusters', 'silhouette_score'])

# Plot the silhouette scores
plt.figure(figsize=(10, 6))
for min_df in min_df_values:
    subset_df = silhouette_scores_df[silhouette_scores_df['min_df'] == min_df]
    plt.plot(subset_df['num_clusters'], subset_df['silhouette_score'],
marker='o', label=f'min_df = {min_df}')

plt.xlabel('Number of Clusters')
plt.ylabel('Silhouette Score')
plt.title('Silhouette Score vs. Number of Clusters for Different min_df
Values')
plt.legend()
plt.grid()
plt.show()
```

In this script, we use the `itertools.product` function to create combinations of `min_df` and `num_clusters` values. We calculate silhouette scores for each combination and store them in the `silhouette_scores` list. Then, we convert the silhouette scores to a DataFrame for easier visualization. The resulting plot shows how the silhouette score varies for different values of `num_clusters` while considering different `min_df` values.

[End of response]

Here is the output of the script:

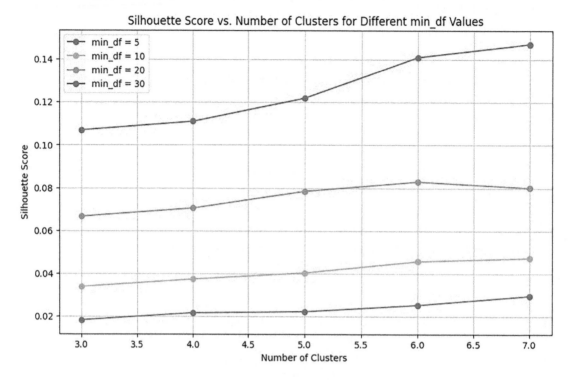

Figure 16.16: Silhouette score versus different min_df values

Let's refine the plot to show the number of features corresponding to the `min_fd` parameter value.

[Prompt]

The plot is good. I would like a small change by adding the number of features for each of the `min_df` values to the `label=f'min_df = {min_df}`

[End of prompt]

[Prompt response]

Certainly! You can add the number of features corresponding to each `min_df` value to the legend labels.

Here's the modified code with that change:

```
# ...

# Store silhouette scores for each combination
silhouette_scores = []
```

```python
# Perform clustering and calculate silhouette scores for different min_df and
num_clusters combinations
for min_df, n_clusters in itertools.product(min_df_values, num_clusters):
    # Preprocess and vectorize the data
    tfidf_df = preprocess_and_vectorize_data(df, min_df)

    # Perform KMeans clustering
    kmeans = KMeans(n_clusters=n_clusters, random_state=42)
    cluster_labels = kmeans.fit_predict(tfidf_df)

    # Calculate silhouette score
    silhouette_scores.append((min_df, n_clusters, silhouette_score(tfidf_df,
cluster_labels)))

# Convert silhouette scores to a DataFrame for easier visualization
silhouette_scores_df = pd.DataFrame(silhouette_scores, columns=['min_df', 'num_
clusters', 'silhouette_score'])

# Plot the silhouette scores
plt.figure(figsize=(10, 6))
for min_df in min_df_values:
    subset_df = silhouette_scores_df[silhouette_scores_df['min_df'] == min_df]

    # Get the number of features for the current min_df value
    num_features = preprocess_and_vectorize_data(df, min_df).shape[1]

    plt.plot(subset_df['num_clusters'], subset_df['silhouette_score'],
marker='o', label=f'min_df = {min_df}, num_features = {num_features}')

plt.xlabel('Number of Clusters')
plt.ylabel('Silhouette Score')
plt.title('Silhouette Score vs. Number of Clusters for Different min_df
Values')
plt.legend()
plt.grid()
plt.show()
```

In this modified script, we calculate the number of features for each `min_df` value using the `shape[1]` attribute of the TF-IDF DataFrame. Then, we include this information in the legend labels for each line on the plot. This change will help you visualize the impact of both `min_df` and the number of features on the silhouette scores.

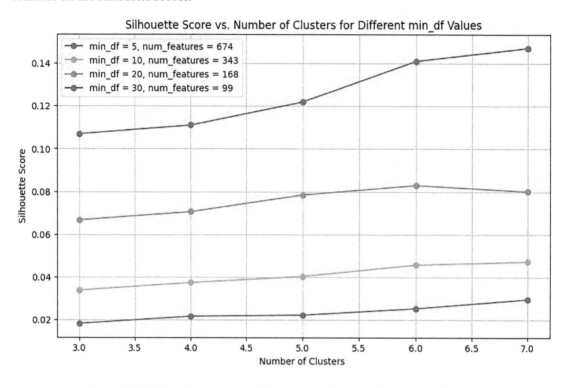

Figure 16.17: Silhouette score versus different min_df values with number of features

[End of response]

Let's proceed with the next prompt.

[Prompt]

I will use the value of `min_df_value` = 20, `num_clusters`= [3, 4, 5, 6]. I would like to know the number of products in each cluster. Can you add a plot `Products per Cluster` to the previous code to show number of products per cluster for `num_clusters_values` in [3, 4, 5, 6]

[End of prompt]

[Prompt response]

Certainly! You can add a plot to visualize the number of products in each cluster for different `num_clusters` values. Here's the modified script with the requested changes:

```
#  ...

# Chosen min_df and num_clusters values
```

```
min_df_value = 20
num_clusters_values = [3, 4, 5, 6]

# Store silhouette scores and number of products per cluster
results = []

# Perform clustering and calculate silhouette scores for chosen min_df and num_
clusters values
for n_clusters in num_clusters_values:
    # Preprocess and vectorize the data
    tfidf_df = preprocess_and_vectorize_data(df, min_df_value)

    # Perform KMeans clustering
    kmeans = KMeans(n_clusters=n_clusters, random_state=42)
    cluster_labels = kmeans.fit_predict(tfidf_df)

    # Calculate silhouette score
    silhouette = silhouette_score(tfidf_df, cluster_labels)

    # Count number of products in each cluster
    cluster_counts = pd.Series(cluster_labels).value_counts().sort_index()

    results.append((n_clusters, silhouette, cluster_counts))

# Convert results to a DataFrame for easier visualization
results_df = pd.DataFrame(results, columns=['num_clusters', 'silhouette_score',
'cluster_counts'])

# Plot the silhouette scores
plt.figure(figsize=(15, 6))

# Silhouette Score plot
plt.subplot(1, 2, 1)
plt.plot(results_df['num_clusters'], results_df['silhouette_score'],
marker='o')
plt.xlabel('Number of Clusters')
plt.ylabel('Silhouette Score')
plt.title('Silhouette Score vs. Number of Clusters')
plt.grid()

# Products per Cluster plot
```

```
plt.subplot(1, 2, 2)
for n_clusters, cluster_counts in results_df[['num_clusters', 'cluster_
counts']].values:
    plt.plot(range(1, n_clusters + 1), cluster_counts, marker='o', label=f'num_
clusters = {n_clusters}')

plt.xlabel('Cluster')
plt.ylabel('Number of Products')
plt.title('Number of Products per Cluster')
plt.legend()
plt.grid()

plt.tight_layout()
plt.show()
```

In this modified script, we calculate the number of products in each cluster using pd.Series(cluster_labels).value_counts().sort_index() and store the results along with silhouette scores in the results list. We then create a DataFrame from the results for easier visualization.

The script includes two plots side by side: the first plot displays the silhouette scores for different num_clusters values, and the second plot displays the number of products in each cluster for the same num_clusters values. This will help you understand the relationship between the number of clusters, silhouette scores, and the distribution of products among clusters.

After running the script, you should see the following output:

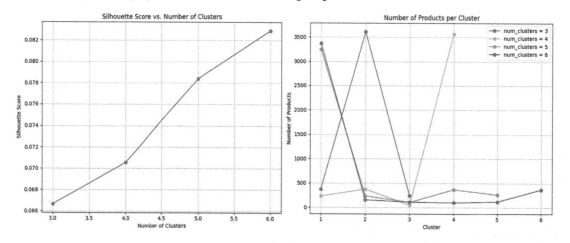

Figure 16.18: Added plot of products per cluster

[End of response]

We will now select the number of clusters and min_df value and proceed with the next prompt.

Interpret clusters and visualize results

We'll be looking into interpreting clusters and visualizing the results. What are the things we should bear in mind?

Interpreting cluster

For cluster interpretation, we should consider things like:

- Cohesion: Ensure data points are similar to each other. You can find this out by examining terms that are the most representative in each cluster.
- Separation: Clusters should be well separated ensuring they are distinct and meaningful.
- Labels: Clusters should also have descriptive labels.
- Outliers: It's important to identify outliers that don't fit well in any cluster.

Visualizing clusters

For visualizing clusters, here are some things to consider:

- Dimensionality reduction: You want to reduce the high-dimensional TF-IDF matrix to 2D or 3D to make it easier to visualize. For this, a technique like PCA comes in handy.
- Scatter plots: Scatter plots are great for visualizing data points; a point can be a document, for example, and colors or shapes could represent different clusters.
- Word clouds: You could also use word clouds if you look at text, to see what the most common words used are.
- Heat maps: Heat maps are another great way to visualize frequency and will help highlight the most important terms per cluster.
- Interactivity: Ensure you allow for exploration to help you drill down into specific data points by using, for example, Plotly.

Next, let's craft a prompt for visualization.

[Prompt]

I will use the value of `min_df_value` = 20 and 5 clusters. I would like to use PCA with 3 components to visualize product clusters on a 3D graph. The colors of clusters should be mapped from the seaborn `color_palette`.

[End of prompt]

[Prompt response]

Certainly! In order to visualize the product clusters in a 3D graph using PCA with 3 components and mapping cluster colors from a seaborn color palette, you can follow these steps:

1. Import necessary libraries.
2. Preprocess the data and perform clustering.
3. Apply PCA to reduce the dimensionality to 3 components.
4. Plot the clusters in a 3D scatter plot with seaborn color palette.

Here's the code to achieve this:

```python
from sklearn.decomposition import PCA
import seaborn as sns
import matplotlib.pyplot as plt
from mpl_toolkits.mplot3d import Axes3D  # Required for 3D plotting

# Selected min_df and num_clusters values
min_df_value = 20
num_clusters = 5

# Preprocess data and perform clustering
tfidf_matrix, tfidf_vectorizer = preprocess_and_vectorize_
data(df['Description'], min_df_value)
kmeans = KMeans(n_clusters=num_clusters, random_state=42)
cluster_labels = kmeans.fit_predict(tfidf_matrix)

# Apply PCA with 3 components
pca = PCA(n_components=3)
pca_result = pca.fit_transform(tfidf_matrix.toarray())

# Create a DataFrame for PCA results
pca_df = pd.DataFrame(data=pca_result, columns=['PC1', 'PC2', 'PC3'])
pca_df['Cluster'] = cluster_labels

# Seaborn color palette for cluster colors
color_palette = sns.color_palette("Set1", n_colors=num_clusters)

# Plot 3D scatter plot
fig = plt.figure(figsize=(10, 8))
ax = fig.add_subplot(111, projection='3d')

for cluster_id in range(num_clusters):
    cluster_points = pca_df[pca_df['Cluster'] == cluster_id]
    ax.scatter(cluster_points['PC1'], cluster_points['PC2'], cluster_
points['PC3'], color=color_palette[cluster_id], label=f'Cluster {cluster_id}')

ax.set_xlabel('PC1')
ax.set_ylabel('PC2')
ax.set_zlabel('PC3')
ax.set_title('Product Clusters in 3D')
ax.legend()
plt.show()
```

[End of response]

This code will preprocess the data, perform clustering, apply PCA to reduce dimensionality to 3 components, and then plot the product clusters in a 3D scatter plot with cluster colors mapped from a seaborn color palette. Adjust the figure size, labels, and other plot parameters as needed to customize the visualization.

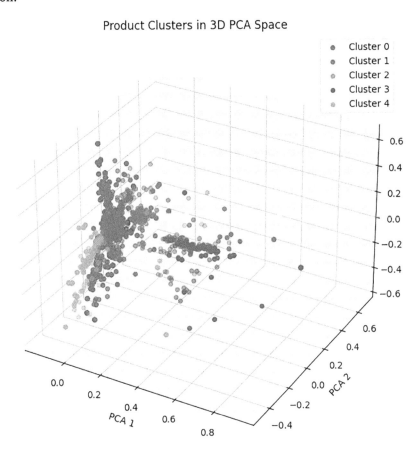

Figure 16.19: Product clusters visualized in 3D space

Creating a word cloud

Now, we will examine the most frequent words in each of the clusters. Let's proceed with the next prompt.

[Prompt]

I would like to visualize the most frequent words occurring in product descriptions assigned to clusters. I would like you to use the word cloud library and create a function that will output word clouds for each of the clusters.

[End of prompt]

[Prompt response]

Sure! To visualize the most frequent words occurring in product descriptions assigned to clusters, you can use the WordCloud library. Here's how you can create a function that generates word clouds for each of the clusters:

```python
from wordcloud import WordCloud

# Create a DataFrame for clustering results
clustering_results = pd.DataFrame(data={'Description': df['Description'],
'Cluster': cluster_labels})

# Function to generate word clouds for each cluster
def generate_wordclouds(dataframe, num_clusters):
    for cluster_id in range(num_clusters):
        cluster_data = dataframe[dataframe['Cluster'] == cluster_id]
        cluster_text = ' '.join(cluster_data['Description'])

        # Create a WordCloud object
        wordcloud = WordCloud(width=800, height=400, background_color='white',
max_words=100).generate(cluster_text)

        # Plot the WordCloud
        plt.figure(figsize=(10, 6))
        plt.imshow(wordcloud, interpolation='bilinear')
        plt.title(f'Cluster {cluster_id} - Most Frequent Words')
        plt.axis('off')
        plt.show()

# Generate word clouds for each cluster
generate_wordclouds(clustering_results, num_clusters)
```

This code defines a function generate_wordclouds that generates word clouds for each cluster based on the product descriptions assigned to that cluster. Adjust the parameters of the WordCloud object (e.g., width, height, background_color, max_words) as needed for your visualization preferences.

The function will plot the word clouds for each cluster.

Figure 16.20: Word cloud for the first cluster

Figure 16.21: Word cloud for the second cluster

Figure 16.22: Word cloud for the third cluster

Figure 16.23: Word cloud for the fourth cluster

[End of response]

Assigning categories to products and evaluating and refining

Neither assigning categories to products nor evaluating and refining steps were in scope for this chapter to solve but let's describe what they are to give you an idea of how you could explore those should you want to.

Our dataset contains invoices, and for us to categorize products, we would first need to understand the use cases we could possibly have. Those could be, for example:

- Organizing inventory
- Improving search functionality
- Enhancing the user experience

As you can see, this is very centered on product data, which means we would probably need a completely different dataset containing product titles, descriptions, and more. Let's describe at a high level what our approach could be using ChatGPT.

[Prompt]

I'm looking at an e-commerce dataset. What can you tell me about the process of assigning categories to products?

[End of prompt]

[Prompt response]

Assigning categories to products in an e-commerce dataset is a crucial task for organizing inventory, improving search functionality, and enhancing the user experience. Here's a step-by-step guide to help you through the process:

Steps to Assign Categories to Products:

Understand the Data:

- **Review Product Descriptions:** Examine the product titles, descriptions, and any other relevant attributes.
- **Identify Existing Categories:** If there are existing categories, review them to understand the current classification system.

Define Categories:

- **Create a Category Hierarchy:** Develop a hierarchical structure of categories and subcategories that makes sense for your products.
- **Ensure Completeness:** Make sure your categories cover all types of products in your dataset.

Feature Extraction:

- **Text Features:** Extract relevant text features from product titles and descriptions using techniques like TF-IDF or word embeddings.

- **Other Features:** Consider other attributes like price, brand, and specifications that might help in categorization.

Manual Labeling:

- **Sample Labeling:** Manually label a sample of products to create a training dataset. This helps in understanding the nuances of each category.

Model Selection:

- **Choose a Classification Model:** Select a machine learning model suitable for text classification, such as Naive Bayes, SVM, or deep learning models like LSTM or BERT.

Training the Model:

- **Train the Model:** Use the labeled data to train your classification model.
- **Evaluate Performance:** Evaluate the model's performance using metrics like accuracy, precision, recall, and F1-score.

Assign Categories:

- **Predict Categories:** Use the trained model to predict categories for the unlabeled products.
- **Review Predictions:** Manually review a subset of the predictions to ensure accuracy.

Iterate and Improve:

- **Refine Categories:** Based on the results, refine your category definitions and model.
- **Continuous Learning:** Continuously update the model with new data to improve its accuracy over time.

Example in Python:

Here's a simplified example using a Naive Bayes classifier for text classification:

```python
import pandas as pd
from sklearn.feature_extraction.text import TfidfVectorizer
from sklearn.model_selection import train_test_split
from sklearn.naive_bayes import MultinomialNB
from sklearn.metrics import accuracy_score

# Sample data
data = {
'Product': ['Red Shirt', 'Blue Jeans', 'Green Hat', 'Black Shoes'],
'Category': ['Clothing', 'Clothing', 'Accessories', 'Footwear']
}

df = pd.DataFrame(data)

# Feature extraction
```

```
vectorizer = TfidfVectorizer()
X = vectorizer.fit_transform(df['Product'])
y = df['Category']

# Train-test split
X_train, X_test, y_train, y_test = train_test_split(X, y, test_size=0.2,
random_state=42)

# Train the model
model = MultinomialNB()
model.fit(X_train, y_train)

# Predict and evaluate
y_pred = model.predict(X_test)
print(f'Accuracy: {accuracy_score(y_test, y_pred)}')
```

This code provides a basic framework for categorizing products based on their names. For a real-world application, you would need a larger dataset and more sophisticated preprocessing and modeling techniques.

If you have any specific questions or need further details, feel free to ask!

[End of response]

We'll leave it up to you to pursue this further. From what you've hopefully seen in this chapter already, start with a high-level prompt explaining what dataset you have (you have to find a dataset for the above problem) and what you aim to do. On the latter, you already have the steps, so you're suggested to craft a prompt explaining what to do for each step and what code to run.

Evaluate and refine

This is also out of scope, but let's get you started on a ChatGPT prompt that you can then keep working on.

[Prompt]

Describe evaluate and refine step in the context of e-commerce data on invoices.

[End of prompt]

[Prompt response]

Sure! Let's break down the evaluate and refine steps in the context of e-commerce data on invoices:

Evaluate Step:

1. Model Performance Metrics:

    • **Accuracy**: Measure how often the model correctly predicts the category of an invoice.

- **Precision and Recall:** Evaluate the precision (correct positive predictions) and recall (ability to find all relevant instances) for each category.
- **F1-Score:** Combine precision and recall into a single metric to balance both aspects.

2. Confusion Matrix:

- **Visualize Predictions:** Use a confusion matrix to see where the model is making correct and incorrect predictions. This helps identify specific categories where the model may be struggling.

3. Cross-Validation:

- **Robust Evaluation:** Perform cross-validation to ensure the model's performance is consistent across different subsets of the data.

4. Error Analysis:

- **Analyze Misclassifications:** Examine the invoices that were misclassified to understand why the model made errors. Look for patterns or common issues.

Refine Step:

1. Feature Engineering:

- **Enhance Features:** Create new features or improve existing ones to provide more relevant information to the model. For example, extracting keywords from invoice descriptions or adding metadata like invoice date and amount.

2. Hyperparameter Tuning:

- **Optimize Model Parameters:** Use techniques like grid search or random search to find the best hyperparameters for your model, improving its performance.

3. Model Selection:

- **Try Different Models:** Experiment with different algorithms (e.g., decision trees, random forests, neural networks) to see if another model performs better.

4. Data Augmentation:

- **Increase Data Variety:** Augment your dataset by generating synthetic data or using techniques like oversampling for underrepresented categories.

5. Regular Updates:

- **Continuous Learning:** Regularly update the model with new invoice data to keep it current and improve its accuracy over time.

Example in Python:

Here's a simplified example of evaluating and refining a model using cross-validation and hyperparameter tuning:

```python
import pandas as pd
from sklearn.feature_extraction.text import TfidfVectorizer
from sklearn.model_selection import train_test_split, GridSearchCV
from sklearn.naive_bayes import MultinomialNB
from sklearn.metrics import classification_report, confusion_matrix
import seaborn as sns
import matplotlib.pyplot as plt

# Sample data
data = {
    'Invoice': ['Invoice for Red Shirt', 'Invoice for Blue Jeans', 'Invoice for
Green Hat', 'Invoice for Black Shoes'],
    'Category': ['Clothing', 'Clothing', 'Accessories', 'Footwear']
}

df = pd.DataFrame(data)

# Feature extraction
vectorizer = TfidfVectorizer()
X = vectorizer.fit_transform(df['Invoice'])
y = df['Category']

# Train-test split
X_train, X_test, y_train, y_test = train_test_split(X, y, test_size=0.2,
random_state=42)

# Model training
model = MultinomialNB()
model.fit(X_train, y_train)

# Model evaluation
y_pred = model.predict(X_test)
print(classification_report(y_test, y_pred))

# Confusion matrix
conf_matrix = confusion_matrix(y_test, y_pred)
sns.heatmap(conf_matrix, annot=True, fmt='d', cmap='Blues')
plt.xlabel('Predicted')
```

```
plt.ylabel('Actual')
plt.title('Confusion Matrix')
plt.show()

# Hyperparameter tuning
param_grid = {'alpha': [0.1, 0.5, 1.0]}
grid_search = GridSearchCV(MultinomialNB(), param_grid, cv=5)
grid_search.fit(X_train, y_train)
print(f'Best parameters: {grid_search.best_params_}')
```

This code provides a framework for evaluating and refining a model using cross-validation and hyperparameter tuning.

If you have any specific questions or need further details, feel free to ask!

[End of response]

Reflection on prompts for this use case

Just like with our first use case in this chapter, we followed a specific method of first setting high-level context of describing our role, the shape of the dataset, and what we were looking to do. Then, we followed the below process to first breaking down the problem in steps, getting code and how we could continue to improve and refine and finally visualize the results:

1. **Step-by-step guidance:** The requests are structured as a series of step-by-step tasks, breaking down the larger problem into manageable components. This makes it easier to follow and implement the solution incrementally.

2. **Specify inputs and requirements:** Provide clear and specific information about the dataset, its columns, and the requirements for preprocessing, clustering, and visualization. This helps ensure that the assistance received is tailored to the particular needs.

3. **Request for code with comments:** Code snippets request to include comments to explain each step and clarify the purpose of the code. This helps in understanding the code and code validation and facilitates learning.

4. **Iteration and refinement:** Iteration of prompts, asking for additional modifications and visualizations after the initial guidance. This iterative approach allows for refining and improving the solution progressively.

5. **Visualization and interpretation:** Visualizing and interpreting the results allows focusing on deriving meaningful insights from the data.

Assignment

In the previous section, we used traditional embedding with TF-IDF to transform text data into numerical representations, which can then be used for various **natural language processing (NLP)** tasks such as clustering. Let's now try and improve the clustering results by using a more advanced embedding technique. We will use the Hugging Face Transformers library to get pre-trained embeddings for our product descriptions:

1. Ask ChatGPT to explain Hugging Face Transformers' advantages over TF-IDF vectorization for clustering use cases.

2. Use ChatGPT to generate and create product clusters using Hugging Face Transformers embeddings.

3. Compare the results with the previous clustering results using TF-IDF vectorization.

Solution

See the solution in the repository: `https://github.com/PacktPublishing/AI-Assisted-Software-Development-with-GitHub-Copilot-and-ChatGPT`

Summary

This chapter focused on clustering and how it could be used to group your data into separate areas. Creating these areas made it easier to understand our data points. Through visualization like heat maps, word clouds, and more, you were given the insight that data benefits from being shown in different ways. You also saw how the clustering process helped identify outliers, that is, data that vastly differs and can't easily be assigned to any one cluster. For the ChatGPT and prompting part, you saw how setting a high-level context describing the dataset helped generate a suitable set of steps you could follow from top to bottom. The same high-level context also helped ChatGPT recommend a clustering algorithm.

Join our community on Discord

Join our community's Discord space for discussions with the author and other readers:

`https://packt.link/aicode`

17

Machine Learning with Copilot

Introduction

Machine learning, or ML, involves data and learning patterns from that said data and using those patterns to make predictions or decisions. Machine learning consists of a series of steps, all the way from loading data and cleaning it to eventually training a model to get the insights you need from said model. All these steps are roughly the same for most problems in this problem space. However, details may differ, like the choice of pre-processing step, the choice of algorithm, etc. An AI tool like GitHub Copilot comes into machine learning from a few different angles:

- **Suggesting workflows:** Thanks to Copilot having been trained in machine learning work flows, it's able to suggest a workflow that fits your problem.
- **Recommending tools and algorithms:** If you provide your AI tool with enough context on what your problem is and the shape of your data, an AI tool like Copilot can suggest tools and algorithms that fit your specific problem.
- **Code assistance:** Another way that Copilot is a great help is by being able to generate code for various steps in the machine learning process.

This chapter will explore an e-commerce dataset, and the chapter will serve as an interesting comparison exercise to the other chapters, which used ChatGPT to solve machine learning problems.

Let's dive in and discover the suggestions from GitHub Copilot.

GitHub Copilot Chat in your IDE

GitHub Copilot Chat is a tool within certain **Integrated Development Environments (IDEs)** that answers coding questions. It helps by suggesting code, explaining code functionality, creating unit tests, and fixing bugs.

How it works

You have two different ways of providing prompts to GitHub Copilot:

- In-editor: In this mode, you provide text comments, and through the *Tab* or *Return* key, Copilot is able to produce an output.
- Chat mode: In chat mode, you type a prompt in the text box, and then GitHub Copilot will treat an open file/files as context (if you use @workspace, then it will look at all files in your directory).

A text file can be, for example, a code file like app.py or a Jupyter Notebook. Copilot can treat both these files as context, together with your typed prompt.

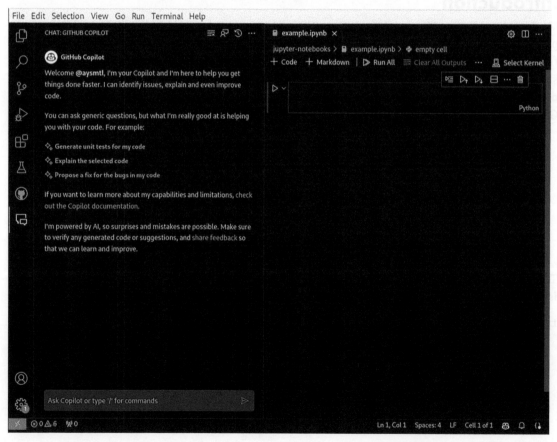

Figure 17.1: GitHub Copilot chat on the left side and an open Jupyter Notebook on the right side

Dataset overview

Let's explore the dataset we're about to use. Like we did in other chapters on machine learning, we start with a dataset, this one being a dataset of Amazon book reviews.

The dataset contains information about different products and their reviews. It includes the following columns:

- `marketplace` (string): Location of the product
- `customer_id` (string): Unique ID of the customer
- `review_id` (string): Review ID
- `product_id` (string): Unique ID of the product
- `product_parent` (string): Parent product
- `product_title` (string): Title of the product reviewed
- `product_category` (string): Different product categories
- `star_rating` (int): Rating of the product out of 5
- `helpful_votes` (int): Number of helpful votes for the product
- `total_votes` (int): Total number of votes for the product
- `review_headline` (string): Heading of the review
- `review_body` (string): Content of the review
- `review_date` (string): Date on which the product was reviewed
- `sentiment` (string): Sentiment of the review (positive or negative)

Steps for data exploration

Performing data exploration helps us understand the dataset and its characteristics. It involves examining the data, identifying patterns, and summarizing key insights. Here are the steps we will follow:

1. **Load the dataset:** Read the dataset into a pandas DataFrame to work with the data effectively.
2. **Inspect the data:** Display the first few rows of the DataFrame to get a glimpse of the data. Check the column names, data types, and any missing values.
3. **Summary statistics:** Calculate summary statistics such as the mean, median, minimum, maximum, and quartiles for numeric columns. This helps in understanding the distribution and range of values.
4. **Explore categorical variables:** Analyze the unique values and their frequencies for categorical variables like `marketplace`, `product_category`, and `sentiment`. Visualizations such as bar plots can be helpful for this analysis.
5. **Distribution of ratings:** Plot a histogram or bar plot to visualize the distribution of `star_ratings`. This helps in understanding the overall sentiment of the reviews.
6. **Temporal analysis:** Analyze the temporal aspect of the data by examining the `review_date` column. Explore trends, seasonality, or any patterns over time.

7. **Review length analysis:** Analyze the length of `review_body` to understand the amount of information provided in the reviews. Calculate descriptive statistics like the mean, median, and maximum length.

8. **Correlation analysis:** Investigate the correlation between numeric variables using correlation matrices or scatter plots. This helps in identifying relationships between variables.

9. **Additional exploratory analysis:** Conduct additional analysis based on specific project requirements or interesting patterns observed during the exploration process.

Note that you can also ask GitHub Copilot which steps to follow when doing machine learning.

Prompt strategy

The prompts we are about to use provide high-level guidance for Copilot, and the outputs/results allow further tailoring of Copilot's responses to match the specific dataset and analysis needs.

The key aspects of the prompting approach are:

- Define the task. Clearly instruct the AI assistant what task we are solving.
- Break down into steps. Breaking the data exploration down into logical steps (like data loading, inspection, summary stats etc.)
- Providing context/intent for each prompt to guide Copilot (like requesting numeric summary statistics)
- Sharing previous results as input. Sharing outputs and results from Copilot's code snippets to further guide the conversation (like printing the summary stats)
- Refine, iteratively refining prompts and conversing with Copilot in a back-and-forth way

Therefore, we will use the TAG (Task-Action-Guidance) prompt pattern described in *Chapter 2*. Let's describe this project to fit this pattern, so we get a sense on how to write our initial prompt:

- **Task:** Data exploration, find patterns and insights into customers reviews in an e-commerce project.
- **Action:** We've described the steps we should take in a previous section; those should be reflected in the prompt we write.
- **Guidance:** The extra guidance we will provide is that we want exploratory techniques suggested as well as code snippets.

Your initial data exploration prompt: Prompt 1, setting the high-level context

Just like in other chapters where we used ChatGPT, our initial prompt sets the high-level context for the problem we're looking to solve, including the domain and the shape of our data. All this context helps the AI tool to provide the correct steps both in text and code.

Below is an initial prompt you can try:

[Prompt]

I am performing data exploration for the AwesomeShop e-commerce project. The dataset contains information about various products and their reviews. I want to gain insights into the data, identify patterns, and understand the characteristics of the reviews. Can you provide me with some exploratory analysis techniques and code snippets to help me uncover interesting insights from the dataset? The dataset for the AwesomeShop E-commerce project contains information about different products and their reviews. It includes the following columns:

- `marketplace` (string): Location of the product
- `customer_id` (string): Unique ID of the customer
- `review_id` (string): Review ID
- `product_id` (string): Unique ID of the product
- `product_parent` (string): Parent product
- `product_title` (string): Title of the product reviewed
- `product_category` (string): Different product categories
- `star_rating` (int): Rating of the product out of 5
- `helpful_votes` (int): Number of helpful votes for the product
- `total_votes` (int): Total number of votes for the product
- `review_headline` (string): Heading of the review
- `review_body` (string): Content of the review
- `review_date` (string): Date on which the product was reviewed
- `sentiment` (string): Sentiment of the review (positive or negative)

But remember that I want to learn step by step, as follows:

1. **Load the Dataset:** Read the dataset into a pandas DataFrame to work with the data effectively.
2. **Inspect the Data:** Display the first few rows of the DataFrame to get a glimpse of the data. Check the column names, data types, and any missing values.
3. **Summary Statistics:** Calculate summary statistics such as the mean, median, minimum, maximum, and quartiles for numeric columns. This helps in understanding the distribution and range of values.
4. **Explore Categorical Variables:** Analyze the unique values and their frequencies for categorical variables like `marketplace`, `product_category`, and `sentiment`. Visualizations such as bar plots can be helpful for this analysis.
5. **Distribution of Ratings:** Plot a histogram or bar plot to visualize the distribution of `star_ratings`. This helps in understanding the overall sentiment of the reviews.
6. **Temporal Analysis:** Analyze the temporal aspect of the data by examining the `review_date` column. Explore trends, seasonality, or any patterns over time.
7. **Review Length Analysis:** Analyze the length of `review_body` to understand the amount of information provided in the reviews. Calculate descriptive statistics like the mean, median, and maximum length.

8. **Correlation Analysis:** Investigate the correlation between numeric variables using correlation matrices or scatter plots. This helps in identifying relationships between variables.

9. **Additional Exploratory Analysis:** Conduct additional analysis based on specific project requirements or interesting patterns observed during the exploration process. Seek feedback from the user after each step.

[End of prompt]

Step 1: Load the dataset

We get quite a wordy response from Copilot, so let's break down the response into parts and explain what we get.

You should receive a response similar to the response below:

[Prompt response]

Sure, let's start with step 1: loading the dataset.

```python
# Step 1: Load the Dataset
import pandas as pd

# Define the file path
file_path = '/path/to/your/file.csv'  # replace with your file path

# Load the dataset
df = pd.read_csv(file_path)

# Display the first few rows of the DataFrame
print(df.head())
```

Please replace `'/path/to/your/file.csv'` with your actual filename or path to the file. Once you've done this, you can run the code to load your dataset.

Let me know once you've successfully loaded the data, and we can proceed to the next step.

[End of response]

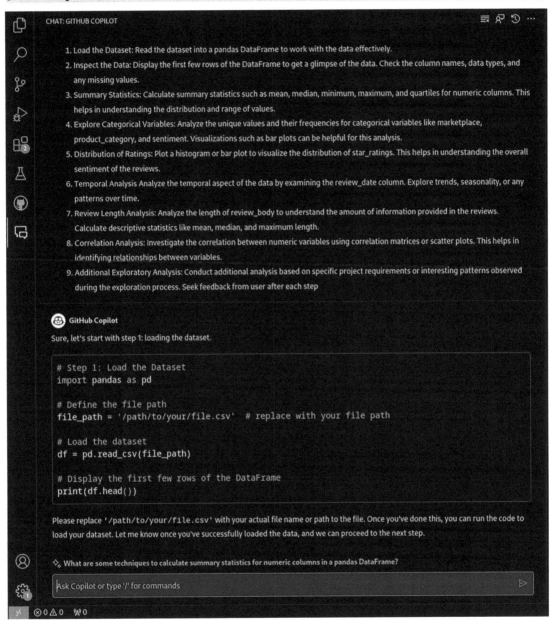

Figure 17.2: Showing part of the Copilot prompt and the start of the Copilot result on loading data

Let's try the output code generated by Copilot and see if it works. Modify the `file_path` variable to point to the location of your dataset, and then execute the code. Note below how we edited the file path to reflect an actual path in our system:

```python
import pandas as pd

# Define the file path
file_path = '../Datasets/amazon_books_Data.csv'

# Load the dataset
df = pd.read_csv(file_path)
```

Running the code for loading data

Let's run the code provided by Copilot. See the below output from our Jupyter Notebook:

```
# Display the first few rows of the DataFrame
print(df.head())
   Unnamed: 0 market_place customer_id       review_id   product_id  \
0           0         "US"  "25933450"  "RJOVP071AVAJO"  "0439873800"
1           1         "US"   "1801372"  "R1ORGBETCDW3AI"  "1623953553"
2           2         "US"   "5782091"  "R7TNRFQAOUTX5"   "142151981X"
3           3         "US"  "32715830"  "R2GANXKDIFZ6OI"  "014241543X"
4           4         "US"  "14005703"  "R2NYB6C3R8LVN6"  "1604600527"

  product_parent                        product_title  \
0    "84656342"  "There Was an Old Lady Who Swallowed a Shell!"
1   "729938122"                            "I Saw a Friend"
2   "678139048"                         "Black Lagoon, Vol. 6"
3   "712432151"                                  "If I Stay"
4   "800572372"                    "Stars 'N Strips Forever"

  product_category  star_rating  helpful_votes  total_votes     vine  \
0          "Books"            1              0            0  0 \t(N)
1          "Books"            1              0            0  0 \t(N)
2          "Books"            1              0            0  0 \t(N)
3          "Books"            1              0            0  0 \t(N)
4          "Books"            1              2            2  0 \t(N)

  verified_purchase                                   review_headline  \
0         1 \t(Y)                                         "Five Stars"
1         1 \t(Y)  "Please buy "I Saw a Friend"! Your children wi...
2         1 \t(Y)                                      "Shipped fast."
```

```
3              0 \t(N)                                      "Five Stars"
4              1 \t(Y)                                      "Five Stars"


                                        review_body review_date  \
0                 "I love it and so does my students!"  2015-08-31
1   "My wife and I ordered 2 books and gave them a...  2015-08-31
2   "Great book just like all the others in the se...  2015-08-31
3                                      "So beautiful"  2015-08-31
4   "Enjoyed the author's story and his quilts are...  2015-08-31


  Sentiment_books review_month review_day  review_year
0        positive       August     Monday         2015
1        positive       August     Monday         2015
2        positive       August     Monday         2015
3        positive       August     Monday         2015
4        positive       August     Monday         2015
```

Step 2: Inspect the data

Next, let's inspect the data. For the inspection prompt, we'll use the output from our code execution and see if we can get Copilot to tell us about the next step we need to take:

[Prompt]

It runs fine; below is the output:

```
Unnamed: 0 market_place customer_id review_id product_id 0 0 "US" "25933450"
"RJOVP071AVAJO" "0439873800"
1 1 "US" "1801372" "R1ORGBETCDW3AI" "1623953553"
2 2 "US" "5782091" "R7TNRFQAOUTX5" "142151981X"
3 3 "US" "32715830" "R2GANXKDIFZ6OI" "014241543X"
4 4 "US" "14005703" "R2NYB6C3R8LVN6" "1604600527"
product_parent product_title 0 "84656342" "There Was an Old Lady Who Swallowed
a Shell!"
1 "729938122" "I Saw a Friend"
2 "678139048" "Black Lagoon, Vol. 6"
3 "712432151" "If I Stay"
4 "800572372" "Stars 'N Strips Forever"
product_category star_rating helpful_votes total_votes vine 0 "Books" 1 0 0 0
\t(N)
1 "Books" 1 0 0 0 \t(N)
2 "Books" 1 0 0 0 \t(N)
3 "Books" 1 0 0 0 \t(N)
4 "Books" 1 2 2 0 \t(N)
```

```
verified_purchase review_headline 0 1 \t(Y) "Five Stars"
1 1 \t(Y) "Please buy "I Saw a Friend"! Your children wi...
2 1 \t(Y) "Shipped fast."
... 1 positive August Monday 2015
2 positive August Monday 2015
3 positive August Monday 2015
4 positive August Monday 2015
```

The output is truncated. View it as a scrollable element or open it in a text editor. Adjust cell output settings...

[End of prompt]

You should receive a response similar to the response below:

[Prompt response]

Great! Now that you've successfully loaded the dataset, let's move on to "inspecting the data."

```python
# Step 2: Inspect the Data

# Check the column names
print("Column Names:")
print(df.columns)

# Check the data types of each column
print("\nData Types:")
print(df.dtypes)

# Check for missing values
print("\nMissing Values:")
print(df.isnull().sum())
```

This code will give you an overview of your dataset, including the names of the columns, the data types of each column, and the number of missing values in each column. Run this code and let me know what you find.

[End of response]

Let's try the code above to inspect the data and see if it works. Run the below code in a code cell in your Jupyter Notebook:

```python
# Display the first few rows of the DataFrame
df.head()

# Check the column names
column_names = df.columns
print(column_names)
```

```
# Check the data types of the columns
data_types = df.dtypes
print(data_types)


# Check for missing values
missing_values = df.isnull().sum()
print(missing_values)
```

You should see an output similar to below:

```
Index(['Unnamed: 0', 'market_place', 'customer_id', 'review_id', 'product_id',
       'product_parent', 'product_title', 'product_category', 'star_rating',
       'helpful_votes', 'total_votes', 'vine', 'verified_purchase',
       'review_headline', 'review_body', 'review_date', 'Sentiment_books',
       'review_month', 'review_day', 'review_year'],
      dtype='object')
Unnamed: 0              int64
market_place           object
customer_id            object
review_id              object
product_id             object
product_parent         object
product_title          object
product_category       object
star_rating            int64
helpful_votes          int64
total_votes            int64
vine                   object
verified_purchase      object
review_headline        object
review_body            object
review_date            object
Sentiment_books        object
review_month           object
review_day             object
review_year            int64
dtype: object
Unnamed: 0             0
market_place          0
customer_id           0
review_id             0
product_id            0
```

```
product_parent          0
product_title           0
product_category        0
star_rating             0
helpful_votes           0
total_votes             0
vine                    0
verified_purchase       0
review_headline         0
review_body             0
review_date             0
Sentiment_books         0
review_month            0
review_day              0
review_year             0
dtype: int64
```

Great! So far, it has served us well when we provide Copilot with a state of where we are going and get it to suggest the next steps; let's keep following that format.

Step 3: Summary statistics

Next, we want to summarize things, so we again provide it with output data in the hope that Copilot will tell us what the next step is:

[Prompt]

There are no missing values; below is the output:

```
Index(['Unnamed: 0', 'market_place', 'customer_id', 'review_id', 'product_id',
'product_parent', 'product_title', 'product_category', 'star_rating', 'helpful_
votes', 'total_votes', 'vine', 'verified_purchase', 'review_headline', 'review_
body', 'review_date', 'Sentiment_books', 'review_month', 'review_day', 'review_
year'], dtype='object') Unnamed: 0 int64 market_place object customer_id object
review_id object product_id object product_parent object product_title object
product_category object star_rating int64 helpful_votes int64 total_votes int64
vine object verified_purchase object review_headline object review_body object
review_date object Sentiment_books object review_month object review_day object
... review_month 0 review_day 0 review_year 0 dtype: int64
```

[End of prompt]

You should receive a response similar to the response below:

[Prompt response]

Great! Now that we've inspected the data, let's move on to step 3: calculating summary statistics for numeric columns. This will help us understand the distribution and range of values.

```
# Step 3: Summary Statistics

# Calculate summary statistics for numeric columns
numeric_columns = ['star_rating', 'helpful_votes', 'total_votes']
print(df[numeric_columns].describe())
```

This code will provide you with the count, mean, standard deviation, minimum, 25th percentile, median (50th percentile), 75th percentile, and maximum of the numeric columns in your dataset. Run this code and let me know what you find.

[End of response]

Let's try this and see if it works. Let's run the code below and call `df.describe`:

```
# Calculate summary statistics
summary_stats = df.describe()
print(summary_stats)
```

You should see the following output:

	Unnamed: 0	star_rating	helpful_votes	total_votes	review_year
count	100.000000	100.000000	100.000000	100.000000	100.0
mean	49.500000	0.840000	0.540000	0.960000	2015.0
std	29.011492	0.368453	1.298173	2.420118	0.0
min	0.000000	0.000000	0.000000	0.000000	2015.0
25%	24.750000	1.000000	0.000000	0.000000	2015.0
50%	49.500000	1.000000	0.000000	0.000000	2015.0
75%	74.250000	1.000000	1.000000	1.000000	2015.0
max	99.000000	1.000000	9.000000	14.000000	2015.0

Great! We're able to see the count, mean value standard deviation, and more. We've continued to use the idea of feeding Copilot the output of our code, and it's been able to understand at which point in the machine learning process it is and what to do next.

Step 4: Explore categorical variables

Just like before, let's construct a prompt consisting of the output of the code we just ran and let Copilot tell us what should happen next:

[Prompt]

Below is the output:

```
Unnamed: 0 star_rating helpful_votes total_votes review_year count 100.000000
100.000000 100.000000 100.000000 100.0 mean 49.500000 0.840000 0.540000
```

```
0.960000 2015.0 std 29.011492 0.368453 1.298173 2.420118 0.0 min 0.000000
0.000000 0.000000 0.000000 2015.0 25% 24.750000 1.000000 0.000000 0.000000
2015.0 50% 49.500000 1.000000 0.000000 0.000000 2015.0 75% 74.250000 1.000000
1.000000 1.000000 2015.0 max 99.000000 1.000000 9.000000 14.000000 2015.0
```

[End of prompt]

You should receive a response similar to the response below:

[Prompt response]

Great! Now that we have the summary statistics, let's move on to step 4: exploring categorical variables. We'll analyze the unique values and their frequencies for categorical variables like market place, product_category, and sentiment.

```python
# Step 4: Explore Categorical Variables
# Analyze the unique values and their frequencies for categorical variables
categorical_columns = ['market_place', 'product_category', 'Sentiment_books']

for column in categorical_columns:
    print("\n" + column)
    print(df[column].value_counts())
```
This code will print the unique values and their frequencies for each of the specified
 categorical columns. Run this code and let me know what you find.

[End of response]

Let's try this and see if it works. Run the below code in a code cell to analyze the categorical variables:

```python
# Analyze categorical variables
categorical_cols = ['market_place', 'product_category', 'Sentiment_books']

for col in categorical_cols:
    unique_values = df[col].unique()
    value_counts = df[col].value_counts()
    print(f"\n{col} unique values:\n{unique_values}\n")
    print(f"{col} value counts:\n{value_counts}")
```

You should see the following output:

```
market_place unique values:
['"US"']

market_place value counts:
market_place
```

```
"US"     100
Name: count, dtype: int64


product_category unique values:
['"Books"']


product_category value counts:
product_category
"Books"    100
Name: count, dtype: int64


Sentiment_books unique values:
['positive' 'negative']


Sentiment_books value counts:
Sentiment_books
positive    84
negative    16
Name: count, dtype: int64
```

Step 5: Distribution of ratings

Next, we want to understand the distribution of ratings. To learn more about the ratings, we will provide the output from the last code execution as a prompt:

[Prompt]

Below is the output:

- `market_place` unique values: ["'US'"]
- `market_place` value counts: `market_place` "US" 100 Name: count, dtype: int64
- `product_category` unique values: ["'Books'"]
- `product_category` value counts: `product_category` "Books" 100 Name: count, dtype: int64
- `Sentiment_books` unique values: ['positive' 'negative']
- `Sentiment_books` value counts: `Sentiment_books` positive 84 negative 16 Name: count, dtype: int64

[End of prompt]

You should receive a response similar to the response below:

[Prompt response]

Great! Now that we've explored the categorical variables, let's move on to step 5: visualizing the distribution of star ratings.

```python
# Step 5: Distribution of Ratings

import matplotlib.pyplot as plt

# Plot a histogram for star ratings
plt.hist(df['star_rating'], bins=5, edgecolor='black')
plt.title('Distribution of Star Ratings')
plt.xlabel('Star Ratings')
plt.ylabel('Frequency')
plt.show()
```

This code will plot a histogram of the star ratings, which will help us understand the overall sentiment of the reviews. Run this code and let me know what you find.

[End of response]

Let's try this and see if it works. Below, we have code for performing visualization; run this code in a code cell:

```python
import matplotlib.pyplot as plt

# Plot the distribution of star ratings
plt.hist(df['star_rating'], bins=5, edgecolor='black')
plt.xlabel('Star Rating')
plt.ylabel('Frequency')
plt.title('Distribution of Star Ratings')
plt.show()
```

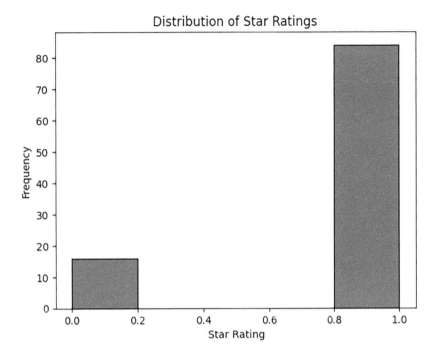

Figure 17.3: Distribution of star ratings

Step 6: Temporal analysis

At this point, we have a good idea of how ratings are distributed; it seems like they are either very low or very high. Let's progress to the next step.

[Prompt]

Proceed to the next step.

[End of prompt]

You should receive a response similar to the response below:

[Prompt response]

Great! Now let's move on to step 6: Temporal Analysis. We'll analyze the `review_date` column to explore trends, seasonality, or any patterns over time.

First, we need to convert the `review_date` column to a datetime format. Then, we can extract the year, month, and day into separate columns for easier analysis.

```
# Step 6: Temporal Analysis

# Convert review_date to datetime format
df['review_date'] = pd.to_datetime(df['review_date'])

# Extract year, month, and day into separate columns
df['year'] = df['review_date'].dt.year
df['month'] = df['review_date'].dt.month
df['day'] = df['review_date'].dt.day

# Check the number of reviews per year
print(df['year'].value_counts().sort_index())

# Check the number of reviews per month
print(df['month'].value_counts().sort_index())

# Check the number of reviews per day
print(df['day'].value_counts().sort_index())
```

This code will print the number of reviews per year, month, and day. Run this code and let me know what you find.

[End of response]

Let's try this code and see if it works. Run the above code in a code cell:

```
# Step 6: Temporal Analysis

# Convert review_date to datetime format
df['review_date'] = pd.to_datetime(df['review_date'])

# Extract year, month, and day into separate columns
df['year'] = df['review_date'].dt.year
df['month'] = df['review_date'].dt.month
df['day'] = df['review_date'].dt.day

# Check the number of reviews per year
print(df['year'].value_counts().sort_index())

# Check the number of reviews per month
print(df['month'].value_counts().sort_index())
```

```
# Check the number of reviews per day
print(df['day'].value_counts().sort_index())
```

You should see an output similar to the below:

```
year
2015    100
Name: count, dtype: int64
month
8    100
Name: count, dtype: int64
day
31    100
Name: count, dtype: int64
```

Step 7: Review length analysis

Let's move forward in our analysis; next up is a review length analysis.

[Prompt]

Below is the output: year 2015 100 Name: count, dtype: int64 month 8 100 Name: count, dtype: int64 day 31 100 Name: count, dtype: int64

[End of prompt]

You should receive a response similar to the response below:

[Prompt response]

Great! Now that we've analyzed the temporal aspect of the data, let's move on to step 7: Review Length Analysis. We'll analyze the length of review_body to understand the amount of information provided in the reviews.

```
# Step 7: Review Length Analysis

# Calculate the length of each review
df['review_length'] = df['review_body'].str.len()

# Calculate descriptive statistics for review length
print(df['review_length'].describe())
```

This code will calculate the length of each review and provide descriptive statistics like mean, median, and maximum length. Run this code and let me know what you find.

[End of response]

At this point, we want to understand what the above code is doing; let's ask Copilot for help:

[Prompt]

Before we move on to step 7, can you please explain how to interpret the output?

[End of prompt]

You should receive a response similar to the response below:

[Prompt response]

Absolutely. The output you've shared indicates the frequency of reviews based on the year, month, and day.

- `year`: All 100 reviews in your dataset were written in the year 2015.
- `month`: All 100 reviews were written in the 8th month, which is August.
- `day`: All 100 reviews were written on the 31st day of the month.

This suggests that all the reviews in your dataset were written on the same date - August 31, 2015.

In a larger, more diverse dataset, you might see reviews spread across different years, months, and days. Analyzing these could help identify trends or patterns over time, such as an increase in reviews during certain periods.

[End of response]

OK, we have a problem – our dataset is limited, and all reviews seem to have taken place at the same point in time, which prevents us from discovering trends. Let's inform Copilot of that and see what we can do next:

[Prompt]

In that case, we cannot explore trends or patterns within this dataset.

[End of prompt]

You should receive a response similar to the response below:

[Prompt response]

That's correct. Since all the reviews in this dataset are from the same date, we won't be able to analyze trends or patterns over time. However, you can still perform other types of analysis. For instance, you can analyze the length of the reviews, the distribution of star ratings, or the frequency of certain words or phrases in the review text.

If you have a larger, more diverse dataset, you could also analyze trends over time, compare different products or categories, or use machine learning to predict star ratings based on the review text.

Let's proceed with the review length analysis as planned:

```
# Step 7: Review Length Analysis

# Calculate the length of each review
df['review_length'] = df['review_body'].str.len()

# Calculate descriptive statistics for review length
print(df['review_length'].describe())
```

This code will calculate the length of each review and provide descriptive statistics like mean, median, and maximum length. Run this code and let me know what you find.

[End of response]

Let's try this code and see if it works. Type this code into a code cell and run it:

```
# Step 7: Review Length Analysis

# Calculate the length of each review
df['review_length'] = df['review_body'].str.len()

# Calculate descriptive statistics for review length
print(df['review_length'].describe())
```

You should see output similar to the below:

```
count     100.000000
mean      253.190000
std       420.934403
min         6.000000
25%        36.000000
50%       104.500000
75%       269.750000
max      2685.000000
Name: review_length, dtype: float64
```

[Prompt]

Below is the output:

count 100.000000 mean 253.190000 std 420.934403 min 6.000000 25% 36.000000 50% 104.500000 75% 269.750000 max 2685.000000 Name: review_length, dtype: float64

[End of prompt]

You should receive a response similar to the response below.

[Prompt response]

Great! The output you've shared provides a summary of the review lengths in your dataset:

- `count`: There are 100 reviews in your dataset.
- `mean`: On average, a review is about 253 characters long.
- `std`: The standard deviation is approximately 421, indicating that the lengths of the reviews vary quite a bit around the mean.
- `min`: The shortest review is 6 characters long.
- 25%: 25% of the reviews are 36 characters long or shorter.
- 50% (or median): Half of the reviews are 104.5 characters long or shorter.
- 75%: 75% of the reviews are 269.75 characters long or shorter.
- `max`: The longest review is 2685 characters long.

This information can be useful to understand the amount of text available for any text analysis or natural language processing tasks.

For the next step, you could consider visualizing this data or analyzing the text content of the reviews. For example, you could create a histogram of review lengths, or you could use a word cloud to visualize the most common words in the reviews. Let me know what you'd like to do next.

[End of response]

Step 8: Correlation analysis

Now, we want to determine the relationship between two or more variables to understand what variables are related. The below prompt shows how we progress in our analysis:

[Prompt]

Proceed to the next step for correlation analysis.

[End of prompt]

You should receive a response similar to the response below:

[Prompt response]

Sure, let's move on to step 8: Correlation Analysis. We'll analyze the correlation between numeric variables like `star_rating`, `helpful_votes`, and `total_votes`.

```
# Step 8: Correlation Analysis

# Calculate the correlation matrix
correlation_matrix = df[['star_rating', 'helpful_votes', 'total_votes']].corr()

# Print the correlation matrix
print(correlation_matrix)
```

This code will calculate and print a correlation matrix, which shows the correlation coefficients between pairs of variables. The correlation coefficient ranges from -1 to 1. A value close to 1 implies a high positive correlation while a value close to -1 implies a high negative correlation. A value close to 0 implies no correlation. Run this code and let me know what you find.

[End of response]

Let's try this code and see if it works. Add the correlation code to a code cell in your Notebook and run it:

```
# Step 8: Correlation Analysis

# Calculate the correlation matrix
correlation_matrix = df[['star_rating', 'helpful_votes', 'total_votes']].corr()

# Print the correlation matrix
print(correlation_matrix)
```

You should see an output similar to the below:

```
               star_rating  helpful_votes  total_votes
star_rating       1.000000      -0.324371    -0.517002
helpful_votes    -0.324371       1.000000     0.659612
total_votes      -0.517002       0.659612     1.000000
```

Next, let's send the above output to Copilot and see if we can get an explanation of the correlations:

[Prompt]

Below is the output: star_rating helpful_votes total_votes star_rating 1.000000 -0.324371 -0.517002 helpful_votes -0.324371 1.000000 0.659612 total_votes -0.517002 0.659612 1.000000

[End of prompt]

You should receive a response similar to the response below:

[Prompt response]

Great! The output you've shared is a correlation matrix, which shows the correlation coefficients between pairs of variables. Here's how to interpret it:

- `star_rating` and `helpful_votes`: The correlation coefficient is -0.324371, indicating a weak negative correlation. This suggests that as the star rating increases, the number of helpful votes tends to decrease slightly, and vice versa.
- `star_rating` and `total_votes`: The correlation coefficient is -0.517002, indicating a moderate negative correlation. This suggests that as the star rating increases, the total number of votes (both helpful and not helpful) tends to decrease, and vice versa.
- `helpful_votes` and `total_votes`: The correlation coefficient is 0.659612, indicating a moderate positive correlation. This suggests that as the number of helpful votes increases, the total number of votes also tends to increase, and vice versa.

For the next step, you could consider visualizing these correlations using a heatmap, or you could move on to another type of analysis. Let me know what you'd like to do next.

[End of response]

Next, we want to look into visualizations of these correlations; a heatmap is one way to do this.

[Prompt]

For Step 8.1, visualize these correlations using a heatmap.

[End of prompt]

You should receive a response similar to the response below:

[Prompt response]

Sure, let's visualize the correlation matrix using a heatmap. We'll use the seaborn library for this.

```python
# Step 8.1: Visualize Correlation Matrix with Heatmap

import seaborn as sns

# Plot a heatmap of the correlation matrix
plt.figure(figsize=(8, 6))
sns.heatmap(correlation_matrix, annot=True, cmap='coolwarm', center=0)
plt.title('Correlation Matrix Heatmap')
plt.show()
```

This code will create a heatmap of the correlation matrix. The colors represent the correlation coefficients: warm colors (towards red) indicate positive correlation, cool colors (towards blue) indicate negative correlation, and neutral colors (around white) indicate no correlation. The annot=True option will display the correlation coefficients on the heatmap. Run this code and let me know what you find.

[End of response]

Let's try this code to create a heatmap visualization using the seaborn library and see if it works. Run the code in a code cell in your Notebook:

```python
# Step 8.1: Visualize Correlation Matrix with Heatmap

import seaborn as sns

# Plot a heatmap of the correlation matrix
plt.figure(figsize=(8, 6))
sns.heatmap(correlation_matrix, annot=True, cmap='coolwarm', center=0)
plt.title('Correlation Matrix Heatmap')
plt.show()
```

You should see output similar to the below:

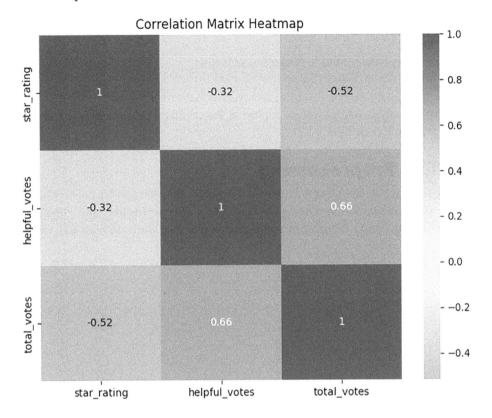

Figure 17.4: Heatmap showing the correlation between three variables: total_votes, helpful_votes, and star_rating

Step 9: Additional exploratory analysis

So, why do we want to perform an additional exploratory analysis? Well, there are some good reasons why we would want to do that:

- Uncovering hidden user patterns: Sometimes, there are trends, patterns, and relationships not immediately discoverable, and taking a second deeper look can find these.
- Validate initial findings: By validating the results from the initial analysis with a second analysis, you ensure robustness and reliability.
- Identify outliers: Not effectively finding outliers can skew the results. Spending more time on finding these can pay off.
- Improve model accuracy: Additional variables can be identified that can improve accuracy.

Above is a non-exhaustive list of reasons why we should do an additional analysis. Let's see how Co-pilot can help us:

[Prompt]

Thank you, I wish to understand if there is any more exploratory analysis for the sentiment analysis of this dataset.

[End of prompt]

You should receive a response similar to the response below:

[Prompt response]

Certainly, sentiment analysis often involves exploring the text data in more depth. Here are a few additional steps you could consider:

Step 10: Text Preprocessing

Before analyzing the text, it's often helpful to clean it up a bit. This can involve converting all text to lower case, removing punctuation, removing stop words (common words like "and", "the", "a", which don't add much meaning), and stemming or lemmatizing (reducing words to their root form).

```python
from nltk.corpus import stopwords
from nltk.stem import PorterStemmer
import re

# Initialize a PorterStemmer object to perform stemming
stemmer = PorterStemmer()

# Define a function to preprocess the text
def preprocess_text(text):
    # Convert to lower case
    text = text.lower()
    # Remove punctuation
    text = re.sub(r'[^\w\s]', '', text)
    # Remove stop words and stem the words
    text = ' '.join([stemmer.stem(word) for word in text.split() if word not in
stopwords.words('english')])
    return text

# Apply the function to the review_body column
df['review_body_clean'] = df['review_body'].apply(preprocess_text)
```

Step 11: Word Frequency Analysis

After preprocessing the text, you can analyze the frequency of words in the reviews. This can help identify common themes or topics.

```python
from collections import Counter

# Count the frequency of words in the reviews
```

```
word_counts = Counter(' '.join(df['review_body_clean']).split())

# Print the 10 most common words
print(word_counts.most_common(10))
```

Step 12: Sentiment Score Calculation

You can calculate a sentiment score for each review using a sentiment analysis tool like TextBlob or Vader. This can provide a more quantitative measure of the sentiment expressed in the reviews.

```
from textblob import TextBlob

# Define a function to calculate sentiment
def calculate_sentiment(text):
    return TextBlob(text).sentiment.polarity

# Apply the function to the review_body_clean column
df['sentiment_score'] = df['review_body_clean'].apply(calculate_sentiment)

# Print the average sentiment score
print(df['sentiment_score'].mean())
```

Please note that you'll need to install the nltk and textblob libraries to run this code, which you can do using pip:

```
pip install nltk textblob
```

Let me know if you'd like to proceed with any of these steps, or if there's something else you'd like to do.

[End of response]

This prompt yielded three steps as a response. Let's try the code from all three steps and see if it works:

Text preprocessing

```
# uncomment if the nltk and textblob are not installed
# !pip install nltk textblob

from nltk.corpus import stopwords
from nltk.stem import PorterStemmer
import re

# Initialize a PorterStemmer object to perform stemming
stemmer = PorterStemmer()

# Define a function to preprocess the text
```

```python
def preprocess_text(text):
    # Convert to lower case
    text = text.lower()
    # Remove punctuation
    text = re.sub(r'[^\w\s]', '', text)
    # Remove stop words and stem the words
    text = ' '.join([stemmer.stem(word) for word in text.split() if word not in
stopwords.words('english')])
    return text


# Apply the function to the review_body column
df['review_body_clean'] = df['review_body'].apply(preprocess_text)
```

Word frequency analysis

```python
from collections import Counter

# Count the frequency of words in the reviews
word_counts = Counter(' '.join(df['review_body_clean']).split())

# Print the 10 most common words
print(word_counts.most_common(10))
```

You should see an output similar to the below:

```
[('book', 80), ('read', 25), ('love', 24), ('great', 24), ('stori', 19),
('good', 17), ('page', 16), ('one', 15), ('like', 14), ('realli', 14)]
```

Next, use the output above and construct the next prompt to understand our situation better:

[Prompt]

For the code below:

```python
from collections import Counter

# Count the frequency of words in the reviews
word_counts = Counter(' '.join(df['review_body_clean']).split())

# Print the 10 most common words
print(word_counts.most_common(10))
```

Below is the output: [('book', 80), ('read', 25), ('love', 24), ('great', 24), ('stori', 19), ('good', 17), ('page', 16),
('one', 15), ('like', 14), ('realli', 14)]

[End of prompt]

You should receive a response similar to the response below:

[Prompt response]

Great! The output you've shared shows the 10 most common words in the cleaned reviews, along with their frequencies:

```
'book': Appears 80 times
'read': Appears 25 times
'love': Appears 24 times
'great': Appears 24 times
'stori': Appears 19 times
'good': Appears 17 times
'page': Appears 16 times
'one': Appears 15 times
'like': Appears 14 times
'realli': Appears 14 times
```

This suggests that most of the reviews are positive, with words like 'love', 'great', and 'good' being quite common. The words 'book', 'read', and 'page' are also common, which is expected in a dataset of book reviews.

For the next step, you could consider calculating a sentiment score for each review to get a more quantitative measure of the sentiment. Alternatively, you could visualize the word frequencies using a bar chart or a word cloud. Let me know what you'd like to do next.

[End of response]

Let's try to run the sentiment score calculation code below:

Sentiment score calculation

```
from textblob import TextBlob

# Define a function to calculate sentiment
def calculate_sentiment(text):
    return TextBlob(text).sentiment.polarity

# Apply the function to the review_body_clean column
df['sentiment_score'] = df['review_body_clean'].apply(calculate_sentiment)

# Print the average sentiment score
print(df['sentiment_score'].mean())
```

Here's the output:

```
0.23785470981747298
```

Next, let's try to interpret the response. As usual, let's create a prompt from the response and see what Copilot thinks of it:

[Prompt]

For the code below:

```
from textblob import TextBlob

# Define a function to calculate sentiment
def calculate_sentiment(text):
return TextBlob(text).sentiment.polarity

# Apply the function to the review_body_clean column
df['sentiment_score'] = df['review_body_clean'].apply(calculate_sentiment)

# Print the average sentiment score
print(df['sentiment_score'].mean())
```

Here is the output: 0.23785470981747298

[End of prompt]

You should receive a response similar to the response below:

[Prompt response]

Great! The output you've shared is the average sentiment score for the reviews in your dataset.

The sentiment score is a number between -1 and 1. A score of -1 represents extremely negative sentiment, a score of 1 represents extremely positive sentiment, and a score of 0 represents neutral sentiment.

The average sentiment score in your dataset is approximately 0.238, which indicates a generally positive sentiment in the reviews. This aligns with the word frequency analysis, which showed that positive words like 'love', 'great', and 'good' are quite common in the reviews.

For the next step, you could consider visualizing the distribution of sentiment scores using a histogram or a box plot. Alternatively, you could analyze the relationship between sentiment score and other variables like star rating or review length. Let me know what you'd like to do next.

[End of response]

[Prompt]

Follow these instructions step by step:

- Visualize the distribution of sentiment scores using a histogram.
- Analyze the relationship between sentiment score and other variables like star rating or review length.

[End of prompt]

You should receive a response similar to the response below.

[Prompt response]

Sure, let's proceed with those steps.

Step 13: Visualize the Distribution of Sentiment Scores

We can use a histogram to visualize the distribution of sentiment scores.

```python
import matplotlib.pyplot as plt

# Plot a histogram of the sentiment scores
plt.figure(figsize=(8, 6))
plt.hist(df['sentiment_score'], bins=20, color='skyblue')
plt.title('Distribution of Sentiment Scores')
plt.xlabel('Sentiment Score')
plt.ylabel('Frequency')
plt.show()
```

Step 14: Analyze the Relationship Between Sentiment Score and Other Variables

We can use scatter plots to visualize the relationship between sentiment score and other variables like star rating and review length.

```python
# Plot a scatter plot of sentiment score vs star rating
plt.figure(figsize=(8, 6))
plt.scatter(df['sentiment_score'], df['star_rating'], alpha=0.5,
color='skyblue')
plt.title('Sentiment Score vs Star Rating')
plt.xlabel('Sentiment Score')
plt.ylabel('Star Rating')
plt.show()

# Plot a scatter plot of sentiment score vs review length
plt.figure(figsize=(8, 6))
plt.scatter(df['sentiment_score'], df['review_length'], alpha=0.5,
color='skyblue')
plt.title('Sentiment Score vs Review Length')
plt.xlabel('Sentiment Score')
plt.ylabel('Review Length')
plt.show()
```

These plots will help you understand if there's any correlation between sentiment score and star rating or review length. Run these codes and let me know what you find.

[End of response]

Let's try the above code and see if it works. Add the below code to a code cell and run it:

Visualize the distribution of sentiment scores

```python
import matplotlib.pyplot as plt

# Plot a histogram of the sentiment scores
plt.figure(figsize=(8, 6))
plt.hist(df['sentiment_score'], bins=20, color='skyblue')
plt.title('Distribution of Sentiment Scores')
plt.xlabel('Sentiment Score')
plt.ylabel('Frequency')
plt.show()
```

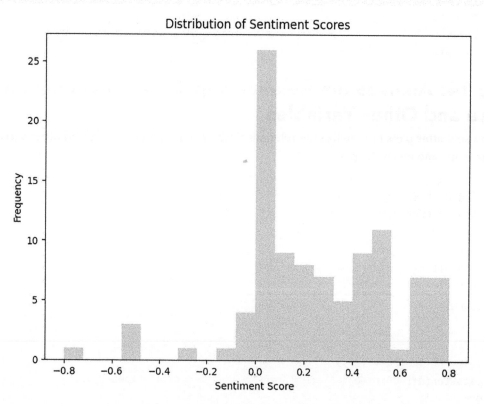

Figure 17.5: Image depicting the distribution of sentiment scores

Analyze the relationship between sentiment score and other variables

```
# Plot a scatter plot of sentiment score vs star rating
plt.figure(figsize=(8, 6))
plt.scatter(df['sentiment_score'], df['star_rating'], alpha=0.5,
color='skyblue')
plt.title('Sentiment Score vs Star Rating')
plt.xlabel('Sentiment Score')
plt.ylabel('Star Rating')
plt.show()

# Plot a scatter plot of sentiment score vs review length
plt.figure(figsize=(8, 6))
plt.scatter(df['sentiment_score'], df['review_length'], alpha=0.5,
color='skyblue')
plt.title('Sentiment Score vs Review Length')
plt.xlabel('Sentiment Score')
plt.ylabel('Review Length')
plt.show()
```

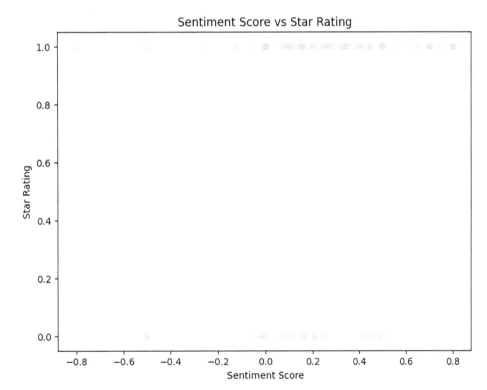

Figure 17.6: Sentiment score versus star rating

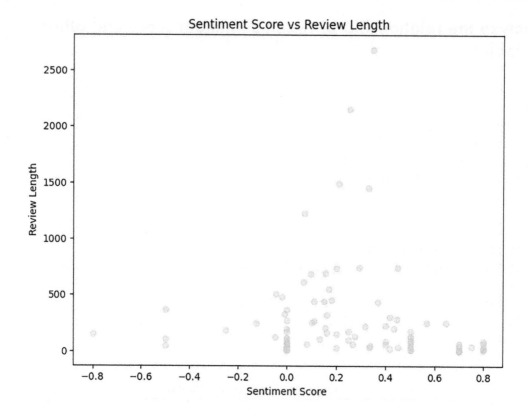

Figure 17.7: Sentiment score versus review length

Assignment

Your assignment is to reflect on the approach taken and go through a similar regression scenario for this dataset on house prices in Boston: `https://www.kaggle.com/datasets/vikrishnan/boston-house-prices`.

Here are some questions you could try answering using the above dataset and regression:

- Price Prediction: What is the estimated price of a house, given its features (e.g., size, location, and number of bedrooms)?
- Feature Importance: Which features have the most significant impact on house prices?
- Price Trends: How do house prices change over time in a specific area?

Solution

The solution is in the repository: `https://github.com/PacktPublishing/AI-Assisted-Software-Development-with-GitHub-Copilot-and-ChatGPT`

Summary

This chapter had one important purpose – to compare and contrast the experience of using ChatGPT with GitHub Copilot and, in this case, its chat function. We used an approach that consisted of providing a lot of upfront information to Copilot, by describing the overall problem and the shape of the dataset. We also provided instructions to let Copilot guide us on what to do, which showed us the steps to take gradually and what code to run. The general conclusion is that we can use roughly the same method using Copilot Chat as we did with ChatGPT.

We also saw how Copilot can help explain our output, understand where in the process we are, and suggest the next step to take.

As a rule, we should always test code and ask our AI assistant to help if it doesn't run or produce the expected output.

Join our community on Discord

Join our community's Discord space for discussions with the author and other readers:

```
https://packt.link/aicode
```

Summary

18
Regression with Copilot Chat

Introduction

The stock of a corporation signifies ownership in the corporation. A single share of the stock represents a claim on the fractional assets and the earnings of the corporation in proportion to the total number of shares. For example, if an investor owns 50 shares of stock in a company that has, in total, 1,000 shares, then that investor (or shareholder) would own and have a claim on 5% of the company's assets and earnings.

The stocks of a company can be traded between shareholders and other parties via stock exchanges and organizations. Major stock exchanges include the New York Stock Exchange, NASDAQ, the London Stock Exchange Group, the Shanghai Stock Exchange, and the Hong Kong Stock Exchange. The prices that a stock is traded at fluctuate essentially due to the law of supply and demand. At any one moment, the supply is the number of shares that are in the hands of public investors, the demand is the number of shares investors want to buy, and the price of the stock moves up and down to attain and maintain equilibrium.

Investors generally want to buy low and sell high. This seems straightforward enough but putting it into practice is exceedingly tough because it is incredibly difficult to predict whether a stock price will increase or decrease. Fundamental analysis and technical analysis are the two main research areas that aim to comprehend the reasons and circumstances that influence price fluctuations or even forecast future stock prices:

- **Fundamental analysis:** This stream focuses on the fundamental elements that affect a company's value and operations, such as the macroeconomic environment, the state of the industry, and the company's management and competitors.
- **Technical analysis:** On the other hand, this uses statistical analysis of historical trading activity, such as price movement, volume, and time, to forecast future price movements.

In this chapter, we will explore the second technique using the Apple dataset to predict stock prices and help investors decide whether to buy or not.

Regression

Let's start by asking Copilot Chat for the definition of regression:

[Prompt]

What is regression?

[End of prompt]

You should receive a response similar to the response below:

[Prompt response]

Regression is a statistical method used in data analysis which investigates the relationship between a dependent (target) and independent variable(s) (predictor). This method is mostly used for forecasting, time series modeling, and finding the causal effect relationship between the variables. For example, the relationship between rainfall and soil erosion or the relationship between salary and years of experience.

[End of response]

You may notice in your chatbox that GitHub Copilot is suggesting the next context, highlighted in blue, asking, "**What are the different types of regression?**". You can click on this to get the answer. This demonstrates how Copilot is a powerful tool that assists users effectively.

Dataset overview

This dataset contains Apple's (AAPL) stock data spanning 10 years. Insights from this data can be used to build useful price forecasting algorithms to aid investment.

We can make the following notes about this dataset:

- Data is collected and aggregated from 25 exchanges.
- Data is updated weekly.
- This dataset contains 1-minute, 5-minute, 30-minute, and 1-hour bars (open/high/low/close/volume) for AAPL.
- Out-of-hours trades are included. Prices are adjusted for splits and dividends. Dataset available at https://www.kaggle.com/datasets/tarunpaparaju/apple-aapl-historical-stock-data.

Explore the dataset

To better illustrate this regression approach, it is necessary to have suitable predictors for our target. The dataset recorded more direct elements to the stock. Five values illustrating movements in the price over one unit of time (usually one day, but it can also be one week or one month) are key trading indicators.

They are as follows:

- **Open**: The starting price for a given trading day

- **Close:** The final price on that day
- **High:** The highest prices at which the stock traded on that day
- **Low:** The lowest prices at which the stock traded on that day
- **Volume:** The total number of shares traded before the market closed on that day

Prompt strategy

In this chapter, we will use the TAG (Task-Action-Guidance) prompt pattern. Here's how we can help frame our project to help us author our initial prompt:

- **Task:** Regression analysis on Apple stock value through history
- **Action:** We will need to instruct the AI assistant to tell us what steps to take
- **Guidance:** The guidance should be us describing the dataset

Your initial prompt

Just like with other chapters in this book, we start with a prompt providing as much context as possible about what we want to do and the shape of the dataset. The idea is that we set a high-level context for our AI tool, which helps guide it throughout the rest of our prompts.

[Prompt]

I'm performing a regression project to forecast stock prices using the Apple Historical Stock dataset. This will aid investors in making informed decisions about buying or not buying stocks. The workflow includes loading the dataset, exploring its contents, splitting the dataset, building a regression model, and evaluating its performance. But remember I want to learn it step by step. Let's start with loading the dataset. I am storing the dataset in `<file path>`. Here's the shape of the dataset:

- **Open:** The starting price for a given trading day
- **Close:** The final price on that day
- **High:** The highest prices at which the stock traded on that day
- **Low:** The lowest prices at which the stock traded on that day
- **Volume:** The total number of shares traded before the market closed on that day

[End of prompt]

You should receive a response similar to the response below:

[Prompt response]

Sure, let's start by loading the dataset. We'll use the pandas library in Python to do this. Replace `<file-path>` with the path where your file is located.

Here's the Python code to load the dataset:

```
import pandas as pd

# Replace <file-path> with the path of your dataset
```

```
file_path = "<file-path>"

# Load the dataset
df = pd.read_csv(file_path)

# Display the first few rows of the dataset
print(df.head())
```

After running this code, you should see the first few rows of your dataset printed out. This will give you a preliminary view of your data.

For the next steps, you might want to explore the dataset, clean the data if necessary, split the dataset into a training set and a test set, build a regression model using the training set, and then evaluate the model's performance using the test set.

[End of response]

Let's try the output generated by Copilot and see if it works. Modify the file_path variable to point to the location of your dataset and then execute the code below in a code cell in a notebook:

```
import pandas as pd

# Replace <file-path> with the path of your dataset
file_path = "/your-path/.csv"

# Load the dataset
df = pd.read_csv(file_path)

# Display the first few rows of the dataset
print(df.head())
```

Here's the output you should see after running the code above:

	Date	Close/Last	Volume	Open	High	Low
0	02/28/2020	$273.36	106721200	$257.26	$278.41	$256.37
1	02/27/2020	$273.52	80151380	$281.1	$286	$272.96
2	02/26/2020	$292.65	49678430	$286.53	$297.88	$286.5
3	02/25/2020	$288.08	57668360	$300.95	$302.53	$286.13
4	02/24/2020	$298.18	55548830	$297.26	$304.18	$289.23

Next, we will focus on historical prices (the five recorded values) and performance to predict future prices. Let's start by checking the data types.

[Prompt]

Check the data types.

[End of prompt]

You should receive a response similar to the response below:

[Prompt response]

To check the data types of the columns in your DataFrame, you can use the dtypes attribute. Here's how you can do it:

```
# Check the data types of each column
print(df.dtypes)
```

This will print out the name of each column along with its data type. This is useful to know because certain operations can only be performed on certain types of data. For example, you can't perform numerical operations on a string.

[End of response]

Let's try this and see if it works. Run the code print(df.types):

```
# Check the data types of each column
print(df.dtypes)
Date          object
Close/Last    object
Volume         int64
Open          object
High          object
Low           object
dtype: object
```

Now, use the above output to query our AI tool.

[Prompt]

Below is the output, Date object Close/Last object Volume int64 Open object High object Low object dtype: object

[End of prompt]

You should receive a response similar to the response below:

[Prompt response]

It appears that the 'Date' column and the price columns ('Close/Last', 'Open', 'High', 'Low') are being read as 'object' type, which is essentially a string in pandas. However, for your analysis, you would want 'Date' to be in a datetime format and the price columns to be of a float type.

Here's how you can convert the data types:

```
# Convert 'Date' to datetime
df['Date'] = pd.to_datetime(df['Date'])

# Remove $ from price columns and convert to float
```

```
price_columns = [' Close/Last', ' Open', ' High', ' Low']
for col in price_columns:
    df[col] = df[col].str.replace('$', '').astype(float)

# Check the data types again
print(df.dtypes)
```

This code first converts the 'Date' column to datetime format using `pd.to_datetime()`. Then it loops over each price column, removes the dollar sign from each value, and converts the column to float type. Finally, it prints out the data types of the columns again to confirm the changes.

[End of response]

Let's try these suggestions above to convert our columns by running the below code:

```
# Convert 'Date' to datetime
df['Date'] = pd.to_datetime(df['Date'])

# Remove $ from price columns and convert to float
price_columns = [' Close/Last', ' Open', ' High', ' Low']
for col in price_columns:
    df[col] = df[col].str.replace('$', '').astype(float)

# Check the data types again
print(df.dtypes)
```

You should see the following output, which is the columns correctly converted to suitable types instead of being strings:

```
Date            datetime64[ns]
Close/Last             float64
Volume                   int64
Open                   float64
High                   float64
Low                    float64
dtype: object
```

Next, let's tell Copilot about the result to ensure it tells us what to do next.

[Prompt]

Below is the output, Date datetime64[ns] Close/Last float64 Volume int64 Open float64 High float64 Low float64 dtype: object

[End of prompt]

You should receive a response similar to the response below:

[Prompt response]

Great! Now your 'Date' column is of type 'datetime64[ns]' and your price columns ('Close/Last', 'Open', 'High', 'Low') are of type 'float64'. This means you can now perform numerical operations on your price columns and time series analysis on your 'Date' column.

The next steps could be to perform exploratory data analysis, such as checking for missing values, visualizing the distribution of your variables, or examining the correlation between different variables. You might also want to split your data into a training set and a test set in preparation for building your regression model.

[End of response]

Exploratory data analysis

Guided by the output on what to do next, we decide to check the missing values in our dataset:

[Prompt]

Check missing values.

[End of response]

You should receive a response similar to the response below:

[Prompt response]

To check for missing values in your DataFrame, you can use the isnull() function along with the sum() function in pandas. Here's how you can do it:

```
# Check for missing values
print(df.isnull().sum())
```

This will print out the number of missing values in each column of your DataFrame. If a column has zero missing values, that means there are no missing values in that column. If a column has a number greater than zero, that's the number of missing values in that column.

[End of response]

The response from Copilot says to check for null values and provides code for how to do so. Let's run the suggested code in a code cell in a Notebook:

```
# Check for missing values
print(df.isnull().sum())
```

Here's the output:

```
Date          0
Close/Last    0
Volume        0
```

```
Open           0
High           0
Low            0
dtype: int64
```

With this output, provide it to Copilot to see what to do next:

[Prompt]

Below is the output, Date 0 Close/Last 0 Volume 0 Open 0 High 0 Low 0 dtype: int64

[End of prompt]

You should receive a response similar to the response below:

[Prompt response]

Great! The output indicates that there are no missing values in your dataset. Each column has 0 missing values. This is good news because it means you don't have to handle missing data, which can be a complex process.

The next step in your analysis could be to perform some exploratory data analysis (EDA). This might include visualizing your data, checking for outliers, or examining the relationships between variables. After that, you can proceed to split your data into a training set and a test set, and then build your regression model.

[End of response]

Great, we had no missing values and it seems like the next steps should be visual analysis and checking for outliers. With that knowledge, let's craft an appropriate prompt.

[Prompt]

Visualize data and check for outliers.

[End of prompt]

You should receive a response similar to the response below:

[Prompt response]

Visualizing the data can be done using various libraries in Python, such as Matplotlib or Seaborn. For checking outliers, boxplots can be very useful. Here's how you can create boxplots for your price columns:

```python
import matplotlib.pyplot as plt
import seaborn as sns

# Set up the matplotlib figure
f, axes = plt.subplots(2, 2, figsize=(15, 10))

# Plot a simple histogram with binsize determined automatically
```

```
sns.boxplot(data=df[' Close/Last'], ax=axes[0, 0])
axes[0, 0].set_title('Close/Last')

sns.boxplot(data=df[' Open'], ax=axes[0, 1])
axes[0, 1].set_title('Open')

sns.boxplot(data=df[' High'], ax=axes[1, 0])
axes[1, 0].set_title('High')

sns.boxplot(data=df[' Low'], ax=axes[1, 1])
axes[1, 1].set_title('Low')

plt.tight_layout()
```

This code will create a 2x2 grid of plots, with each plot being a boxplot of one of your price columns. Boxplots are useful for visualizing the distribution of data and identifying potential outliers. In a box-plot, an outlier is typically represented as a point that is located outside the whiskers of the boxplot.

[End of response]

The code above suggests using the matplotlib and seaborn libraries and also contains code to create a boxplot visualization; let's run said code:

```
import matplotlib.pyplot as plt
import seaborn as sns

# Set up the matplotlib figure
f, axes = plt.subplots(2, 2, figsize=(15, 10))

# Plot a simple histogram with binsize determined automatically
sns.boxplot(data=df[' Close/Last'], ax=axes[0, 0])
axes[0, 0].set_title('Close/Last')

sns.boxplot(data=df[' Open'], ax=axes[0, 1])
axes[0, 1].set_title('Open')

sns.boxplot(data=df[' High'], ax=axes[1, 0])
axes[1, 0].set_title('High')

sns.boxplot(data=df[' Low'], ax=axes[1, 1])
axes[1, 1].set_title('Low')

plt.tight_layout()
```

You should see results similar to the following boxplots:

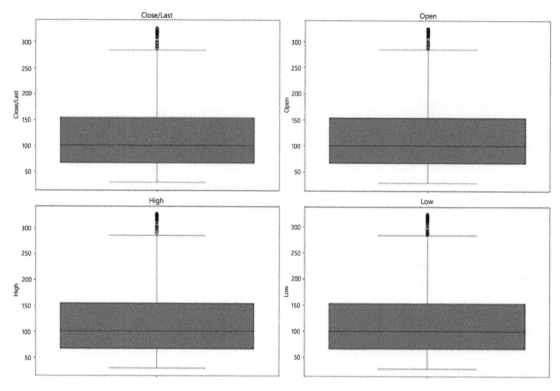

Figure 18.1: Boxplots of our dataset

Next, we want to learn more about our variables and their relationship.

[Prompt]

Examine the relationships between variables.

[End of prompt]

You should receive a response similar to the response below:

[Prompt response]

To examine the relationships between variables, you can use a correlation matrix and a heatmap. The correlation matrix will give you numerical values that represent how closely related two variables are, while the heatmap will give you a visual representation of these relationships.

Here's how you can do it:

```
# Calculate the correlation matrix
corr = df.corr()

# Plot the heatmap
```

```
sns.heatmap(corr, annot=True, cmap='coolwarm')
```

```
plt.show()
```

This code first calculates the correlation matrix using the corr() function, which returns a DataFrame where each cell represents the correlation coefficient between two variables. Then it plots a heatmap using this correlation matrix. The annot=True argument allows the correlation coefficients to be plotted on the heatmap, and the cmap='coolwarm' argument sets the color scheme of the heatmap.

The correlation coefficient ranges from -1 to 1. A value close to 1 implies a high positive correlation while a value close to -1 implies a high negative correlation. A value close to 0 implies no correlation.

[End of response]

The response says we should create a correlation matrix and visualize it via a heatmap. Let's try the suggested code above and see what we get:

```
# Calculate the correlation matrix
corr = df.corr()
```

```
# Plot the heatmap
sns.heatmap(corr, annot=True, cmap='coolwarm')
```

```
plt.show()
```

Here's the output from the code above:

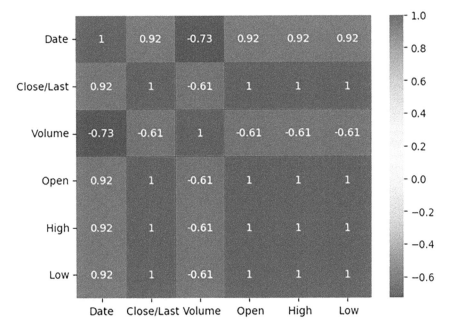

Figure 18.2: Heatmap

In the heatmap, we can see:

- The diagonal is always 1 because it shows the correlation of each variable with itself.
- Close/Last, Open, High, and Low have a high positive correlation with each other (0.92), indicating that as one of these variables increases, the others tend to also increase. This is typical for stock data, as these prices move closely together throughout the trading day.
- Volume shows a negative correlation with Close/Last, Open, High, and Low (-0.61). This suggests that on days when the volume of shares traded is higher, the prices may tend to be lower, or vice versa.

As shown in the screenshot below, Copilot recommends the next step following the analysis of variable relationships. We will choose this and see what it says.

Let's ask Copilot what to do next.

[Prompt]

What is the next step after examining the relationships between variables?

[End of prompt]

You should receive a response similar to the response below:

[Prompt response]

The next step after examining the relationships between variables is typically to prepare your data for modeling. This can involve several sub-steps:

- **Feature Selection:** Based on your correlation analysis, you might decide to drop some features that are not correlated with your target variable, or to avoid multicollinearity, drop one of two features that are highly correlated with each other.
- **Data Splitting:** You'll need to split your data into a training set and a test set. A common split is 80% of the data for training and 20% for testing.
- **Data Scaling:** Depending on the model you plan to use, you might need to scale your data so that all features have a similar range of values.

Once your data is prepared, you can proceed to build your regression model.

[End of response]

Data splitting

At this point, let's prepare for the creation of the model. Before we can create the model, we need to split up our data into training data and test sets to verify the model later.

[Prompt]

Let's move on to the step of splitting the data.

[End of prompt]

You should receive a response similar to the response below:

[Prompt response]

Absolutely, splitting the data into a training set and a test set is a crucial step in preparing your data for modeling. We'll use the `train_test_split` function from `sklearn.model_selection` to do this.

Assuming that we are going to predict the 'Close/Last' price, here's how you can split your data:

```python
from sklearn.model_selection import train_test_split

# Define the feature variables and the target variable
X = df.drop(' Close/Last', axis=1)
y = df[' Close/Last']

# Split the data into training set and test set
X_train, X_test, y_train, y_test = train_test_split(X, y, test_size=0.2,
random_state=42)
```

This code first defines the feature variables X and the target variable y. Then it splits these into a training set and a test set, with 80% of the data going to the training set and 20% going to the test set. The `random_state` parameter is used for reproducibility - using the same `random_state` will ensure that you get the same train/test split every time you run the code.

[End of response]

In short, the code above shows us how to split up our dataset; let's try this code next:

```python
from sklearn.model_selection import train_test_split

# Define the feature variables and the target variable
X = df.drop(' Close/Last', axis=1)
y = df[' Close/Last']

# Split the data into training set and test set
X_train, X_test, y_train, y_test = train_test_split(X, y, test_size=0.2,
random_state=42)
```

At this point, we don't have an output to show as we assigned the results to variables. Let's, however, print that next.

[Prompt]

Print the shape of samples.

[End of prompt]

You should receive a response similar to the response below:

[Prompt response]

To print the shape of your training and test samples, you can use the shape attribute. Here's how you can do it:

```python
# Print the shape of the training set and the test set
print("Training set (X):", X_train.shape)
print("Training set (y):", y_train.shape)
print("Test set (X):", X_test.shape)
print("Test set (y):", y_test.shape)
```

This will print out the number of rows and columns in your training set and test set. The number of rows should be the same between X_train and y_train, and between X_test and y_test. The number of columns in X_train and X_test should be the same, and y_train and y_test should each have just one column (since they represent the target variable).

[End of response]

The suggested code is straightforward, as it consists of a set of print statements. Let's try said code by running it in a code cell:

```python
# Print the shape of the training set and the test set
print("Training set (X):", X_train.shape)
print("Training set (y):", y_train.shape)
print("Test set (X):", X_test.shape)
print("Test set (y):", y_test.shape)
```

You should see output similar to the below:

```
Training set (X): (2014, 5)
Training set (y): (2014,)
Test set (X): (504, 5)
Test set (y): (504,)
```

Build a regression model

Now that we've split up the data, let's train the model next, or at least that's what we expect Copilot to say if we ask it for the next step. Let's create a prompt asking just that:

[Prompt]

What is the next step after splitting the data?

[End of prompt]

You should receive a response similar to the response below:

[Prompt response]

After splitting the data, the next step is to create and train your regression model using the training data. Depending on the nature of your data and the problem you're trying to solve, you might choose a simple linear regression model, or a more complex model like polynomial regression or ridge regression.

Once the model is trained, you can use it to make predictions on the test data. Then, you evaluate the performance of the model by comparing these predictions to the actual values in the test data. Common metrics for evaluating regression models include Mean Absolute Error (MAE), Mean Squared Error (MSE), and R-squared.

[End of response]

Okay, just as we thought, the next step is to train the model. Let's create a prompt asking for more detailed information on how to train the model:

[Prompt]

Create and train a regression model.

[End of prompt]

You should receive a response similar to the response below:

[Prompt response]

Sure, let's create and train a simple Linear Regression model using the training data. We'll use the `LinearRegression` class from `sklearn.linear_model` to do this.

Here's how you can create and train your model:

```
from sklearn.linear_model import LinearRegression

# Create a Linear Regression model
model = LinearRegression()

# Train the model
model.fit(X_train, y_train)
```

This code first creates a Linear Regression model. Then it trains the model using the fit method and the training data. After this step, your model is ready to make predictions on unseen data.

Please note that if your data has a non-linear relationship, you might need to use a more complex model like Polynomial Regression or a tree-based model. Also, if your features are not on the same scale, you might need to scale your data before training the model.

[End of response]

We've received a response on using linear regression and the sklearn library. Note that you might need to install said library before proceeding. Once you've ensured sklearn is installed, proceed to run the suggested code below:

```
from sklearn.linear_model import LinearRegression

# Create a Linear Regression model
model = LinearRegression()
```

```
# Train the model
model.fit(X_train, y_train)
```

Here's the output from running the code:

```
---------------------------------------------------------------------
DTypePromotionError                          Traceback (most recent call last)

File ~/.conda/envs/myenv/lib/python3.12/site-packages/sklearn/base.py:1152, in
_fit_context.<locals>.decorator.<locals>.wrapper(estimator, *args, **kwargs)
   1145     estimator._validate_params()
   1147 with config_context(
   1148     skip_parameter_validation=(
   1149         prefer_skip_nested_validation or global_skip_validation
   1150     )
   1151 ):
-> 1152     return fit_method(estimator, *args, **kwargs)


File ~/.conda/envs/myenv/lib/python3.12/site-packages/sklearn/linear_model/_
base.py:678, in LinearRegression.fit(self, X, y, sample_weight)
   674 n_jobs_ = self.n_jobs
   676 accept_sparse = False if self.positive else ["csr", "csc", "coo"]
--> 678 X, y = self._validate_data(
   679     X, y, accept_sparse=accept_sparse, y_numeric=True, multi_
output=True
   680 )
   682 has_sw = sample_weight is not None
   683 if has_sw:


File ~/.conda/envs/myenv/lib/python3.12/site-packages/sklearn/base.py:622, in
BaseEstimator._validate_data(self, X, y, reset, validate_separately, cast_to_
ndarray, **check_params)
   620         y = check_array(y, input_name="y", **check_y_params)
   621     else:
--> 622         X, y = check_X_y(X, y, **check_params)
   623     out = X, y
   625 if not no_val_X and check_params.get("ensure_2d", True):


File ~/.conda/envs/myenv/lib/python3.12/site-packages/sklearn/utils/validation.
py:1146, in check_X_y(X, y, accept_sparse, accept_large_sparse, dtype, order,
copy, force_all_finite, ensure_2d, allow_nd, multi_output, ensure_min_samples,
ensure_min_features, y_numeric, estimator)
```

```
     1141          estimator_name = _check_estimator_name(estimator)
     1142      raise ValueError(
     1143          f"{estimator_name} requires y to be passed, but the target y is
None"
     1144      )
-> 1146 X = check_array(
     1147      X,
     1148      accept_sparse=accept_sparse,
     1149      accept_large_sparse=accept_large_sparse,
     1150      dtype=dtype,
     1151      order=order,
     1152      copy=copy,
     1153      force_all_finite=force_all_finite,
     1154      ensure_2d=ensure_2d,
     1155      allow_nd=allow_nd,
     1156      ensure_min_samples=ensure_min_samples,
     1157      ensure_min_features=ensure_min_features,
     1158      estimator=estimator,
     1159      input_name="X",
     1160 )
     1162 y = _check_y(y, multi_output=multi_output, y_numeric=y_numeric,
estimator=estimator)
     1164 check_consistent_length(X, y)
```

File ~/.conda/envs/myenv/lib/python3.12/site-packages/sklearn/utils/validation.
py:795, in check_array(array, accept_sparse, accept_large_sparse, dtype, order,
copy, force_all_finite, ensure_2d, allow_nd, ensure_min_samples, ensure_min_
features, estimator, input_name)

```
     791 pandas_requires_conversion = any(
     792      _pandas_dtype_needs_early_conversion(i) for i in dtypes_orig
     793 )
     794 if all(isinstance(dtype_iter, np.dtype) for dtype_iter in dtypes_orig):
--> 795      dtype_orig = np.result_type(*dtypes_orig)
     796 elif pandas_requires_conversion and any(d == object for d in dtypes_
orig):
     797      # Force object if any of the dtypes is an object
     798      dtype_orig = object
```

DTypePromotionError: The DType <class 'numpy.dtypes.DateTime64DType'> could not
be promoted by <class 'numpy.dtypes.Float64DType'>. This means that no common
DType exists for the given inputs. For example they cannot be stored in a
single array unless the dtype is `object`. The full list of DTypes is: (<class

```
'numpy.dtypes.DateTime64DType'>, <class 'numpy.dtypes.Int64DType'>, <class
'numpy.dtypes.Float64DType'>, <class 'numpy.dtypes.Float64DType'>, <class
'numpy.dtypes.Float64DType'>)
```

We're clearly getting an error back, so let's see if Copilot can help with this error. As usual, include context like the error text to get a good response.

[Prompt]

I am getting this error after running the code,

```
Cell 39 line 7 4 model = LinearRegression() 6 # Train the model ----> 7 model.
fit(X_train, y_train)
File ~/.conda/envs/myenv/lib/python3.12/site-packages/sklearn/base.py:1152, in
_fit_context..decorator..wrapper(estimator, *args, **kwargs) 1145 estimator._
validate_params() 1147 with config_context( 1148 skip_parameter_validation=(
1149 prefer_skip_nested_validation or global_skip_validation 1150 ) 1151 ): ->
1152 return fit_method(estimator, *args, **kwargs)
File ~/.conda/envs/myenv/lib/python3.12/site-packages/sklearn/linear_model/
base.py:678, in LinearRegression.fit(self, X, y, sample_weight) 674 n_jobs =
self.n_jobs 676 accept_sparse = False if self.positive else ["csr", "csc",
"coo"] --> 678 X, y = self._validate_data( 679 X, y, accept_sparse=accept_
sparse, y_numeric=True, multi_output=True 680 ) 682 has_sw = sample_weight is
not None 683 if has_sw: ... 796 elif pandas_requires_conversion and any(d ==
object for d in dtypes_orig): 797 # Force object if any of the dtypes is an
object 798 dtype_orig = object
DTypePromotionError: The DType <class 'numpy.dtypes.DateTime64DType'> could
not be promoted by <class 'numpy.dtypes.Float64DType'>. This means that no
common DType exists for the given inputs. For example they cannot be stored in
a single array unless the dtype is object. The full list of DTypes is: (<class
'numpy.dtypes.DateTime64DType'>, <class 'numpy.dtypes.Int64DType'>, <class
'numpy.dtypes.Float64DType'>, <class 'numpy.dtypes.Float64DType'>, <class
'numpy.dtypes.Float64DType'>)
```

[End of prompt]

You should receive a response similar to the response below:

[Prompt response]

The error message suggests that the model is having trouble handling the 'Date' column because it's in datetime format, and the model expects numerical input.

One common approach to deal with datetime data is to extract features from it, such as the year, month, day, etc. Here's how you can do it:

```
# Extract features from 'Date'
X_train['Year'] = X_train['Date'].dt.year
X_train['Month'] = X_train['Date'].dt.month
```

```
X_train['Day'] = X_train['Date'].dt.day

# Drop the original 'Date' column
X_train = X_train.drop('Date', axis=1)

# Do the same for the test set
X_test['Year'] = X_test['Date'].dt.year
X_test['Month'] = X_test['Date'].dt.month
X_test['Day'] = X_test['Date'].dt.day
X_test = X_test.drop('Date', axis=1)


# Now try to fit the model again
model.fit(X_train, y_train)
```

This code first extracts the year, month, and day from the 'Date' column and adds them as new columns in the DataFrame. Then it drops the original 'Date' column. Finally, it tries to fit the model again.

Please note that this is a simple approach and might not be the best way to handle datetime data for your specific problem. The best approach depends on the nature of your data and the problem you're trying to solve.

[End of response]

So, our Date column was the problem. The model training can only handle numerical data. It seems the response suggested we should extract features from the Date column though, like year, month, and day, to preserve the info, but in numerical form. Additionally, we should then drop the Date column as we got what we wanted from it.

Let's try running the suggested code:

```
# Extract features from 'Date'
X_train['Year'] = X_train['Date'].dt.year
X_train['Month'] = X_train['Date'].dt.month
X_train['Day'] = X_train['Date'].dt.day

# Drop the original 'Date' column
X_train = X_train.drop('Date', axis=1)

# Do the same for the test set
X_test['Year'] = X_test['Date'].dt.year
X_test['Month'] = X_test['Date'].dt.month
X_test['Day'] = X_test['Date'].dt.day
X_test = X_test.drop('Date', axis=1)

# Now try to fit the model again
model.fit(X_train, y_train)
LinearRegression()
```

You should now see your code running without any issues. Let's tell Copilot about this fact and see if it suggests how we can proceed.

[Prompt]

Thanks, that works.

[End of prompt]

You should receive a response similar to the response below:

[Prompt response]

You're welcome! I'm glad to hear that it worked. Now that your model is trained, the next step is usually to use the model to make predictions on your test data. After that, you can evaluate the performance of your model by comparing these predictions to the actual values in your test data. If you have any more questions or need further assistance, feel free to ask.

[End of response]

Evaluate the model

As suggested by the response, Copilot recommends asking the following: What are some common metrics for evaluating regression models? Let's select this and see what it says.

Evaluation metrics

Let's ask Copilot about evaluation metrics.

[Prompt]

What are some common metrics for evaluating regression models?

[End of prompt]

You should receive a response similar to the response below:

[Prompt response]

There are several common metrics for evaluating the performance of regression models:

- **Mean Absolute Error (MAE)**: This is the average of the absolute differences between the predicted and actual values. It gives an idea of how wrong the predictions were.
- **Mean Squared Error (MSE)**: This is the average of the squared differences between the predicted and actual values. Squaring the differences amplifies the impact of large errors.
- **Root Mean Squared Error (RMSE)**: This is the square root of the MSE. It has the same units as the output variable, making it easier to interpret than the MSE.
- **R-squared (R^2)**: This is the proportion of the variance in the dependent variable that is predictable from the independent variables. It provides a measure of how well the model's predictions fit the actual data. A value of 1 means the model perfectly predicts the actual values, while a value of 0 means the model does not predict the actual values at all.

- **Adjusted R-squared:** This is a modified version of R-squared that has been adjusted for the number of predictors in the model. It increases only if the new term improves the model more than would be expected by chance.

Each of these metrics has its own strengths and weaknesses, and the choice of which to use depends on the specific problem and the goals of the analysis.

[End of response]

Now that we know how to evaluate and with what metrics, let's make predictions next given our testing data, and see what we get in response.

[Prompt]

Make predictions and evaluate the model using different metrics.

[End of prompt]

You should receive a response similar to the response below:

[Prompt response]

Sure, let's use the trained model to make predictions on the test data. Then, we'll evaluate these predictions using Mean Absolute Error (MAE), Mean Squared Error (MSE), Root Mean Squared Error (RMSE), and R-squared (R^2). We'll use the metrics module from sklearn to calculate these metrics.

Here's how you can do it:

```python
from sklearn import metrics
import numpy as np

# Make predictions on the test data
y_pred = model.predict(X_test)

# Calculate MAE, MSE, RMSE, and R2
mae = metrics.mean_absolute_error(y_test, y_pred)
mse = metrics.mean_squared_error(y_test, y_pred)
rmse = np.sqrt(mse) # or metrics.mean_squared_error(y_test, y_pred,
squared=False)
r2 = metrics.r2_score(y_test, y_pred)

# Print the metrics
print("Mean Absolute Error (MAE):", mae)
print("Mean Squared Error (MSE):", mse)
print("Root Mean Squared Error (RMSE):", rmse)
print("R-squared (R2 ):", r2)
```

This code first uses the model to make predictions on the test data. Then it calculates the MAE, MSE, RMSE, and R^2 by comparing these predictions to the actual values in the test data. Finally, it prints out these metrics.

[End of response]

The code contains both metrics and calls a `predict()` function that produces a response from the model; let's try this and see if it works.

```
from sklearn import metrics
import numpy as np

# Make predictions on the test data
y_pred = model.predict(X_test)

# Calculate MAE, MSE, RMSE, and R2
mae = metrics.mean_absolute_error(y_test, y_pred)
mse = metrics.mean_squared_error(y_test, y_pred)
rmse = np.sqrt(mse) # or metrics.mean_squared_error(y_test, y_pred,
squared=False)
r2 = metrics.r2_score(y_test, y_pred)

# Print the metrics
print("Mean Absolute Error (MAE):", mae)
print("Mean Squared Error (MSE):", mse)
print("Root Mean Squared Error (RMSE):", rmse)
print("R-squared (R2 ):", r2)
```

You should see a response similar to the one below:

```
Mean Absolute Error (MAE): 0.458844690389933
Mean Squared Error (MSE): 0.4236006011305136
Root Mean Squared Error (RMSE): 0.6508460656180642
R-squared (R2 ): 0.999868004623502
```

Let's provide Copilot with the response below to learn what we should do next.

[Prompt]

```
Below is the output, Mean Absolute Error (MAE): 0.458844690389933 Mean
Squared Error (MSE): 0.4236006011305136 Root Mean Squared Error (RMSE):
0.6508460656180642 R-squared (R2 ): 0.999868004623502
```

[End of prompt]

You should receive a response similar to the response below:

[Prompt response]

Great! The output shows the calculated metrics for your regression model.

- **Mean Absolute Error (MAE):** The average absolute difference between the predicted and actual values is approximately 0.46. This means that on average, your predictions are about 0.46 units away from the actual values.
- **Mean Squared Error (MSE):** The average squared difference between the predicted and actual values is approximately 0.42. This metric is more sensitive to large errors than MAE because it squares the differences.
- **Root Mean Squared Error (RMSE):** The square root of the MSE is approximately 0.65. This metric is in the same units as the output variable, making it easier to interpret than the MSE.
- **R-squared (R^2):** The proportion of the variance in the dependent variable that is predictable from the independent variables is approximately 0.9999. This is very close to 1, which indicates that your model explains almost all of the variability of the response data around its mean.

Overall, these metrics suggest that your model is performing very well on the test data.

[End of response]

Next, we want to have a sense of how well the model is performing by comparing predicted values to actual values, so let's create a prompt to reflect that request.

[Prompt]

Display a comparison of predicted values versus actual values.

[End of prompt]

You should receive a response similar to the response below:

[Prompt response]

Sure, you can compare the predicted values with the actual values by visualizing them in a plot. Here's how you can do it using matplotlib:

```python
import matplotlib.pyplot as plt

# Plot the actual values
plt.scatter(X_test.index, y_test, color='blue', label='Actual')

# Plot the predicted values
plt.scatter(X_test.index, y_pred, color='red', label='Predicted')

plt.title('Actual vs Predicted')
plt.xlabel('Index')
plt.ylabel('Target')
plt.legend()
plt.show()
```

This code creates a scatter plot where the x-axis represents the index of the test set and the y-axis represents the target variable. The actual values are plotted in blue and the predicted values are plotted in red. This allows you to visually compare the predictions made by the model to the actual values.

[End of response]

The suggested code seems to want to create a scatter plot to better compare our predicted values compared to our test data:

```python
import matplotlib.pyplot as plt

# Plot the actual values
plt.scatter(X_test.index, y_test, color='blue', label='Actual')

# Plot the predicted values
plt.scatter(X_test.index, y_pred, color='red', label='Predicted')

plt.title('Actual vs Predicted')
plt.xlabel('Index')
plt.ylabel('Target')
plt.legend()
plt.show()
```

Here's the output from running the above code:

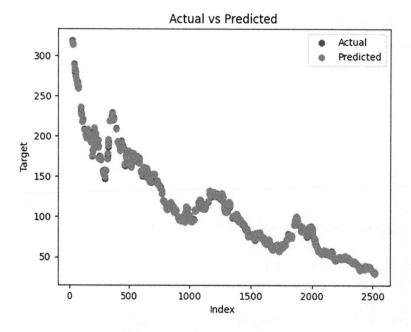

Figure 18.3: Actual versus predicted data

We can see how the predicted data matches the actual data quite well. Let's try to sum up our learning next.

Assignment

Instead of using regression to predict a value, let's take the same data but treat it as a classification problem and predict whether the stock price will go up or down the next day.

Summary

Regression is a fundamental concept in machine learning used to predict a continuous outcome variable based on one or more predictor variables. It involves identifying the relationship between a dependent variable (often called the target) and one or more independent variables (features). We saw that, given our dataset, we were able to find correlations for certain variables. We also found that we could include columns like Date, but to include these, we needed to extract the important numerical parts from those columns, namely the year, month, and date.

Regression has many applications in other sectors, like healthcare and marketing. From a prompt perspective, it's a good idea to set the context early on and show Copilot the shape of the data, which will then help you ask Copilot what to do next.

In the next chapter, we will use the same dataset while using GitHub Copilot to help us write some code.

Join our community on Discord

Join our community's Discord space for discussions with the author and other readers:

`https://packt.link/aicode`

19

Regression with Copilot Suggestions

Introduction

In the previous chapter, we used GitHub Copilot Chat to build a regression problem and explored how AI can assist in coding. In this chapter, we'll take a different approach. We will write code with the help of GitHub Copilot, allowing it to guide us through coding and adding helpful comments. This will be an interactive experience, combining our coding skills with Copilot's suggestions to effectively tackle a regression problem. Let's see how GitHub Copilot can enhance our coding process in real time.

In the task, we will use the Apple dataset to predict stock prices and help investors decide whether to buy or not. This is the same dataset we used in *Chapter 18*, *Regression with Copilot Chat*, where we used Copilot Chat to analyze it.

Dataset overview

This dataset provides us with a wealth of information about Apple's stock (traded under AAPL) over the past decade, starting from the year 2010. This data is incredibly valuable because it can help us develop forecasting algorithms to predict the future price of Apple's stock, which is crucial for making investment decisions. The data in this set has been collected and aggregated from 25 different stock exchanges.

To effectively use this data for forecasting, we need to understand the key elements: the features that influence our target, which is predicting stock prices.

The dataset includes five important values that indicate how the stock price changes over a specific period of time, which is typically one day, but it could also be one week or one month. These values are:

- **Open:** This is the stock price at the beginning of the trading day.
- **Close:** This is the stock price at the end of the trading day.
- **High:** This value shows the highest price the stock reached during the trading day.

- **Low:** This indicates the lowest price the stock hit during the trading day.
- **Volume:** This is the total number of shares that were traded throughout the day before the market closed.

Our focus will be on using historical price data, which includes these five recorded values, along with the stock's past performance, to make predictions about its future prices.

Prompt strategy

In this chapter, we'll use the "Exploratory prompt pattern" as described in *Chapter 2*. We feel pretty confident on what actions we want to take in general but is interested in what the AI assistant will generate in case we need to pivot.

Start coding with Copilot's help

With GitHub Copilot installed, you're ready to start coding your regression problem in Python. The approach of using suggestions in an open file is a bit different from using the chat window. The main difference is that we will rely on typing comments and use the *Tab* key to get Copilot to provide us with suggestions. This technique works equally well in Jupyter Notebook and normal text files. Here's how it works:

```
# generate import statements for libraries to use with a Regression problem
```

Here, we have an open text file. We've added comments to generate `import` statements. To get Copilot to generate a response, we need to use the *Return* key followed by the *Tab* key to accept the suggestion. Here's how the above text file could change:

```
# generate import statements for libraries to use with a Regression problem
import pandas
import numpy
import scikit-learn
```

The `import` statement is what is generated by Copilot when pressing *Tab* followed by *Return*.

 The AI assistant helps by providing code completion, but remember to review and understand each suggestion before accepting it.

Step 1: Import libraries with Copilot's assistance

We could start with a prompt suggestion comment that describes the problem upfront, the dataset, and more, just like we did with Copilot Chat in other chapters in this book. Then, the prompt could look like so:

```
# generate the steps I need to follow for performing a Regression problem,
here's my dataset and its columns
```

However, we will try an approach where we ask for everything we need.

Let's begin. Let's create our first comment (this is equivalent to typing in a chat window):

[Prompt]

import pandas

[End of prompt]

Accept the suggestion with *Tab*. You should see the following bold code:

[Prompt response]

```
# import pandas
import pandas as pd
```

[End of response]

Great! We have imported the libraries we need. Let's load and explore the dataset next.

Step 2: Load and explore the dataset

In the next step, we want to load the dataset and explore the data features. Keep working in the same file and add the below prompt:

[Prompt]

```
# Load the dataset into a pandas DataFrame
```

[End of prompt]

At this point, Copilot understands what we're trying to do, so we don't need to type more than the above prompt comment. So, we just need to press *Return* followed by *Tab* a number of times, and we should get the content below:

[Prompt response]

```
# Load the dataset into a pandas DataFrame
df = pd.read_csv('enter-your-file-path')

# Print the first 5 rows of the DataFrame
print(df.head())
```

[End of response]

Ensure you have downloaded the dataset from Kaggle (https://www.kaggle.com/ datasets/varpit94/apple-stock-data-updated-till-22jun2021) and that you have replaced the path in read_csv to point to where the file is in your system.

If you run the suggested code, you should see similar output to:

```
        Date    Close    Volume       Open     High      Low
0  02/28/2020  $273.36  106721200   $257.26  $278.41  $256.37
1  02/27/2020  $273.52   80151380    $281.1     $286  $272.96
2  02/26/2020  $292.65   49678430   $286.53  $297.88   $286.5
3  02/25/2020  $288.08   57668360   $300.95  $302.53  $286.13
4  02/24/2020  $298.18   55548830   $297.26  $304.18  $289.23
```

If you see the above, that means the data was loaded successfully.

Get types and columns

Great! Now that we've successfully loaded the data, let's learn more about the loaded dataset, such as what columns and column types it has. As usual, let's keep working on the same file and add a prompt as a comment like so:

[Prompt]

```
# Get the data types of the columns in the dataset
```

[End of prompt]

You should see the below results:

[Prompt response]

```
# Get the data types of the columns in the dataset
print(df.dtypes)
```

[End of response]

Now, let's run the code. It should show our columns and their data types:

```
Date        object
Close       object
Volume       int64
Open        object
High        object
Low         object
dtype: object
```

Great! We see the columns, but many of the columns have the object type. That's not good; they need to be numerical to be used in machine learning training. Let's see if we can address this shortly, but first, let's learn more about the shape of the dataset.

Shape of the dataset

Let's learn more about our dataset in terms of structure, like how many columns and how many rows it consists of. This will help us assess its complexity, see how much data we have, and whether it's enough to train a model to be reliable. Let's write our next prompt comment:

[Prompt]

```
# Get the shape of the dataset
```

[End of prompt]

You should see the below suggestion:

[Prompt response]

```
# Get the shape of the dataset
print(df.shape)
```

[End of response]

Running the code above should provide the response below:

```
(2518, 6)
```

This response tells us we have 2518 rows and 6 columns.

Addressing the column types

At this point, we know we need more numerical columns, so let's deal with the ones that aren't numerical. First, let's identify those non-numerical columns:

[Prompt]

```
# print the columns in the dataset
```

[End of prompt]

You should see a suggestion like below:

[Prompt response]

```
# print the columns in the dataset
print(df.columns)
Index(['Date', 'Close', 'Volume', 'Open', 'High', 'Low'], dtype='object')
```

[End of response]

It's interesting that although we just asked to print the columns, Copilot makes the decision to show us only the columns of the object type. It's not really surprising because Copilot has been trained on machine learning and is able to deduce what will happen next, which in this case is converting columns for use in model training.

Next, let's be a bit prescriptive and ask for columns to be converted to numerical versions with the below prompt comment:

[Prompt]

```
# Replace the $ symbol with an empty string and convert the column to float
data type
```

[End of prompt]

You should see the below code, which turns several columns into numerical versions.

[Prompt response]

```
# Replace the $ symbol with an empty string and convert the column to float
data type
df['Open'] = df['Open'].replace({'\$': ''}, regex=True).astype(float)
df['Close'] = df['Close'].replace({'\$': ''}, regex=True).astype(float)
df['High'] = df['High'].replace({'\$': ''}, regex=True).astype(float)
df['Low'] = df['Low'].replace({'\$': ''}, regex=True).astype(float)
```

[End of response]

Great! Let's inspect the columns next to ensure the conversion has been carried out correctly.

[Prompt]

```
# Print the first 5 rows of the DataFrame to confirm the changes
```

[End of prompt]

You should see a response similar to this:

[Prompt response]

```
# Print the first 5 rows of the DataFrame to confirm the changes
print(df.head())
```

[End of response]

If you run the above code, you should see the response below:

```
        Date    Close     Volume    Open    High     Low
0  02/28/2020  273.36  106721200  257.26  278.41  256.37
1  02/27/2020  273.52   80151380  281.10  286.00  272.96
2  02/26/2020  292.65   49678430  286.53  297.88  286.50
3  02/25/2020  288.08   57668360  300.95  302.53  286.13
4  02/24/2020  298.18   55548830  297.26  304.18  289.23
```

We can clearly see that the dollar signs have been removed and the columns are now numerical, save for the Date column, which we can deal with later.

Statistical summary

Next, let's learn a bit more about the dataset by asking for a statistical summary. We can expect to see these values:

- **Count:** The number of non-null entries
- **Mean:** The average value

- **Standard Deviation (std):** The spread of the data
- **Minimum (min):** The smallest value
- **25th Percentile (25%):** The value below which 25% of the data falls
- **Median (50%):** The middle value, also known as the 50th percentile
- **75th Percentile (75%):** The value below which 75% of the data falls
- **Maximum (max):** The largest value

With that in mind, let's write a prompt comment:

[Prompt]

```
# get the statistical summary of the dataset
```

[End of prompt]

You should see an output similar to this:

[Prompt response]

```
# get the statistical summary of the dataset
print(df.describe())
```

[End of response]

If you run the code, you will see data similar to this:

	Close	Volume	Open	High	Low
count	2518.000000	2.518000e+03	2518.000000	2518.000000	2518.000000
mean	114.769522	7.258009e+07	114.728443	115.766415	113.690582
std	60.662405	5.663113e+07	60.546893	61.134456	60.085105
min	29.835700	1.136205e+07	29.392800	29.928600	28.464300
25%	66.822475	3.053026e+07	66.877150	67.475300	66.372950
50%	101.090000	5.295469e+07	101.115000	102.085000	100.350000
75%					

Check for missing values

It's crucial to identify missing values to assess the quality of your dataset. High numbers of null values might indicate issues with data collection or entry and may affect our model, so we need a way to handle them:

[Prompt]

Check for missing values

[End of prompt]

You should see a response similar to this:

[Prompt response]

```
# check for missing values
print(df.isnull().sum())
```

[End of response]

Great! So, what does the code do? Well, let's explain. Let's say you have the following dataset:

```
data = {'A': [7, 99, None, 3, None],
        'B': [5, None, 6, 8, 9],
        'C': [10, 15, 12, None, 11]}
```

Running the suggested code would summarize the number of missing values per column, and you would see a response like this:

```
A: 2
B: 1
C: 1
```

What you can do is replace the missing value with a value that doesn't affect the overall score. One way to do so is to add the mean value and replace None with that.

Check for duplicates

Another way to clean up the data is to remove duplicated data, because you don't want that data to create a reinforcing effect on the model. Let's create a comment for that and see if Copilot can help us:

[Prompt]

```
print(df.duplicated().sum())
```

[End of prompt]

At this point, Copilot understands what we're trying to do, that is, identify and remove duplicates. So, you should see suggested code for both operations below:

[Prompt response]

```
# check for duplicates
print(df.duplicated().sum())

# drop duplicates
df.drop_duplicates(inplace=True)
```

[End of response]

Scale numerical features

Next, we're going to scale values, so they fall into a specific range, 0–1. This type of preprocessing will have beneficial effects on a number of things, such as algorithm performance, convergence speed, interpretability, and preventing a group of values from dominating. Let's create a prompt for scaling features:

[Prompt]

```
# Scale numerical features
```

[End of prompt]

Note that when there's more than one row in the response, you may need to press *Return* and *Tab* repeatedly. You should see output similar to this:

[Prompt response]

```
# Scale numerical features
# import StandardScaler
from sklearn.preprocessing import StandardScaler

scaler = StandardScaler()
df[['Open', 'Close', 'High', 'Low', 'Volume']] = scaler.fit_
transform(df[['Open', 'Close', 'High', 'Low', 'Volume']])

# Print the first 5 rows of the DataFrame to confirm the changes
print(df.head())
```

[End of response]

Running the suggested code should result in the below output:

	Date	Close	Volume	Open	High	Low
0	02/28/2020	2.614832	0.602988	2.354536	2.660953	2.375094
1	02/27/2020	2.617470	0.133721	2.748359	2.785130	2.651257
2	02/26/2020	2.932884	-0.404481	2.838059	2.979494	2.876649
3	02/25/2020	2.857534	-0.263366	3.076269	3.055571	2.870490
4	02/24/2020	3.024063	-0.300800	3.015313	3.082566	2.922093

Visualization

Next, we want to visualize our data. We could give vague instructions on how to do it, but in this case, a scatter plot is a good tool to use, so let's reflect that in the prompt:

[Prompt]

```
# Create a scatter plot of the Open and Close columns
```

[End of prompt]

You should see a response similar to this:

[Prompt response]

```
import matplotlib.pyplot as plt
```

```
# Create a scatter plot of the Open and Close columns
plt.scatter(df['Open'], df['Close'])
plt.xlabel('Open')
plt.ylabel('Close')
plt.title('Relationship between Open and Close')
plt.show()
```

[End of response]

Running the code above should result in a scatter plot like this:

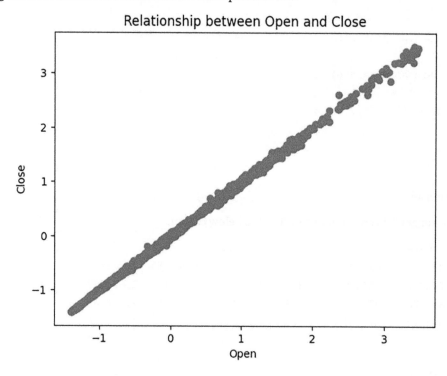

Figure 19.1: Scatter plot showing the relation between the Open and Close columns

Step 3: Split data into training and testing sets

Before we can train the model, we need to split the data into training data and test data. Let's create a prompt to help with this:

[Prompt]

"use train_test_split from scikit-learn to split the dataset"

[End of prompt]

You should see an output similar to:

[Prompt response]

```
# Use train_test_split from scikit-Learn to split the dataset
from sklearn.model_selection import train_test_split

# Drop the Date column from the DataFrame
df = df.drop('Date', axis=1)

# Split the dataset into training and testing sets
X = df.drop('Close', axis=1)
y = df['Close']
X_train, X_test, y_train, y_test = train_test_split(X, y, test_size=0.2,
random_state=42)
```

[End of response]

```
# Print the shapes of the training and testing sets
print('X_train shape:', X_train.shape)
print('y_train shape:', y_train.shape)
print('X_test shape:', X_test.shape)
print('y_test shape:', y_test.shape)
```

If you run the code above, you should see a response similar to:

```
X_train shape: (2014, 4)
y_train shape: (2014,)
X_test shape: (504, 4)
y_test shape: (504,)
```

Asking questions

Just like in the chat experience of Copilot, it's possible to ask questions on a specific topic. If you prefix a question with "Q:", Copilot understands it's a question. Let's try this to find out our next step:

[Prompt]

Q: what is the next step after splitting the data into training and testing sets?

[End of prompt]

You should see a response similar to:

[Prompt response]

```
# Q: what is the next step after splitting the data into training and testing
sets?
# A: train the model using the training set and test the model using the tesing
set
```

[End of response]

Step 4: Build a regression problem

The time has come to train the model. You could be pretty vague here and just ask Copilot to perform training. It's recommended, however, to suggest the type of training you want. In this case, we want linear regression, so let's create a prompt that includes that:

[Prompt]

"initialize a LinearRegression model".

[End of prompt]

You should see a response similar to this:

[Prompt response]

```
# initialize a LinearRegression model
# import LinearRegression
from sklearn.linear_model import LinearRegression

# Instantiate LinearRegression as lr
lr = LinearRegression()
```

[End Suggestion Response]

Great! We have some code that ensures we use linear regression. We haven't carried out any training, though, so that's next.

Step 5: Train the model

With the type of training specified, let's train the model next:

[Prompt]

"fit the model"

[End of prompt]

You should see a response similar to this:

[Prompt response]

```
# Fit lr to the training data
lr.fit(X_train, y_train)

# Predict the labels of the test set
y_pred = lr.predict(X_test)
```

[End of response]

Step 6: Evaluate model performance

Great! We have trained the model, but we don't know anything about how well it performs, and that's something we should address next:

[Prompt]

Evaluate the performance metrics like MSE or R-squared.

[End of prompt]

You should see an output similar to this:

[Prompt response]

```
#evaluate the performance metrics like MSE or R-squared

from sklearn.metrics import mean_squared_error

# Calculate the Mean Squared Error (MSE) of the model on the testing set
mean_squared_error = mean_squared_error(y_test, y_pred)
print('Mean squared error:', mean_squared_error)

# Calculate the Root Mean Squared Error (RMSE) of the model on the testing set
root_mean_squared_error = np.sqrt(mean_squared_error)
print('Root mean squared error:', root_mean_squared_error)
```

[End of response]

If you run the above code, you should see a response like this:

```
MSE: 0.00011569609998631774
RMSE: 0.010756212157926123
```

The output we get represents two different errors: mean squared error and root mean squared error.

A lower MSE indicates a better fit of the model to the data. In this case, the MSE is quite low, suggesting that the model's predictions are very close to the actual values.

The RMSE value is also very low, reinforcing that the model's predictions are highly accurate. Great! Let's go over this chapter's assignment, and then summarize what we have learned about using Copilot to help us with machine learning.

Assignment

Try to solve this problem using a prompting approach where you provide a lot of information upfront. We suggest constructing a prompt like so:

- "Carry out regression on a dataset with the following shape:
- Open: This is the stock price at the beginning of the trading day.

- Close: This represents the stock price at the end of the trading day.
- High: This value shows the highest price the stock reached during the trading day.
- Low: This indicates the lowest price the stock hit during the trading day.
- Volume: This is the total number of shares that were traded throughout the day before the market closed.

Suggest all the steps from loading and pre-processing the data to training and evaluating the model. You must show code for each step."

Then see what the response is and try to run the suggested code snippet for each step. If you encounter any issues, indicate the error to Copilot with a question prompt like so:

- "Q: the below/above code doesn't work, please fix"

Don't forget to press *Return* and *Tab* to accept the completion.

Summary

In this chapter, we wanted to use the suggestion feature of GitHub Copilot, meaning we would type comments and use the *Return* and *Tab* keys to receive suggestions from Copilot. There's a bit of a trick to it because sometimes you need to repeatedly press *Return* and *Tab* to get the full response. It's also an AI experience that's well suited to whenever you actively write code. GitHub Copilot Chat also has a place. In fact, the two different experiences complement one another; choose how much of each approach you want to use. Also, always test the code suggested by Copilot and ask Copilot to fix the code output if needed.

Join our community on Discord

Join our community's Discord space for discussions with the author and other readers:

```
https://packt.link/aicode
```

20

Increasing Efficiency with GitHub Copilot

Introduction

So far, you've been using the knowledge you were taught at the beginning of the book about GitHub Copilot and ChatGPT. This foundational knowledge was enough to teach you how to write prompts and accept them. It was also enough to let you start work on creating solutions for machine learning, data science, and web development. In the case of web development, you also discovered Copilot is an efficient tool when working with existing code bases. In this chapter, we want to take your AI tool knowledge to the next level, as there are more features that you may want to leverage.

There are a lot of things that can be done to increase efficiency; you will see later in the chapter how there are features within Copilot that let you scaffold files, and you will learn more about your workspace and even Visual Studio Code as an editor, which are all time-saving features. This chapter will cover some of the most important features.

In this chapter, we will:

- Learn how to use Copilot to generate code.
- Use Copilot commands to automate tasks, like generating a new project.
- Apply techniques to debug and troubleshoot code.
- Review and optimize code using Copilot.

Code generation and automation

At its core, Copilot is a code generator. It can generate text for you that is either part of documentation or source code.

There are two primary ways to generate code with Copilot:

- Copilot's active editor via prompts as comments.
- Copilot Chat, which lets you type in a prompt.

Copilot's active editor

When you're in the active editor, Copilot can generate code. To generate code, you need to write a prompt as a comment. There are different ways to add comments to your programming language code. In JavaScript and C#, for example, you use //, while you would type <!-- if you're in HTML.

Let's see an example of this:

[Prompt]

Create a new function called add that takes two parameters.

[End of prompt]

```
//Create a new function called add that takes two parameters
```

Above, we have a prompt as a comment. Copilot looks at this prompt and attempts to generate code based on it. At this point, Copilot sends the generated code back as a "suggestion," which you can accept using the Tab key. Here's what it looks like in the editor:

```
// Create a new function called add that takes two parameters

function add(num1, num2) {
    throw new Error('Function not implemented.');
}
```

At this point, you get no suggestions. You have a couple of options:

- You can press the Return key to get more suggestions.
- Start typing part of the code you want to generate, and Copilot will suggest code based on what you type.

Copilot Chat

Copilot Chat is a way to interact with Copilot using a chat interface. To activate Copilot Chat, click on the icon in the bottom-left corner of Visual Studio Code (or VS Code), which will open up a chat window.

Figure 20.1: Showing the left menu in Visual Studio Code with the "Chat" icon from Copilot Chat

Upon clicking the above chat icon, the below image will be shown.

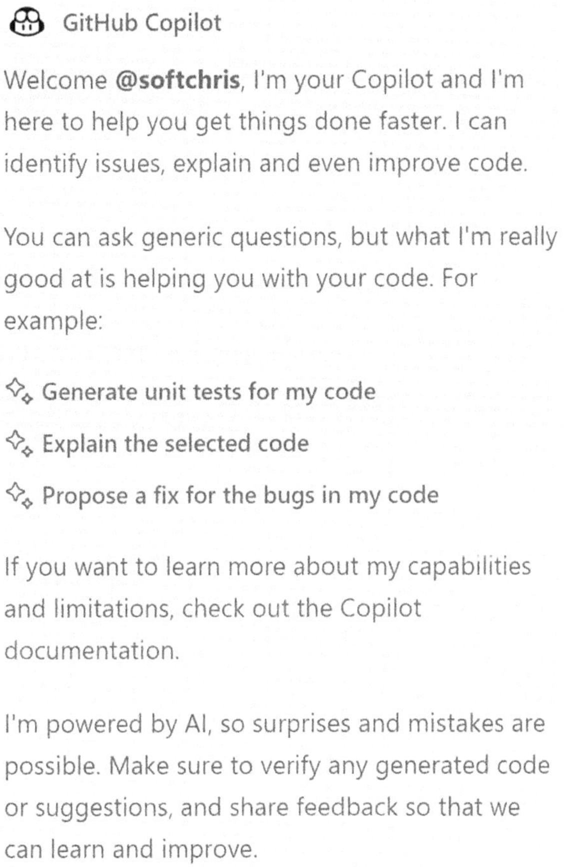

GitHub Copilot

Welcome **@softchris**, I'm your Copilot and I'm here to help you get things done faster. I can identify issues, explain and even improve code.

You can ask generic questions, but what I'm really good at is helping you with your code. For example:

✧ Generate unit tests for my code

✧ Explain the selected code

✧ Propose a fix for the bugs in my code

If you want to learn more about my capabilities and limitations, check out the Copilot documentation.

I'm powered by AI, so surprises and mistakes are possible. Make sure to verify any generated code or suggestions, and share feedback so that we can learn and improve.

Figure 20.2: The image above shows the chat window that opens when you click the Chat icon in the left menu in Visual Studio Code

Let's try to generate some code based on the same prompt as before. Let's use the input text field in the chat window and type in the prompt:

[Prompt]

Create a new function called add that takes two parameters

[End of prompt]

The output comes in two parts, a text instruction and a code suggestion. First, the text instruction:

[Prompt response]

Sure, here's an example of a function called add that takes two parameters and returns their sum:

```
function add(a, b) {
  return a + b;
}
```

[End of response]

It even shows you an example of how to use the function:

```
const result = add(2, 3);
console.log(result); // Output: 5
```

Copilot commands

If you start typing / in the chat window, you will see a list of commands that you can use with Copilot.

@terminal	Ask how to do something in the terminal
@vscode	Ask about VS Code
/api	@vscode
@workspace	Ask about your workspace
/explain	@workspace
/fix	@workspace
/new	@workspace
/newNotebook	@workspace
/tests	@workspace
/help	
/clear	

Figure 20.3: Available commands

There are quite a few available commands, and we will focus on a few of them in this chapter.

Creating a Notebook

With this command, you can create a new notebook. A notebook is a place where you can store code snippets and text. To create a notebook, type in /newNotebook, and also provide a name for the notebook, for example, products.

@workspace /newNotebook products

 GitHub Copilot used @workspace /newNotebook

Here's an outline for a Jupyter notebook on handling product data:

- **Import Required Libraries**
- **Load Product Data**
- **Data Exploration**
- **Data Cleaning**
- **Data Analysis**
- **Visualize Product Sales**

Create Notebook

Figure 20.4: Creating a Notebook

The above image shows what's displayed when you type the /newNotebook command; you're asked to confirm the scaffolding of a notebook by clicking **Create Notebook**.

This will create a new notebook with commonly used code snippets for products. Let's inspect the output next.

Your notebook, at a high level, contains the following:

- import, which contains all the imports needed to work with a dataset; here's what the content looks like:

```
import pandas as pd # Import Pandas library
import numpy as np # Import NumPy library
import matplotlib.pyplot as plt # Import Matplotlib library for data
visualization
import seaborn as sns # Import Seaborn library for data visualization
```

- Load data, which contains code to load data from a CSV file (the CSV file `product_data.csv` doesn't exist, but Copilot assumes that you have such a file; adjust this part of the code to fit the name of the CSV file that you do have):

```python
# Load product data from CSV file into a Pandas DataFrame
product_data = pd.read_csv('product_data.csv')

# Load product data from JSON file into a Pandas DataFrame
# product_data = pd.read_json('product_data.json')

# Display the first 5 rows of the DataFrame
print(product_data.head())
```

- Explore product data, which contains operations to inspect the data:

```python
# Use Pandas functions to explore the product data
# Display the last 5 rows of the DataFrame
print(product_data.tail())

# Display the summary information of the DataFrame
print(product_data.info())

# Display the statistical summary of the DataFrame
print(product_data.describe())
```

- Filter product data, which contains operations to filter the data:

```python
# Filter product data based on specific criteria using boolean indexing
filtered_data = product_data[(product_data['category'] == 'electronics')
& (product_data['price'] < 100)]

# Display the filtered data
print(filtered_data)
```

- Sorting data, which contains sorting operations:

```python
# Sort the product data based on one or more columns using the sort_
values() function
# Sort by price in ascending order
product_data.sort_values(by='price', ascending=True, inplace=True)

# Sort by category in ascending order, then by price in descending order
product_data.sort_values(by=['category', 'price'], ascending=[True,
False], inplace=True)
```

```
# Display the sorted data
print(product_data)
```

- Aggregating data; often, you want to aggregate data to get a better understanding of it:

```
# Group the product data by category and calculate the total price for
each category
category_total_price = product_data.groupby('category')['price'].sum()


# Display the total price for each category
print(category_total_price)


# Group the product data by category and calculate the average price for
each category
category_avg_price = product_data.groupby('category')['price'].mean()


# Display the average price for each category
print(category_avg_price)


# Group the product data by category and calculate the number of
products in each category
category_product_count = product_data.groupby('category')['product_id'].
count()


# Display the number of products in each category
print(category_product_count)
```

In summary, that's a lot of code you don't have to write yourself. You can use this notebook as a starting point to work with product data.

Creating a project

Another really useful command is being able to create a project. Usually, we either create files by hand, which takes time, or we rely on CLI tools to create projects for us. With Copilot, you can create a project by typing in /new in the chat window. To use the command, type /new and then provide a description for it, for example, **React**. This will create a new project with a React project template. Let's inspect the output:

```
my-react-app
├── public
│   ├── index.html
│   └── favicon.ico
├── src
│   ├── App.js
│   ├── index.js
```

```
|       ├── components
|       |       ├── Customer.js
|       |       ├── Product.js
|       |       ├── CustomerList.js
|       |       └── ProductList.js
|       ├── data
|       |       ├── customers.json
|       |       └── products.json
|       └── styles
|               ├── App.css
|               ├── Customer.css
|               ├── Product.css
|               ├── CustomerList.css
|               └── ProductList.css
├── package.json
└── README.md
```

The files created above are typical of what's expected for a React project. It contains:

- `public`, which contains the `index.html` file that references the JavaScript file indicating the location of your app.
- `src`, which contains all the application files and is itself divided into different folders for components, data, and CSS styles.

All of this constitutes a starting point. You might want to change files to fit your liking.

Debugging and troubleshooting

Being able to debug and troubleshoot code is an important skill to have. When you develop code, it seldom does what you need it to do the first time. You need to be able to debug and troubleshoot code to figure out what's wrong with it. The same applies if you have a reported bug; you need to be able to diagnose at what point it goes wrong.

Copilot can help, and a good approach is using Copilot chat and asking it to add support for debugging and troubleshooting.

The following is a piece of sample code you've been given. It's a REST API in the framework Flask for Python. It's working code, but it might not be so easy to work with from a debugging and troubleshooting standpoint:

```python
from flask import Flask, jsonify, request
import sqlite3

app = Flask(__name__)

# Create a connection to the database
```

```python
conn = sqlite3.connect('products.db')
c = conn.cursor()

# Create a table for products if it doesn't exist
c.execute('''CREATE TABLE IF NOT EXISTS products
             (id INTEGER PRIMARY KEY AUTOINCREMENT,
              name TEXT,
              price REAL)''')
conn.commit()

@app.route('/products', methods=['GET'])
def get_products():
    # Retrieve all products from the database
    c.execute('SELECT * FROM products')
    products = c.fetchall()

    # Convert the products to a JSON response
    response = []
    for product in products:
        response.append({
            'id': product[0],
            'name': product[1],
            'price': product[2]
        })
    return jsonify(response)

@app.route('/products', methods=['POST'])
def add_product():
    # Retrieve the product data from the request body
    data = request.get_json()
    name = data['name']
    price = data['price']

    # Insert the product into the database
    c.execute('INSERT INTO products (name, price) VALUES (?, ?)', (name,
price))
    conn.commit()

    # Return a success message
    return jsonify({'message': 'Product added successfully'})

if __name__ == '__main__':
    app.run(debug=True)
```

The above code works, but it doesn't support debugging and troubleshooting; let's see how we can add support for that by using Copilot Chat:

[Prompt]

Add support for troubleshooting and debugging

[End of prompt]

Copilot chat answers us with both text and code:

[Prompt response]

Sure, here's an updated version of the Flask API that includes support for troubleshooting and debugging:

```python
from flask import Flask, jsonify, request
import sqlite3


app = Flask(__name__)

# Create a connection to the database
conn = sqlite3.connect('products.db')
c = conn.cursor()

# Create a table for products if it doesn't exist
c.execute('''CREATE TABLE IF NOT EXISTS products
             (id INTEGER PRIMARY KEY AUTOINCREMENT,
              name TEXT,
              price REAL)''')
conn.commit()


@app.route('/products', methods=['GET'])
def get_products():
    try:
        # Retrieve all products from the database
        c.execute('SELECT * FROM products')
        products = c.fetchall()

        # Convert the products to a JSON response
        response = []
        for product in products:
            response.append({
                'id': product[0],
                'name': product[1],
```

```
                    'price': product[2]
            })
        return jsonify(response)
    except Exception as e:
        # Log the error and return an error message
        app.logger.error(str(e))
        return jsonify({'error': 'An error occurred while retrieving
products'})


@app.route('/products', methods=['POST'])
def add_product():
    try:
        # Retrieve the product data from the request body
        data = request.get_json()
        name = data['name']
        price = data['price']

        # Insert the product into the database
        c.execute('INSERT INTO products (name, price) VALUES (?, ?)', (name,
price))
        conn.commit()

        # Return a success message
        return jsonify({'message': 'Product added successfully'})
    except Exception as e:
        # Log the error and return an error message
        app.logger.error(str(e))
        return jsonify({'error': 'An error occurred while adding the product'})


if __name__ == '__main__':
    app.run(debug=True)
```

The improvements are:

- Added a try/except block around the code in the get_products() function.
- Added logger statements to log errors.
- Added debug=True to the app.run() statement.

These changes will help us troubleshoot and debug the code.

[End of response]

Let's look at how we can use Copilot to help us with code reviews and optimizations next.

Code review and optimization techniques

Right now, we have code that works, but it's not optimized. For example, it's usually a good idea to separate code into different files. Let's see what Copilot suggests to improve the code.

[Prompt]

Improve the selected code

[End of prompt]

As usual, we get the Copilot chat response in terms of text and code:

[Prompt response]

Sure, here are some improvements you could make to the selected code:

- Use a context manager to handle the database connection and cursor. This ensures that the connection is properly closed when the code is finished executing, even if an exception occurs.
- Use a list comprehension to convert the products to a JSON response. This is more concise and can be faster than using a for loop.
- Use the json parameter of the Response object to return a JSON response. This is more concise than using the jsonify function.
- Use the request.json attribute to retrieve the product data from the request body. This is a more concise and Pythonic way to do it.

and the resulting code:

```python
from flask import Flask, Response, request
import sqlite3


app = Flask(__name__)


# Create a table for products if it doesn't exist
with sqlite3.connect('products.db') as conn:
    c = conn.cursor()
    c.execute('''CREATE TABLE IF NOT EXISTS products
                (id INTEGER PRIMARY KEY AUTOINCREMENT,
                name TEXT,
                price REAL)''')
    conn.commit()


@app.route('/products', methods=['GET'])
def get_products():
    try:
        # Retrieve all products from the database
        with sqlite3.connect('products.db') as conn:
```

```python
        conn.row_factory = sqlite3.Row
        c = conn.cursor()
        c.execute('SELECT * FROM products')
        products = c.fetchall()

        # Convert the products to a JSON response
        response = [{'id': product['id'], 'name': product['name'], 'price':
product['price']} for product in products]
        return Response(response=response, status=200, mimetype='application/
json')
    except Exception as e:
        # Log the error and return an error message
        app.logger.error(str(e))
        return Response(response={'error': 'An error occurred while retrieving
products'}, status=500, mimetype='application/json')


@app.route('/products', methods=['POST'])
def add_product():
    try:
        # Retrieve the product data from the request body
        data = request.json
        name = data['name']
        price = data['price']

        # Insert the product into the database
        with sqlite3.connect('products.db') as conn:
            c = conn.cursor()
            c.execute('INSERT INTO products (name, price) VALUES (?, ?)',
(name, price))
            conn.commit()

        # Return a success message
        return Response(response={'message': 'Product added successfully'},
status=201, mimetype='application/json')
    except Exception as e:
        # Log the error and return an error message
        app.logger.error(str(e))
        return Response(response={'error': 'An error occurred while adding the
product'}, status=500, mimetype='application/json')


if __name__ == '__main__':
    app.run(debug=True)
```

The biggest change above was using a context manager to handle the database connection and cursor. This ensures that the connection is properly closed when the code has finished executing, even if an exception occurs.

We still want to separate the code into different files; let's see what Copilot suggests for that.

Let's start with a prompt:

[Prompt]

Separate the code into separate files by responsibility

[End of prompt]

and the resulting code:

[Prompt response]

```python
# app.py
from flask import Flask
from products import products_bp


app = Flask(__name__)
app.register_blueprint(products_bp)


if __name__ == '__main__':
    app.run(debug=True)
# database.py
import sqlite3


def get_db():
    db = sqlite3.connect('products.db')
    db.row_factory = sqlite3.Row
    return db
# products.py
from flask import Blueprint, jsonify, request
from database import get_db


products_bp = Blueprint('products', __name__)


@products_bp.route('/products', methods=['GET'])
def get_products():
    try:
        # Retrieve all products from the database
```

```python
        db = get_db()
        products = db.execute('SELECT * FROM products').fetchall()

        # Convert the products to a JSON response
        response = [{'id': product['id'], 'name': product['name'], 'price':
product['price']} for product in products]
        return jsonify(response)
    except Exception as e:
        # Log the error and return an error message
        app.logger.error(str(e))
        return jsonify({'error': 'An error occurred while retrieving
products'}), 500


@products_bp.route('/products', methods=['POST'])
def add_product():
    try:
        # Retrieve the product data from the request body
        data = request.json.get('data', {})
        name = data.get('name', '')
        price = data.get('price', 0)

        # Insert the product into the database
        db = get_db()
        db.execute('INSERT INTO products (name, price) VALUES (?, ?)', (name,
price))
        db.commit()

        # Return a success message
        return jsonify({'message': 'Product added successfully'}), 201
    except Exception as e:
        # Log the error and return an error message
        app.logger.error(str(e))
        return jsonify({'error': 'An error occurred while adding the
product'}), 500
```

[End of response]

 If you receive any errors while running the code, consult Copilot, tell it there's an error, and ask it to address the issue. Remember that Copilot is more than a code generator.

What we're seeing now is a separation of concerns. The app.py file is responsible for starting the application and registering the blueprint. The database.py file is responsible for handling the database connection. The products.py file is responsible for handling the products API. This code is something we can work with and maintain.

This code can be improved further by changing database.py to use a context manager:

```python
import sqlite3

def get_db():
    with sqlite3.connect('products.db') as db:
        db.row_factory = sqlite3.Row
        return db

def init_db():
    with sqlite3.connect('products.db') as db:
        db.execute('''CREATE TABLE IF NOT EXISTS products
                        (id INTEGER PRIMARY KEY AUTOINCREMENT,
                        name TEXT,
                        price REAL)''')
        db.commit()

# other code omitted for brevity
```

Here, you saw how Copilot can review your code in steps, splitting a single file into multiple files, and then improving the code.

Workspace

Your workspace is all the files you have open in a directory. You want your AI assistant to consider all these files when giving you a recommendation. Let's look at the following web project where the following files exist:

```
src/
  app.py
  utils.py
```

`app.py` contains an API and `utils.py` contains an email validation function. Here's the code for `app.py`:

```python
# create a web api using Flask, should have a products GET route


from flask import Flask, jsonify
app = Flask(__name__)


@app.route('/customers, methods=['GET'])
def get_customers():
    return jsonify({'customers': ['item1', 'item2', 'item3']})
# TODO, create a POST route for products
# Run the app
if __name__ == '__main__':
    app.run(debug=True)
```

Note the `TODO` comment; we're about to add a route to store a customer. When storing this customer, we need to ensure that the customer data contains a valid email. Luckily, the `utils.py` file already contains such a function, but can we get Copilot to use it? Let's see.

Change the comment in `app.py` to say the following:

[Prompt]

TODO, create a POST route for customers. It should validate the request body, and ensure it has a valid email address.

[End of prompt]

You get a basic function that doesn't really do what it's supposed to:

[Prompt response]

```python
@app.route('/customers', methods=['POST'])
def post_customers():
    return jsonify({'message': 'success'})
```

[End of response]

To help with this, you resort to GitHub Chat and type in the following prompt:

[Prompt]

Validate the request body and ensure that it has a valid email address

[End of prompt]

[Prompt response]

To validate the request body and ensure it has a valid email address, you can use the `request` object from Flask and a regular expression. Here's how you can modify your `post_customers` function:

```python
from flask import request
import re

@app.route('/customers', methods=['POST'])
def post_customers():
    data = request.get_json()

    if 'email' not in data:
        return jsonify({'message': 'No email provided'}), 400

    email = data['email']
    pattern = r'\b[A-Za-z0-9._%+-]+@[A-Za-z0-9.-]+\.[A-Z|a-z]{2,}\b'

    if not re.match(pattern, email):
        return jsonify({'message': 'Invalid email format'}), 400

    return jsonify({'message': 'success'})
```

[End of response]

While the above code works, it doesn't leverage our existing `utils.py` file, in which there is a function already solving validating an email. So how do we get Copilot to consider that file? The answer lies in a command called @workspace. The @worskspace command considers all the files. Here's how it can be used:

[Prompt]

@workspace improve selected code to validate request body to ensure it contains a valid email address, use primarily functionality from other files in the workspace to solve the problem.

[End of prompt]

> @workspace improve selected code to validate request body to ensure it contains a valid email address, use primarily functionality from other files in the workspace to solve the problem

---

    👾   </>   **GitHub Copilot** used @workspace   👍 👎

Used 3 references   >

You can modify the `post_customers` function in your `app.py` to use the `validate_email` function from `utils.py`. Here's how you can do it:

```python
from flask import request
from utils import validate_email

@app.route('/customers', methods=['POST'])
def post_customers():
    data = request.get_json()

    if 'email' not in data:
        return jsonify({'message': 'No email provi

    email = data['email']

    if not validate_email(email):
        return jsonify({'message': 'Invalid email

    return jsonify({'message': 'success'})
```

Figure 20.5: Image from Copilot Chat showing how using the @workspace command leverages existing code and code files in the workspace to solve a problem, rather than creating new code.

Let's also show the response in code and discuss what we can see:

[Prompt response]

```python
from flask import request
from utils import validate_email


@app.route('/customers', methods=['POST'])
def post_customers():
    data = request.get_json()

    if 'email' not in data:
        return jsonify({'message': 'No email provided'}), 400

    email = data['email']

    if not validate_email(email):
        return jsonify({'message': 'Invalid email format'}), 400

    return jsonify({'message': 'success'})
```

[End of response]

In the code above, `validate_email`, residing in the file `utils.py`, is used to validate an email. This is important as the first attempt, and solving this problem led to Copilot duplicating code. For that reason, using @workspace is recommended when you want Copilot to consider all code in your workspace when suggesting a solution.

Visual Studio Code lookup

Another powerful feature of Copilot is being able to quickly look up how to do something in Visual Studio Code. Rather than consulting official documentation, you may want to quickly find what you need without leaving your code editor. To use this feature, there's a @vscode command. Let's ensure we have the chat window open and see how it works with the following prompt:

[Prompt]

@vscode How do I open a terminal window?

[End of prompt]

GitHub Copilot used @vscode

You can open a terminal window in VS Code by using the **Terminal: Create New Terminal** command.

Show in Command Palette

Figure 20.6: Copilot response to the above prompt

There are two things worth noting here:

- Copilot tells you how to do something and where to find it.
- It offers to visually show you how to find what you need if you click the **Show in Command Palette** button.

Terminal

The last really great feature we will show you is terminal commands. In theory, you could use terminal without resorting to this specific command, but it helps if you don't have to prefix your question with "Show me how to do something in the terminal." To use this command, prefix your prompt with @terminal like so:

[Prompt]

@terminal show me how to create a remote called upstream in Git that points to a remote repo.

[End of prompt]

[Prompt response]

To create a remote called "upstream" that points to a remote repository in Git, you can use the git remote add command. Here's the command:

- git remote add upstream {remote_repo_url}
- Replace {remote_repo_url} with the URL of the remote repository.
- This command adds a new remote named "upstream" that points to the specified remote repository. You can then fetch from or push to the "upstream" remote as needed.
- {remote_repo_url}: The URL of the remote repository. This could be a URL on GitHub, GitLab, Bitbucket, or any other Git server.

[End of response]

As you can see, you get both the command you need and a detailed explanation of how to type.

Assignment

See if you can improve the code further by adding, for example, documentation, tests, or maybe an ORM (object-relational mapper). Remember to use the commands covered in this chapter.

Challenge

Check out the other commands that Copilot Chat supports, and see if you can use them to improve your workflow.

Quiz

What can Copilot help with?

    a.   Code generation, automation, debugging, troubleshooting, code review, and optimization

    b.   Deployment

    c.   None of the above

Summary

In this chapter, we covered some more advanced functionality available in Copilot. You learned how to use `@workspace` to enable Copilot to consider all your files. The `@vscode` command was another useful command in that it showed you how to work with Visual Studio Code.

We also looked at scaffolding – specifically, how to scaffold files for a web project – and how to create a Notebook with starter code. Such commands are likely to save you hours when you first start with a project. Copilot has quite a few commands, and I recommend trying them out.

Join our community on Discord

Join our community's Discord space for discussions with the author and other readers:

`https://packt.link/aicode`

21

Agents in Software Development

Introduction

This chapter will introduce you to the concept of agents in software development. We'll cover what agents are, how they work, and how you can use them in your projects. We'll also cover some of the most popular agents' frameworks and how you can get started with them.

Let's introduce the problems that agents can solve. The general idea is to have a program that can act on your behalf. Examples of this could be automating tasks, making decisions, and interacting with other agents and humans. Programs like these can save you time and make your life easier or your business more efficient.

In this chapter, we will do the following:

- Introduce the concept of agents in software development.
- Explain what agents are and how they work.
- Discuss the different types of agents and how they can be used.

What are agents?

As mentioned previously, agents are programs that can act on your behalf. They can perform tasks, make decisions, and interact with other agents and humans. Agents can be used in a wide range of applications.

Several things make a program an agent program versus just a program:

- **Agent programs have a clear goal:** For instance, take a thermostat keeping the temperature at 25 degrees and taking appropriate actions to keep it there, or an agent managing finances and trying to maximize your profit.
- **Autonomous:** An agent makes necessary decisions to ensure it meets a goal as defined previously. For a finance agent, that could mean buying and selling stocks when they meet a specific trigger condition.

- **Has sensors:** Sensors are either physical or could be an API in software, something that enables an agent to understand "what the world is like." For a thermostat, a sensor is a temperature indicator, but for a finance agent, a sensor can be an API toward the stock market that enables the agents to decide their goals.

How do agents work?

Agents work by receiving input, processing it, and producing output. They can be programmed to perform specific tasks, make decisions, and interact with other agents and humans. Agents can also learn from their interactions and improve their performance over time.

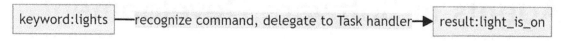

Figure 21.1: Process for simple agent: keyword, recognize, perform task

Simpler agents versus agents using AI

Agents are not a new thing. They have been around for a long time. What's new is that agents are now being powered by AI. Let's compare the two:

- **Simpler agents:** Traditional agents are programmed to perform specific tasks and make decisions based on predefined rules and logic.
- **Agents using AI:** Agents powered by AI can perform more complex tasks and make more intelligent decisions. They can understand natural language, learn from their interactions, and improve their performance over time.

Simpler agents

Simpler agents, as mentioned in the previous sections, are limited in that they are made for specific tasks. Interacting with them is usually also limited – you either use keywords or the way you can express yourself is limited.

An example of a simple agent is a chatbot. Such chatbots are programmed to understand a limited set of keywords and phrases.

For example, "Tell me more about your products," or "What's your return policy?". Any attempts at conversation outside of these keywords and phrases will result in the chatbot not understanding the user.

A simple agent is not a great conversationalist

When you have a conversation with a human, you expect them to know a few topics well and at least to be able to talk about other topics. For a simpler agent, we might end up in the following conversation:

- User: "Tell me about your products."

- Agent: "We have a wide range of products, including electronics, clothing, and accessories. Please indicate your interest."
- User: "I'm interested in clothes, something fitting the current weather."
- Agent: "I can advise on **clothes** for sure, but I don't know the **current weather**."

There are two interesting things we can observe here:

- The conversation feels short, and the important information is either at the end of a sentence or just before a comma, which indicates that simpler parsing is used to extract the important information.
- It doesn't handle non-product information like weather, which could help filter down the response.

Improved conversation with tool calling and large language models (LLMs)

An LLM is an improvement in that it's good at sounding more natural, but also that it can parse out and recognize intent from fluent text. You can also provide the LLM with additional knowledge thanks to something called tool calling, where you tell the LLM about various capabilities like the clothes API, weather API, and so on, which can handle the conversation better, and resemble a conversation with a human. Let's take that same conversation with an LLM and highlight the difference:

- User: "What are your products?"
- Agent: "We have a wide range of products, including electronics, clothing, and accessories."
- User: "Great, I'm interested in clothes, something fitting the current weather. What can you recommend?"
- Agent: "Can you tell me your location so I can advise you better on clothes?"
- User: "Sure, I'm based in Phoenix, Arizona."
- Agent: "I see it's currently 90F in Phoenix at the moment. Might I suggest these shorts?"

The reason this conversation fared better is that this LLM expresses itself more naturally thanks to the tool calling that called its weather API with Phoenix as input and then proceeded to call the clothes API with the weather response as a filter.

The anatomy of a conversational agent

A conversational agent typically consists of the following components:

- **Input:** The input to the agent, typically in the form of natural language. It should be said this can be a lot of different spoken languages, not just English, which you have had to hardcode in the past.
- **Processing:** The processing of the input, typically using **natural language processing (NLP)** techniques.

- **Delegation:** The delegation of the input to the appropriate component of the agent. The component it's delegated to can be an agent for a specific task, for example, to book a flight or to answer a question.

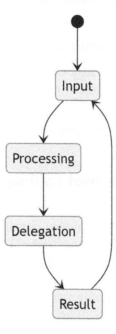

Figure 21.2: Conversational agents process steps

The preceding diagram indicates a loop where you go from input to processing to delegation to result, so why is there a loop? An agent doesn't have the concept of an end; it sits there and waits for the user to provide input and reacts to it. As mentioned earlier in this chapter, an agent works toward a goal, and if the goal is to manage finances, it's a continuous job.

More on tool calling in LLMs

We've mentioned tool calling previously in this chapter but let's try to show how it works to add capabilities to the LLM.

The LLM only knows what it has been trained on, and for things it hasn't been trained on, it will, in many cases, try to provide you with an answer that isn't always correct as it makes it up; this is known as a hallucination. To improve areas where you want the LLM to provide more accurate responses, you can present it with a tool. The process of providing a tool consists of the following components:

- A JSON description of a function
- A description of the function so the LLM knows when this function should be called

Once you've provided the preceding components, let's say you provide a function capable of fetching the weather; the LLM can now use its built-in features to semantically interpret all the following inputs to mean that the user wants to know about the weather:

- "What's the weather like today in Salt Lake City?"
- "What's the temperature in San Francisco?"
- "Is it going to rain in New York tomorrow?"
- "What's the weather like in London?"
- "Is it warm outside?"

Adding capabilities to GPT using tools

How it works is that you provide a function specification in a JSON format. This JSON function format is a schema the GPT model understands. The GPT model will essentially do two things for you:

- Extract parameters from the prompt.
- Determine whether to call a function and which function to call, as you can tell it about more than one function.

As a developer, you need to then actively call the function if the LLM thinks it should be called.

Your function format follows this schema:

```json
{
    "type": "function",
    "function": {
        "name": "get_current_weather",
        "description": "Get the current weather",
        "parameters": {
            "type": "object",
            "properties": {
                "location": {
                    "type": "string",
                    "description": "The city and state, e.g. San Francisco, CA",
                },
                "format": {
                    "type": "string",
                    "enum": ["celsius", "fahrenheit"],
                    "description": "The temperature unit to use. Infer this from the users location.",
                },
            },
            "required": ["location", "format"],
        },
    }
}
```

In the preceding JSON schema, there are a few things you're telling the GPT model:

- There's a function called `get_current_weather`.
- The description is `"Get the current weather"`.
- The function takes two parameters, `location` and `format`.
- There's also a description of the parameters, their types, and allowed values.

Let's describe how this would work in practice, given the following prompt:

[Prompt]

"What's the weather like today in Salt Lake City?"

[End of prompt]

Here's what the GPT model can extract from the prompt:

- Location: Salt Lake City.
- Format: This is not provided, but the GPT can infer this from the user's location.
- Function to call: `get_current_weather`.

What you need to do as a developer is to call the function indicated with the extracted parameter values. The following is code that could be used to connect to the GPT model, where a function description is provided, and parse the response:

```python
import open

def get_current_weather(location, format):
    # Call weather API
    response = requests.get(f"https://api.weather.com/v3/wx/forecast/
daily/5day?location={location}&format={format}
    return response.json()

# Call the GPT model

tool = {
        "type": "function",
        "function": {
            "name": "get_current_weather",
            "description": "Get the current weather",
            "parameters": {
                "type": "object",
                "properties": {
                    "location": {
                        "type": "string",
                        "description": "The city and state, e.g. San Francisco,
```

```
CA",
                        },
                    "format": {
                        "type": "string",
                        "enum": ["celsius", "fahrenheit"],
                        "description": "The temperature unit to use. Infer this
from the users location.",
                        },
                    },
                "required": ["location", "format"],
                },
            }
        }


prompt = "What's the weather like today in Salt Lake City?"

response = openai.Completion.create(
    model="text-davinci-003",
    prompt=prompt,
    max_tokens=150,
    tools= [tool]
)


# Parse the response
function_response = response.choices[0].function_response # here we learn what
function to call
location = function_response.parameters.location # extracting parameter value
for location
format = function_response.parameters.format # extracting parameter value for
format
weather = get_current_weather(location, format) # here we get the response from
the API
```

This is probably the most basic example of how you can create a conversational agent using GPT.

However, we expect a bit more from an advanced agent. What if we want to do something more complex, like booking a flight, hotel, car, and restaurant?

Advanced conversations

It's easy to think you can just add more functions to the GPT model and that might work for a time. However, as the conversation becomes more complex, the GPT model needs to remember the context of the conversation and keep track of the state of the conversation.

For more advanced conversations, it quickly becomes more complex.

Imagine going into a travel agent's office and the following back-and-forth conversation taking place between two humans:

User: "I want to go on a vacation."

Agent: "Sure."

User: "I want to go to a warm place."

Agent: "Sure, tell me more about what you're looking for."

User: "I want somewhere with a beach."

Agent: "Sure, any more details?"

User: "I want there to be at least 25 degrees."

Agent: "Sure, any more details?"

User: "No, that's it."

Agent: "I found three places that match your criteria. Can I present them to you?"

User: "Yes, please."

Agent: "Here are the three places. Which one do you want to know more about?"

User: "I want the first one."

Agent: "Here's more information about the first place."

User: "Cool, can you book a hotel and flight for the first place?"

Agent: "Sure, I'll get that done for you."

Agent: "I've booked the hotel and flight for you."

User: "Thanks, ooh, I need to rent a car as well."

Agent: "Sure, any specific car you're looking for?"

User: "Not really; my budget is $100 per day."

Agent: "I found five cars that match your criteria. Can I present them to you?"

User: "Yes, please. I want the fifth one."

Agent: "I've booked the car for you."

Agent: "You're all set for your vacation."

User: "Thanks, but wait, I need help booking a restaurant for the first night."

At this point, it stands clear that this conversation can go on for quite a while. The agent needs to remember the context of the conversation and keep track of the state.

There are also many different tasks that the agent needs to delegate to other agents or services, like booking a hotel, flight, car, and restaurant, and the weather API, sightseeing API, and more.

The point is that there's more to an agent than just understanding the initial prompt and delegating the task to another agent or service. You need to think of this conversation as a state machine and an orchestration of different agents and services.

Modeling advanced conversations

We mentioned that a more advanced conversation involves remembering both context and state. Let's inspect a subset of the example conversation and see how the state changes:

User: "I want to go on a vacation."

Agent: "Sure."

At this point, the agent hasn't remembered anything more than the user's intention, which is to go on vacation. It's just acknowledged the user's prompt.

User: "I want to go to a warm place."

Agent: "Sure, tell me more about what you're looking for."

Now things are getting interesting. The agent has remembered "warm" as a piece of criteria and needs to translate "warm" into a temperature range it can use to filter out places that are too cold.

User: "I want somewhere with a beach."

Agent: "Sure, any more details?"

This is another step forward; the agent has remembered "beach" as an additional piece of criteria to use when filtering out places.

User: "I want it to be at least 25 degrees."

An additional criterion, "25 degrees," has been added. Let's see the earlier piece of criteria, "warm," which was defined as 20–40 Celsius – this adjusts the range to 25–40 Celsius.

Agent: "Sure, any more details?"

User: "No, that's it."

At this point, the agent recognizes that the user has no more criteria to add, and a search/decision can take place with the filters of "warm," "beach," and "25–40 Celsius." Now, an API is called to get a list of places and the agent can present the list to the user for selection.

Agent: "I found three places that match your criteria. Can I present them to you?"

What's important to add is that not only are criteria remembered for this specific trip retrieval but they need to be remembered for the next steps as well unless the user changes the criteria.

Hopefully, you can see from the preceding example that the state is built up slowly, and the agent needs to remember the context of the conversation.

It can be helpful to think of a more advanced conversation as consisting of the following steps:

1. **Input:** The input to the agent, typically in the form of natural language.
2. **Processing:** The processing of the input, typically using NLP techniques.
3. **Determine the next step:** The agent needs to determine the next step in the conversation based on the input and the current state of the conversation. Answers here can be to ask for more information, present a list of options, book something, and so on.
4. **End conversation or continue (ask for user input):** The agent needs to determine whether the conversation should end or continue. If it should continue, it needs to ask for user input.

Pseudo code for advanced conversations

The agent might have a few different states, for example:

- **Ask for a task:** This would typically be asked when the conversation starts or when a task has been performed and a user selection has been done.

- **Ask the user for more information on a task:** This would typically be asked before a task is performed to ensure the agent has all the information it needs.

- **Present a list of options to the user:** This would typically be asked after a task has been performed to present the user with things to choose from.

- **Perform a task:** Here, the agent would perform a task, like booking a hotel, flight, car, or restaurant.

- **End the conversation:** The agent moves to this state when the conversation is over, and the user has somehow indicated that the conversation is over.

This is how this might look in pseudo code:

```python
# enum
class State(Enum):
    ASK_FOR_TASK = 1
    ASK_FOR_MORE_INFORMATION = 2
    PRESENT_TASK_RESULT = 3
    PERFORM_TASK = 4
    END_CONVERSATION = 5


# initial state
state = State.ASK_FOR_TASK

def ask_for_task():
    # ask the user for a task
    pass


def ask_for_more_information(task):
    # store filter criteria
```

```python
        pass

    def present_task_result(task):
        # presents the result so the user can choose
        pass

    def perform_task(task):
        # Perform a task
        pass

    def end_conversation():
        # End the conversation
        pass

    while state != State.END_CONVERSATION:
        if state == State.ASK_FOR_TASK:
            # Ask for a task
            task = ask_for_task()
            state = State.ASK_FOR_MORE_INFORMATION
        elif state == State.ASK_FOR_MORE_INFORMATION:
            # Ask the user for more information on a task
            task = ask_for_more_information(task)
            state = State.PERFORM_TASK
        elif state == State.PRESENT_TASK_RESULT:
            # Present a list of options to the user
            task = present_task_result(task)
            state = State.ASK_FOR_MORE_INFORMATION
        elif state == State.PERFORM_TASK:
            # Perform a task
            perform_task(task)
            state = State.PRESENT_TASK_RESULT
        elif state == State.END_CONVERSATION:
            # End the conversation
            end_conversation()
```

The preceding code is a decent starting point for a more advanced conversation. However, we should remember that humans are not always predictable, and the agent needs to be able to handle the unexpected. For example, humans can change their minds or add new criteria at any point.

Autonomous agents

Autonomous agents are agents that can act on their own without human intervention. They can perform tasks, make decisions, and interact with other agents and humans without human input. Autonomous agents can be used in a wide range of applications, from self-driving cars to virtual assistants.

Examples of autonomous agents include the following:

- **Self-driving cars:** Self-driving cars are autonomous agents that can drive themselves without human intervention. They can navigate roads, avoid obstacles, and make decisions based on their surroundings.

- **Virtual assistants:** Virtual assistants are autonomous agents that can perform tasks, make decisions, and interact with humans without human input. They can understand natural language, learn from their interactions, and improve their performance over time. Imagine an example of this where you have a financial agent; you might have given it a high-level goal to manage your finances and ensure an 8% value increase per year. You might have given this agent the go-ahead to buy and sell stocks under a certain value but to consultant you on larger purchases and sales over a certain limit.

We are likely to see a rise in both conversational agents as well as autonomous agents in the future. There are a lot of interesting areas where these agents can be used, from customer service to healthcare, finance, and transportation. Imagine having an autonomous agent that can help you with your taxes, book a vacation, or help you with your health while knowing your medical history, your preferences, and more.

Assignment

Given the following conversation, deduce which type of agent is likely involved in the conversation and how would you model the conversation:

User: "I want to bake a cake."

Agent: "Sure, what type of cake are you looking to bake?"

User: "I want to make a chocolate cake."

Agent: "Sure, do you have a recipe in mind?"

User: "No, can you help me find a recipe?"

Agent: "Sure, anything I should know in terms of allergies or preferences?"

User: "I'm allergic to nuts and I prefer a recipe that's easy to make. Oh, I also want to make a cake that's vegan."

Agent: "Got it! I found three recipes that match your criteria. Can I present them?"

User: "Yes, please."

Agent: "Here are the three recipes. Which one do you want?"

User: "I want number 2."

Agent: "Is that all?"

User: "No, do I need to buy the ingredients? Also, can you help me set the oven temperature?"

Agent: "Yes, looks like you're missing a few ingredients. I can help you place an order for the ingredients. I can also help you set the oven temperature. When do you need it set?"

User: "Yes, place the order, and let's set the oven as soon as the order arrives."

Agent: "I've placed the order and am waiting for the delivery. I'll set the oven temperature as it arrives."

User: "Thanks."

Agent: "You're welcome, that's it?"

User: "Yes."

Challenge

Can you think of a problem that can be solved using agents? How would you use agents to solve this problem? What type of agents would you use?

Quiz

Q: What's tool calling in LLMs?

   a.   It's when the LLM calls a built-in tool to provide a response.

   b.   It's when you let the LLM know of a new capability by providing it with a function description in JSON and a semantic description that indicates when this function should be called.

   c.   It's when you use functions to fine-tune the LLM.

Summary

In this chapter, we introduced the concept of agents in software development. We explained what agents are and how they work. We discussed the different types of agents and how they can be used. We hope that you now have a glimpse of the future to see where LLMs like GPT are heading and how your future is about to change.

References

It's worth checking out some resources on agents if you're curious:

   •   Autogen: https://github.com/microsoft/autogen

   •   Semantic Kernel: https://learn.microsoft.com/en-us/semantic-kernel/overview/

   •   Join our Discord: https://discord.gg/pAbnFJrkgZ

Join our community on Discord

Join our community's Discord space for discussions with the author and other readers:

`https://packt.link/aicode`

22

Conclusion

Huge thanks to you, dear reader, for getting this far into the book. We hope that you're now at a point where you can confidently use AI tools like GitHub Copilot and ChatGPT in your projects.

Recap of the book

Let's recap on what we've covered in this book. We started by introducing you to the world of AI and how we got to **large language models (LLMs)**. We then introduced you to GitHub Copilot and ChatGPT, two of the most popular AI tools in the world today. Not only are these two tools popular, but they're also interesting to compare and contrast. ChatGPT comes with a chat interface and is built so that it can tackle a range of tasks. GitHub Copilot also comes with a chat interface and an in-editor mode but is more dedicated to solving problems around software development. An important aspect that unites these two tools is the fact you can use prompts and natural language input, they can be used as input, and the end user receives an output that hopefully brings them closer to solving their problem. Because both of these two tools rely on prompt input, it allows us to decide what type of prompts and how many prompts are needed, tweak the prompts, and even use prompts to validate the AI tool's response.

Then, we presented you with a prompt strategy to ensure you use these AI tools effectively. After that, we showed how this prompt strategy was put into practice in a web development project spanning from the frontend to the backend over several chapters. We then showed how the very same prompt strategy applied to data science and machine learning projects. These two problem domains have been chosen at random; the point of the book is to demonstrate the capability of generative AI tools, and knowing how to pair that with a prompt strategy will greatly empower you.

The impact of using an AI tool is that you now have a tool that does much of the heavy lifting around code development regardless of the problem domain. What this means for you as a developer is that you can now focus to a higher degree on being declarative, to state how you want things rather than typing every line of code. Using AI tools and using them efficiently is likely to speed up the coding part of your job considerably.

Before rounding up the book, we presented you with a glimpse of the future, namely agents, which are programs that can act on your behalf and represent where we think AI is headed next.

Finally, we covered the AI tools and their features more in detail to set you up for success in your future projects.

Major conclusions

So, what are the major conclusions that can be drawn from this book? They are as follows:

- AI tools like GitHub Copilot and ChatGPT are here to stay and are only going to get better with time.
- The world is shifting toward a more declarative way of programming; ask the AI to do much of the heavy lifting for you. Your new role is to work with your AI tool iteratively for the best results.
- You should have a prompt strategy in place to approach problems within your chosen domain regardless of whether you're a web developer, data scientist, or machine learning engineer.
- Prompting is quickly becoming a skill in its own right, even if we think that improved models will make it less important in the future. For now, it's a skill that you should master, and we hope this book is helping you on this road to becoming proficient in prompting.

What's next

What we discussed in our chapter on agents (*Chapter 21*) is where things are going, and you should keep an eye on that. Agents are already part of the curriculum at the University of Oxford; check out this course link to learn more `https://conted.ox.ac.uk/courses/artificial-intelligence-generative-ai-cloud-and-mlops-online`.

Autogen, as mentioned in *Chapter 21*, is a highly interesting project that introduces agents. We recommend having a look at it and, if so inclined, leveraging it in your own projects: `https://github.com/microsoft/autogen`.

At last

The world of AI is moving quickly. Yesterday's perfect tools and strategies might not be the best ones in a few months. It's therefore our ambition to keep this book updated with the latest findings and insights. A heartfelt thanks to you, dear reader, and we hope this book has proved valuable to you.

Join our community on Discord

Join our community's Discord space for discussions with the author and other readers:

`https://packt.link/aicode`

packt.com

Subscribe to our online digital library for full access to over 7,000 books and videos, as well as in-dustry leading tools to help you plan your personal development and advance your career. For more information, please visit our website.

Why subscribe?

- Spend less time learning and more time coding with practical eBooks and Videos from over 4,000 industry professionals
- Improve your learning with Skill Plans built especially for you
- Get a free eBook or video every month
- Fully searchable for easy access to vital information
- Copy and paste, print, and bookmark content

At www.packt.com, you can also read a collection of free technical articles, sign up for a range of free newsletters, and receive exclusive discounts and offers on Packt books and eBooks.

Other Books You May Enjoy

If you enjoyed this book, you may be interested in these other books by Packt:

Python Machine Learning By Example

Yuxi (Hayden) Liu

ISBN: 9781835085622

- Follow machine learning best practices throughout data preparation and model development
- Build and improve image classifiers using convolutional neural networks (CNNs) and transfer learning
- Develop and fine-tune neural networks using TensorFlow and PyTorch

- Analyze sequence data and make predictions using recurrent neural networks (RNNs), transformers, and CLIP
- Build classifiers using support vector machines (SVMs) and boost performance with PCA
- Avoid overfitting using regularization, feature selection, and more

Unlocking the Secrets of Prompt Engineering

Gilbert Mizrahi

ISBN: 9781835083833

- Explore the different types of prompts, their strengths, and weaknesses
- Understand the AI agent's knowledge and mental model
- Enhance your creative writing with AI insights for fiction and poetry
- Develop advanced skills in AI chatbot creation and deployment
- Discover how AI will transform industries such as education, legal, and others
- Integrate LLMs with various tools to boost productivity
- Understand AI ethics and best practices, and navigate limitations effectively
- Experiment and optimize AI techniques for best results

Packt is searching for authors like you

If you're interested in becoming an author for Packt, please visit authors.packtpub.com and apply today. We have worked with thousands of developers and tech professionals, just like you, to help them share their insight with the global tech community. You can make a general application, apply for a specific hot topic that we are recruiting an author for, or submit your own idea.

Share your thoughts

Now you've finished *AI-Assisted Programming for Web and Machine Learning*, we'd love to hear your thoughts! Scan the QR code below to go straight to the Amazon review page for this book and share your feedback or leave a review on the site that you purchased it from.

https://packt.link/r/1835086055

Your review is important to us and the tech community and will help us make sure we're delivering excellent quality content.

Index

Download a free PDF copy of this book

Thanks for purchasing this book!

Do you like to read on the go but are unable to carry your print books everywhere?

Is your eBook purchase not compatible with the device of your choice?

Don't worry, now with every Packt book you get a DRM-free PDF version of that book at no cost.

Read anywhere, any place, on any device. Search, copy, and paste code from your favorite technical books directly into your application.

The perks don't stop there, you can get exclusive access to discounts, newsletters, and great free content in your inbox daily.

Follow these simple steps to get the benefits:

1. Scan the QR code or visit the link below:

https://packt.link/free-ebook/9781835086056

2. Submit your proof of purchase.
3. That's it! We'll send your free PDF and other benefits to your email directly.

Milton Keynes UK
Ingram Content Group UK Ltd.
UKHW050111171024
449681UK00003B/8